COASTERS GO TO WAR
Military Sailings to the Continent, 1939-1945

John de S. Winser

Ships in Focus Publications

Published in the UK in 2009 by Ships in Focus Publications,
18 Franklands, Longton
Preston PR4 5PD
ISBN 978-1-901703-56-6

Printed by Amadeus Press, Cleckheaton, Yorkshire

COASTERS GO TO WAR
Military Sailings to the Continent, 1939-1945

John de S. Winser

Contents

Title page: Possibly for the first time in their young lives, French children, liberated from German occupation, enjoy the Arromanches beach in July 1944, undeterred by the discharge of military supplies into the assembled US Army trucks. *[Imperial War Museum, A24674]*

Opposite: Seen on passage to arrive at Juno beachhead on D+1 Day (7th June 1944), the coaster *Southport* carried 560 tons of ammunition from London's Tilbury Dock and 39 troops who had embarked during the ship's short stay in the Solent. *[Riksarkivet, Oslo]*

Introduction

The extraordinary diversity in size and design of ships of the coasting type gives them a fascination all of their own and the role they played during the Second World War makes them particularly worthy of study. Under the supervision of what became the Sea Transport Division's Military Cargo Branch at the British Ministry of War Transport, the cross-Channel military coaster fleet story started immediately war was declared in September 1939: within eight days, a dozen ships had been requisitioned to sail from the Bristol Channel to just two ports in western France. By June 1940, this coaster fleet had grown to more than 160 ships and had involved sailings to no less than 15 ports in France, Belgium and Norway. It would not have been impossible, at the outbreak of war, to forecast that coasters might convey a quarter of a million tons of military cargo to the troops on the Continent over the subsequent nine months: this was merely the, admittedly often more hazardous, wartime equivalent of the cargo for which they had been designed. What would have been totally unpredictable was that, at the end of that time, around 40,000 soldiers would owe their cross-Channel rescue to coasters. The Dunkirk story and the troop evacuations from other French ports would not be complete without paying tribute to the very significant contribution made by the coasters, as will be apparent from Part I of this book.

The Military Cargo Branch was responsible for arranging movement by sea in merchant ships of all service cargo from its reception at the loading port to its delivery at destination, including the organisation of the ships involved. It faced no greater challenge than to meet the military requirements of the Normandy invasion in June 1944. In addition to their usual consignments of ammunition, cased petrol and stores, coasters crossing to France as part of the greatest amphibious operation in history also carried more than 2,000 vehicles and 12,500 soldiers in the initial stages. An average of 38 coasters reached the Normandy beachheads every day immediately after D-Day and naval reports credit them as being the perfect aid to a rapid stores build-up, because of the ease with which they could be beached, dried out and discharged. Equally vital was their ability to discharge in ports too small to handle larger ocean-going cargo vessels. Part II of the book details the cross-Channel voyages performed during the first three months after D-Day, some of the cargoes carried and the hazards encountered, before going on to outline the salient events involving the coasters during the subsequent nine months up to the end of the war in Europe in May 1945. Over 460 military cargo coasters, representing ten different nationalities, crossed the Channel in 1944-45, sailing initially to the Normandy beaches, then serving an ever widening range of ports in France, Belgium, the Netherlands, Germany and Norway, as these became available: this then is their story.

Acknowledgements

I would like to express my very sincere appreciation to all those whose photographs have been selected. The appearance of the vessels in their peacetime role provides a fascinating contrast to the illustrations depicting ships in their sombre war paint schemes. Despite the conditions of almost total secrecy which understandably surrounded all wartime shipping movements and the Admiralty instruction that names of ports of call should be omitted from ships' logs, it is remarkable how much data is available. It is appropriate therefore to recognise the foresight of those who ensured that so many original wartime documents were retained for posterity and to applaud the facilities provided for researchers at The National Archives at Kew; the Guildhall Library in the City of London and elsewhere. Certain individuals very kindly devoted their valuable time to assisting me and special thanks are due to Bob Todd and David Hodge of the National Maritime Museum and to my youngest daughter Helen, a senior production editor on international journals.

John de S Winser

Above: The London-loaded cased petrol coaster *Ebbrix* in convoy EWC1B (confirmed by the flag signals) left the Solent for Normandy on D-Day (6th June 1944) after embarking 40 dock operating personnel: the tent-cover, clearly visible over the cargo hatch, served as the troops' overnight accommodation. The scene, also showing *Southport* to the right, was photographed from the *Vestmanrod* by Norwegian News Agency's O.F. Backer. *[Riksarkivet, Oslo]*
Opposite page: This map indicates the main places in Britain and the near Continent which relate to the events of 1939-40 and 1944-45 referred to in this book.

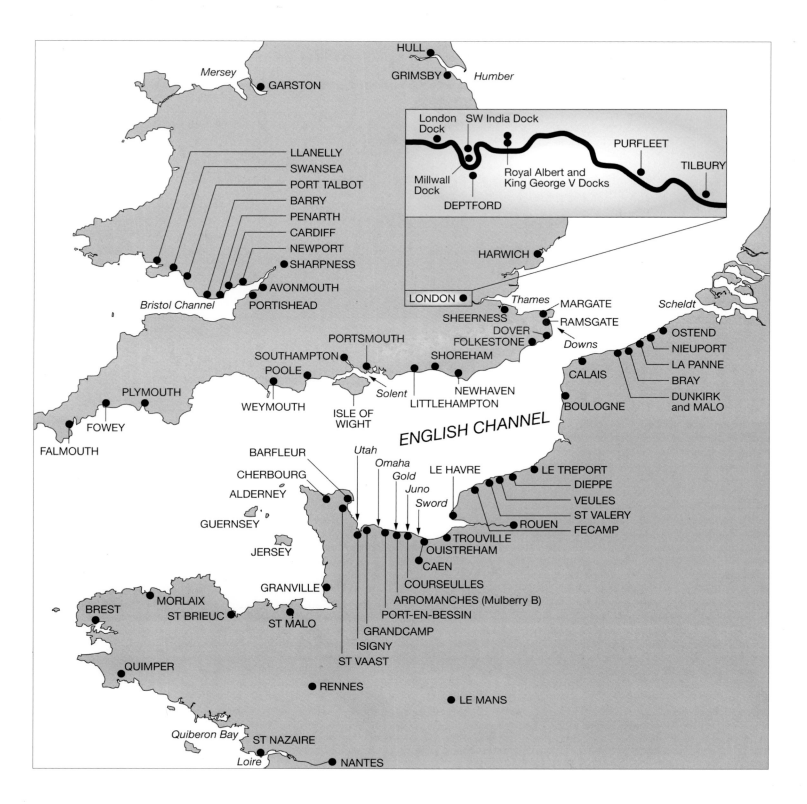

HULL

Mersey
GARSTON
GRIMSBY
Humber

London
Dock
SW India Dock
PURFLEET
TILBURY
Millwall
Dock
Royal Albert and
King George V Docks
DEPTFORD

LLANELLY
SWANSEA
PORT TALBOT
BARRY
PENARTH
CARDIFF
NEWPORT
SHARPNESS
AVONMOUTH
PORTISHEAD

HARWICH

Bristol Channel

LONDON

Thames
MARGATE
Scheldt
SHEERNESS
RAMSGATE
DOVER
FOLKESTONE
OSTEND
NIEUPORT
Downs

PORTSMOUTH
SOUTHAMPTON
SHOREHAM
LA PANNE
POOLE
CALAIS
BRAY
WEYMOUTH
NEWHAVEN
BOULOGNE
DUNKIRK
and MALO
PLYMOUTH
ISLE OF
WIGHT
Solent
LITTLEHAMPTON

FOWEY
FALMOUTH

ENGLISH CHANNEL

BARFLEUR
Utah
Omaha
LE HAVRE
LE TREPORT
CHERBOURG
Gold
DIEPPE
ALDERNEY
Juno
VEULES
Sword
ST VALERY
GUERNSEY
ROUEN
FECAMP
JERSEY
TROUVILLE
OUISTREHAM
GRANVILLE
CAEN
COURSEULLES
MORLAIX
ARROMANCHES (Mulberry B)
BREST
ST BRIEUC
PORT-EN-BESSIN
ST MALO
GRANDCAMP
QUIMPER
ISIGNY
ST VAAST

RENNES
LE MANS

Quiberon Bay
ST NAZAIRE
Loire
NANTES

In the early days of the Second World War in September 1939, coasters were taken up for the carriage of ammunition and cased petrol to the British Expeditionary Force in France. The Gibson coaster *Eildon* was assigned to transport the latter and sailed in the first military cargo convoy to leave the Bristol Channel for Brest and Nantes. She continued these sailings until May 1940, returning from her final crossing one day prior to the start of the British evacuations from Dunkirk. *[J. and M. Clarkson collection]*

The British and Continental Steam Ship Company's *Ousel* was taken up as an ammunition ship at Liverpool and left there on 25th September 1939 to load at Newport: her service was completed after two departures for France, the first in September to Brest and the second in November to St Nazaire. *[Fotoflite incorporating Skyfotos]*

Part I
The Early War Months

Section 1
Supplying the British Army in France and Norway
September 1939-May 1940

On 1st August 1939, the British Secretary of State for War informed the Committee of Imperial Defence that two military divisions could be in France within one month of the outbreak of war and that a further two divisions could follow within four weeks. Planning for the movement of the British Expeditionary Force (BEF) had begun in Spring 1939 and had been worked out in minute detail, with four cargo discharge berths being assigned at Cherbourg; a dozen at Brest, including one for ammunition and three for petrol, and others at St Nazaire and Nantes on the River Loire but none at Le Havre, which was at that stage regarded as too vulnerable. It was the threat of attack from air and sea which had prompted the initial decision to route almost all BEF supplies through western France, in preference to the Channel ports. Coasters were assigned by the Ministry of Shipping for the carriage of the ammunition and cased petrol cargoes and, to achieve a planned despatch of 8-10 ships each week from the Bristol Channel to Brest or Nantes, the first was taken up on 3rd September 1939, the very day war was declared. By the end of that month, this fleet had grown to 29 vessels, ranging in gross tonnage from the 1,931 of *Adjutant* to the 394 of *Cairngorm*, with all but two being of recent construction. The inaugural convoy of 16 cargo ships from the Bristol Channel left for France on 11th September and included the cased petrol carriers *Clyde Coast* and *Eildon* from Swansea and *Jacinth* and *Ngakoa* from Avonmouth: following up during September were six further convoy departures, involving 24 coasters in all. Because, by mid-October, transportation for the BEF had been reduced to a maintenance basis, most of the merchant ships in outbound cargo convoy BC14 (Bristol Channel No 14) were coasters. This convoy comprised the cased petrol carriers *Coxwold*, *Jade*, *Lochee*, *Pacific Coast* and *Pembroke Coast*; the ammunition coasters *Adjutant* and *Ousel* and four ocean-going ships, two carrying vehicles and two

with stores: HM destroyers *Express*, *Vesper* and *Vivacious* formed the convoy escort. BC14 was the third outward BEF convoy for *Pacific Coast*: it also proved to be her last. Unconnected with enemy action, her cased petrol cargo exploded as she reached Brest on 9th November and the vessel was towed outside the port, where she remained on fire for four days.

Supply convoys continued from the Bristol Channel until the end of May 1940 but the individual ships often sailed relatively infrequently and some only once. The early cargo convoys were primarily composed of ocean-going ships with a service speed in excess of that of many coasters. Consequently, some of the coasters introduced into service were adjudged unsuitable for further such convoys and were either released or were transferred to the English Channel, where, augmented by others, they crossed to France independently and unescorted. For these sailings, Poole was the main loading port for the cased petrol carriers and their usual continental destination was Caen. For the ships assigned to carry ammunition, the initial primary loading ports were Newhaven and Littlehampton with the French discharge ports being Dieppe and Fecamp, although sailings were later introduced between Fowey and St Malo. For the first eight months of the war, the only reported enemy activity affecting these ships was an unsuccessful 27th February bombing attack on *Sandhill*, one of the coasters sailing independently to France from Newhaven. Alarms had, however, been raised earlier that month when the cased petrol coaster *Spinel* failed to reach her destination during her return crossing from Caen: an air search was called for and the ship, disabled by engine trouble, was finally towed into Brixham by a Belgian trawler. By the end of April, 37 military cargo coasters, including eight owned by Coast Lines Ltd., had, at some stage, been employed in support of the BEF in France and six of those 37, joined by *Redcar*, were assigned in April and May to serve the British forces on military operations in Norway, in their endeavour to prevent German forces from occupying the country. The Norwegian operation began on 10th April with the British Government's decision to despatch a Field Force and the first movement sailed for Narvik, well inside the Arctic Circle, and Namsos on 12th April, followed four days later by the first sailing for Andalsnes. Thereafter reinforcements and supplies crossed every few days until British forces were withdrawn in early June. Of the seven coasters supporting the Army in Norway, the cased petrol carrier *Pembroke Coast* was lost as a result of air attacks at Harstad and the outward voyage of *Coxwold*, carrying mines and fuel, was seriously delayed by the ship striking rocks: although she was finally able to complete her voyage, she brought more than half her cargo back. *Redcar* and *Ronan* completed uneventful round trips; *Lochee* reached her destination, despite sustaining damage at Scapa when another ship dragged her anchors in a gale; *Yewmount* was ordered to return home from Harstad without unloading any of her cased petrol and *Pizarro* sustained such extensive damage in a collision with a French coaster that her sailing had to be aborted.

In France, the British Army's front line was on the borders with neutral Belgium in the extreme north-east of the country and on 10th May German forces launched their long-awaited attack on the Netherlands, Belgium and Luxembourg. Apart from the coaster terminals of Dieppe and Fecamp,

During the Norwegian campaign, bombs ignited the oil berth at Harstad in May 1940: fire spread to *Pembroke Coast*, still fully loaded with aviation and vehicle fuel, and it proved impossible to prevent her loss. [B. and A. Feilden/J. and M. Clarkson collection]

Coxwold completed eight round voyages to Western France with cased petrol between September 1939 and April 1940 and was then ordered into the Arctic Circle to support the British Army in Norway. [F.W. Hawks/J. and M. Clarkson collection]

supplies for the BEF were still entering France through ports from Rouen westwards as far as Brest, with the result that lines of communication, utilising the railway system, stretched the entire width of the country. The speed of the German advance was such that by 15th May the real possibility existed that the BEF front line might become severed from its established supply system. To cover this situation, plans were formulated for vital cargoes to be shipped directly through the ports nearest the British fighting troops, namely Boulogne, Calais and Dunkirk. Up to the middle of May, no more than 23 coasters had been needed at any one time to cover the military cargo commitments to France. In response to the threat to the existing supply lines, the number of coasters allocated to BEF service had more than quadrupled by 27th May to over 100, 36 of which

Heavy air raids prevented cargo discharge at Dunkirk: consequently *Clewbay* returned to Littlehampton in May 1940 with her 578 tons of ammunition still on board. *[World Ship Society Ltd.]*

had been ordered to load over 26,000 tons of ammunition, cased petrol and stores at Poole, Littlehampton, Newhaven and London. A schedule drawn up on 20th May called for *Firth Fisher* to leave with stores and for *Glamis* to sail with cased petrol that same day; for *Spinel* to follow with cased petrol the next day; for *Sodality*, *Williamstown* and *Worthtown* to leave with stores and *Clewbay*, *Sandhill* and *Scottish Co-operator* with ammunition on 22nd May, followed the day after by *Nephrite* and *Lowick*, with stores and ammunition respectively. In implementing the 20th May plan, *Firth Fisher* arrived off Boulogne on 21st May but, activating a magnetic mine, broke her back and immediately went down. *Glamis* was held on stand-by in the Downs anchorage, between Dover and Ramsgate: *Spinel*, having initially crossed to Boulogne, was re-routed to Dunkirk, where she became trapped in the harbour as a result of air raids and subsequently had to be abandoned. *Sodality* and *Williamstown* safely completed their round trips to Dunkirk and Calais respectively: *Worthtown* discharged part of her cargo at Boulogne and, when the port was subjected to artillery fire, moved to Dunkirk but there became a victim of bombing attacks. Because of the intensity of these air attacks, *Clewbay* was unable

to discharge at Dunkirk and brought her cargo back, whereas *Sandhill* successfully landed hers. *Scottish Co-operator* was able to unload only part of her consignment at Boulogne; *Nephrite* was given permission on 31st May to jettison her cargo and *Lowick*, after setting out for Dunkirk, was turned back. During this period, two coasters were directed to Ostend with food supplies: *The Marquis* successfully completed her round trip but, on her homeward crossing, *Abukir* was subjected to E-boat attack, was hit by a torpedo and quickly went down, the heavy loss of life being exacerbated by the dastardly machine-gunning of survivors in the water. Forty of the newly requisitioned vessels were small Dutch coasters, ranging in gross tonnage from the 121 of *Bornrif* to the 435 of *Bart*. After escaping from the Netherlands, at least 58 were lying at Poole and London and were earmarked to cross the Strait of Dover having loaded military supplies, the former group at Southampton (New Docks) and the latter at London (Deptford), after their Dutch crews had been replaced by Royal Navy personnel. Some of these vessels proved not to be immediately available or suitable and the list was whittled down to a total of 41, all of which were commissioned at Poole, London (Tilbury) or Sheerness.

Section 2
Evacuation Operations, May and June 1940

Operation "Dynamo". In his history of the Second World War, Winston Churchill records that, at a meeting of the War Cabinet on 20th May, it was acknowledged that a successful fighting retreat by the British Army to the River Somme might leave some units cut off and a troop evacuation of some sort from the French coast might become unavoidable. In response, on 21st May six stores coasters were dispatched in ballast to the Downs anchorage a full five days before any rescue operation was initiated. The vessels selected were *Beal*, *Bullfinch*, *Gateshead*, *Sequacity*, *Yewdale* and *Yewglen* and, as emergency evacuation vessels, were fitted with drinking water tanks in their holds and fully stocked up with supplies of the Army's staple diet of bully beef, biscuits and milk. Many of the recently-requisitioned coasters were still at their loading ports when the British military situation deteriorated significantly: Boulogne fell to the advancing German forces on 24th May and Calais was captured two days later. With the Army being forced to fall back on the Dunkirk area, the requirement to send supplies to the BEF was overtaken by the overwhelming need for a mass evacuation fleet to rescue all the beleaguered troops: the operation to set this in motion, code named "Dynamo", was put into effect at 1857 on 26th May. That day, additional coasters, including six General Steam vessels at London, were placed on 24 hours' notice for evacuation service. Of the 41 Dutch coasters mentioned earlier, only *Abel Tasman*, *Alice*, *Bart*, *Kaap Falga*, *Oranje* and *Tiny* actually loaded military supplies, with the cargo put aboard *Bart* including over 12,000 packages of food. Early on 27th May, the first two of the original six evacuation coasters were ordered to leave for Dunkirk using the shortest route. However, two miles off Calais, *Sequacity* came within range of recently-deployed German field guns and accurate shelling finally sank her: crew members were taken aboard the accompanying coaster *Yewdale*, which survived despite having her rafts and lifeboat destroyed by bullets from attacking aircraft. *Yewdale* was to sustain far greater damage on her return from Dunkirk two days later, when a massive air attack killed five of her 940 troops and wounded 78 others. Meanwhile, whilst outward bound with stores for Dunkirk on 28th May, *Dorrien Rose* went to the assistance of the troopship *Queen of the Channel* which had been straddled by bombs and, with her back broken, was sinking 10 miles north of Ostend. Before she went down, her 904 troops and crew were safely transferred to *Dorrien Rose*, which had manoeuvred alongside. The stricken ship was designed to carry 1,600 excursion passengers and could therefore accommodate all the troops below decks: just how they fared during their nine-hour crossing to Dover in a coaster, still with an outward cargo in her holds, was not officially recorded.

Sequacity became an early coaster casualty of the Dunkirk evacuations: whilst outward bound on 27th May 1940, she was sunk by accurate fire from German field guns newly-deployed on the French coast near Calais. *[National Maritime Museum, P12968]*

Nevertheless, the following day *Dorrien Rose* was able to cross to Dunkirk to rescue a further 637 troops. Returning on 29th May from the Dunkirk beaches, where she had involuntarily been aground all day, *Bullfinch* had her steering gear damaged by bombs but reached Ramsgate, despite the loss of her compasses which had been rendered inoperative by the explosions. The shallow draught of the coasters allowed them to anchor close inshore or beach to the east of Dunkirk, at Malo(-les-Bains), Bray or across the Franco-Belgian border at La Panne or Nieuport. The damage in Dunkirk harbour was such that the only possible alongside berths for British ships were at the East Pier,

Manned by the Royal Navy, the Dutch *Patria* is credited with carrying no fewer than 1,400 troops on two evacuation crossings to Margate. She is seen arriving at Portsmouth on 12th October 1955. *[J. and M. Clarkson collection]*

or Mole, which, having been designed only as a breakwater, was totally unsuitable for mass troop evacuations. While the Red Ensign coasters made their contribution to the success of the evacuation, the service performed by some of the Dutch White Ensign coasters proved even more impressive, not only in respect of carrying troops back to England but also in ferrying them from the Dunkirk beaches to larger ships. *Patria* is credited with having landed 1,200 troops at Margate on 30th May, a remarkable achievement and certainly a record as far as Dunkirk coaster evacuations is concerned. *Patria*'s operational report describes the two solid phalanxes of men, holding hands, wading out to the ship to board by nets, ladders and ropes, the embarkation being completed in just over two hours: it does not record conditions on board during a crossing, extended to over nine hours, because of the shortage of disembarkation facilities on the ship's arrival off the English coast. During her first stay off the Dunkirk beaches on 28th-29th May, it is estimated that *Hilda* transported more than 1,000 troops to waiting destroyers and some of her 'sister' ships also played a significant part in similar ferrying operations. *Tilly* crossed to Dunkirk on no fewer than five occasions, whilst *Hondsrug*, *Oranje* and *Pascholl* completed four round trips each. *Alice*, which had loaded food supplies at Southampton, sustained damage in air attacks at Dunkirk and had to be abandoned on 28th May and a similar fate, as a result of grounding, befell *Sursum Corda* three days later and *Lena* on 3rd June. The evacuation was officially brought to an end on 4th

June and three of the ships reaching Ramsgate that morning were *Bornrif*, *Hondsrug* and *Pascholl*, between them carrying 659 French servicemen and bringing the total rescued by 52 coasters during the operation to more than 28,000. Before Dunkirk, the prospect of evacuating over 300,000 men from a harbour breakwater and nearby beaches, under constant attack from the air, would have been regarded as a near impossibility but, by the implementation of impromptu measures, the feat had been achieved. It had been a period of courage, determination and tragedy, with perhaps the occasional lighter moment, not apparently shared by the Belgian major who proved difficult owing to the inability of the rescuing coaster *Vrede* to dry his corsets!

Operation "Cycle". Attention was next directed to the deteriorating predicament affecting around 25,000 British troops, including the 51st Highland Division and a local garrison of 5,000, facing the German advance towards the River Seine. An evacuation fleet was placed on stand-by on 8th June and, on receiving the order to commence Operation "Cycle" the following day, vessels set sail for Le Havre but were soon recalled, so as not to conflict with the French shipping movements from the port. On 10th June, British destroyers patrolling the French coast between Le Havre and Dieppe were subjected to gunfire from the shore: this showed that German forces had already reached the coast and that, for 12,000 British troops, the escape route to their embarkation port of Le Havre had been severed and a beach rescue operation would be essential. Accordingly, that and the following night, 24 coasters were amongst the assorted armada of small ships and boats which set out across the Channel destined for the St Valery(-en-Caux) area, between Dieppe and Fecamp. *Corinia* and *Sandhill* sailed from Newhaven, towing a total of 24 boats; *Goldfinch* and the War Department coaster *Sir Evelyn Wood*, each with six ships' lifeboats in tow, left Southampton and 13 Royal Navy-manned Dutch coasters, all but one Dunkirk veterans, set sail from Poole, Portsmouth or Newhaven, some loaded with supplies for the troops. *Lowick* was one of the ships carrying naval beach parties which discovered, on reaching French waters on 11th June, that the British troops had been delayed and that the first ships had come under enemy fire. In consequence, the fleet withdrew seawards only to find itself subjected to heavy bombing that afternoon and evening. The evacuation was now to take place that night but thick fog severely disrupted efforts to organise the seaborne force. With their shallow draughts, some of the coasters were ordered to go close inshore in the area of Veules(-les-Roses) and *Guernsey Queen* even touched bottom in her efforts to comply with this requirement. Small numbers of British and French troops did manage to get away on the 12th: *Goldfinch* ferried 500 soldiers to a troopship and *Cameo* and *Guernsey Queen* between them embarked 494

and continued to do so, until being forced to retire under fire from machine-guns and field artillery being moved into commanding positions by the advancing German Army. The naval report after the operation conceded that the Dutch coasters were ineffective, partly because their Royal Navy crews could not establish their ship's positions in the prevailing conditions and partly because, without radio equipment, they could not be directed to beaches where Allied soldiers might be assembling: for a variety of reasons, most of these vessels totally lost contact in the fog. An exception to this generalisation was *Pascholl* which went close inshore and, under heavy fire, waited until the last boat-loads of troops had reached her, before sailing with 333 British and French servicemen aboard. This achievement was particularly praiseworthy in view of the fact that her Captain reported afterwards that the ship was his first command and that the machinery was in the hands of a young engine room artificer who knew nothing about diesel engines and had been given an instruction book in a foreign language he could not understand. Three of the Dutch coasters did not survive the operation. *Twente*, loaded with ammunition and cased petrol, sustained three shell hits and sank on 12th June, at the same time that *Hebe II*, after ferrying soldiers to a troopship, went firmly aground on a falling tide and had to be abandoned: the following day, *Abel Tasman*, fourth in a line of ships entering Poole Harbour, was blown to pieces by mine.

When it became obvious that no further rescue attempts would be successful, returning ships were ordered to turn back any vessels still heading for the French coast. Some nevertheless slipped through, including the sister ships *Roebuck* and *Sambur*. Treacherously reassured by a French fishing boat that it was safe to make land off St Valery, both vessels found themselves lured into a trap and heavy artillery fire caused damage to the ships and serious casualties amongst their crews. The St Valery part of the operation proved to be a bitter contrast to the achievements of Dunkirk and, for years after the war ended, some of the many thousands of British soldiers captured, unaware of the strenuous efforts made to rescue them, were convinced that they had

Goldfinch was the first vessel to arrive off Veules during Operation "Cycle" in June 1940: she helped in the rescue of the small number of troops to reach that part of the French coast. *[Ships in Focus]*

This 1937 view of *Hebe* (II), right of picture with Ostend fishing boat *O280*, gives an indication of the small size of the Dutch coasters which made them admirably suited for troop embarkations from the Dunkirk beaches in May-June 1940. *[Captain J. F. van Puyvelde]*

pressed into service, some being loaded with emergency Army stores. Ten of the 18 evacuation vessels departing St Malo on 16th June were coasters, mostly carrying line of communication troops from the Rennes and Le Mans area. The following day a further seven coasters left the Breton port, including *Alt*, *Farfield*, *Ouse* and *Perelle*, which had been preparing to load potatoes at Jersey until HM destroyer *Wild Swan* anchored off the island with orders that all available shipping should follow her to St Malo. Of a total of 30,600 servicemen lifted from St Malo – 10,600 more than expected – nearly one-third travelled in coasters each of which on paper had a troop capacity of 500: this did not prevent 1,200 troops being assigned to travel to Weymouth in the 870 gross-ton *Corinia* and 2,000 to board

been badly let down by the Navy. Although valuable stores at Le Havre, which could have been saved, were abandoned, the troop evacuation from that port, aided by coasters already in the area on commercial voyages, was successful. Most of the troops were transported not to the UK but to Cherbourg, including 370 aboard a coaster, *The Countess*, on 12th June. Next day, this evacuation was completed when the coasters *Emerald*, still with some outward cargo in her holds, and *Theems* embarked from motor boats the rearguard troops, who had been manning the road blocks, and the demolition teams: they sailed for Cherbourg at 0500 and were the last evacuation ships to leave.

Operation "Aerial". Even after the completion of "Cycle", up to 140,000 British servicemen were still in active units in western France. Consequently, Operation "Aerial" was initiated on 15th June to evacuate all remaining members of the BEF, on the basis of lifting around 30,000 from Cherbourg; 20,000 from St Malo and the remainder from Brest, Nantes, St Nazaire and La Pallice. Troops were ordered to move to the above ports, with the immediate embarkation of non-fighting personnel, who constituted half of the above totals. In all, 58 coasters sailed in support of the operation, with 11 of the Royal Navy-manned Dutch coasters again being

the slightly larger *Alt*, which left the Breton port at 2135 on 17th June for a crossing of more than 15 hours to Southampton. Sailing about an hour earlier, but destined for Jersey, had been *Farfield* carrying the ground equipment and 188 personnel of two RAF squadrons, whose fighters, temporarily based in Jersey, were to provide air cover for the Cherbourg evacuations. The final official evacuation vessel to leave St Malo at 2210 that night was *Ouse* with naval ratings and military headquarters personnel: she only just managed to get away, clearing the lock with only 6in of water beneath her keel. Even though ocean-going cargo and cross-Channel passenger ships could easily embark troops at Cherbourg, coasters were still sent to assist, although not always used, and the first to leave there on 16th June were *Alnwick*, *Camroux IV*, *Empire Jonquil* and *Jaba*: at least 3,000 British troops were aboard the 19 coaster departures from the port mainly for Poole and Weymouth, before these evacuations finished on 18th June. Elsewhere, *Afon Gwili* had been ordered to the Bay of Biscay port of La Pallice, south of St Nazaire, but, after a 21-hour wait on 17th June, found no troops to embark. That same day, *Sparta*, in Brest to discharge a cargo of commercial coal, was requisitioned to carry 500 troops to Falmouth and the next day *Glendinning*, with troops from Nantes, joined a homeward convoy of nine evacuation ships. There was real concern that German air attacks might close the ports of Brest and St Nazaire to the large troopships and ocean-going cargo vessels which had been directed there and, in consequence, troop evacuations would be needed from the beaches or small ports. To cover this eventuality, 17 coasters proceeded to Brest or Quiberon Bay, near St Nazaire, and others were placed on stand-by. In the event, they were not used but the reality of the danger became alarmingly clear on 17th June when the troopship *Lancastria*, embarking servicemen whilst at anchor off St Nazaire, was sunk with disastrous loss of life. Freed from military sailings but still on

government service, some of the coasters then joined the evacuation fleet sent to the Channel Islands to evacuate civilians from Jersey and Guernsey between 20th and 22nd June and from Alderney on the 19th and 23rd, the latter evacuees having fled to that island from France. Operation "Aerial" was brought to an end on 25th June, the coasters once again having played a significant part, particularly at St Malo. It would be almost exactly four years before coasters would once again be setting out for the Continent from British ports and the historic events relating to this are the subject of Part II.

TABLE 1
COASTERS KNOWN TO HAVE REACHED THE FRENCH COAST AS PART OF
OPERATIONS "DYNAMO" (D) – Dunkirk 26th May-4th June
"CYCLE" (C) – St Valery and Le Havre 9th-13th June
AND "AERIAL" (A) – Cherbourg westwards 15th-25th June

Ship	D	C	A	Lost
ABEL TASMAN	D	C		Lost
AEGIR	D			
AFON GWILI		C	A	
ALICE	D			Lost
ALNWICK			A	
ALT			A	
AMAZONE	†D			
ANTIQUITY			A	
ANTJE	D			
ATLANTIC	D	C	A	
BEAL	D			
BETSWOOD			A	
BORNRIF	D			
BULLFINCH	D			
CAMEO		†C		
CAMROUX IV			A	
CARIBIA	D		A	
CLEWBAY			A	
CONTINENTAL COASTER			A	
CORINIA		C	A	
DAGMAR			A	
DEAL			A	
DELTA	D			
DESPATCH II	D	C	A	
DOGGERSBANK	†D		A	
DOMINENCE			A	
DONA FLORA			A	
DORRIEN ROSE	D			
EMERALD		C		

Ship	D	C	A
EMPIRE JONQUIL			A
ESKBURN	D		
FARFIELD			A
FELIXSTOWE			A
FELSPAR			A

Ship	D	C	A
FERMAIN			A
FIRECREST			A
FOAM QUEEN	D		
FREDANJA	†D		A
FRISO	D	C	A

Many of the Dutch coasters taken up in May 1940 performed invaluable service under the White Ensign during the troop evacuations. Seen at Thornycroft's yard, Northam in 1940 *Caribia* was no exception, rescuing around 900 soldiers on four crossings from France. *[National Maritime Museum, N12413]*

Name	D	C	A	Lost
GLEN TILT			A	
GLENDINNING			A	
GLENGARRIFF	D			
GOLDFINCH		†C		
GORECHT	D			
GUERNSEY QUEEN		†C		
HEBE II	D	†C		Lost
HILDA	†D			
HODDER			A	
HONDSRUG	†D		A	
HORST	D			Lost
HULL TRADER			A	
HYTHE	D		A	
JABA	D	C	A	
JADE		C		
JUTLAND	D		A	
KAAP FALGA	D	C		
KILRAE			A	
KINGSTOWN			A	
LADY SHEILA	D			
LENA	†D			Lost
LEVENWOOD	D			
LOWICK		C	A	
MAIDSTONE			A	
MALRIX			A	

Name	D	C	A	Lost
MARSWORTH			A	
MURRAYFIELD			A	
NEPHRITE	D		A	
NGAROMA	D			
NYROCA			A	
OBSIDIAN			A	
ORANJE	D			
OUSE			A	
PACIFIC	D	C		
PARKNASILLA		C		
PASCHOLL	D	†C		
PATRIA	†D			
PERELLE			A	
PINGUIN			A	
POLGRANGE			A	
RAVONIA		C	A	
REIGER	†D			
RIAN	D			
RIKA	D			
ROEBUCK	D	C		
RUJA	D			
SAMBUR		C		
SAN ANTONIO	D	C		
SANDHILL	D	C		
SCHELDT		C		

Name	D	C	A	Lost
SCOTTISH CO-OPERATOR	D		A	
SEINE	D			
SEQUACITY	D			Lost
SILVER COAST		C		
SIR EVELYN WOOD		C		
SPARTA			A	
SUFFOLK COAST			A	
SURSUM CORDA	D			Lost
THE BARON			A	
THE COUNTESS		C		
THEEMS		C		
TILLY	D			
TINY	D			
TWENTE	†D	C		Lost
VREDE	D			
WEGA		C	A	
WEST COASTER			A	
WESTOWN	D			
WHITSTABLE	D			
YEWDALE	D			
YEWPARK			A	
ZEUS	†D	C		

† Following the operations, award made to member(s) of ship's company

One of the 41 small Dutch coasters commissioned for Operation "Dynamo" in May 1940 was *Rian*: she rescued 257 British soldiers from Dunkirk. *[Captain J. F. van Puyvelde]*

Section 3
Ships' Service Record to France, Belgium and Norway
September 1939-June 1940

SHIP'S NAME gross tonnage/year built, nationality (owners/*managers, if British) – date taken up and intended cargo
Loading Port; sailing Date; cargo (dwt); supplementary information
Notes:
   1. The destination of Bristol Channel (BC) convoys was Brest, St Nazaire or Nantes
   2. Commissioned vessels were manned by Royal Navy personnel
   3. The Downs anchorage, between Dover and Ramsgate, was the departure area for ships crossing the Strait of Dover, unless otherwise indicated
   4. Vessels not shown as released continued in military service elsewhere

ABEL TASMAN 314/37 Dutch – commissioned 25/5/40 for Ammunition
• Left Dover for Dunkirk 1900 27/5 with 300 tons of ammunition on Operation "Dynamo"; beached at La Panne 0500 28/5; cargo not required; Captain wounded during air attack 1400 28/5; vessel refloated and left Dunkirk 1745 28/5 with 244 British Army drivers and 20 French staff officers (total 264); arrived Dover 0810 29/5, then moved to Newhaven for cargo discharge
• **Lost.** Left Poole for the St Valery area 10/6 on Operation "Cycle"; in position off the French coast 11/6 but lost contact in fog; returned without troops; arrived Poole 13/6; although fourth in line of ships entering harbour to berth, vessel blown to pieces by mine 1030 13/6 with the loss of all 11 crew

ABUKIR 694/20 British, ex-Egyptian (Ministry of Shipping/*General Steam) – taken up 28/2/40 for Stores
• **Lost.** Left Southampton 24/5 with 750 tons of biscuits for the Belgian Army; left the Downs 25/5 for Ostend, which found to be in ruins and undergoing half-hourly air attacks; cargo discharged by crew members and Dutch and Belgian sailors; loaded motor-cycles, five Army lorries and two staff cars; embarked passengers, including pilots and Belgian evacuees; left Ostend 2300 27/5; subjected to two torpedo attacks, the second, when vessel 50 miles NE of N Foreland at 0130 28/5, resulted in a hit amidships in the engine room; stern burst into flames, vessel broke in two, quickly sank to the bottom and turned over; survivors in the water were machine-gunned; of a total of 220 on board, Master and 30 others rescued by HMS *Codrington*, then transferred to fellow destroyer *Grenade* 0700 28/5 for Dover; ship's report claims attacker was U-boat but sinking officially attributed to E-boat action; 189 lives lost, including 15 crew

A mine explosion sank *Abel Tasman*, despite her being the fourth in line to enter Poole harbour on 13th June 1940. *[Ben Scholten collection]*

ADJUTANT 1,931/22 British (General Steam) – taken up 3/9/39 for Ammunition
• Left Newport and BC 15/9 in convoy BC2; arrived Brest 17/9
• Left Newport 26/9 and BC 27/9 in convoy BC6; arrived Brest 29/9
• Left Newport 15/10 and BC 16/10 in convoy BC11; arrived St Nazaire 18/10
• Left Newport and BC 7/11 in convoy BC14; arrived St Nazaire 12/11; returned to Newport 21/11
• Left Newport 25/1 and BC 26/1 in convoy BC24; arrived St Nazaire 28/1; returned to Fowey 10/2
• Left Fowey 7/3 in convoy AXF2; arrived St Malo 8/3; returned to Fowey 13/3

• Left Fowey 21/4 in convoy AXF4; arrived St Malo 21/4; returned to Fowey 27/4
• Left Fowey 31/5 in convoy AXF7; arrived St Malo 1/6; left St Malo 6/6 with retrieved ammunition; arrived Fowey 8/6; made available 15/6 for Operation "Aerial" but not used

In February 1940, the ammunition loading port for *Adjutant* was moved from Newport to Fowey, to facilitate sailings to St Malo. *[W. H. Brown/J. and M. Clarkson collection]*

AEGIR 277/39 Dutch – commissioned 25/5/40 for Stores
• Left Sheerness for Dunkirk 27/5 on Operation "Dynamo"; left Dunkirk with 247 troops; arrived Dover 1430 29/5
• Returned to Dunkirk; embarked 355 troops; arrived Margate 1555 30/5
• Returned to Dunkirk; embarked 350 troops; arrived Margate 1815 31/5
• Returned to Dunkirk; embarked 130 men, including survivors from HM destroyer *Havant*; arrived Margate 1650 1/6. (Total number evacuated: 1,082.) Paid off 5/6

AFON GWILI 874/20 British (Afon Lliedi/*Coombs) – taken up 24/5/40 for Stores
• Three-quarters loaded at Southampton for the Dunkirk area by 26/5 but cargo not required
• Left Southampton 9/6; called Le Havre 0755 10/6-1120 11/6; left for Cherbourg and Brest with evacuees during Operation "Cycle"; arrived Brest 1830 14/6; left Brest 2000 15/6 on Operation "Aerial"; arrived La Pallice 2330 16/6; waited for soldiers requiring evacuation but none arrived; left La Pallice 2030 17/6 without troops; arrived Falmouth Roads 19/6; released 17/7

AFON TOWY 684/19 British (Afon Lliedi/*Coombs) – taken up 12/6/40 for Stores
• Left Sheerness 17/6; arrived Newhaven 19/6 on Operation "Aerial" stand-by; released 26/6

ALICE 291/39 Dutch – commissioned 25/5/40 for Stores
• **Lost.** Left Southampton 26/5, via Dover, for Dunkirk with 300 tons

of food supplies on Operation "Dynamo"; four miles from French coast, rescued an RAF Hurricane pilot; beached at La Panne 0500 28/5; subjected to air attack; damage to ship revealed when vessel refloated and engines seized up; anchored and abandoned with ballast tanks flooded to allow water into the engine room through the damaged hull; crew transferred to coaster *Kaap Falga*

ALNWICK 508/36 British (Tyne-Tees) – taken up 12/6/40 for Stores
• Arrived Newhaven from London 13/6; left Newhaven for Cherbourg 1500 15/6 on Operation "Aerial"; left Cherbourg 1300 16/6 with British troops; arrived Poole 2200 16/6
• Left Poole 1520 17/6; called Cherbourg 0500-1310 18/6; arrived Poole 1945 18/6; released 28/6 after a crossing from Alderney to Weymouth with civilian evacuees. (Vessel also participated in Operation "Overlord" in 1944: see Part II)

Disembarking at Southampton after completion of their 15-hour crossing from St Malo are some of the 2,000 British troops evacuated by *Alt* in June 1940. *[Imperial War Museum, H1839]*

ALT 1,004/11 British (LMS) – taken up 16/6/40 for Stores
• Arrived Jersey on a commercial voyage from Holyhead 13/6; left Jersey 0330 17/6 on Operation "Aerial"; called St Malo 0730-2135 17/6; left with 2,000 British troops; arrived Southampton 1315 18/6; released same day

AMAZONE 250/39 Dutch – commissioned 25/5/40 for Stores
• Left Poole 25/5; left Dover for Dunkirk 1300 28/5 on Operation "Dynamo"; beached bows in at Bray with ship's boats assisting embarkation; left Dunkirk 0300 29/5 with 190 troops; arrived Dover 1420 29/5

• Left for Dunkirk 0230 30/5 with drinking water for the troops; arrived Bray beach 1000 30/5; cargo discharged; left Dunkirk 1915 30/5 with 320 British and 18 French troops; attacked by aircraft 2010-2030 30/5; four soldiers injured by machine-gun strafing; arrived Ramsgate 0645 31/5

• Left for Dunkirk 1215 31/5; assisted the bringing down of an aircraft already damaged by destroyers 1440 31/5; anchored inshore two miles E of Dunkirk 1530 31/5 with ship's dinghy aiding embarkation; moved one mile further eastwards 1845 31/5; launch *Enterprise* commandeered for ferrying troops until running aground and being abandoned; left Dunkirk 2315 31/5 with 111 French troops; arrived Ramsgate 0500 1/6. (Total number evacuated: 639.) Paid off. (Vessel also participated in Operation "Overlord" in 1944: see Part II)

On 7th October 1939, *Anglian Coast* left Southampton to load cased petrol at Swansea for the British Army at Nantes. *[B. and A. Feilden/J. and M. Clarkson collection]*

ANGLIAN COAST **594/35 British (Coast)** – taken up 30/9/39 for Cased Petrol
• Left Swansea and BC 22/10 in convoy BC12; arrived Nantes 24/10; returned to Swansea 3/11 for release 4/12

ANTIQUITY **311/33 British (Everard)** – taken up 12/6/40 for Stores
• Fitted out at London (Deptford) for emergency evacuation; left Newhaven 15/6 on Operation "Aerial"; called Granville but no troops to evacuate; moved to St Malo 18/6; approached a sandy beach crowded with evacuees but all British troops already evacuated; left St Malo without passengers 19/6; arrived Weymouth Bay 19/6; released 28/6 after a crossing from Jersey to Weymouth with civilian evacuees. (Vessel also participated in Operation "Overlord" in 1944: see Part II)

ANTJE **157/12 Dutch** – commissioned 26/5/40 for Stores
• Left Sheerness on Operation "Dynamo"; left Dunkirk with 443 troops; arrived Margate 1850 31/5
• Returned to Dunkirk; embarked 150 troops; arrived Margate 2100 1/6. (Total number evacuated: 593.) Paid off 5/6

Antiquity anchored off St Malo for the night of 18th-19th June 1940 to await British troops but all had already been evacuated. *[Fotoflite incorporating Skyfotos]*

ARTHUR WRIGHT **1,091/37 British (*Stephenson Clarke)** – taken up 12/6/40 for Stores
• Left Shoreham 15/6; arrived Plymouth 16/6 on Operation "Aerial" stand-by; released 21/6

ASSURITY **164/21 British (Everard)** – taken up 25/5/40 for Stores
• Requisitioned at Southampton for Operation "Dynamo" but not used; released

ATLANTIC **221/30 Dutch** – commissioned 25/5/40 for Stores
• Left Poole 25/5; left Dover for Dunkirk 0900 29/5 on Operation "Dynamo"; beached at La Panne 0300 30/5; used two ship's lifeboats for embarkation; left Dunkirk 1000 30/5 with 78 British and 162 French troops (total 240); arrived Ramsgate 1935 30/5
• Left for Dunkirk 2300 30/5; anchored at Malo beach; embarkation slowed by strong tide and cross wind; as tide fell, engines failed to start, so vessel towed to deeper water by coaster *Ruja*; ship's lifeboats taken away for another assignment, so employed a whaler and the Thames motor launch *Lansdowne*, until latter's propeller became fouled; left Dunkirk 0400 1/6 with *Lansdowne* in tow; rescued troops and crew of naval drifter *Fair Breeze*, sinking after striking a sunken wreck 0425 1/6; *Lansdowne* broke adrift and was abandoned; arrived Ramsgate 1100 1/6 with 71 troops. (Total number evacuated from Dunkirk: 311)
• Left Poole for the St Valery area 10/6 on Operation "Cycle"; in position off the French coast 11/6 but lost contact in fog; with fuel running short, left for Solent without troops 0700 12/6
• Left for France on Operation "Aerial"; arrived Weymouth with troops 0700 18/6; paid off 2/7 after a crossing from Jersey to Weymouth with civilian evacuees

ATLANTIC COAST **890/34 British (Coast)** – taken up 13/10/39 for Cased Petrol
• Left Swansea and BC 30/10 in convoy BC13; arrived Nantes 1/11
• Left Avonmouth 30/11 and BC 1/12 for Brest in convoy BC17; returned to Swansea 13/12
• Left Swansea and BC 12/2 in convoy BC26; arrived Nantes 15/2
• Left Swansea and BC 7/3 in convoy BC29; arrived Nantes 9/3
• Left Swansea and BC 7/4 in convoy BC33; arrived Nantes 9/4
• Left Swansea and BC 1/5 in convoy BC36; arrived Nantes 3/5; returned to Swansea 13/5
(Vessel also participated in Operation "Overlord" in 1944: see Part II)

Nantes and Brest were the October 1939-May 1940 discharge ports for six sailings by the cased petrol carrier *Atlantic Coast*. [B. and A. Feilden/J. and M. Clarkson collection]

BART **435/38 Dutch** – commissioned 23/5/40 for Stores
• Left Sheerness 1830 27/5 with 12,436 packages of food, 400 cases of oil and paraffin, 320 lifebelts and two special gang planks; arrived Dover and loaded a further 240 gallons of paraffin; left Dover for Dunkirk 1400 28/5 on Operation "Dynamo"; cargo not required, so anchored in the Downs; returned to Thames to discharge 7/6; paid off 11/6

BEAL **504/36 British (Tyne-Tees)** – taken up 21/5/40 for Stores
• Fitted out at London for emergency evacuation; arrived in the Downs 21/5; left for Dunkirk 27/5 on Operation "Dynamo"; turned back as route had become within range of German field guns near Calais; re-anchored in the Downs 27/5; left 2245 28/5 by a more northerly route to Dunkirk with coasters *Bullfinch* and *Yewdale*; arrived La Panne 0500 29/5; left Dunkirk 1530 29/5 with 364 British troops; arrived Ramsgate 0825 30/5; released 5/6. (Vessel also participated in Operation "Overlord" in 1944: see Part II)

BETSWOOD **1,051/36 British (France, Fenwick)** – taken up 23/5/40 for Stores
• Commenced loading 1,250 tons at Southampton for the Dunkirk area 23/5 but cargo not required
• Left Shoreham 15/6, via Plymouth, for Quiberon Bay on Operation "Aerial"; returned to Plymouth 18/6 without troops; released 21/6

BORNRIF **121/00 Dutch** – commissioned 25/5/40 for Stores
• Left London (Tilbury) for Dunkirk 1330 27/5 on Operation "Dynamo"; on approaching French coast, departing ships misleadingly signalled that the port was in enemy hands, so turned back; arrived the Downs 1100 28/5
• Left for Dunkirk 1700 28/5; arrived Malo beach 0100 29/5; towed incapacitated coaster *Hondsrug* off the beach and left Dunkirk 0300 29/5 with 50 troops and *Hondsrug* in tow; arrived Ramsgate 1400 29/5
• Left 1500 3/6; arrived Dunkirk West Pier 2230 3/6; failed to tow off grounded coaster *Lena*; left Dunkirk 0100 4/6 with 96 French troops; arrived Ramsgate and grounded off the harbour entrance in thick fog 0700 4/6; troops disembarked by motor boat. (Total number evacuated: 146.) Paid off 6/6

Bornrif abandoned her first crossing to Dunkirk, after receiving incorrect information that the port had been captured by the Germans. [J. and M. Clarkson collection]

BRANDARIS **249/38 Dutch** – commissioned 25/5/40 for Stores
• From Sheerness, left for Dunkirk 1500 27/5 on Operation "Dynamo"; on approaching French coast with *Bornrif* and others, departing ships misleadingly signalled that the port was in enemy hands, so turned back. Unconfirmed reports indicate that vessel landed 166 troops on 29/5 and a further 164 on 30/5; paid off 6/6

BRITISH COAST **889/34 British (Coast)** – taken up 5/10/39 for Cased Petrol
• Left Swansea and BC 30/10 in convoy BC13; arrived Nantes 1/11; returned to Avonmouth 12/11

Photographed here in the Mersey, *British Coast* loaded military cargo in the Bristol Channel for discharge at ports in western France until April 1940: she resumed sailings to the Continent in July 1944 to supply the Allied Armies liberating France. *[B. and A. Feilden/J. and M. Clarkson collection]*

• Left Swansea and BC 18/1 in convoy BC23; arrived Brest 20/1
• Left Swansea 20/2 and BC 21/2 in convoy BC27; arrived Nantes 23/2
• Left Swansea and BC 14/3 in convoy BC30; arrived Nantes 17/3
• Left Swansea and BC 7/4 in convoy BC33; arrived Brest 9/4
• Left Swansea and BC 23/4 in convoy BC35; arrived Nantes 25/4; returned to Swansea 5/5, then left for Stornoway to recover cargo from damaged coaster *Pizarro* (qv). (Vessel also participated in Operation "Overlord" in 1944: see Part II)

BROADHURST 1,013/35 British (Stephenson Clarke)
• Made available at Shoreham 26/5/40 to evacuate 200 troops during Operation "Dynamo" but vessel not taken up and left for Sunderland same day

BULLFINCH 433/36 British (General Steam) – taken up 11/9/39 for Cased Petrol
• Left Avonmouth 20/9 and BC 21/9 for W France in convoy BC4; arrived 23/9; returned to Avonmouth 5/10; with a speed of 8 knots, adjudged

Bullfinch was fortunate to survive the Dunkirk evacuations: she was involuntarily aground for over 11 hours, then sustained bomb damage. *[J. and M. Clarkson collection]*

unsuitable for BC convoys and released 10/10
• Taken up 22/5/40 and fitted out at London for emergency evacuation; left London 22/5; left for Dunkirk 27/5 on Operation "Dynamo"; turned back as route had become within range of German field guns near Calais; re-anchored in the Downs 27/5; left for Dunkirk 2245 28/5 with coasters *Beal* and *Yewdale* by a more northerly route; arrived La Panne beach 0450 29/5; went aground fore and aft 0645 29/5, due failure of kedge anchor to hold; refloated with the assistance of troopship *Royal Sovereign* and left Dunkirk 1815 29/5 with British troops; delayed for repairs after steering gear damaged by concussion from bomb explosions; two aircraft brought down during further attacks; both compasses rendered inoperative by bombs; arrived Ramsgate 1100 30/5; two small vessels from Dunkirk disembarked troops at the same time as *Bullfinch*; the total landed was 913 but the exact number from each ship is not known; released 18/6

CAIRNGORM 394/38 British (Robertson) – taken up 11/9/39 for Cased Petrol
• Left Swansea and BC 27/9 for W France in convoy BC6; arrived 30/9; returned to Swansea 5/10; with a speed of 10 knots, adjudged unsuitable for BC convoys and released 16/10. (Vessel also participated in Operation "Overlord" in 1944: see Part II)

CAMEO 946/37 British (Robertson) – taken up 7/9/39 for Cased Petrol
• Left Swansea and BC 15/9 in convoy BC2; arrived Nantes 17/9
• Left Swansea and BC 6/10 for W France in convoy BC9; arrived 8/10
• Left Swansea and BC 15/11 in convoy BC15; arrived Nantes 18/11; returned to Swansea 27/11
• Arrived Poole from Swansea 13/12; from Poole, arrived Caen 22/12, 14/1, 10/3, 26/3, 7/4, 18/4
• Arrived Swansea from Poole 22/4; left Swansea and BC 1/5 in convoy BC36; arrived Nantes 3/5; returned to Swansea 13/5
• Arrived Poole from Swansea 23/5 on stand-by to load 1,050 tons for the Dunkirk area but cargo not required

Cameo's crew manned two lifeboats to help evacuate 402 troops from the French beaches on 12th June 1940. [E.N. Taylor/J. and M. Clarkson collection]

• Left Poole for the St Valery area 2000 10/6 on Operation "Cycle"; encountered thick fog; subjected to shore gunfire near Fecamp 0800 11/6 but shells fell short; moved to the St Valery area 1100 11/6; shelling restarted, so moved near Fecamp which seen to be in flames; ordered to Veules beach 0300 12/6; crew utilised two ship's lifeboats, making three trips to augment other boats ferrying troops; operation abandoned when boats subjected to machine-gun fire; left Veules 1000 12/6 with 226 British and 176 French troops (total 402); to receive provisions and drinking water and to transfer six wounded soldiers, at 1900 12/6 went alongside HM cruiser *Cardiff*, on stand-by to provide bombardment support; arrived Poole Bay 0830 13/6, berthed Poole 1130 13/6; released 8/8. (Vessel also participated in Operation "Overlord" in 1944: see Part II)

CAMROUX IV 590/38 British (Newcastle) – taken up 12/6/40 for Stores
• Left Newhaven 2025 15/6 on Operation "Aerial"; called Cherbourg 0640-1127 16/6; left with British troops; arrived Poole 2200 16/6
• Left Poole 1530 17/6; called Cherbourg 0445-1315 18/6; arrived Poole 1120 19/6; released 26/6 after a crossing from Alderney to Weymouth with civilian evacuees

CARIBIA 312/36 Dutch – commissioned 26/5/40 for Stores
• Left London (Tilbury) 0315 27/5, via Sheerness, for Dunkirk on Operation "Dynamo"; approaching French coast, embarked troops from a naval drifter then went alongside East Pier; left Dunkirk 0400 29/5 with 320 troops; arrived Margate 1445 29/5
• Left for Dunkirk 1930 29/5; arrived La Panne beach 0500 30/5, then moved to Bray; left Dunkirk 1000 30/5 with 263 British troops; subjected to shore gunfire for 45 minutes; arrived Ramsgate 1735 30/5
• Left 1500 31/5; came under air attack; arrived Dunkirk 2230 31/5 but no troops for evacuation from harbour or beaches; left Dunkirk 0130 1/6 without troops; arrived Ramsgate 0900 1/6. (Total number evacuated from Dunkirk: 583)
• Left for St Malo on Operation "Aerial"; left St Malo 0700 16/6 with about 300 British troops; arrived Weymouth 1515 17/6; paid off 2/7 after a crossing from Jersey to Weymouth with civilian evacuees

CLEWBAY 645/04 British (Kelly/*Clint) – taken up 26/11/39 for Ammunition
• From Newhaven, arrived Fecamp 12/12, 2/1, 7/1, 13/1, 19/1, 25/1, 3/2, 11/2, 20/2; arrived Le Havre 21/3; arrived Fecamp 29/3, 13/4, 29/4, 7/5
• Left Newhaven 2345 22/5 with 578 tons; anchored in the Downs 1410 23/5; left 1515 24/5; arrived Dunkirk harbour 2359 24/5; severity of air raids prevented cargo discharge; left Dunkirk 0020 25/5; arrived the Downs 1040 25/5; arrived Littlehampton 30/5 for cargo discharge
• Left Littlehampton for St Malo 9/6; left St Malo 11/6; arrived Fowey 12/6
• Left Southampton 15/6 on Operation "Aerial"; called Brest 17/6; returned without troops; arrived Falmouth 18/6 and released

CLYDE COAST 511/38 British (Coast) – taken up 6/9/39 for Cased Petrol
• Left Swansea and BC 11/9 in convoy BC1; arrived Nantes 13/9
• Left Avonmouth 2/10 and BC 3/10 in convoy BC8; arrived Brest 8/10; returned to Avonmouth 16/10; with a speed of 9.5 knots, adjudged unsuitable for further BC convoys
• Arrived Poole from Avonmouth 26/10; from Poole, arrived Caen 1/11, 11/11; returned to Poole 14/11 for release 27/11

CONIDA 413/36 British (*Dundee, Perth & London) – taken up 25/5/40 for Stores
• Fully loaded at London for the Dunkirk area 26/5 but cargo not required; vessel released 5/6

CONTINENTAL COASTER 555/07 British (British Isles) – taken up 11/6/40 for Stores
• Left Newhaven for St Malo 14/6 on Operation "Aerial"; left St Malo 0700 16/6 with 284 British troops; arrived Weymouth 2150 16/6; released 28/6

CORINIA 870/28 British (Northwest) – taken up 22/5/40 for Ammunition
• Loaded 1,100 tons at Littlehampton 23-26/5; left 27/5; arrived the Downs 28/5 during Operation "Dynamo"; cargo not required; returned to Littlehampton 6/6
• Left Newhaven for the St Valery area 2200 10/6 towing nine motor yachts and three fishing boats on Operation "Cycle"; arrived off St Valery 1400 11/6; no other ships sighted, so left the French coast without troops 1600 11/6; arrived Newhaven 0930 12/6
• Left Newhaven for St Malo 13/6 on Operation "Aerial"; left St Malo 1900 17/6 with 1,200 British troops; arrived Weymouth 0950 18/6; released 1/7 after a crossing from Guernsey to Weymouth with civilian evacuees

CORMORANT 1,220/27 British (General Steam)
• Made available at London 26/5/40 on 24 hours' notice for Operation "Dynamo" but not taken up

COXWOLD 1,124/38 British (Yorkshire Dale/*Atkinson & Prickett) – taken up 17/9/39 for Cased Petrol
• Left Avonmouth 20/9 and BC 21/9 for Nantes in convoy BC4
• Left Avonmouth 14/10 and BC 16/10 for Brest in convoy BC11
• Left Avonmouth 6/11 and BC 7/11 for Brest in convoy BC14
• Left Avonmouth 30/11 and BC 1/12 for Brest in convoy BC17
• Left Avonmouth and BC 10/1 in convoy BC22; arrived Nantes 12/1
• Left Swansea and BC 12/2 in convoy BC26; arrived Nantes 15/2
• Left Swansea and BC 14/3 in convoy BC30; arrived Nantes 17/3
• Left Swansea and BC 7/4 in convoy BC33; arrived Nantes 9/4; returned to Avonmouth 20/4
• Left Avonmouth for Norway 28/4 with mines and 1,000 tons of cased aviation and vehicle fuel; damaged by striking rocks 7/5; arrived Scapa for inspection 8/5; left Scapa for Harstad in convoy NS4, as replacement for lost coaster *Pembroke Coast*; arrived Narvik area 27/5; ordered to return 7/6 after only 400 tons of cargo discharged; arrived Glasgow 17/6 and BC 19/6. (Vessel also participated in Operation "Overlord" in 1944: see Part II)

DAGMAR 844/22 British, ex-Danish (Ministry of Shipping/*Robertson) – taken up 10/6/40 for Stores
• Left Shoreham 15/6, via Plymouth, for Quiberon Bay on Operation "Aerial"; returned without troops 19/6; released same day

At London, *Cormorant* was placed on stand-by for Dunkirk evacuation service. [*Ships in Focus*]

On 16th June 1940, *Deal* embarked 450 British troops at St Malo for a 10-hour crossing to Plymouth. [*J. and M. Clarkson*]

DEAL 691/28 British (Southern Railway) – taken up 29/5/40 for Stores
• From Plymouth, arrived St Malo 10/6; left St Malo 12/6; arrived Southampton 13/6
• Left Southampton for Guernsey 14/6; left Guernsey for St Malo 15/6 on Operation "Aerial"; left St Malo 1253 16/6 with 450 British troops; arrived Plymouth 2340 16/6; released 19/6 prior to a crossing from Guernsey to Weymouth with civilian evacuees

DELTA 200/34 Dutch – commissioned 24/5/40 for Stores
• Crossed to Dunkirk in ballast on Operation "Dynamo"; left Dunkirk with 203 troops; arrived Margate 1820 30/5
• Returned to Dunkirk; embarked 79 troops; arrived Ramsgate 1000 1/6. (Total number evacuated: 282.) Paid off 5/6

DESPATCH 199/31 Dutch – commissioned 25/5/40 as **DESPATCH II** for Stores
• Left for Dunkirk 0930 29/5 on Operation "Dynamo"; anchored two miles W of La Panne beach 2000 29/5; left Dunkirk 0400 30/5 with 263 French troops and two French civilians; developed engine trouble, so re-anchored for repairs; proceeded, came under fire from shore guns, then survived two bomb explosions in an air attack; arrived Ramsgate 1910 30/5
• Left Ramsgate 0915 31/5; arrived off Dunkirk whilst air attack in progress; anchored three miles E of Dunkirk 1725 31/5; further air attacks; left Dunkirk 0001 1/6 with 139 British and 26 French troops (total 165); arrived Ramsgate 1030 1/6. (Total number evacuated from Dunkirk: 430)
• Left Poole for the St Valery area 10/6 on Operation "Cycle"; in position off the French coast 11/6; ordered to follow troopship *Amsterdam* 2100 11/6 but became detached in fog; left 2130 12/6 without troops; arrived Poole 0915 13/6
• Left Poole for Cherbourg 18/6 on Operation "Aerial"; left Cherbourg 18/6; arrived Poole 19/6; paid off 2/7 after a crossing from Jersey to Weymouth with civilian evacuees

DEVON COAST 646/36 British (Coast) – taken up 11/9/39 for Cased Petrol
• Left Swansea and BC 15/9 for W France in convoy BC2; arrived 17/9
• Left Swansea and BC 3/10 for W France in convoy BC8; arrived 5/10
• Left Swansea and BC 22/10 in convoy BC12; arrived Nantes 24/10
• Left Swansea and BC 15/11 in convoy BC15; arrived Nantes 18/11; returned to Swansea 27/11 for release 16/12

DOGGERSBANK 208/39 Dutch – commissioned 26/5/40 for Stores
• Left Sheerness for Dunkirk 1600 27/5 on Operation "Dynamo"; beached at Bray 1200 28/5 but depth of water proved too great for troops to wade out; boat and raft sent inshore but were initially rushed and swamped; craft righted and Army authorities took charge of embarkation; 450 troops ferried to HM destroyers, including *Grafton*, 2310 28/5; returned

to Bray beach 0750 29/5; boats sent inshore were mobbed and capsized by revolver-wielding French troops; ferried troops to HM destroyer *Codrington*; beached at low water to enable soldiers to walk out to the ship; refloated and left Dunkirk 30/5 with 308 troops; arrived Margate 2100 30/5
• Crossed overnight to Dunkirk 30-31/5; left Dunkirk 31/5 with 400 troops; arrived Margate 1855 31/5. (Total number evacuated from Dunkirk: 708)
• The ship reported a further round trip to Dunkirk on 2-3/6, disembarking 50 troops at Margate but no confirmation found elsewhere
• Left for St Malo on Operation "Aerial"; left St Malo 0700 16/6 with about 300 British troops; arrived Weymouth 1610 17/6
• Left Weymouth for Cherbourg 1830 17/6; left Cherbourg 18/6 with British troops; arrived Weymouth 2300 18/6; paid off after a crossing from Guernsey to Weymouth with civilian evacuees. (Vessel also participated in Operation "Overlord" in 1944: see Part II)

A Royal Navy Lieutenant and crew took over *Doggersbank* from her Dutch owner/captain at Gravesend on 26th May 1940. *[Ben Scholten collection]*

DOMINENCE 261/40 British (London & Rochester) – taken up 10/6/40 for Stores
• Left Newhaven 15/6 on Operation "Aerial"; called St Malo 16-17/6; arrived Weymouth 18/6 and released

DONA FLORA 1,179/24 British (Kingdon/*Donking) – taken up 12/6/40 for Stores
• Left Newhaven 0825 16/6 on Operation "Aerial"; arrived Cherbourg 2220 16/6; left 1200 17/6 with British troops; arrived Weymouth 2230 17/6
• Left Weymouth 0200 18/6; called Cherbourg 1220-1400 18/6; arrived Poole 1108 19/6; released 29/7. (Vessel also participated in Operation "Overlord" in 1944: see Part II)

In June 1940, *Dona Flora* made two crossings in support of the successful evacuation of Cherbourg. *[World Ship Society Ltd.]*

DORRIEN ROSE 1,039/22 British (Hughes) – taken up 21/5/40 for Stores
• Loaded 1,200 tons of stores below and cased petrol on deck at Newhaven 22-23/5; arrived the Downs 26/5; left for Dunkirk 1430 27/5 on Operation "Dynamo"; anchored off the Belgian coast until 0300 28/5; subjected to air attack 0420 28/5; went alongside, port bow to starboard bow, troopship *Queen of the Channel*, bombed and sinking 10 miles N of Ostend 0505 28/5; embarked 904 troops and crew and took four lifeboats in tow, two of which later broke away; left the scene 0525 28/5; escorted part way by HM destroyer *Greyhound*; arrived Dover 1420 28/5
• Left for Dunkirk 1340 29/5; struck a submerged wreck 1610 29/5; anchored for repairs after water entered engine room bilges; proceeded 1830 29/5; came under fire from enemy surface craft 0400 30/5; arrived Dunkirk East Pier 0650 30/5; landed half her cargo of provisions but this created such congestion on the pier that further unloading abandoned; left Dunkirk 1220 30/5 with 637 troops; two bombs narrowly missed ship on leaving port; arrived Folkestone 2045 30/5 then moved to Newhaven for repairs. (Total number evacuated: 1,541.) Released 9/7. (Vessel also participated in Operation "Overlord" in 1944: see Part II)

DORSET COAST 646/36 British (Coast) – taken up 14/9/39 for Cased Petrol
• Left Swansea and BC 21/9 in convoy BC4; arrived Nantes 23/9
• Left Swansea and BC 9/10 in convoy BC10; arrived Brest 11/10
• Left Swansea and BC 30/10 in convoy BC13; arrived Nantes 1/11; returned to Swansea 12/11
• Left Swansea and BC 7/3 in convoy BC29; arrived Nantes 9/3
• Left Swansea and BC 30/3 in convoy BC32; arrived Nantes 1/4
• Left Swansea and BC 1/5 in convoy BC36; arrived Nantes 3/5; returned to Avonmouth 13/5; released 23/7

EILDON 1,447/36 British (Gibson) – taken up 4/9/39 for Cased Petrol
• Left Swansea and BC 11/9 in convoy BC1; arrived Brest 13/9
• Left Avonmouth and BC 24/9 in convoy BC5; arrived Nantes 26/9
• Left Avonmouth 8/10 and BC 9/10 in convoy BC10; arrived Nantes 11/10
• Left Avonmouth 29/10 and BC 30/10 in convoy BC13; arrived Brest 1/11
• Left Avonmouth 22/11 and BC 23/11 in convoy BC16; arrived Brest 25/11; left Brest 29/11 but turned back to Camaret Bay for shelter; returned to Avonmouth 5/12
• Left Swansea and BC 10/1 in convoy BC22; detached to Rouen, arrived 13/1
• Left Newport 4/2 and BC 6/2 in convoy BC25; arrived Brest 8/2
• Left Newport 13/3 and BC 14/3 in convoy BC30; detached to St Malo, arrived 17/3
• Left Swansea and BC 23/4 in convoy BC35; arrived Nantes 25/4
• Left Swansea and BC 16/5 in convoy BC38; arrived Nantes 18/5; called Brest 24/5; returned to Swansea 25/5. (Vessel also participated in Operation "Overlord" in 1944: see Part II)

EMERALD 736/04 British (Robertson) – taken up 9/6/40 for Stores
• Arrived Le Havre from Cardiff with commercial coal 8/6; left Le Havre 2000 9/6 on Operation "Cycle" with British troops and 150 tons of undischarged cargo; arrived Cherbourg 10/6
• Returned to Le Havre 2030 11/6; embarked 40 British demolition and rearguard troops from motor boats in Havre Roads; left 0500 13/6; arrived Cherbourg 2000 13/6 and released

EMPIRE JONQUIL 369/39 British (Ministry of Shipping/*Monroe) – taken up 12/6/40 for Stores
• Left Newhaven 1455 15/6 on Operation "Aerial"; called Cherbourg 0600-1140 16/6; left with British troops; arrived Poole 2200 16/6
• Left Poole 1340 17/6; called Cherbourg 0600-1115 18/6; arrived Poole 1940 18/6; released 25/6 after a crossing from Alderney to Weymouth with civilian evacuees. (Vessel also participated in Operation "Overlord" in 1944: see Part II)

ESKBURN 472/17 British (British Isles) – Taken up 29/5/40 for Stores
• Left Southampton 29/5 and the Downs 2300 30/5 on Operation "Dynamo"; arrived Dunkirk 0830 31/5; embarked 27 Belgian troops; left Dunkirk 2345 31/5; arrived Folkestone 0845 1/6 and released

FARFIELD 468/21 British (Coppack) – taken up 17/6/40 for Stores
• At Jersey, having arrived from Plymouth 16/6; left Jersey for St Malo 1100 17/6 on Operation "Aerial"; left St Malo 2030 17/6 with 188 RAF personnel and ground equipment of Nos 17 and 501 Squadrons, whose fighters temporarily based in Jersey to cover the Cherbourg evacuations; arrived Jersey 0505 18/6; released after a crossing from Jersey to Weymouth with civilian evacuees

FAUVETTE 614/35 British (General Steam)
• Made available at London 26/5/40 on 24 hours' notice for Operation "Dynamo" but not taken up

Six General Steam vessels were on 24 hours' notice for Dunkirk, including *Fauvette*, seen her in 1953. *[Ships in Focus]*

FAXFLEET 863/16 British (Ouse/*Atkinson) – taken up 23/5/40 for Stores
• Loaded 1,100 tons at Newhaven for the Dunkirk area 24-26/5 but cargo not required; vessel released 4/6

FELIXSTOWE 892/18 British (LNER) – taken up 10/6/40 for Stores
• Left Newhaven 0720 16/6 on Operation "Aerial"; called Cherbourg 1850-2115 16/6; left with British troops; arrived Poole 0550 17/6
• Left Poole 1533 17/6; called Cherbourg 2050-2250 17/6; left with British troops; arrived Poole 0500 18/6 and Weymouth 2145 18/6; released 26/6 after a crossing from Guernsey to Weymouth with civilian evacuees

Unable to sail to her normal ports after the fall of Belgium, *Felixstowe* was about to serve the Channel Islands when requisitioned. *[J. and M. Clarkson collection]*

FELSPAR 799/08 British (Robertson) – taken up 21/5/40 for Ammunition
• Loaded 890 tons at Newhaven for the Dunkirk area 23-24/5; left Newhaven 26/5; arrived in the Downs 27/5 during Operation "Dynamo"; cargo not required; left the Downs 5/6; arrived Newhaven 6/6
• Left Newhaven 7/6; arrived St Malo 2200 9/6; left 2000 12/6 with retrieved ammunition; arrived Littlehampton 1900 14/6
• Left Littlehampton for St Malo 16/6 on Operation "Aerial" stand-by; off St Malo 1840 17/6-1725 18/6; arrived Weymouth 1155 19/6; released 4/7 after a crossing from Jersey to Weymouth with civilian evacuees. (Vessel also participated in Operation "Overlord" in 1944 but as a naval collier)

FERMAIN 759/20 British (Dorey) – taken up 12/6/40 for Stores
• Left Newhaven 16/6, via Plymouth, on Operation "Aerial"; arrived St Nazaire 18/6; directed to embark Belgian troops but no contact made; returned without troops; arrived Falmouth 19/6; released 28/6

FIRECREST 538/29 British (Paul) – taken up 11/6/40 for Stores
• Left London 11/6; arrived Plymouth 16/6; left 0330 17/6 for St Nazaire on Operation "Aerial"; did not enter port and left 19/6 without troops; arrived Plymouth 1000 21/6; released 22/6

FIRTH FISHER 574/19 British (Fisher) – taken up 20/5/40 for Stores
• **Lost.** Left Littlehampton 20/5 with 460 tons; left the Downs for Boulogne 21/5; when E of the Boulogne pierhead at 1840 21/5, detonated a magnetic mine; vessel broke in two and immediately went down; seven crew members lost; pilot and three others rescued by commercial coaster *Sparta*, which then damaged by 12 attacking aircraft

FOAM QUEEN 811/22 British (British Channel Islands) – taken up 24/5/40 for Stores
• Loaded 1,050 tons at Littlehampton for the Dunkirk area 24-26/5 but cargo not required, so discharged; left Littlehampton 29/5; left the Downs for Dunkirk 31/5 on Operation "Dynamo"; left Dunkirk 0300 1/6 with 98 French troops; arrived Ramsgate 0910 1/6; released 9/6

FREDANJA 277/36 Dutch – commissioned 25/5/40 for Stores
• Left Newhaven 2200 27/5 on Operation "Dynamo"; went alongside Dunkirk East Pier 0015 29/5; left Dunkirk 0415 29/5 with 230 troops; arrived Dover 1435 29/5
• Left Dover for Dunkirk 0800 30/5 with 20 tons of stores and drinking water for the troops; arrived Malo beach 1400 30/5; discharged cargo; left Dunkirk with 450 troops 1900 30/5; air attack with bombs and machine-gun fire caused six casualties and damaged engine and compass 2030 30/5; arrived Ramsgate 0645 31/5. (Total number evacuated from Dunkirk: 680)
• Left for Cherbourg on Operation "Aerial"; arrived Weymouth with troops 1230 18/6; paid off 3/7

FRISO 250/39 Dutch – commissioned 25/5/40 for Stores
• Left Dover for Dunkirk 1230 28/5 with a lifeboat in tow on Operation "Dynamo"; sailed along the coast eastwards from Dunkirk but found no troops to evacuate; went alongside Dunkirk East Pier 0030 29/5; left Dunkirk with 138 troops; arrived Dover 1400 29/5
• Left Dover for Dunkirk 2100 29/5 with stores and drinking water for the troops; subjected to air attack with one bomb exploding 250yds from ship's starboard bow; entered Dunkirk harbour but no troops waiting and port being shelled; moved to the beaches; left Dunkirk 1230 30/5 with 357 troops; took in tow a naval drifter 1330 30/5; bomb exploded between drifter and *Friso* causing slight damage to auxiliary machinery and compass 1400 30/5; subjected to shelling from shore guns 1430 30/5; encountered thick fog 1830 30/5; arrived Dover 0045 31/5. (Total number evacuated from Dunkirk: 495)
• Left Poole for the St Valery area 10/6 on Operation "Cycle"; in position off the French coast 11/6 but lost contact in fog; returned 13/6 without troops
• Left for Cherbourg on Operation "Aerial"; left Cherbourg 18/6; arrived Southampton 0130 19/6; paid off 5/7

During the Dunkirk evacuations, the Dutch coaster *Friso* survived four attacks by shells or bombs. *[World Ship Society Ltd.]*

GALACUM 585/15 British (Northwest) – taken up 24/5/40 for Stores
• Loaded 750 tons at London (Deptford) for the Dunkirk area 24-26/5 but cargo not required; released 5/6. (Vessel also participated in Operation "Overlord" in 1944: see Part II)

GATESHEAD 744/19 British (Tyne-Tees) – taken up 21/5/40 for Stores
• Fitted out for emergency evacuation; left London and arrived in Downs 22/5; left for Dunkirk 27/5 on Operation "Dynamo"; ordered to turn back; at anchor in the Downs 27/5-3/6; released 5/6. (Vessel also participated in Operation "Overlord" in 1944: see Part II)

GLAMIS 555/36 British (Dundee, Perth & London) – taken up 5/9/39 for Cased Petrol
• Left Swansea and BC 21/9 for W France in convoy BC4
• Left Swansea and BC 6/10 for W France in convoy BC9; returned to Swansea 19/10; with a speed of 9 knots, adjudged unsuitable for further BC convoys
• Left Swansea 22/10; from Poole, arrived Caen 30/10, 9/11, 23/11, 14/12, 7/1, 28/1; arrived Alderney 18/2; arrived St Malo 19/2; arrived Caen 8/3, 22/3, 4/4, 17/4, 26/4, 7/5, 16/5
• Loaded 500 tons for the Dunkirk area; left Poole 1920 20/5 to anchor in the Downs; cargo not required; returned to Poole 0820 1/6
• Made available at Poole 8/6 for Operation "Cycle"
• Left Poole 12/6; called Brest 15/6; returned to Poole 17/6. (Vessel also participated in Operation "Overlord" in 1944: see Part II)

It became clear that, with a speed of only nine knots, *Glamis* could become a liability in escorted convoys to France. *[Ships in Focus]*

GLEN TILT 871/20 British (South Georgia) – taken up 6/40 for Stores
• At anchor off Le Havre 4/6 on a commercial voyage, brought down an attacking aircraft with her third 12pdr round; arrived Granville 9/6 for commercial cargo; before cargo loaded, taken up for Operation "Aerial" and left Granville 1432 15/6; arrived St Malo 1950 15/6; left St Malo 1430 16/6 with 500 British troops; arrived Weymouth 1225 17/6; released after a crossing from Alderney and another from Guernsey, both to Weymouth with civilian evacuees

GLENDINNING 1,927/21 British (Gibson) – taken up 18/6/40 for Stores
• At Nantes having arrived on a commercial voyage from Middlesbrough 12/6; left Nantes 0400 and St Nazaire 1100 18/6 on Operation "Aerial" in convoy of nine transports, all carrying British troops; arrived Plymouth 1300 20/6 and released. (Vessel also participated in Operation "Overlord" in 1944: see Part II)

Glendinning was requisitioned at Nantes in June 1940 and joined a convoy of nine vessels evacuating British troops from western France. *[National Maritime Museum, P22833]*

GLENGARRIFF 868/36 British (Kelly) – taken up 5/40 for Stores
• Left Portsmouth 28/5 and the Downs 0100 31/5 for Dunkirk on Operation "Dynamo"; arrived off Bray beach 0600 31/5; left Dunkirk 1530 31/5 with 64 British troops; arrived Dover 2255 31/5 and released. (Vessel also participated in Operation "Overlord" in 1944: see Part II)

GOLDFINCH 454/37 British (General Steam) – taken up 12/9/39 for Cased Petrol
• Left Swansea 26/9 and BC 27/9 for W France in convoy BC6; returned to Avonmouth 5/10; with a speed of 9 knots, deemed unsuitable for BC convoys
• Arrived Southampton from Avonmouth 17/10; from Southampton, arrived Caen 27/10, 3/11, 12/11, 1/12
• From Poole, arrived Caen 19/1, 3/2, 11/2, 18/2, 4/3, 17/3; with RAF cargo, arrived Guernsey 7/4, Jersey 8/4; arrived Caen 14/4, 25/4, 5/5, 15/5, 19/5
• Made available at Poole to load 490 tons of cased petrol for the Dunkirk area 24/5 but cargo not required; at anchor in the Downs in ballast during Operation "Dynamo"; returned to Poole Bay 1/6, berthed Poole 5/6
• Left Southampton for the St Valery area 0400 11/6 towing two powered and four other ships' lifeboats on Operation "Cycle"; arrived off the French coast 2300 11/6; went close inshore 12/6; using ship's boats at Veules, ferried 500 soldiers to troopship *Princess Maud*; came under fire from shore guns 0815 12/6; two direct hits caused damage; naval rating killed and buried at sea that night; left 12/6 without troops; arrived Southampton 1245 13/6. (Vessel also participated in Operation "Overlord" in 1944: see Part II)

GORECHT 187/27 Dutch – commissioned 27/5/40 for Stores
• Left for Dunkirk on Operation "Dynamo"; left Dunkirk with 47 troops, arrived Dover 1000 30/5; paid off after a crossing from Guernsey to Weymouth with civilian evacuees

GORSEFIELD 628/22 British (Zillah/*Savage) – taken up 28/12/39 for Ammunition
• From Newhaven, arrived Fecamp 10/1, 16/1, 24/1, 31/1, 10/2, 18/2, 5/3
• From Littlehampton/Newhaven, arrived Rouen 14/3, 26/3; arrived Fecamp 31/3; arrived Rouen 9/4; arrived Dieppe 22/4
• From Southampton, arrived Rouen 1/5, 8/5, 13/5, 19/5
• Commenced loading 600 tons at Littlehampton for the Dunkirk area 24/5 but cargo not required
• Made available at Littlehampton for Operation "Cycle" 8/6; assigned to leave Newhaven for Granville 15/6 on Operation "Aerial"

In 1940, *Gorsefield* initially served as an ammunition carrier, crossing from Newhaven to Fecamp independently and without escort. *[World Ship Society Ltd.]*

GRIT 501/34 British (Everard) – taken up 12/9/39 for Cased Petrol
• Left Swansea and BC 18/9 in convoy BC3; arrived Nantes 20/9; returned to Swansea 25/9; with a speed of 9 knots, adjudged unsuitable for BC convoys and released 4/10

Being regarded as unsuitable for sailings in convoy at the end of her first crossing to Nantes, *Grit* was released from military service. *[J. and M. Clarkson collection]*

GUERNSEY QUEEN **567/39 British (British Channel Islands)** – taken up 20/9/39 for Cased Petrol
• Left Swansea and BC 6/10 for W France in convoy BC9; arrived 8/10; returned to Swansea 14/10
• Arrived Poole from Swansea 18/10; from Poole, arrived Caen 22/10, 3/11, 14/11, 21/11, 5/12, 17/12, 11/1, 9/2, 21/2, 15/3, 29/3, 11/4, 24/4, 1/5, 8/5, 14/5, 18/5
• Made available at Poole to load 560 tons for the Dunkirk area 24/5 but cargo not required
• Left Poole for the St Valery area on Operation "Cycle"; arrived off the French coast 0030 12/6; proceeded so close inshore at Veules that vessel touched bottom; shells from field guns damaged water tanks, funnel, lifeboat and hull; left 12/6 with 37 British and 55 French troops (total 92); arrived Poole 1030 13/6; left Poole 1905 17/6; called Guernsey 0940-1630 18/6; called Jersey 2000 18/6-0530 19/6 and Guernsey again 0830-2215 19/6; arrived Poole 1420 20/6. (Vessel also participated in Operation "Overlord" in 1944: see Part II)

GWENTHILLS **868/37 British (Mordey)** – taken up 5/6/40 for Stores
• At Le Havre having arrived on a commercial voyage from Newport and Rouen 4/6; left Le Havre 1700 8/6 with retrieved stores; arrived Southampton 1100 9/6; released 14/6. (Vessel also participated in Operation "Overlord" in 1944: see Part II)

HEBE **176/32 Dutch** – commissioned 25/5/40 as ***HEBE II*** for Stores
• Left for Dunkirk 27/5 on Operation "Dynamo"; arrived off the beaches 0030 28/5 but no troops awaiting evacuation; went alongside Dunkirk East Pier; embarked 67 troops; arrived Dover 1510 29/5
• Left Dover 2000 29/5; found Dunkirk East Pier to be deserted, so moved eastwards and beached to allow soldiers to wade out and climb on board 30/5; ferried 300 troops to a destroyer, followed by another load to HM minesweeper *Fitzroy*; attempted to tow coaster *Sursum Corda* off beach but only succeeded in grounding herself; refloated and embarked 250 troops who, together with men rescued from the water and from small boats, ferried to a destroyer; left Dunkirk 2300 30/5 with 270 troops; arrived Dover 1020 31/5. (Total number evacuated from Dunkirk: 337)
• **Lost.** Left Poole for the St Valery area 10/6 on Operation "Cycle"; in position off the French coast 11/6; despite heavy fire, ferried 80 troops from Veules beach to troopship *Princess Maud* 0200-0400 12/6; went inshore again 0630 12/6 for further embarkations but firmly grounded on a falling tide and had to be abandoned

HILDA **250/39 Dutch** – commissioned 26/5/40 for Stores
• Left Sheerness 1800 27/5 on Operation "Dynamo"; arrived Dunkirk East Pier 1200 28/5, then moved to Bray beach, where exhausted troops experienced difficulty in climbing aboard; ferried 500 troops to a destroyer 1900 28/5; embarked further troops brought out by ship's boat; ship

stuck firmly aground; further 400 troops waded out to board 0130 29/5; refloating enabled embarked troops to be ferried to a destroyer, probably HMS *Esk*; embarked another 100 troops, some severely wounded, and ferried them to a destroyer; moved to La Panne to ferry troops from grounded paddle steamer, probably *Gracie Fields*, to destroyers; left Dunkirk 1900 29/5 with 385 troops; arrived Dover 0815 30/5
• Left for Dunkirk 31/5 with naval boat crews embarked and motor boats *Britannic, Gipsy King, Golden Spray II, Lady Haig, Moss Rose* and *Rose Marie* and two ships' lifeboats in tow; arrived La Panne beach which being subjected to gunfire 1600 31/5; ferried 600 troops to HM destroyer *Scimitar* 2030 31/5; embarked further troops 0400 1/6; in near proximity to HM destroyer *Keith* and HM minesweeper *Skipjack* when both were bombed and sunk 0830-0850 1/6; rescued survivors, including two British Brigadiers and one French General; left Dunkirk, stopped on passage to rescue a few survivors from the crippled troopship *Scotia* and paddle minesweeper *Brighton Queen*; disembarked 416 British and 82 French troops (total 498) on arrival Ramsgate 1800 1/6
• Left for Dunkirk 1900 2/6 with two boats in tow; arrived off the beaches 0130 3/6 but no troops awaiting evacuation; returned to Ramsgate 0900 3/6. (Total number evacuated: 883.) Paid off 5/6

HODDER **1,016/10 British (LMS)** – taken up 17/6/40 for Stores
• At Jersey having arrived on a commercial voyage from Holyhead 14/6; left Jersey 0330 17/6 on Operation "Aerial"; called St Malo 0730-2359 17/6; found no troops awaiting evacuation; sighted German aircraft laying magnetic mines 0230 18/6; took in tow coaster *Jutland*; arrived Jersey 1050 18/6; released 21/6 after a crossing from Jersey to Southampton with 150 men of the Royal Jersey Militia and wives of staff officers

At Jersey to load potatoes for Holyhead, *Hodder* was ordered to proceed to St Malo as part of the evacuation fleet. *[J. and M. Clarkson collection]*

HONDSRUG **227/37 Dutch** – commissioned 24/5/40 for Stores
• Left Sheerness 0300 and the Downs 1500 27/5 for Dunkirk on Operation "Dynamo"; on approaching French coast, misleadingly signalled by departing ships that the port was in enemy hands, so turned back; arrived in the Downs 1000 28/5
• Left for Dunkirk 1815 28/5; beached to embark troops 0200 29/5 but screw became fouled; left Dunkirk in tow of coaster *Bornrif* with 500 troops; arrived Ramsgate 1400 29/5
• After screw cleared, left for Dunkirk 0730 31/5; arrived off the beaches whilst heavy bombing in progress 1500 31/5; beached but water too deep for troops to wade out, so moved to anchorage and embarked troops from motor boats 2300 31/5; moved to Dunkirk East Pier 0330 1/6; left Dunkirk 0600 1/6 with 141 British and 83 French troops (total 224); on departure, machine-gunned by a low flying aircraft; arrived Ramsgate 1135 1/6
• Left for Dunkirk 1530 1/6; entered the harbour 2130 1/6 during air raid; left Dunkirk 2200 1/6 with 421 French troops; arrived Ramsgate 0445 2/6
• Left for Dunkirk 1600 3/6; left Dunkirk West Pier 0001 4/6 with 297 French soldiers and 11 French sailors (total 308); arrived Ramsgate in fog 0540 4/6. (Total number evacuated from Dunkirk: 1,453)
• Left for St Malo on Operation "Aerial"; left St Malo 0700 16/6 with about 300 British troops; arrived Weymouth 1525 17/6; paid off 2/7 after a crossing from Jersey to Weymouth with civilian evacuees. (Vessel also participated in Operation "Overlord" in 1944: see Part II)

HORST **400/39 Dutch** – commissioned 25/5/40 for Stores
• Left for Dunkirk 28/5 on Operation "Dynamo"; left Dunkirk with 350 troops; arrived Margate 1640 29/5
• Returned to Dunkirk; embarked 800 troops; arrived Margate 0005 31/5. (Total number evacuated: 1,150)
• **Lost.** Left for Dunkirk 1315 31/5; arrived La Panne beach 1800 31/5; embarked troops; when about to weigh, cable became fouled, donkey engine broke down and ship sustained damage from nearby explosion; troops transferred to another vessel and *Horst* abandoned with auxiliary machinery deliberately left running to seize up

HULL TRADER **717/17 British (Free Trade Wharf)** – taken up 11/6/40 for Stores
• Left Newhaven 15/6 and Littlehampton 16/6 for St Malo on Operation "Aerial"; left St Malo 1900 17/6 with 150 British troops; arrived Weymouth 1240 18/6; released 27/6

HYTHE **688/25 British (Southern Railway)** – taken up 29/5/40 for Stores
• Left Southampton 29/5 and the Downs 0230 31/5 for Dunkirk on Operation "Dynamo"; relied on a military road map for inshore navigation; Dunkirk approach channels under air attack and being subjected to shore gunfire as vessel arrived 0634 31/5; surf proved too rough for beach embarkation, so moved to Dunkirk East Pier 0800 31/5; harbour entrance

In the absence of a naval chart, *Hythe* resorted to a military road map for navigation off Dunkirk in May 1940: her success in this regard is confirmed by her safe rescue of 749 Belgian, French and British troops. *[Fotoflite incorporating Skyfotos]*

subjected to heavy gunfire from the shore; with intermittent bombing in progress and shelling becoming more accurate, despite space remaining on forecastle head for 20-30 more men, ship ordered to leave Dunkirk at 0920 31/5 with 2 Belgian, 4 French and 743 British troops (total 749), including 18 wounded; arrived Dover 1445 31/5
• Left Southampton 12/6 on Operation "Cycle" stand-by; returned to Southampton 13/6
• Left Southampton 15/6 and Plymouth 17/6 on Operation "Aerial"; called St Nazaire 18/6; returned to Plymouth 19/6 without troops; released same day

JABA **200/37 Dutch** – commissioned 25/5/40 for Stores
• Left for Dunkirk on Operation "Dynamo"; left Dunkirk with 199 troops; arrived Dover 1437 29/5
• Returned to Dunkirk; embarked 173 troops; arrived Ramsgate 0845 31/5
• Returned to Dunkirk; embarked 95 British and 201 French troops (total 296); arrived Ramsgate 1250 1/6. (Total number evacuated from Dunkirk: 668)
• Left Poole for the St Valery area 10/6 on Operation "Cycle"; in position off the French coast 11/6 but lost contact in fog; returned without troops 12/6
• Left for Cherbourg on Operation "Aerial"; left Cherbourg 1200 16/6 with British troops; arrived Poole 16/6
• Left Poole for Cherbourg 17/6; left Cherbourg 18/6; arrived Poole 19/6; paid off 5/7 after a crossing from Jersey to Weymouth with civilian evacuees

Assigned to transport cased petrol, *Jacinth* participated in the very first military cargo convoy from the Bristol Channel to western France. *[J. and M. Clarkson]*

JACINTH **650/37 British (Robertson)** – taken up 6/9/39 for Cased Petrol
• Left Avonmouth and BC 11/9 in convoy BC1; arrived Nantes 13/9
• Left Swansea and BC 27/9 in convoy BC6; arrived Nantes 30/9; returned to Avonmouth 8/10; with a speed of 9 knots, adjudged unsuitable for BC convoys
• Arrived Poole from Avonmouth 20/10; from Poole, arrived Caen 26/10, 7/11, 20/11, 2/12; released after return to Poole 5/12

JADE **930/38 British (Robertson)** – taken up 4/9/39 for Cased Petrol
• Left Swansea and BC 16/10 for W France in convoy BC11
• Left Swansea and BC 7/11 for W France in convoy BC14; returned to Swansea 21/11
• Arrived Poole 12/12; from Poole, arrived Caen 31/12, 21/1, 4/2, 16/2, 25/2, 7/3, 20/3, 2/4, 13/4, 20/4, 28/4, 10/5
• Made available at Poole to load 1,050 tons for the Dunkirk area 24/5; left Poole 25/5; cargo not required; returned to Poole 27/5
• Left Poole for the St Valery area 9/6 with naval officer embarked on Operation "Cycle"; arrived off Fecamp 11/6 to discover port in flames; subjected to machine-gun fire from the shore off St Valery 12/6; returned without troops; arrived Swansea 15/6. (Vessel also participated in Operation "Overlord" in 1944: see Part II)

JAVA **341/36 Dutch** – commissioned 25/5/40 for Stores
• Left Southampton 29/5 and Dover 1945 1/6 for Dunkirk on Operation "Dynamo"; engine failed 16 miles from destination 2359 1/6; restarted and proceeded a further five miles towards French coast, then turned back to Dover; arrived London 5/6 in tow of coaster *Bornrif*; paid off 6/6

JOLLY GIRLS **483/36 British (Horlock)** – taken up 13/9/39 for Cased Petrol
• Left Avonmouth and BC 24/9 for W France in convoy BC5; returned to Avonmouth 2/10; with a speed of 9 knots, adjudged unsuitable for BC convoys and released 16/10

JUTLAND **357/37 Dutch** – commissioned 24/5/40 for Stores
• Left Sheerness for Dunkirk 0500 27/5 on Operation "Dynamo"; arrived off French coast; after waiting three hours for orders, returned without troops; arrived in the Downs 1000 28/5
• Left for Dunkirk 1730 28/5; arrived at the beaches but no troops to evacuate; left Dunkirk 0250 29/5; arrived Ramsgate 0830 29/5
• Left for Dunkirk 1000 29/5; subjected to air attack on approaches to French coast 1715 29/5; arrived La Panne and embarked 275 French troops; embarked a further 40 troops from damaged HM paddle minesweeper *Gracie Fields* (total 315); left Dunkirk 2130 29/5; arrived Ramsgate 0600 30/5
• Left Ramsgate for Dunkirk 1530 30/5 with motor boat *Constant Nymph*, Dutch eel boat *Johanna*, a cutter and a whaler in tow; arrived off the beaches 2330 30/5; left Dunkirk 0300 31/5 with 205 French troops aboard and five boats in tow; on passage handed over boats and took disabled coaster *Rian* in tow to the Downs; arrived Ramsgate 1100 31/5. (Total number evacuated from Dunkirk: 520)
• Arrived St Malo with cased petrol and ammunition on Operation "Aerial"; on return, engines broke down; taken in tow towards Jersey by coaster *Hodder* 18/6; arrived Weymouth 2140 19/6; paid off 2/7

KAAP FALGA 378/38 Dutch – commissioned 25/5/40 for Stores
• Left Southampton 2030 26/5 with 300 tons of food supplies on Operation "Dynamo"; left the Downs for Dunkirk 2030 27/5; arrived La Panne beach 0800 28/5; landed some cargo; attacked by 20 bombers 1400 28/5; left Dunkirk with crew of abandoned coaster *Alice* and five troops 1700 28/5; arrived Ramsgate 0300 29/5; arrived Dover 1200 31/5 to land undischarged cargo
• Left Portsmouth for the St Valery area 1830 11/6 on Operation "Cycle"; arrived eight miles off Fecamp 0415 12/6; sustained shell hit on port quarter; rescued crew from sinking coaster *Twente* 0630 12/6; left without troops 1300 12/6; arrived Newhaven 0130 13/6; paid off 3/7

During the 1940 evacuations, *Kaap Falga* was attacked by 20 bombers on 28th May and damaged by shell fire on 12th June. She was photographed off Tower Stairs Pier on 11th June 1954. *[J. and M. Clarkson collection]*

KILREA 767/12 British (Mersey Ports Stevedoring) – taken up 11/6/40 for Stores
• Left Southampton 0425 16/6 on Operation "Aerial"; called Brest 1515-2000 17/6; returned without troops; arrived Belfast 19/6; released 21/6

KINGSTOWN 628/10 British (Barkley/*Clint) – taken up 17/6/40 for Stores
• At St Malo having arrived on a commercial voyage from Glasgow 11/6; left St Malo 2000 17/6 with 283 troops on Operation "Aerial"; arrived Weymouth 1430 18/6 and released

LADY SHEILA 216/35 British (Bradley) – taken up 25/5/40 for Stores
• Requisitioned at Southampton; left the Downs for Dunkirk 1350 30/5 on Operation "Dynamo"; arrived 2130 30/5; left Dunkirk 2250 30/5 with 185 British troops; arrived Dover 0627 31/5 and released

For service in the event of a Dunkirk-style evacuation becoming necessary, *Kilrea* was a member of the coaster fleet ordered to Brest. *[J. and M. Clarkson]*

LENA 383/38 Dutch – commissioned 25/5/40 for Stores
• After correcting defective engine, left Sheerness for Dunkirk 0430 27/5 on Operation "Dynamo"; arrived off the beaches 2130 27/5; ferried 120 troops to a destroyer 28/5; left Dunkirk with 353 troops; anchored off Ramsgate 2330 28/5; went alongside 0700 29/5
• Left for Dunkirk 1600 29/5; arrived off the beaches for embarkation using ship's boats; left Dunkirk with 304 troops, including 67 wounded, several of whom did not survive the crossing; arrived Ramsgate 0635 30/5
• Left for Dunkirk 0545 1/6 with a cargo of 25 small kedge anchors; arrived off the beaches 1300 1/6; air attack caused one minor casualty and slight damage to ship; left Dunkirk 2145 1/6 with 340 British and six French troops; arrived Ramsgate 0535 2/6. (Total number evacuated: 1,003)
• **Lost.** Left for Dunkirk 1530 3/6; grounded whilst going alongside at Dunkirk 2300 3/6; efforts to tow vessel off proved unsuccessful; ship abandoned with crew transferring to other vessels

LESRIX 703/24 British (Rix) – taken up 5/40 for Stores
• Loaded 850 tons of stores at Southampton for the Dunkirk area 24/5 but cargo not required; vessel released 6/6

LEVENWOOD 803/24 British (Constantine) – taken up 22/5/40 for Stores
• Loaded 400 tons of stores at London (Deptford) 23/5; left London 24/5; discharged cargo at Dunkirk 26/5, prior to the full implementation of Operation "Dynamo"; returned without troops; anchored in the Downs 27/5
• Left for Dunkirk 0600 31/5 on Operation "Dynamo"; arrived off the

beaches 1130 31/5; embarked troops using ship's boats until vessel could beach at 1430; brought down an attacking aircraft; left Dunkirk 2000 31/5 with 51 British troops; arrived Dover 1850 1/6; released 14/6

LOCHEE 964/37 British (Dundee, Perth & London) – taken up 5/9/39 for Cased Petrol
• Left Swansea and BC 18/9 in convoy BC3; arrived Nantes 20/9; returned to Swansea 28/9
• Left Swansea and BC 16/10 in convoy BC11; arrived Nantes 18/10
• Left Swansea and BC 7/11 in convoy BC14; arrived Nantes 10/11
• From Swansea with stores, arrived Dieppe 22/12; from Port Talbot, arrived Trouville 1/1; from Swansea, arrived Rouen 11/1; from Barry, arrived Rouen 21/1; from Cardiff, arrived Le Havre 29/1; from Swansea, arrived Rouen 8/2; returned to Swansea 11/2
• Left Swansea and BC 29/2 with cased petrol in convoy BC28; arrived Nantes 3/3
• Left Swansea and BC 22/3 in convoy BC31; arrived Nantes 24/3; returned to Swansea 3/4
• Left Swansea for Norway 9/4; sustained damage to hull, rigging and a lifeboat at Scapa as a result of ocean-going cargo vessel *Lombardy* dragging her anchors in a gale 14/4; left Scapa 17/4 in convoy NSM1; arrived Narvik area 24/4; arrived Harstad 3/5; left Harstad 8/5; arrived Greenock 17/5 and Avonmouth 20/5. (Vessel also participated in Operation "Overlord" in 1944: see Part II)

In 1939-40, *Lochee* transported cased petrol to ports on the Continent as far north as Harstad inside the Arctic Circle: in 1942-43, she was part of the North African, Sicilian and Salerno invasion fleets, before returning to sail to Normandy in 1944. *[Graeme Somner collection]*

LOTTIE R 972/37 British (*Stone & Rolfe) – taken up 10/9/39 for Cased Petrol
• Left Avonmouth 14/9 and BC 15/9 in convoy BC2; arrived Nantes 17/9
• Left Avonmouth 14/10 and BC 16/10 in convoy BC11; arrived Brest 17/10
• Left Avonmouth 22/11 and BC 23/11 in convoy BC16; arrived Brest 24/11; returned to Avonmouth 4/12 for release 19/12
• Taken up 11/3/40; left Swansea and BC 15/4 in convoy BC34; arrived Nantes 17/4
• Left Swansea and BC 9/5 for Nantes in convoy BC37; returned to Swansea 19/5. (Vessel also participated in Operation "Overlord" in 1944: see Part II)

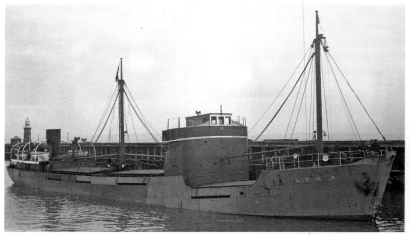

Lottie R, seen here at Avonmouth, made three round voyages from that port to western France in the early war months. *[J. and M. Clarkson collection]*

On 9th June 1940, *Lowick* embarked 79 personnel to organise beach evacuations from the St Valery area of the French coast. *[Roy Fenton collection]*

LOWICK 586/37 British (Tyne-Tees) – taken up 12/9/39 for Cased Petrol
• Left Swansea 23/9 and BC 24/9 for Brest in convoy BC5
• Left Avonmouth 5/10 and BC 6/10 for W France in convoy BC9
• Left Avonmouth 29/10 and BC 30/10 for W France in convoy BC13; returned to Avonmouth 13/11
• Arrived Newhaven 26/12; with ammunition from Newhaven, arrived Fecamp 4/1, 11/1, 18/1, 4/2, 16/2; arrived Rouen 1/3
• From Littlehampton, arrived Rouen 11/3, 21/3, 30/3, 7/4; arrived Dieppe 14/4, 6/5
• Loaded 850 tons of ammunition at Littlehampton 22-23/5; left 24/5; arrived in the Downs 25/5; left for Dunkirk 27/5 during Operation "Dynamo"; cargo not required, so ordered to turn back; re-anchored in the Downs 27/5; arrived Newhaven 28/5
• Left Newhaven for the St Valery area 1750 9/6 with a 79-strong naval and military beach party embarked on Operation "Cycle"; diverted when full evacuation seen to be impossible; called Le Havre 2125 10/6-0325 13/6; embarked 13 troops; called Cherbourg for orders 2250 13/6-1030 14/6; arrived Portsmouth 1820 14/6 and Southampton 15/6
• Left Southampton 0350 16/6 on Operation "Aerial"; left Brest 1800 17/6 without troops; arrived Falmouth 18/6

MAIDSTONE 688/26 British (Southern Railway) – taken up 16/6/40 for Stores
• At St Malo having arrived 14/6 but unable to discharge outward commercial cargo from Southampton owing to proximity of German forces; left St Malo 0520 16/6 with 450 troops and undischarged cargo on Operation "Aerial"; arrived Plymouth 1857 16/6; released 19/6 prior to a crossing from Guernsey to Weymouth with civilian evacuees

MALLARD 352/36 British (General Steam) – taken up 12/9/39 for Cased Petrol
• Left Poole 27/10; arrived Caen 30/10; returned to Poole 1/11; released 20/11
• Made available 26/5 on 24 hours' notice for Operation "Dynamo" but not taken up

MALRIX 703/23 British (Rix) – taken up 21/5/40 for Ammunition
• At Littlehampton 22/5 to load 850 tons for the Dunkirk area but requirement changed; left Littlehampton 1310 22/5; called Fecamp 0100 23/5-0110 24/5; returned with retrieved ammunition; arrived Fowey 0015 25/5
• Left Fowey 31/5 in convoy AXF7; arrived St Malo 1400 2/6; left St Malo 0900 7/6 with retrieved ammunition; arrived Fowey 0900 8/6
• Left Southampton 15/6 and Plymouth 0330 17/6 on Operation "Aerial"; called St Nazaire 1100-1300 19/6; returned without troops; arrived Plymouth 0630 21/6; released 22/6

MARSWORTH 366/25 British (Grand Union) – taken up 11/6/40 for Stores
• Left Southampton 15/6 and Plymouth 0330 17/6 on Operation "Aerial"; called St Nazaire 0001-0030 19/6; returned without troops; arrived Plymouth 0620 21/6; released 22/6. (Vessel also participated in Operation "Overlord" in 1944: see Part II)

MONS 641/19 British (Consolidated Fisheries/*Marsden) – taken up 22/5/40 for Stores
• Loaded 800 tons at Newhaven for the Dunkirk area 23-26/5 but cargo not required; released 5/6

MOUNT 118/38 British (Pickfords) – taken up 25/5/40 for Stores
• Requisitioned in Solent area for Operation "Dynamo" but not used and released

Her small size did not preclude Pickfords' *Mount* from being added to the list of vessels taken up for possible Dunkirk service. *[Tom Rayner/J. and M. Clarkson collection]*

MURRAYFIELD 576/08 British (Border) – taken up 22/5/40 for Stores
• Assigned to load 600 tons for the Dunkirk area but requirement changed; left the Solent 22/5; called Fecamp 1200 23/5-1200 24/5; returned with retrieved ammunition; arrived Fowey 1220 25/5
• Left Fowey 29/5 in convoy AXF6; arrived St Malo 1410 30/5; left St Malo 1640 2/6 with retrieved ammunition; arrived Fowey 0940 3/6
• Arrived Shoreham 10/6; left Shoreham 15/6 and Plymouth 0130 17/6 on Operation "Aerial"; in Quiberon Bay 0950-2100 18/6; returned without troops; arrived Plymouth 2345 19/6; released 21/6

NEPHRITE 927/27 British (Stephenson Clarke) – taken up 20/5/40 for Stores
• Left London (Deptford) with 1,000 tons; anchored in the Downs 24/5;

left 0600 31/5 on Operation "Dynamo"; permission given to jettison cargo to accommodate troops; arrived Dunkirk 1130 31/5; left Dunkirk 1830 31/5 with 430 British and 74 French troops (total 504); arrived Folkestone 0835 1/6
• Left Newhaven 15/6, via Plymouth, on Operation "Aerial"; arrived St Nazaire 1100 16/6; returned without troops; arrived Plymouth 0540 21/6; released 24/6. (Vessel also participated in Operation "Overlord" in 1944: see Part II)

***NGAKOA* 507/38 British (W Wilson)** – taken up 4/9/39 for Cased Petrol
• Left Avonmouth and BC 11/9 in convoy BC1; arrived Nantes 13/9; returned to Swansea 18/9; with a speed of 9.5 knots, deemed unsuitable for BC convoys and released 30/11

***NGAROMA* 503/31 British (W Wilson)** – taken up 21/5/40 for Stores
• Loaded 640 tons of food at Littlehampton 22/5; left the Downs 24/5; discharged cargo in Dunkirk harbour despite air attacks; moved to the beaches 1200 26/6; slightly damaged by air attack; left Dunkirk 0130 27/5 on Operation "Dynamo" with 30 British troops; arrived Dover 1630 27/5
• Chief and two other engineers refused to sail 1520 29/5; armed guard sent to ship 1730 29/5; left the Downs for Dunkirk 1820 29/5; encountered fog 0300 30/5; hit by shore gunfire off the French coast 0715 30/5; four crew members killed, another wounded and ship damaged; turned back 0815 30/5; arrived Dover 1300 30/5

***NYROCA* 786/18 British (British & Continental)** – taken up 23/5/40 for Stores
• Loaded 1,000 tons for the Dunkirk area at Newhaven 23-26/5 but cargo not required
• Left Southampton 0430 16/6, via Plymouth, on Operation "Aerial"; arrived Brest 17/6; involved in collision which holed HMS *Westcott*'s No 3 fuel tank and reduced the destroyer's speed to 8 knots; left Brest 1800 17/6 without troops; arrived Barry 20/6; released 22/6

***OBSIDIAN* 811/22 British (Robertson)** – taken up 11/6/40 for Stores
• Left Newhaven 0300 16/6 on Operation "Aerial"; called Brest 1400-2000 17/6; left without troops for Glasgow, arrived 22/6; released 24/6. (Vessel also participated in Operation "Overlord" in 1944: see Part II)

***OCEAN COAST* 1,173/35 British (Coast)** – taken up 24/4/40 for Cased Petrol
• Left Swansea and BC 16/5 in convoy BC38; arrived Nantes 18/5
• Left Avonmouth 27/5 and BC 29/5 in convoy BC39; arrived Nantes 31/5; returned to Avonmouth 6/6. (Vessel also participated in Operation "Overlord" in 1944: see Part II)

***ORANJE* 231/37 Dutch** – commissioned 23/5/40 for Stores
• Loaded 200 tons of stores at London (Deptford) and further supplies

Although not utilised for troop evacuations from France in 1940, *Obsidian* went on to play a full part in Operation "Overlord" four years later. *[Ships in Focus]*

Nine Coast Lines' vessels carried cased petrol to the British Army on the Continent in 1939-40: one of these was *Ocean Coast*, which in 1942 was also a participant in the landing operations at Algiers, followed, two years later, by those at Normandy. *[B. and A. Feilden/J. and M. Clarkson]*

from a lighter at Dover; left for Dunkirk 1500 27/5 on Operation "Dynamo"; on passage subjected to 'friendly' rifle fire from passing merchant ship 0100 28/5; bomb exploded 50yds from the ship 0400 28/5, when offering assistance to the sinking troopship *Queen of the Channel*; continued towards Bray beach but cargo not required; embarked five soldiers and returned with cargo still aboard; arrived Ramsgate 1630 28/5
• Left for Dunkirk 1930 28/5; arrived off La Panne beach and rescued one man from raft 0430 29/5; beached stern first and commenced discharge of 150 tons of stores 0730 29/5; left Dunkirk 0415 30/5 with 501 troops; arrived Margate 1750 30/5

• Left for Dunkirk 2230 30/5 with two boats in tow; boats broke adrift and were lost; ferried troops to HM destroyer *Basilisk*; when La Panne subjected to fire from shore guns, moved to Bray beach; left Dunkirk with 100 troops; arrived off Margate 2300 31/5; went alongside 0400 1/6
• Left for Dunkirk 0800 1/6 with four boats in tow; crossed at slow speed because of fouled screw; subjected to air attacks, during which wheelhouse window shattered; ship not required for troop evacuation, so returned towing one of the original four boats; arrived Margate 2200 1/6. (Total number evacuated: 606.) Paid off 6/6

ORTOLAN 489/20 British (General Steam)
• Made available at London 26/5/40 on 24 hours' notice for Operation "Dynamo" but not taken up. (Vessel participated in Operation "Overlord" in 1944: see Part II)

OUSE 1,004/11 British (LMS) – taken up 16/6/40 for Stores
• At Jersey having arrived on a commercial voyage from Holyhead 15/6; left Jersey 0200 17/6 on Operation "Aerial"; arrived St Malo 0530 17/6; left 2210 17/6 with 100 naval ratings and military headquarters personnel and was last official evacuation ship to leave, clearing the lock with only 6in of water beneath the keel; arrived Southampton 1635 18/6; released same day

OUSEL 1,533/22 British (British & Continental) – taken up 20/9/39 for Ammunition
• Left Newport 29/9 and BC 30/9 in convoy BC7; arrived Brest 4/10
• Left Newport and BC 7/11 in convoy BC14; arrived St Nazaire 11/11; returned to Newport 21/11 for release 29/11

PACIFIC 362/38 Dutch – commissioned 25/5/40 for Stores
• Left Poole 26/5 and Dover 1300 28/5 for Dunkirk on Operation "Dynamo"; beached on sandbank off La Panne 2300 28/5; refloated on rising tide; left Dunkirk 0430 29/5 with 57 troops; arrived Dover 1440 29/5
• Left for Dunkirk 0240 30/5; anchored off Malo beach 0900 30/5; left Dunkirk 1600 30/5 with 30 Army officers and 493 other ranks (total 523); arrived Ramsgate 2100 30/5
• Left for Dunkirk 0230 31/5; anchored off Malo beach in a heavy swell; left Dunkirk 2100 31/5 with 272 British and 142 French troops (total 414); arrived Ramsgate 0410 1/6. (Total number evacuated from Dunkirk: 994)
• Left Poole for the St Valery area 2000 10/6 with 43 cases of petrol on Operation "Cycle"; in position off the French coast 11/6; ordered to follow troopship *Amsterdam* 2030 11/6 but became detached in fog; developed engine trouble as a result of air attacks, so returned without troops; arrived Poole 2100 12/6; paid off 29/6. (Vessel also participated in Operation "Overlord" in 1944: see Part II)

PACIFIC COAST 1,210/35 British (Coast) – taken up 20/9/39 for Cased Petrol
• Left Swansea and BC 30/9 for Brest in convoy BC7
• Left Avonmouth 21/10 and BC 22/10 for W France in convoy BC12
• **Lost.** Left Avonmouth 6/11 and BC 7/11 in convoy BC14; arrived Brest 9/11; after berthing and whilst removing hatch prior to unloading, suffered an explosion due to spontaneous combustion 9/11; Master, Mate and seven crew members killed, 2nd officer and six others survived; vessel towed out of port by tug *Abeille 22* and beached on a mud bank in Brest Roads; continued to burn for four days; all but forecastle head submerged at high tide and all structure above the water destroyed; wreck eventually refloated; in tow of tug *Sun X*, arrived Falmouth 3/5

Spontaneous combustion caused the cased petrol cargo aboard *Pacific Coast* to explode at Brest on 9th November 1939: fire then gutted the vessel. *[B. and A. Feilden/J. and M. Clarkson]*

PARKNASILLA 846/32 British (Kelly/*Clint) – taken up 6/40 for Stores
• At Cherbourg having arrived on a commercial voyage from Cardiff and Le Havre 10/6; left Cherbourg 1200 11/6 on Operation "Cycle"; called Le Havre 0300 12/6-0300 13/6; arrived Cherbourg 1600 13/6 with the evacuation fleet but without troops and released. (Vessel also participated in Operation "Overlord" in 1944: see Part II)

PASCHOLL 257/31 Dutch – commissioned 25/5/40 for Stores
• Left Portsmouth 27/5 and Dover 1400 28/5 for Dunkirk on Operation "Dynamo"; arrived La Panne beach 2230 28/5; ferried 400 troops to HM destroyer *Wolsey* 0400 29/5; left Dunkirk without troops; arrived the Downs 1200 29/5
• Left Dover for Dunkirk 1900 29/5; arrived La Panne beach 0230 30/5; left Dunkirk 1030 30/5 with 157 British and 145 French troops (total 302); two men wounded in air attack 1400 30/5; arrived Ramsgate 1815 30/5

Two hours before the departure of the last evacuation ship on 13th June 1940, *Parknasilla* was ordered to leave Le Havre for Cherbourg. *[J. and M.Clarkson collection]*

Pascholl was the only Royal Navy-manned Dutch coaster to achieve any success in the Operation "Cycle" evacuations in June 1940. *[B. and A. Feilden/J. and M. Clarkson collection]*

• Left for Dunkirk 31/5; arrived La Panne beach 31/5; left Dunkirk with 101 British and 37 French troops (total 138); arrived Ramsgate 1630 31/5
• Left for Dunkirk 1500 3/6; arrived 2300 3/6; left Dunkirk 0030 4/6 with 255 French troops; arrived Ramsgate 0815 4/6. (Total number evacuated from Dunkirk: 695)
• *Pascholl*, the Captain's first command, was armed only with a Lewis gun, carried food, drinking water and 250 lifebelts for the troops and her machinery was in the hands of a young engine room artificer, who knew nothing about diesel engines and had been given an instruction book in a foreign language he did not understand. Nevertheless, vessel left Poole for the St Valery area 2143 10/6 on Operation "Cycle"; ordered to anchor close inshore at Veules 2100 11/5; beaches came under intense fire from both ends 0830 12/6; waited in the anchorage for the last boat-loads of troops; left the French coast 1130 12/6 with 333 French troops and British gunners and 25 naval personnel (total 358); arrived Southampton 1135 13/6; paid off 19/6

PATRIA **343/37 Dutch** – commissioned 24/5/40 for Stores
• From Sheerness, left the Downs for Dunkirk 1330 27/5 on Operation "Dynamo"; anchored off Nieuport; moved to Dunkirk East Pier 2315 28/5 for embarkation; left Dunkirk 0330 29/5 with 200 troops; towed coaster *Tilly* out of harbour; arrived in the Downs 0845 29/5 and went alongside at Margate 1430 29/5
• Left for Dunkirk 29/5; arrived Bray 2300 29/5 and beached to enable troops to wade out and climb aboard; refloated 0430 30/5 and left Dunkirk with 1,200 troops; arrived off Ramsgate 1015 30/5; went alongside at Margate 1350 30/5. (Total number evacuated: 1,400.) Paid off 6/6

PEMBROKE COAST **625/36 British (Coast)** – taken up 14/9/39 for Cased Petrol
• Left Avonmouth 17/9 and BC 18/9 in convoy BC3; arrived Brest 20/9

• Left Swansea and BC 9/10 for W France in convoy BC10; arrived 11/10
• Left Swansea and BC 7/11 in convoy BC14; arrived Nantes 10/11; returned to Swansea 21/11
• Arrived Newhaven from Swansea 31/12; with stores from Newhaven, arrived Le Havre 12/1, 25/1, 6/2, arrived Rouen 17/2
• Arrived Swansea from Newhaven 24/2; with cased petrol, left Swansea and BC 22/3 for Nantes in convoy BC31; left Quiberon Bay for Swansea 1/4
• Left Swansea and BC 23/4 for Nantes in convoy BC35; returned to Avonmouth 6/5
• **Lost.** Left Avonmouth for Norway 8/5 with 700 tons of reserve cased aviation and vehicle fuel; arrived Greenock 10/5; left Clyde 12/5 in convoy NS3 to arrive Harstad 19/5; still fully loaded, caught fire after bombs ignited adjoining oil berth at Harstad night of 20-21/5; vessel beached; crew repatriated in troopship *Dunluce Castle*

PERELLE **659/22 British (Dorey)** – taken up 17/6/40 for Stores
• At Jersey having arrived on a commercial voyage from St Malo 16/6; left for St Malo 17/6 on Operation "Aerial"; left St Malo 1900 17/6 with 800 British troops; arrived Weymouth 0900 18/6; released after a crossing from Jersey to Weymouth with civilian evacuees

PINGUIN **197/34 Dutch** – commissioned 15/6/40
• At Portsmouth having arrived 14/6; left for Cherbourg on Operation "Aerial"; left Cherbourg 18/6 with troops; arrived Weymouth 2050 18/6; paid off after a crossing from Jersey to Weymouth with civilian evacuees

PIZARRO **1,367/23 British (MacAndrews)** – taken up 5/10/39 for Cased Petrol
• Left Swansea and BC 22/10 in convoy BC12; arrived Nantes 24/10

Pinguin was at Goole until 1st June 1940 and was not therefore amongst the first batch of Dutch coasters to be commissioned. *[Ben Scholten]*

• Left Swansea and BC 15/11 in convoy BC15; arrived Nantes 18/11; returned to Swansea 27/11
• Left Avonmouth 25/1 and BC 26/1 in convoy BC24; arrived Nantes 29/1
• Left Swansea and BC 29/2 in convoy BC28; arrived Nantes 3/3
• Left Swansea and BC 30/3 in convoy BC32; arrived Nantes 1/4; returned to Swansea 12/4
• Left Avonmouth for Norway 22/4; left the Clyde for Andalsnes in convoy TSM2; on passage, involved in collision with French coaster *Paul Emile Javary* 16 miles ENE of Stornoway 28/4; beached inside Stornoway harbour with extensive damage port side aft and holed in No 3; settled by the stern; refloated 10/5 but had to be re-beached; broke from moorings but was re-moored 21/5; cargo discharged overside to coaster *British Coast*; left Stornoway 31/5; arrived Glasgow 3/6; released 27/7

PLOVER 352/36 British (General Steam)
• Made available at London 26/5/40 on 24 hours' notice for Operation "Dynamo" but not taken up

POLGLEN 795/15 British (Brunswick/*Pollexfen) – taken up 23/5/40 for Stores
• Loaded 950 tons at Littlehampton for the Dunkirk area 23-26/5 but cargo not required; vessel released 5/6. (Vessel also participated in Operation "Overlord" in 1944: see Part II)

POLGRANGE 804/20 British (Brunswick/*Pollexfen) – taken up 11/6/40 for Stores
• Left Southampton 0400 16/6 on Operation "Aerial"; called Brest 2100-2115 17/6; returned without troops; released 21/6

POLPERRO 403/37 British (Polpen/*Hannan, Samuel) – taken up 16/9/39 for Cased Petrol
• Left Swansea and BC 3/10 in convoy BC8; arrived Nantes 5/10; returned to Swansea 11/10 for release 18/10

Taken up for cased petrol, *Polperro* reached Swansea on 21st September 1939 to load for Nantes and was released after just one crossing. *[Roy Fenton collection]*

PORTSLADE 1,091/36 British (Stephenson Clarke) – taken up 24/5/40 for Stores
• Commenced loading 1,350 tons at Newhaven for the Dunkirk area 24/5 but cargo not required, so vessel released

After *Portslade* had started loading military stores for Dunkirk, the priority changed from supplying the Army to rescuing it. *[J. and M. Clarkson collection]*

RAVONIA 813/25 British (Northwest) – taken up 24/5/40 for Stores
• Left Newhaven for Dunkirk 1530 29/5 on Operation "Dynamo"; ordered to turn back; arrived Newhaven 1620 30/5
• Left Newhaven 1730 9/6 on Operation "Cycle"; called Le Havre 0700-0800 10/6; returned without troops; arrived Newhaven 1745 10/6
• Left Newhaven for the St Valery area 2340 11/6; in position off the

French coast 0545-1115 12/6; returned without troops; arrived Newhaven 0800 13/6
• Left Newhaven 1850 15/6 on Operation "Aerial"; called Brest 1435-2000 17/6; returned without troops; arrived Belfast 19/6; released 25/6

Although ordered to France on four occasions during the 1940 troop evacuations, *Ravonia* was not one of the coasters actually utilised. *[J. and M. Clarkson collection]*

REDCAR 1,475/20 British (P&O) – taken up 27/4/40 for Stores
• Left Leith for Norway 12/5 with 1,200 tons of Army and Fleet Air Arm stores, bombs and ammunition; joined convoy NS3; arrived Harstad 22/5; ordered to return 7/6; arrived Scapa 8/6; arrived Glasgow 17/6; released 30/6. (Vessel also participated in Operation "Overlord" in 1944: see Part II)

In May 1940, *Redcar* was ordered to northern Norway with stores, bombs and ammunition for the Army and Fleet Air Arm. *[Ships in Focus]*

REIGER 155/24 Dutch – commissioned 26/5/40 for Stores
• Left Sheerness for Dunkirk 2000 27/5 on Operation "Dynamo"; on approaching French coast, departing ships misleadingly signalled that Dunkirk was in enemy hands 1100 28/5, so turned back to the Downs
• Left for Dunkirk 1400 28/5; arrived off the beaches 2300 28/5; embarked 70 stretcher cases; transferred 58 of the wounded troops to HM cruiser *Calcutta*, then left Dunkirk 0300 29/5 with the remaining 12; arrived Sheerness 29/5
• Left 0400 30/5; crossing delayed by fog; arrived Dunkirk East Pier 2000 30/5; left Dunkirk 2100 30/5 with 250 troops; arrived Sheerness 1300 31/5
• Left Sheerness for Dunkirk 1100 1/6; attacked by three bombers but survived unscathed; entered the harbour 2130 1/6; left Dunkirk 2215 1/6 with 330 French troops; took in tow a motor launch and MTB, until latter could proceed independently; arrived Sheerness 0930 2/6. (Total number evacuated: 592.) Paid off 6/6

RIAN 232/34 Dutch – commissioned 5/40 for Stores
• From Poole, left for Dunkirk on Operation "Dynamo"; left Dunkirk with 257 British troops; arrived Ramsgate 1120 31/5; paid off 6/6

RIKA 197/35 Dutch – commissioned 27/5/40 for Stores
• Left Sheerness for Dunkirk 0500 29/5 on Operation "Dynamo"; severely shaken in two dive-bombing attacks 1644 29/5; took aboard 295 troops from HM destroyer *Jaguar*, bombed and badly damaged outside the harbour 1815 29/5; arrived Dover 0830 30/5
• Left Dover 0700 1/6 towing four motor launches; arrived Dunkirk Roads 1300 1/6; whilst returning, intercepted by French destroyer *Branlebas* and took aboard French and British survivors, including wounded, 1340 1/6; cast off motor launches to proceed independently; arrived Ramsgate 1800 1/6 and disembarked 200
• Left for Dunkirk 2000 2/6 with launch and boat in tow; arrived 0115 3/6 but no troops for evacuation, so returned; arrived Ramsgate 0800 3/6; paid off 5/6

ROEBUCK 776/25 British (GWR) – taken up 29/5/40 for Stores
• Left Weymouth 29/5 and Dover 0200 31/5 on Operation "Dynamo"; on approach to Dunkirk, stern slightly damaged in collision with HM destroyer *Wolsey* 0703 31/5; anchored off La Panne beach 0811 31/5 but no embarkation possible; berthed alongside at Dunkirk 1050 31/5; left Dunkirk 1525 31/5 with 689 troops including 119 wounded, many on stretchers; arrived Dover 2055 31/5
• Left Weymouth for the St Valery area 1700 12/6 on Operation "Cycle" in company with sister ship *Sambur*; arrived five miles off St Valery 0200 13/6 but found no naval vessel on station to issue orders; Master, unaware that operation had ended, received encouragement to proceed inshore from crew of a French fishing boat at 0415 13/6; this proved to be a trap and ship came under concentrated artillery fire from the shore at 0440

13/6; hull, bridge and deck holed by bullets and shells; Second Officer and a seaman killed, another man died later, Chief Officer and one seaman wounded; aided by fog, ship zigzagged out of range at full speed; arrived Newhaven 13/6; released 22/8

RONAN 1,489/38 British (Gibson) – taken up 14/9/39 for Cased Petrol
• Left Avonmouth 29/9 and BC 30/9 in convoy BC7; arrived Nantes 2/10
• Left Avonmouth 21/10 and BC 22/10 in convoy BC12; arrived Brest 23/10
• Left Avonmouth 14/11 and BC 15/11 in convoy BC15; arrived Brest 17/11; returned to Avonmouth 25/11
• From Swansea with stores, arrived Rouen 23/12, arrived Dieppe 5/1; returned to Barry 11/1
• Left Avonmouth 11/2 and BC 12/2 in convoy BC26; arrived Brest 13/2
• Left Avonmouth 6/3 and BC 7/3 in convoy BC29; arrived Brest 8/3; returned to Avonmouth 20/3
• Left Swansea for Norway 15/4 with 1,663 tons of cased aviation and vehicle fuel; left Greenock 18/4 in convoy TM1, via Scapa; called Namsos 1200 23/4-0330 24/4; at Lofoten Islands 25-26/4; in Romsdal Fiord 27-28/4; called Scapa 1/5-3/5; returned to Swansea 6/5
• Left Avonmouth 8/5 and BC 9/5 in convoy BC37; arrived Brest 10/5
• Left Avonmouth 26/5 and BC 29/5 in convoy BC 39; arrived Nantes 31/5; returned to Avonmouth 6/6. (Vessel also participated in Operation "Overlord" in 1944: see Part II)

Ronan completed nine round voyages to France and one to Norway in 1939-40: she saw Mediterranean service in support of the North African landings in 1942, before returning to form part of the 1944 Normandy invasion fleet. *[W. H. Brown/J. and M. Clarkson collection]*

RUJA 175/26 Dutch – commissioned 25/5/40 for Stores
• Left for Dunkirk on Operation "Dynamo"; anchored N of the Goodwins with defective engine 29/5; continued to the French coast; embarked troops from the beaches; left Dunkirk with 217 British troops; arrived Ramsgate 1015 1/6; paid off

SAMBUR 776/25 British (GWR) – taken up 10/6/40 for Stores
• Left Weymouth for the St Valery area 1700 12/6 on Operation "Cycle"; proceeded in company with sister ship *Roebuck* (qv); *Sambur* sustained similar damage 13/6; two men killed, Chief Officer and one seaman seriously wounded, two others injured; arrived Newhaven 13/6; released 22/8

Two crew members were killed and four wounded by shore gunfire when *Sambur* was approaching the French town of St Valery during the post-Dunkirk evacuations in June 1940. *[J. and M. Clarkson collection]*

SAN ANTONIO 410/09 Dutch – commissioned 25/5/40 for Stores
• Left Poole 25/5 and the Downs 28/5 for Dunkirk on Operation "Dynamo"; left Dunkirk East Pier 0300 29/5 with 217 troops; arrived Dover 1400 29/5
• Left for Dunkirk 30/5; damaged by delayed-action bomb 2045 30/5; sustained damage in contact with Dunkirk pier 0115 31/5; left with 214 British troops; arrived Ramsgate 0620 31/5. (Total number evacuated: 431)
• Left Poole for the St Valery area 10/6 on Operation "Cycle"; in position off the French coast 11/6 but lost contact in fog; returned 12/6 without troops; paid off 3/7

SANDHILL 586/38 British (Tyne-Tees) – taken up 17/9/39 for Cased Petrol
• Left Avonmouth and BC 27/9 in convoy BC6; arrived Brest 29/9
• Left Swansea and BC 30/10 in convoy BC13; arrived Nantes 1/11; returned to Swansea 12/11
• Arrived Poole from Swansea 18/11; from Poole, arrived Caen 29/11
• Arrived Newhaven from Southampton 8/2; with stores from Newhaven, arrived Rouen 14/2, 22/2; vessel attacked by aircraft but not hit 27/2; arrived Le Havre 6/3; arrived Fecamp with ammunition 22/3, 28/3, 5/4, 11/4, 18/4, 23/4, 30/4, 9/5; collision with Fecamp pier on departure 10/5 caused indentation to steel plates and damage to frames; arrived Fecamp 16/5
• Loaded 940 tons of ammunition at Newhaven 22-23/5; left 2345 23/5;

arrived Dunkirk 1430 24/5; after discharging cargo, left Dunkirk 2320 26/5 without troops, shortly after the start of Operation "Dynamo"; anchored in the Downs; returned to Newhaven 1/6
• Left Newhaven for Le Havre 1740 9/6 on Operation "Cycle" but turned back; arrived Newhaven 2020 10/6
• Left Newhaven for the St Valery area 2200 10/6 towing the boats *Adeline*, *Falcon II*, *Hawfinch*, *Hibernia*, *Lady Doris*, *Montego Bay*, *My Lassie*, *Ocean Gift*, *Ocean Spray*, *Silver Spray*, *Three Brothers* and *White Spray* for beach rescue; *Ocean Spray* abandoned as untowable 0820 11/6; arrived off St Valery 1430 11/6; at 1930 11/6 ordered to close troopship *Amsterdam* but unable to do so owing to fog; bombardment from shore artillery in progress, so left without troops 1300 12/6; arrived Newhaven 0600 13/6. (Vessel also participated in Operation "Overlord" in 1944: see Part II)

SCHELDT 497/38 British (Vianda) – taken up 16/5/40 for Cased Petrol
• Fully loaded, left Poole 1935 26/5 on the starting date of the Dunkirk evacuation; cargo not required; returned to Poole 0755 4/6
• Left Poole for the St Valery area 2200 10/6 with naval officer embarked on Operation "Cycle"; arrived off St Valery 0900 11/6; attempted to reach Fecamp but met with shore gunfire which caused slight damage 1130 11/6; proceeded westwards; sailed close inshore near St Valery 0030 12/6; rescued eight French and two British troops from two open boats 0600-0700 12/6; subjected to shore artillery fire 0705 12/6, so retired seawards; left the French coast 2130 12/6; arrived Poole 0830 13/6; released 25/7. (Vessel also participated in Operation "Overlord" in 1944: see Part II)

Twenty-six coasters, including *Scheldt*, were ordered to the St Valery area of the French coast in June 1940: high hopes of achieving substantial British troop evacuations were regrettably dashed. *[J. and M. Clarkson collection]*

SCOTTISH CO-OPERATOR 513/39 British (Scottish Co-operative) – taken up 14/2/40 for Ammunition
• From Newhaven, arrived Rouen 7/3, 16/3, 28/3, 5/4, 11/4; arrived Dieppe 28/4, 8/5; arrived Fecamp 14/5

• Left Newhaven 22/5 with 600 tons; arrived Boulogne 22/5; ammunition only part discharged; proximity of German forces prompted premature return; arrived Newhaven 23/5
• Loaded further ammunition at Newhaven 26/5 but cargo not required; left the Downs for Dunkirk in ballast 2000 30/5 on Operation "Dynamo"; entered the harbour 0600 31/5; embarked 50 stretcher cases and 150 walking wounded who were transferred to a hospital carrier, probably *Paris*; left Dunkirk 1030 31/5 with 525 British troops, including seven stretcher cases; arrived Margate 1450 31/5; severed degaussing cable on leaving Margate Pier
• Left Newhaven for Cherbourg 16/6 on Operation "Aerial"; left Cherbourg 17/6 with British troops; arrived Weymouth 2105 17/6

SEINE 179/26 British (London & Rochester) – taken up 29/5/40 for Stores
• Left Sheerness for Dunkirk 1800 29/5 with drinking water for the troops and a naval officer and four ratings embarked on Operation "Dynamo"; arrived off Nieuport 1500 30/5; moved first to Bray then to La Panne beach; left Dunkirk 1900 30/5 with 280 British and 13 French troops (total 293); subjected to air attack on passage; arrived Ramsgate 0730 31/5
• Ship's report and logbook records another round voyage, arriving at Dunkirk 1700 31/5, leaving at 2000 31/5 and landing 320 troops at Ramsgate at 0900 1/6 but this not confirmed in naval records and ship's dates appear anyway to be one day astray
• Left for Dunkirk 1200 1/6; entered the harbour 2000 1/6; air raids in progress for one hour; left Dunkirk 2130 1/6 with 250 British troops; arrived Ramsgate 0520 2/6. (Total number evacuated: 543-863.) Released

SEQUACITY 870/37 British (Everard) – taken up 21/5/40 for Stores
• **Lost.** Fitted out at London for emergency evacuation 21/5; arrived in the Downs 21/5; left 0400 27/5 by the shortest route to Dunkirk on Operation "Dynamo"; became the target for recently-deployed German field guns two miles E of Calais 0640 27/5; one shell entered the main hold on port side on water-line and exited starboard side, another did likewise through the engine room and a third entered the wheelhouse, went into the hatches and out through the ship's bottom; vessel reversed course and was attacked with machine-gun fire from 11 aircraft; Chief Engineer wounded as a result of further shore gunfire; vessel, making water, listed to starboard; crew transferred to lifeboat 1010 27/5; ship sank by the head at 1020 27/5; 13 survivors taken aboard accompanying coaster *Yewdale*

SILVER COAST 606/38 British (Merchants) – taken up 22/5/40 for Cased Petrol
• Left Poole for the St Valery area 2200 10/6 on Operation "Cycle"; arrived off St Valery 0500 11/6; in clearing fog, met by shells from field guns ashore, so moved to seaward; approached the coast again at 1400 11/6 despite continuing gunfire; waited three hours with engines stopped; moved out to sea; subjected to air attack; picked up three British and two French troops from a raft; arrived Poole 0815 12/6; released 23/7

SIR EVELYN WOOD 850/96 British (War Department) – Stores

• From Southampton; arrived Rouen 12/1/40, 26/1, 7/2, 18/2, 3/3, 10/3; arrived Le Havre 19/3, 31/3, 6/4; arrived Rouen 13/4, 20/4, 26/4, 3/5, 8/5, 13/5; return delayed by five days owing to magnetic mines in the Seine
• Left Southampton for the St Valery area 0410 11/6 towing six lifeboats on Operation "Cycle"; arrived off Veules 0400 12/6; returned to Solent without troops towing HM drifter *Golden Harvest*; arrived Southampton 1315 13/6. (Vessel also participated in Operation "Overlord" in 1944: see Part II)

SODALITY 829/38 British (Everard) – taken up 6/9/39 for Cased Petrol

• Left Avonmouth 17/9 and BC 18/9 in convoy BC3; arrived Brest 20/9
• Left Swansea and BC 16/10 in convoy BC11; arrived Nantes 18/10; returned to Swansea 28/10 after dropping astern of homeward convoy and being unable to catch up
• Arrived Poole from Swansea 5/11; from Poole, arrived Caen 16/11, left Caen 18/11 for London and release 27/11
• Taken up 20/5/40; loaded 1,000 tons of stores at London (Deptford); left London 21/5; left the Downs for Dunkirk 1300 21/5 in the company of troopship *St Helier* and with HM destroyers *Wild Swan* and *Wolsey* as escort; arrived 1800 21/5; discharged cargo and embarked six soldiers, prior to the start of Operation "Dynamo"; left Dunkirk 0415 24/5, landed troops at Dover by tender; arrived London 24/5
• Part loaded with stores at London (Deptford) for Dunkirk by 26/5 but cargo not required; vessel released 3/6. (Vessel also participated in Operation "Overlord" in 1944: see Part II)

Based at Southampton, the 1896-built *Sir Evelyn Wood* was the only War Department vessel on cross-Channel cargo service. Here she sails from Preston. *[World Ship Society Ltd.]*

Unable to maintain the required convoy speed in October 1939, *Sodality* was transferred the following month to sail independently from Poole to Caen with cased petrol. *[Ships in Focus]*

SPARTA 708/00 British (Bennett) – taken up 17/6/40 for Stores
• On a commercial voyage, rescued crew of coaster *Firth Fisher* (qv) off Boulogne 21/5
• At Brest having arrived from Cardiff with commercial cargo of coal 13/6; left Brest 1110 17/6 on Operation "Aerial" with 500 British troops; arrived Falmouth 1815 18/6 and released

SPINEL 650/37 British (Robertson) – taken up 6/9/39 for Cased Petrol
• Left Avonmouth 14/9 and BC 15/9 for W France in convoy BC2; returned to Swansea 25/9; with a speed of 9 knots, adjudged unsuitable for BC convoys
• Arrived Southampton from Swansea 16/10; from Southampton, arrived Caen 23/10, 5/11, 20/11
• From Poole, arrived Caen 5/1, 26/1, 7/2; sailed Caen 8/2; disabled by engine trouble; air search called for; vessel towed into Brixham by Belgian trawler *Strijd voor Christus* 11/2
• From Poole, arrived Caen 28/2, 13/3, 27/3, 10/4, 11/5
• **Lost.** Left Poole 21/5 with 600 tons; left the Downs 22/5; arrived Boulogne 22/5; cargo discharge deemed unsafe owing to near proximity of German forces; returned to the Downs 23/5; re-routed to Dunkirk; berthed 1100 24/5, despite air attack off the French coast; port continually bombed, so shifted berth to avoid fires; bombing raids on 25/5 created fires alongside vessel and wounded two crew members; shifted berth whilst under air attack from machine-guns and bombs; discharged 60 tons of cased petrol 1500-2000 26/5; port heavily bombed 0900 27/5; damage to the harbour bridge prevented departure from the port, so ship abandoned; all crew, except hospitalised bosun, repatriated in troopship *Royal Daffodil*; vessel fell into German hands

After being abandoned at Dunkirk in May 1940 as a result of air attacks, *Spinel* was taken over by the Germans and saw out the remainder of the war based in the German-occupied Channel Islands. *[J. and M. Clarkson collection]*

SUFFOLK COAST 535/38 British (Coast) – taken up 11/6/40 for Stores
• Left Southampton for St Malo 14/6 on Operation "Aerial"; left St Malo 1430 16/6 with 767 British troops; arrived Weymouth 1100 17/6; released 28/6 after a crossing from Jersey and another from Alderney, both to Weymouth with civilian evacuees

SURSUM CORDA 199/33 Dutch – commissioned 25/5/40 for Stores
• Left for Dunkirk 1400 28/5 on Operation "Dynamo"; berthed at East Pier 2230 28/5; western side of harbour ablaze; left Dunkirk 0330 29/5 with 277 British troops; arrived Dover 1425 29/5
• **Lost.** Left for Dunkirk 2100 29/5; arrived Malo beach 0430 30/5; troops embarked over ship's bows and were ferried to HM warships; vessel became overloaded and went securely aground; despite persistent attempts, refloating impossible and engines became damaged in the process; troops and crew transferred to other vessels 0520 31/5 and ship abandoned

SWIFT 936/30 British (General Steam)
• Made available at London 26/5/40 on 24 hours' notice for Operation "Dynamo" but not used

THE BARON 820/27 British (Hay) – taken up 16/6/40 for Stores
• At St Malo having arrived on a commercial voyage from the Clyde; left St Malo 1730 16/6 with 522 troops on Operation "Aerial"; arrived Weymouth 1210 17/6; released 28/6 after a crossing from Jersey to Weymouth with civilian evacuees. (Vessel also participated in Operation "Overlord" in 1944: see Part II)

Seventeen coasters assisted the St Malo evacuation in June 1940, including *The Baron* which brought back 522 British soldiers: she returned to cross-Channel service in June 1944 in support of the Normandy landings. *[Captain J. F. van Puyvelde]*

THE COUNTESS 824/28 British (Hay) – taken up 12/6/40 for Stores
• At Le Havre having arrived on a commercial voyage from Liverpool to Rouen 10/6; left Le Havre 1300 12/6 with 370 British troops on Operation "Cycle"; arrived Cherbourg 2100 12/6 and released

The fleet evacuating troops from Le Havre on 12th June 1940 consisted of six cross-Channel passenger steamers and this coaster, *The Countess*. [J. and M. Clarkson collection]

THE MARQUIS 795/24 British (Hay) – taken up 22/5/40 for Stores
• Left London for Ostend 1600 22/5 with food supplies; arrived 1630 24/5; left Ostend 2220 27/5 with 59 evacuees; anchored in the Downs, arrived Dover 1630 28/5; released 6/6. (Note: coaster *Abukir* (qv), which left Ostend shortly after *The Marquis*, was sunk in an E-boat attack)

THEEMS 553/20 British (Walford) – taken up 10/6/40 for Stores
• At Cherbourg having arrived on a commercial voyage from London and Le Havre 10/6; left Cherbourg 1200 11/6 on Operation "Cycle"; arrived Le Havre 2046 12/6; left 0500 13/6 with 60 British rearguard troops and was last evacuation ship to sail; arrived Cherbourg 2000 13/6 and released

TILLY 381/39 Dutch – commissioned 25/5/40 for Stores
• Left London 25/5 and the Downs 1500 27/5 for Dunkirk on Operation "Dynamo"; on approaching French coast, misleadingly signalled by departing ships that the port was in enemy hands 2300 27/5, so turned back
• Left for Dunkirk 1745 28/5; berthed at East Pier 2359 28/5; towed out of port stern first by coaster *Patria* 0330 29/5, then proceeded independently with 107 troops; arrived Ramsgate 0845 29/5
• Left for Dunkirk 29/5 towing two cutters; arrived Bray beach 30/5; left Dunkirk with one French soldier and 294 British troops; arrived Ramsgate 0940 30/5
• Left for Dunkirk 31/5 again towing two cutters; arrived off the beaches 31/5; left Dunkirk 1/6; arrived Ramsgate 0705 1/6; three other vessels from Dunkirk disembarked troops at the same time as *Tilly*, the total landed was 743 but the exact number from each ship is not known
• Left for Dunkirk 1/6; arrived but found no troops for evacuation, so returned with a disabled lighter in tow; arrived Ramsgate 2359 1/6
• Left 1830 2/6; arrived Dunkirk but ordered to return without troops; arrived Ramsgate 0800 3/6; paid off 6/6. (Vessel also participated in Operation "Overlord" in 1944: see Part II)

TINY 351/39 Dutch – commissioned 23/5/40 for Stores
• Left Southampton for Dunkirk 28/5 with stores on Operation "Dynamo"; left Dunkirk with 259 British and two French troops; arrived Ramsgate 1550 31/5; paid off 6/6

TWENTE 239/37 Dutch – commissioned 25/5/40 for Stores
• Left Sheerness for Dunkirk 27/5 on Operation "Dynamo"; when approaching French coast, ordered to turn back 0330 28/5; attacked from the air 0400 28/5; arrived Ramsgate 28/5
• Left for Dunkirk 1745 28/5; entered the harbour 2345 28/5; fierce fires blazed in the port; left Dunkirk with 390 troops; arrived Ramsgate 29/5
• Left for Dunkirk 29/5; on passage went alongside HM paddle minesweeper *Gracie Fields*, which badly bombed and unable to stop her engines 0130 30/5; took aboard 160 troops, including many wounded, and turned back; arrived Ramsgate 0515 30/5
• Left 30/5; anchored off Dunkirk Roads 2230 30/5; embarked troops from a motor boat, cutter and whaler; left Dunkirk 0500 31/5 with 350 troops; arrived Margate 1845 31/5. (Total number evacuated: 900)
• **Lost.** Left Newhaven for the St Valery area 1915 11/6 with ammunition and cased petrol on Operation "Cycle"; arrived eight miles off Fecamp at 0415 12/6; sustained one shell hit in the stern and two on the water-line on the starboard side amidships 0620 12/6; water pouring into the holds rapidly caused ship to list to starboard; crew transferred to coaster *Kaap Falga*; *Twente* sank 0632 12/6

VREDE 400/32 Dutch – commissioned 26/5/40 for Stores
• Left Sheerness 0430 28/5 and the Downs 1400 28/5 for Dunkirk on Operation "Dynamo"; aground on a sandbank 2300 28/5-0400 29/5; arrived off the beaches 0500 29/5; embarked troops, then moved to the East Pier; left Dunkirk with 473 troops, including a Belgian major who proved difficult, owing to the ship's inability to dry his corsets; arrived Dover 0450 30/5
• Left for Dunkirk 1100 30/5 towing motor boats; two miles out, engines broke down; motor boats sent back and ship towed to Dover; paid off 6/6

WALMER CASTLE 906/36 British (Union-Castle) – taken up 25/5/40 for Stores
• Loaded 950 tons for the Dunkirk area at London (Deptford) 25-26/5 but cargo not required; vessel released 4/6

WEGA 192/27 Dutch – commissioned 25/5/40 for Stores
• Left Poole for the St Valery area 10/6 on Operation "Cycle"; in position off the French coast 11/6 but lost contact in fog; arrived Solent 1200 12/6 without troops; arrived Poole 0915 13/6, then proceeded to berth at 1030 13/6, immediately ahead of coaster *Abel Tasman* which was blown up by mine
• Left Poole for Cherbourg 17/6 on Operation "Aerial"; left Cherbourg 18/6; arrived Poole 19/6; paid off 2/7

When the Army appeared to be in need of supplies in May 1940, Union-Castle Line's *Walmer Castle* was loaded ready to sail for Dunkirk. *[J. and M. Clarkson collection]*

Nine coasters disembarked troops at Weymouth on 17th June 1940, one of which was *West Coaster* seen here in her peacetime colours. *[J. and M. Clarkson collection]*

WEST COASTER 361/38 British (British Isles) – taken up 12/6/40 for Stores
• Left Southampton for St Malo 14/6 on Operation "Aerial"; left St Malo 0700 16/6 with 90 British troops; arrived Weymouth 1110 17/6; released 26/6 after a crossing from Jersey to Weymouth with civilian evacuees

WESTOWN 710/21 British (Brook/*Comben Longstaff) – taken up 23/5/40 for Stores
• Commenced loading 950 tons at Littlehampton 24/5; left 1700 27/5; arrived in the Downs 28/5; on Operation "Dynamo" was off Dunkirk 1230-2130 31/5; left after embarking troops; arrived off Ramsgate 0600 1/6; this movement is not recorded in naval records but 21 troops were landed at 0845 1/6 from an unknown vessel, possibly a tender from *Westown*; released 29/6. (Vessel also participated in Operation "Overlord" in 1944: see Part II)

WHITSTABLE 787/25 British (Southern Railway) – taken up 29/5/40 for Stores
• Left Southampton 29/5 and the Downs 0350 31/5 for Dunkirk on Operation "Dynamo"; anchored close inshore off Bray beach 0820 31/5; all evacuating soldiers were being ferried to waiting destroyers until, at 1430 31/5, a small boat came alongside *Whitstable*; anchorage subjected to heavy air attacks, with dogfights taking place overhead; shells began to explode in the anchorage and exit channel; with boiler water running low, left Dunkirk 1530 31/5 with 14 troops; arrived Dover 2020 31/5 and landed troops by tender
• Left Southampton 1257 12/6 on Operation "Cycle" stand-by; returned to Southampton 1425 13/6
• Left Southampton 1755 15/6 on Operation "Aerial" stand-by; arrived Plymouth 2320 17/6; released 23/6 after a crossing from Jersey to Weymouth with civilian evacuees

Despite seeing thousands of troops on the beaches, the Master of *Whitstable* was understandably irritated that only 14 were ferried to his ship during a six-hour stay at Dunkirk. This photograph was taken in 1953. *[J. and M. Clarkson collection]*

WILLIAMSTOWN 793/37 British (Williamstown/*Comben Longstaff) – taken up 21/5/40 for Stores
• Loaded 700 tons at Littlehampton; left 0010 22/5; arrived Calais 1800 23/5; discharged cargo; left Calais 0300 24/5 with 292 British troops; arrived Folkestone 0715 24/5, prior to the start of Operation "Dynamo"
• Left Newhaven 1530 29/5 during Operation "Dynamo" but returned 1600 30/5; released 4/6

WORTHTOWN 868/39 British (Williamstown/*Comben Longstaff) – taken up 19/5/40 for Stores
• Loaded 650 tons at Newhaven; left Newhaven 21/5 and the Downs 22/5; arrived Boulogne 1400 23/5; landed part cargo 1600-1930 23/5; when port came under shell fire, returned to the Downs with undischarged stores

• **Lost.** Left for Dunkirk 24/5; shelled from the French coast off Calais and attacked by two aircraft, one of which was brought down; three bombs exploded between the piers at Dunkirk as ship entered 24/5; berthed near coaster *Spinel* for cargo discharge; bombing raids continued but vessel undamaged until 27/5, by which time only 10 tons still remained aboard; at 2130 27/5 bombs caused an outbreak of fire and vessel sank, dashing the immediate repatriation hopes of 350 British troops waiting on the quayside; vessel fell into German hands

YEWDALE 823/29 British (Stewart) – taken up 21/5/40 for Stores
• Fitted out at London for emergency evacuation; arrived in the Downs 22/5; left for Dunkirk 0400 27/5 on Operation "Dynamo"; subjected to shore gunfire two miles off Calais 0700 27/5; picked up five men from a raft from Calais 0820 27/5; turned back; attack by 10 aircraft, using bombs and machine-guns, destroyed rafts and a lifeboat; embarked survivors from accompanying coaster *Sequacity* which sunk by gunfire 1020 27/5; arrived in the Downs 1230 27/5
• Left for Dunkirk 2245 28/5 with coasters *Beal* and *Bullfinch*; arrived La Panne beach 0430 29/5; embarked troops using all available craft including ship's boats; left Dunkirk with 940 British troops 1600 29/5; subjected to massive air attacks 1650-1800 29/5; 5 men killed, 78 wounded and 6 jumped overboard; wheelhouse severely damaged, vessel's sides holed in several places; radio and compass destroyed, so used small field compass for navigation; ship's gun brought down one attacking aircraft; anchored in the Downs 2310 29/5; required to wait until 0600 30/5 for a doctor to board; arrived Ramsgate 0815 30/5; released 26/6

YEWGLEN 607/15 British (Stewart) – taken up 21/5/40 for Stores
• Fitted out at London for emergency evacuation; left London 21/5; at anchor in the Downs 22/5-5/6 on Operation "Dynamo" stand-by; returned to London 5/6; released 6/6. (Vessel also participated in Operation "Overlord" in 1944: see Part II)

YEWMOUNT 859/39 British (Stewart) – taken up 30/9/39 for Cased Petrol
• Left Swansea and BC 22/10 for W France in convoy BC12; arrived 24/10; returned to Swansea 3/11
• Arrived Poole from Swansea 17/11; from Poole, arrived Caen 25/11, 26/12
• With stores from Southampton, arrived Rouen 21/1, 3/2, 14/2, 24/2, 6/3, 15/3; arrived Le Havre 16/3, 27/3, 4/4; arrived Rouen 10/4, 17/4, 23/4; left Rouen for the Mersey 25/4
• Loaded cased petrol at Greenock for Norway; left Clyde 28/5 in convoy NS4; arrived Harstad 4/6; ordered to return 7/6 with cargo undischarged;

arrived Glasgow 19/6 and Llanelly 20/6. (Vessel also participated in Operation "Overlord" in 1944: see Part II)

YEWPARK 827/30 British (Stewart) – taken up 10/6/40 for Stores
• Left Weymouth 1740 15/6 and Plymouth 0410 17/6 on Operation "Aerial"; off St Nazaire 1210-1245 19/6; returned without troops; arrived Plymouth 0615 21/6; released 24/6. (Vessel also participated in Operation "Overlord" in 1944: see Part II)

ZAAFARAN 1,563/21 British, ex-Egyptian (Ministry of Shipping/*General Steam) – taken up 14/3/40 for Stores
• From Glasgow, arrived Rouen 18/5; left Le Havre for Southampton 26/5
• Left Southampton 1915 1/6; arrived St Malo 2/6; left St Malo with retrieved ammunition 9/6; arrived Fowey 11/6
• Made available at Fowey 15/6 for Operation "Aerial" but not used

The Egyptian *Zaafaran*, when taken up for British government service, was managed by General Steam, her previous owners. *[Peter Newall collection]*

ZEUS 200/27 Dutch – commissioned 25/5/40 for Stores
• Left Poole 1700 25/5 and Dover 1300 28/5 for Dunkirk on Operation "Dynamo"; berthed at the East Pier 0130 29/5; left Dunkirk 0400 29/5 with 200 troops and two female aliens dressed in soldier's overcoats and wearing steel helmets; arrived Margate 1520 29/5
• Left for Dunkirk 2000 29/5; arrived Bray beach 0500 30/5; left Dunkirk 0900 30/5 with one French soldier and 400 British troops; arrived Ramsgate 1800 30/5. (Total number evacuated from Dunkirk: 603)
• Left Poole for the St Valery area 10/6 on Operation "Cycle"; in position off the French coast 11/6 but lost contact in fog; arrived Solent 1115 12/6 without troops; paid off 3/7 after a crossing from Guernsey to Weymouth with civilian evacuees

Part II
The Liberation of the Continent
Section 1
Preparations for D-Day

The successful conclusion of operations in North Africa and their 1943 extension across Sicily onto the Italian mainland opened the Mediterranean to Allied shipping and enabled plans for a cross-Channel assault to be confirmed. Administrative planning for Operation "Overlord", the Allied landings in Northern France, had been carried out since May 1942 and, in the autumn of 1943, discussions took place at the Ministry of War Transport (as the Ministry of Shipping had by then become) to establish the suitability of including military cargo coasters in the 1944 invasion fleet. Several coasters, including *Cameo*, had already been considered for conversion to fighter direction tenders for the operation but, because of their small size, had been rejected in favour of tank landing ships. As had been demonstrated during the 1940 evacuations from the Continent, coasters were likely to be invaluable to the success of the landings, because of their ability to anchor close inshore or be beached, thereby reducing cargo transit time between ship and shore. This type of vessel also possessed the enormous asset of being able to enter ports with limited depth

of water, not only on the Continent but also in the UK. In the event of enemy air attacks during loading operations, the mere fact that the ships would be spread over a large number of ports would be advantageous, although it was acknowledged that this would add to the complexity of providing port labour and of maintaining control over the loading programmes. Concerns were expressed that a mass of small coasters might cause confusion and delay; that their handling gear could prove unreliable; that their crews would be able to offer little help with cargo discharge and that, with their limited range compared with ocean-going ships, they might overburden the bunkering and servicing facilities. The demands for vessels of the coaster type far exceeded the number readily available, the likelihood being that one-third of the total coaster tonnage might be required for "Overlord". The varying types of coasters being sought included those with derricks which could be strengthened to lift 5- or 10-ton vehicles; those suitable for carrying cased petrol or ammunition; small stores coasters (up to 500 tons dwt); medium stores coasters (500-1,250 tons) and large coasters (over 1,250

With a gross tonnage of just under 3,000, the collier *Mr Therm* was the largest coastal vessel serving the Normandy beachheads: on her first voyage she carried 32 vehicles and 128 troops from London's South West India Dock. *[National Maritime Museum, P23518]*

tons). In preparation for the operation, over a thousand vessels were examined, with details being noted of their derrick equipment; cargo space in measurement and deadweight; bunker capacity and consumption; speed; dimensions; hatch openings and fresh water storage.

The ships initially selected ranged in gross tonnage from the 2,974 of *Mr Therm* down to the 258 of *Ebbrix*; in age from the 49-year-old *Oranmore* to those only recently completed and in deadweight cargo capacity from around 3,800 tons downwards. Large-scale exercises were held to establish exactly how the coasters could best be employed, with five ships being used in London's Royal Docks to test the loading organisation and another vessel undertaking beaching experiments in Swansea Bay, to assess the best method of refloating and of preventing vessels from broaching to. These exercises were followed by trials in the Bristol Channel during which 40 coasters tested loading arrangements, procedures for beaching and discharging and general shore organisation, with experience also being gained in the discharge of cargo into DUKWs (2·5 ton 6x6-wheeled amphibious trucks). Quite obviously, no ship would be allowed to take on board any cargo which she could not discharge with her own appliances at the destination beachhead. It was planned that 54 coasters, most of which were assigned to carry general stores in the sustained movement phase, would between them convey over 2,000 military vehicles on their early crossings and their derricks were therefore strengthened accordingly. Cased petrol carriers were fitted out with special plastic armour; where possible, ships' bridges were strengthened with concrete blocks; machine-guns were mounted on the bridge and forecastle and, for the use of the ferry craft operating between ship and shore in the assault area, all vessels were instructed to carry a deck cargo of diesel, petrol, water and lubricating oil. A total of 331 coasters was selected for loading ammunition, cased petrol, general stores and vehicles during the three weeks prior to the

landings, 163 for the US and 168 for the British beachheads. Table 2 shows the ports utilised, the main cargoes loaded and the total number of coasters allocated to each loading port. Although all the coasters in this pre-loading fleet were under British control, it was an impressively international enterprise. Nearly two-thirds of the ships were of British origin and these were joined by four ships of Belgian origin, eight of Canadian, 12 of Danish, 19 of Dutch, five of Estonian, seven of French, 33 of Norwegian, six of Polish

TABLE 2		
PRE-LOADED COASTER PORT ALLOCATIONS		
Loading port	**Number of coasters allocated**	**Main cargo**
FOR THE US AREA		
GARSTON Berths 1 & 2	8	cased petrol
SWANSEA Prince of Wales Dock, Berths A & B	16	ammunition and stores
Prince of Wales & King's Docks	29	vehicles
PORT TALBOT Talbot Wharf, Berths A & B	14	cased petrol and stores
Crown Wharf	8	cased petrol
Talbot Wharf	3	vehicles
BARRY No 2 Dock, Berths 1 & 3	12	stores
PENARTH North Side, Berths 1-3	16	ammunition and stores
CARDIFF Royal Dock	7	stores
NEWPORT North Quay Berths 1-3	12	ammunition
SHARPNESS Berths A & B	14	cased petrol and stores
AVONMOUTH Berths S & T	17	stores
PORTISHEAD	<u>7</u>	ammunition and stores
	163	
FOR THE BRITISH AREA		
LONDON: Millwall, Berths F, G, J, K and M	6	vehicles
King George V Dock, Berths 3-5, 7-10 and 12	34	cased petrol, stores and vehicles
Royal Albert Dock, Berths 5, 7-25 & 27	43	stores and vehicles
South West India Dock, Berths K & L	2	vehicles
Purfleet A & B	19	cased petrol
Tilbury River Jetty, Berths A & C	11	ammunition
Tilbury Dock, Berths 5, 7, 11, 13, 14, 17-19 and 33	42	ammunition and stores
GRIMSBY	<u>11</u>	stores
	168	

An age of 49 years did not preclude *Oranmore* from playing a full part in Operation "Overlord" and surviving mine damage on 17th July 1944. *[Harry Stewart/J. and M. Clarkson collection]*

anchorage, extending from Hurst Castle in the west to Bembridge in the east, had been allocated in the run-up to D-Day. In it, anchorage positions had originally been required for 100 coasters, half in the west and half in the east. The pressure on space had resulted in places being found for only 55, all in the west, comprising the first two convoys for the US area (Force O3 and EWC1A) and the first two (Force L1 and EWC1B) for the British (Eastern Task Force) beachheads of Gold, Juno and Sword. These ETF ships had loaded at London or Grimsby, with around 125 of them then occupying lay-by berths in the 20-mile stretch of the Thames between Blackwall and Tilbury, before all proceeded downstream to their convoy assembly area in the Thames Estuary, off Southend. Ships leaving the Solent for the US beachheads were required to sail to the west of the Isle of Wight through the Needles gateway, whilst those heading for the British beachheads used the Spithead gate and proceeded down the east coast of the island. Whether originating in the Bristol Channel, the Solent or the Thames, all made for a designated area

and 24 of United States origin, the latter on bareboat charter from their War Shipping Administration. These totals do not include the vessels only starting "Overlord" service in the build-up phase. The emphasis on origin in this context is relevent because the American, Danish, Estonian and French ships had been re-registered in Britain and had therefore become Red Ensign vessels bareboat chartered to the Ministry of War Transport, although the Danes had been given dispensation to fly their ensign as a house flag. The British Sea Transport organisation was responsible for the provision and maintenance of all British controlled ships, including those on charter, but the loading of those on American service was in the hands of the US Army authorities.

It was ultimately intended to supply US forces directly from ports in the United States and for this reason the Americans were allocated the most westerly landing areas. Consequently, ships destined for the US (Western Task Force) beachheads of Utah and Omaha sailed from the Bristol Channel convoy assembly areas (Barry Roads and the Mumbles) either direct to Normandy or to west Solent anchorage positions to await their scheduled cross-Channel convoy departure. Every available space in the vast Solent

south of the Isle of Wight from which specially mine-cleared and marked channels led southwards to the five Normandy beachheads. The positioning convoys to the Solent were WP Special, which sailed out of the Bristol Channel on 30th May; CW273, which left the Thames on 31st May, and follow-up convoys EBC1 from the Bristol Channel and ETC1 from the Thames. Designators of the subsequent Normandy convoys were made up as follows –
1st letter: E for convoys forming in England, as opposed to F for France on the return
2nd letter: B for those forming in the Bristol Channel; C for Cornwall and Devon; P for Portland; T for the Thames Estuary or W (Isle of Wight) for the Solent
3rd letter: C for coaster, L for landing ship or M for ocean-going (MT) cargo ship convoys
Figure: the numerical sequence of the convoy
In the event of the division of a convoy into more than one part, a suffix letter was used, with W indicating the Solent portion of a divided convoy.

Even the best laid plans are subject to change. D-Day was originally planned for May, then changed to 5th June, before at the last moment suffering a further 24 hour postponement because weather conditions were unfavourable. All ships actually under way when the second delaying order was given were turned back or diverted, with coaster convoy EBC1, already on passage from the Bristol Channel to the Solent, being instructed to anchor in Poole Bay. Other factors also caused amendments to the plan. The ex-Danish coaster *Valborg*, in WP Special convoy, required the services of a rescue tug for a tow into Plymouth, after another Normandy-bound coaster collided with her, whilst both were on passage from the Bristol Channel to the Solent; *Eaglescliffe Hall*, scheduled to load vehicles in London, was found to be in need of substantial repairs and a replacement was allocated at short notice and *Watson Ferris*, assigned as a Grimsby loader, had to be switched to London because her cargo of stores had been inadvertently routed to the wrong port. In some instances, the military authorities changed the composition of the early convoys at a very late stage and the US decided that seven coasters, due to load vehicles in Swansea, would not be required and the vessels were therefore repositioned ready for use as part of the build-up fleet.

Masters of merchant ships were instructed to ensure that their ships were blacked-out efficiently; that no navigation lights were used and that funnel smoke was reduced to a minimum, by day and night. The importance of proper station keeping was emphasised to give escorts the best possible chance of protecting the convoy.

Ships which became separated from their convoy could jeopardise the operation and, at night, might be regarded as hostile and fired upon accordingly. Masters of any ships in danger of sinking were required to make every effort to get their vessel clear of the channel and, if possible, to beach to save their cargo. A communication, dated 24th May 1944, from the Minister of War Transport to the masters of merchant ships taking part in Operation "Overlord" was worded thus – 'You are about to engage in the greatest amphibious operation of all time and in an enterprise which will profoundly affect the outcome of the war. Nothing matters except that the operation should be a success. In normal times, one of the first duties of a Master is to secure the safety of his ship. Now, risks must be taken and the ship must even be sacrificed if the needs of the operation require it. The orders of the Naval Authorities must be obeyed. You know what your ship can do and it is your duty to advise the Naval Authorities on the results of carrying out their orders, whenever you think they have over-estimated the capabilities of your ship or engines. But the final decision lies with the Naval Officer in command and you must obey his orders. I can promise that if you have to hazard your ship under Naval orders, no reflection will on that account be cast upon your professional competence, nor will you be prejudiced professionally in any way by implicit obedience to the instructions of the Naval Authorities during the operation. May God be with you as you go forth on your great adventure.'

One representative of the coasters of each of the 10 different countries of origin, which participated in Operation "Overlord" is illustrated on this and the following two pages.
More than sixty per cent of the coasters were of British origin, including *Highwear* seen here. She arrived at Omaha beachhead with a cargo of ammunition on 12th June 1944: the Channel storm which struck a week later drove her aground causing serious damage not only to her propeller, framing and rudder but also to 90 bottom plates. The storm also affected a considerable number of other vessels and caused massive disruption to the carefully prepared schedule of supplies to the Allied forces in action. *[National Maritime Museum, P22946]*

The Norwegian *Sollund* (right) pictured in 1938: she left London on 7th June 1944 with over 1,000 tons of ammunition for Sword beachhead. *[Captain J. F. van Puyvelde]*
The 1908-built *Juta* (below), was one of five Estonian ships which made their contribution to the Normandy invasion, all being allocated to the pre-loading phase. *[National Maritime Museum, P23078]*

The Belgian *Henri Gerlinger* (above) was allocated to load cased petrol at Sharpness for the American troops at Utah beach. *[Captain J. F. van Puyvelde]*
The distinctive shape of the Canadian *Winona (left)* dominates the foreground of this view, recording the coaster arrivals off the French coast on 7th June 1944. *[Imperial War Museum A24036]*

Crescendo (right), one of 19 pre-loaded coasters sailing under the Dutch flag, carried cased petrol from Port Talbot: nine other Dutch coasters then joined to supplement the build-up fleet. *[Captain J. F. van Puyvelde]*
The US-built, British-flag, *Charles Treadwell* (middle left) was based on Bristol Channel ports for loading US Army stores. *[National Maritime Museum]* Grounding on a sunken Army tank on her first visit to the Normandy beaches caused such extensive damage to the Polish *Poznan* (middle right) that she could no longer be retained in service. *[J. and M. Clarkson]*
The ex-French *Leoville* (bottom left) arrived in Normandy on D+1 Day (7th June 1944) carrying stores from London and troops from the Solent. *[Captain J. F. van Puyvelde]*
Fylla (bottom right) was one of a dozen ex-Danish steamers in the invasion fleet. *[Captain J. F. van Puyvelde]*

Section 2
Supplying the Allied Armies in Normandy
June-August 1944

Leaving their anchorages in the Solent during the evening of 5th June, the first coasters crossed the Channel to arrive off the Normandy coast from 1650 onwards on D-Day, 6th June. Force O3, making for the US beaches, included the former French coaster *Bidassoa*, the Norwegian *Edle, Heien, Mari* and *Skarv* and the British *Sarnia* and *The President,* all carrying ammunition, the British cased petrol carriers *Cameo, Empire Cape, Lottie R* and the Dutch *Starkenborgh*. Participants in Force L1, destined for the British beachheads, included the Belgian *Marcel*, the Dutch *Westland* and the British *Apricity, Northgate, Sedulity* and *Signality*, all with cased petrol, and the British *Broomlands, Glengarriff, Monkstone, Polglen, Skelwith Force* and *Stanley Force,* with a main cargo of ammunition. Although coasters were assigned to carry a particular type of main cargo, in reality they also loaded a number of other categories as well. For instance, the cased petrol ship *Signality* carried 60 tons of petrol, oil and lubricants, of which 15 tons was for the RAF, with the remaining 116 tons of cargo consisting of Royal Engineers' stores, Royal Signals' equipment, general supplies and a small quantity of coal. *Skelwith Force* carried 233 tons of ammunition for 25pdr, 105mm and 3·7in guns, as well

as mortar bombs, grenades and Bangalore torpedoes. Her cargo also comprised 52 tons of miscellaneous items, mainly Engineers' stores. All the coasters in the first two convoys and many in the early follow-up convoys carried dock operating troops for working cargo on arrival in France, with up to 140 personnel per ship being embarked either at the loading port or in the Solent. Those ships carrying vehicles had on board four men per vehicle, with the result that coasters were responsible for delivering more than 12,500 drivers and dock operating personnel to the Normandy beaches. There being no accommodation below deck, these soldiers brought their own equipment and rations: they set up field kitchens on deck and slept under tent-covers erected on the ship's hatches. Masters of the vessels concerned were requested to do everything possible to reduce the troops' discomfort during the period these soldiers were on board, which could be as long as a week for those embarking at Bristol Channel ports. On arrival in France, the men went ashore to establish defensive positions and, in many instances, immediately came under enemy fire. Work commenced on unloading the first

Viewed here in 1938, the Norwegian *Skarv* became a D-Day veteran by reaching Omaha beachhead on 6th June 1944. *[Captain J. F. van Puyvelde]*

The first outward voyage to Normandy by the Dutch *Starkenborgh* was marred by ramming the stern of another coaster in the same convoy. *[Dick Gorter collection]*

cargoes into DUKWs and landing craft late on the evening of D-Day, the whole scene in places being illuminated by fires, which burnt brightly all night, but a combination of bad weather and the fact that the ships were anchored some way from the shore prolonged the discharge operation and very slow progress was initially achieved.

The Master of one of the early coasters considered it too dangerous to continue to unload into landing craft but later elected to comply with his instructions, after being threatened by a supervising officer. Some heavy equipment, such as bridging, was brought to the beach in landing craft where the services of mobile cranes were needed but these were in short supply and tended easily to get bogged down. A shortage of DUKWs highlighted the urgency for beaching the coasters and, in Juno area, 13 were beached on 8th June, all Masters being issued with directives covering this procedure. They stated that only small and medium coasters would beach, provided this was the most economical method of cargo discharge or when an emergency, such as bad weather, prevented

unloading at anchor. To deter low flying enemy aircraft, ships in the anchorage were to fly barrage balloons at a height of 1,000ft and, on arrival off the beaching area, the procedure was for vessels to be boarded by the Coaster Berthing Master or Ferry Control Officer, who would issue instructions for beaching, speed of approach, transit marks etc. The general guide stated that the approach should be at high speed if the beach was soft sand or mud; at about four knots if the beach was hard and at the lowest speed at which the ship could be kept under control if the beach was shingle. It was stressed that ship's engines should not be run astern when beaching, as the propeller kick to port might cause the vessel to broach to. As soon as possible after taking the ground, a craft would be detailed to take the stern lines to the warping buoys before the coaster again became waterborne, with coaster berths being clearly marked by means of numbers in black on a white background as high up the beach as possible. During their stay off the French coast, no merchant service personnel were permitted to go ashore except on duty. The first coaster experiencing the effects of enemy action

The Normandy scene on 7th June 1944 with *Sherwood* beached to land her cargo of 37 vehicles and accompanying troops, at the conclusion of their two-day crossing from London. *[Imperial War Museum, A24012]*

Waldo Hill, one of the US-built ships, is seen beached for cargo discharge at Gold in mid-June 1944, between two of her sister ships, *Tully Crosby* and *Cyrus Sears*. [Imperial War Museum, A24364]

was *Northgate* which was subjected to an air attack at 2330 on 6th June, with one of the three bombs exploding a mere 40 feet from her: nevertheless she managed to be the first coaster to return to England, doing so in a tank landing ship convoy the following day. The considerable variation in cargo discharge times, especially in the US area, is reflected by the following arrival dates for reloading at UK ports of Force O3 convoy participants – on 12th June, *Sarnia*, *Skarv* and *The President* at Fowey; on 13th June, *Edle* at Fowey, *Empire Cape* at Portishead and *Heien* at Swansea; on 14th June, *Mari* at Fowey and *Lottie R* at Port Talbot; on 16th June *Starkenborgh* at Sharpness and, on 18th June, *Bidassoa* at Fowey and *Cameo* at Portishead. By the latter date, *Northgate* had already made a further round trip to the British area, as had five other L1 convoy participants, namely *Apricity*, *Marcel*, *Sedulity*, *Signality* and *Stanley Force*.

Prior to the landings, detailed coaster sailing plans had been drawn up to ensure that a smooth and sustained build-up of military equipment and supplies reached the beachheads. Garston and Avonmouth no longer featured as loading ports but Llanelly, on the Bristol Channel, and the English south coast ports of Fowey, Plymouth, Poole, Southampton, Portsmouth (temporarily only),

TABLE 3		
BUILD-UP COASTER PORT ALLOCATIONS FOR THE US AREA		
Loading port	Number of coasters allocated	Main cargo
LLANELLY	11	cased petrol
SWANSEA	13	ammunition
	7	stores
PORT TALBOT	14	cased petrol
BARRY	14	stores
PENARTH	14	ammunition
CARDIFF	14	stores
NEWPORT	14	ammunition
SHARPNESS	13	cased petrol
PORTISHEAD	7	cased petrol
FOWEY	8	ammunition
PLYMOUTH	11	cased petrol
POOLE	8	cased petrol
SOUTHAMPTON	12	cased petrol
	13	stores
	173	

TABLE 4					
BUILD-UP COASTER PORT ALLOCATIONS FOR THE BRITISH AREA					
Loading port	Number of coasters allocated	Main cargo	Number of loading berths	Loading days	Sailing frequency
POOLE	10	cased petrol	2	1-2	4 every 3 days
SOUTHAMPTON	18	ammunition	6	2	3 every day
	25	cased petrol	10	2	5 every day
	29	stores	10	2	5 every day
PORTSMOUTH	10	vehicles			10 sailings only
LITTLEHAMPTON	5	ammunition	2	2	1 every day
NEWHAVEN	10	ammunition	4	2	2 every day
LONDON: Millwall	11	stores	3	4	1 every day
King George V Dock	10	cased petrol	5	2	3 every 2 days
	10	stores	4	6	2 every 3 days
Royal Albert Dock	20	stores	8	4	2 every day
Purfleet	7	cased petrol	2	2	1 every day
Tilbury Dock	8	ammunition	3	3	1 every day
	5	stores	2	6	1 every 3 days
Tilbury Dock & Jetty	10	ammunition	4	4	1 every day
GRIMSBY	<u>13</u>	stores	6	4	1 every day
	201				

On her first voyage carrying ammunition to Normandy, *Brackenfield* was one of three coasters sunk when their convoy was attacked by E-boats in the English Channel on 10th June 1944. *[B. and A. Feilden/J. and M. Clarkson collection]*

Littlehampton and Newhaven (North Quay) were brought into use to supplement the previous Bristol Channel, Thames and East Coast terminals. Coasters loading in Fowey and Plymouth joined convoys from the Bristol Channel as they passed; vessels from Grimsby moved to the Thames Estuary to form up with those originating at London; ships from Littlehampton and Newhaven usually joined convoys on passage from the Thames and loaders from Poole, Portsmouth and Southampton formed up in the Solent, then either crossed to Normandy as a separate entity or attached themselves to one of the through convoys from the Bristol Channel or Thames. No fewer than 97 coasters were based at Southampton, with the vessels sailing to the US area using the Old Docks and those loading for the British area being allocated New Docks' Berths 101/102 for ammunition, 104/105 for stores and 107/108 for cased petrol. The cased petrol loaders at Poole also served both the US Western and the British Eastern Task Force areas, whereas coasters sailing from ports west of Poole exclusively served the US area and those from ports east of Southampton headed only to the British area. The coaster build-up plan, in Tables 3 and 4, details the loading location of the 173 vessels allocated to the US area and the 201 to the British beachheads.

It was not until the early hours of 10th June that the first coaster losses occurred, when convoy ETC4W was attacked by E-boats as it crossed to Normandy from the Solent: three London-loaded vessels were torpedoed and sunk – *Ashanti*, loaded with cased petrol from King George V Dock, and the ammunition carriers *Brackenfield* and *Dungrange*, both from Tilbury Dock. A survivor of that convoy was *Flathouse*, which was the first of 10 coasters to discharge at Mulberry B on that day. Mulberry B was the prefabricated port towed across the Channel and established at Arromanches, after which the port was subsequently renamed and which became the destination of 373 military cargo coaster sailings by the end of August. In addition, the small ports of Ouistreham and Port-en-Bessin, both in the assault areas, were also available for cargo by 10th June. *Beal*, another survivor of ETC4W, reached Port-en-Bessin on its opening day and was the first of 167 coaster sailings, bringing to the port 21 vehicles, 161 tons of ammunition, 13,500 tons of cased petrol and over 40,500 tons of stores in the first three months. Coasters were also able to use Grandcamp, Barfleur, St Vaast and Isigny in the US area and amongst the first ships to enter the latter were *Eskwood*, *Kylebank* and *Wooler*. After their arrivals in Juno sector on 8th and 9th June, *Torquay* and *Polly M* were directed to Courseulles to discharge their cargoes: use of these small harbours on the Normandy coast proved a particularly welcome development, not least because it reduced the urgency of liberating ports in Brittany. Access to them did at times prove hazardous in unfavourable weather conditions, with a number of encounters with the river bank or instances of bottom damage. A coaster casualty, unconnected with enemy action, occurred in the darkness of 13th June when the Norwegian *Reias*, after unloading at Sword beachhead, was rammed by the southbound coaster *Folda* and had to be abandoned. Given the conditions in which the vessels were required to navigate and the fact that initially there were no fewer than 16 convoys and 16 landing craft groups at sea in the Channel at any one time, it was highly praiseworthy that so few such accidents occurred. At Omaha on 17th June *Nesttun* was severely disabled as a result of settling on a mine and a further coaster loss was suffered the following day. Carrying ammunition from Penarth, the Canadian *Albert C Field* became the victim of an aerial torpedo attack,

TABLE 5 COMPARISON BETWEEN PLANNED AND ACTUAL TURN-ROUND DAYS OF SOME BRITISH AREA SHIPS AFFECTED BY THE 19th-22nd JUNE STORM					
Ship	Date started loading	Loading port	Main cargo	Turn-round days Planned	Actual
CORBRIDGE	6/6	London	stores	11	18
SLEMISH	10/6	London	stores	9	13
KNOWLTON	11/6	London	ammunition	13	17
BALDUIN	12/6	Southampton	stores	8	14
CUSHENDUN	13/6	Southampton	ammunition	8	11
MOELFRE ROSE	13/6	Southampton	ammunition	9	12
POLLY M	14/6	Southampton	cased petrol	7	12
KYLE CASTLE	15/6	Southampton	ammunition	10	13
SODALITY	15/6	London	cased petrol	9	12
ASSIDUITY	16/6	Southampton	cased petrol	6	9
CHANNEL QUEEN	16/6	London	cased petrol	9	12
RINGEN	16/6	London	stores	9	12
ROCKVILLE	16/6	Southampton	stores	6	10
SAINT ANGUS	16/6	Southampton	cased petrol	5	10
SERENITY	16/6	London	cased petrol	10	11
GUERNSEY QUEEN	17/6	London	cased petrol	9	11
ELIDIR	18/6	Southampton	stores	5	9
ULSTER HERO	19/6	Southampton	stores	5	6

Despite the impact of the June 1944 storm which struck as *Serenity* reached Normandy, remarkably her round voyage from London was completed only one day later than scheduled: she is seen here in 1959. *[Captain J. F. van Puyvelde]*

After only a single crossing to Normandy, the ammunition coaster *Eilian Hill* was released, following extensive damage in the June 1944 storm. *[W. H. Brown/J. and M. Clarkson collection]*

for extensive repairs, as were *Berryden*, *Eilian Hill* and *Regfos*. On the evening of 22nd June, *Dunvegan Head* was hit by shells from German field gun batteries whilst discharging at Sword and the ensuing fire burned for two days. This not only resulted in the vessel ultimately being condemned but in the decision that Sword beach, which had handled 161 coaster arrivals on the eastern flank of the invasion area, should be closed down on 1st July, with incoming ships being diverted westwards to discharge out of range of enemy guns. On 24th June, two coaster casualties resulted from convoy ETC17 being straddled by long-range shells from the French coast as it transitted the Strait of Dover. *Empire Lough* caught fire and became a total loss, despite being beached: *Gurden Gates* was affected less seriously but

as she commenced the final leg of her passage from the Bristol Channel to Utah.

The worst storm during any June for 40 years struck the Normandy coast on 19th June causing untold disruption to the carefully planned convoy schedules, some of which is apparent from Table 5 showing ships' turn-round days. Registering up to Force 7, with waves more than eight feet high, the storm lasted four days and resulted in damage of varying proportions to more than 28 coasters, many through grounding or by out-of-control craft being thrown against them. During this time, *Bailey Foster* and *Paul Emile Javary* each lost one anchor: *Capito*, *Monksville*, *Wallace Rose* and *Westown* were even more precariously placed after losing both theirs. In saving the ship, its cargo and crew, the Master of *Wallace Rose* glowingly commended the Mate for exceptional courage and bravery, unparalleled in his 18 years in command. *Westdale* was irreparably damaged after going ashore as a result of a mine explosion; *Kylegorm* was in danger of sinking, until pumped out by a salvage vessel, and *Eilian Hill* sustained extensive damage by striking the quay, then grounding at Port-en-Bessin. Even after the storm abated and routine convoys had resumed, it was several weeks before *Broomlands*, *Grangetoft*, *Highwear*, *Regfos* and *The President* were in a fit condition to leave the beachhead: the latter vessel, in the tow of a US tug, was further damaged in a collision south of the Isle of Wight. *Asa Eldridge* also required a tow back across the Channel and, on reaching a home port, was withdrawn

nevertheless had to be diverted to the Solent for repairs. German long-range shelling was one hazard: a subsequent one turned out to be blast damage from enemy flying bombs, aimed at the English mainland but hit by British anti-aircraft guns deployed on the Kent coast. By the end of June, over 400 military cargo coasters had been employed on Operation "Overlord", seven of which had been lost whilst in service. It was fully realised that ships would not always work to the designated ports and some amendments to the sustained loading plan would be inevitable, due to enemy action or bad weather. However, unforeseen difficulties were being experienced mainly in the US area where instances were occurring of cargoes being selectively discharged, instead of being unloaded in bulk. Not only did this delay the ship's return but also resulted in some vessels running out of the 14 days of supplies issued for the crew. Other instances were reported of ships not being included in the first available return convoys and, on several occasions, of the American authorities ordering coasters to return to ports without regard to the plan. This resulted in *Justin Doane* and *Lysland* being directed to the Bristol Channel, despite the plan calling for them to be routed elsewhere, the former to Grimsby, where *Saint-Enogat* had become the first sustained loader. *Lysland* had been scheduled to be one of the earliest vessels to be switched from London's Royal Albert Dock to Harwich (Parkeston Quay), which was being inaugurated for Normandy stores on 26th June. Harwich brought its own problems because its closure for cargo work since

1940 meant that all skilled workers had long since moved away. Consequently, it was decided that the port should concentrate on loading ammunition, which could be handled more expeditiously, so in mid-July *Watson Ferris* left Harwich with the final cargo of general stores and *Thornaby* with the first exclusively ammunition cargo. On the Thames, from 16th June, coaster loading berths were allocated for cased petrol and ammunition at London Dock's East Quay, in place of two berths in King George V Dock and one at Tilbury, and early in July, further changes were made to the arrangements with considerably fewer ships (284 instead of 374) being used on an amended loading pattern, as shown in Table 6.

This plan involved the deletion of Llanelly, Barry, Cardiff, Newport, Sharpness and Portishead and the placing of greater emphasis on Swansea, Fowey, Plymouth and particularly Southampton, the latter despite what was regarded as limited rail capacity to supply the port. The extra sailing time involved in using Bristol Channel ports was considered worthwhile in an attempt to eliminate the Severn Rail Tunnel bottleneck, while, for the British area, the inclusion of Harwich reduced the reliance on London loading. The fleet suffered losses on consecutive days in July, the first being *Ringen* which was sunk by mine on the 4th when bound for Sword beachhead. The following day, *Glendinning* was torpedoed by a U-boat whilst in homeward-bound convoy FTC27 (France Thames Coaster No 27), composed of 22 coasters, including the severely damaged *Westdale* under tow by a tug. The 'Thames' element of the convoy designator did not show the ultimate destination of all of its component vessels: only eight were in fact routed there, the others being detached to Poole, Southampton, Littlehampton and Newhaven.

In July, there was a requirement for small coasters to be put into service to ferry, to small French ports, the loads brought over by the fleet of Liberty and other ocean-going cargo ships. Amongst the first to be so assigned was *Aridity*, which left the Solent on the 8th, and *Hawarden Bridge*, which followed three days later. This was a stopgap arrangement pending the allocation of small Dutch coasters, including *Amazone* and *Pacific* which had featured in the 1940 evacuations from France but which, in 1944, were manned by their Dutch crews. As a result of the mining by the German forces of its outer and inner harbours, the obstruction of its berths by scuttled ships and the systematic demolition of its facilities, the major port of Cherbourg was not available for cargo for many weeks after its liberation and, as regards heavy lifts, for even longer. Six ammunition coasters were able to enter Cherbourg on 22nd

TABLE 6 JULY COASTER PORT ALLOCATIONS			
Loading port	Number of coasters allocated	Main cargo	Turn-round days
FOR THE US AREA			
SWANSEA	28	stores	13
PORT TALBOT	8	cased petrol	14
PENARTH	13	ammunition	13
FOWEY	10	ammunition	9
PLYMOUTH	7	cased petrol	8
	13	stores	9
POOLE	10	cased petrol	6
SOUTHAMPTON	58	stores	6-8
	147		
FOR THE BRITISH AREA			
POOLE	10	cased petrol	7
SOUTHAMPTON	24	cased petrol	6-9
	40	stores	5-7
LITTLEHAMPTON	6	ammunition	5
NEWHAVEN	13	ammunition	8
LONDON: Purfleet	11	cased petrol	10
Tilbury	10	ammunition	12
HARWICH	12	ammunition	14
GRIMSBY	11	stores	14
	137		

July and a few days later *Ashbel Hubbard*, *Benjamin Sherburn*, *Cassard*, *Claudius Magnin*, *Elkanah Crowell* and *Marsden* headed for Cherbourg from the Bristol Channel. They were, however, diverted to the Solent and, joined by *Thyra III* and *Waldo Hill* from London, were required to languish at anchor for between two and five weeks awaiting orders, on receipt of which most were then directed to other discharge locations in Normandy. After unloading their outward cargoes, coasters normally returned in ballast, although a few ships were reloaded before being despatched northbound. On 24th June *Busiris* had left Arromanches (Mulberry B) with four tons of mail and 25 tons of empty gas cylinders and, the following month, *Empire Estuary* carried empty ammunition

In July 1944, the US-built *Ashbel Hubbard* loaded stores in Swansea for Cherbourg. However, she was diverted to wait at anchor in the Solent for over four weeks before crossing to France. *[National Maritime Museum, P21483]*

Accumulated arrears of maintenance ultimately took its toll on ships' serviceability: the ex-French *Cassard* was under repair at Antwerp for more than nine weeks from 24th February 1945. *[National Maritime Museum, P21774]*

The French *Claudius Magnin* was transferred to Port Talbot registry for war service and was based in the Bristol Channel for her initial Normandy sailings. *[National Maritime Museum, P22126]*

boxes from Port-en-Bessin, following in the wake of *Empire Jonquil* which left Courseulles with salvaged engines and landing craft spare parts. In addition to normal outward military cargoes, there was also a need to supply coal from the Humber to feed Cherbourg Power Station, which was now cut off from France's own supplies. During August, coasters for the US military were still serving the beachhead areas of Omaha and Utah, which between them received 426 coaster arrivals that month, as opposed to Cherbourg's 109: however, the combined total of these was slightly less than the number of coasters handled during the same period at the small ports of St Vaast (230), Isigny (161), Barfleur (132) and Grandcamp (38). As envisaged in the original planning, the ability to use these smaller Normandy ports underlined the unique contribution the coaster fleet was able to make. There soon followed the possibility that Granville, St Malo and ports to the west would be opened, in contrast to Juno beach in the British area which was about to be closed down. From time to time, crossings were inevitably affected by accidents, such as on 7th August when *Channel Fisher* damaged her bows in collision with a US Liberty ship off the French coast: despite this, the coaster could not be spared for repairs until after she had completed one more round trip to the beaches. *Empire Factor*, the first of 25 prefabricated coasters which were a dry cargo version of the Chant tankers, arrived in the British area after her third Channel crossing on 18th August but became badly damaged when she broached to while beached. U-boats scored some successes in August, sinking the Juno-bound *Saint-Enogat* on the 19th and catching *Coral* the following day, as she was returning from Arromanches, after completing nine crossings to Normandy with ammunition. On the 26th, a U-boat torpedo also awaited *Ashmun J Clough* as she was heading from Barry with stores for Utah: she went down 23 miles north of Cherbourg. Coaster convoy speeds were normally seven knots, which happened to coincide with the critical speed of some of the coasters on charter from the USA. As these could easily attain 11-12 knots, ships, such as *Justin Doane*, *Richard Bearse*, *Watson Ferris* and *William Howland*, as well as the British-built *Bucklaw*, were at times assigned to faster cross-Channel

M convoys composed of ocean-going cargo ships. At the end of August, military achievements necessitated a major reorganisation in the cross-Channel supply system and details of this are outlined in Section 4. By this time, aided by size and the consequent shorter cargo working time, one small coaster, *Staley Bridge*, had been able to make a remarkable 14 round trips to Normandy, with five others each completing 13.

Above: In August 1944, *Bucklaw*'s superior speed enabled her to sail with ocean-going vessels on ETM convoys from the Thames to Normandy. *[J. and M. Clarkson collection]*

On 31st August 1944, *Staley Bridge* arrived back at Southampton to load cased petrol for her 15th crossing to France, thereby achieving an average turn round-time at the lower end of the target of six to nine days. This peacetime view shows the ship in Birkenhead Docks. *[J. and M. Clarkson collection]*

Section 3
Ships' Service Record to Normandy
June–August 1944

SHIP'S NAME gross tonnage/year built, nationality (owners/*managers, if British) – Date taken up and intended cargo (known variations are shown in the listings accordingly)
• Loading Port (and Dock, if London); Sailing Date; Cargo (dwt); Supplementary Information

	Convoy Departure Area, Date and Designation	Destination and Arrival Date at Anchorage

(Abbreviations: BC = Bristol Channel; MoWT = Ministry of War Transport)
Notes: 1. D-Day was 6/6/44
2. The severe storm which swept the English Channel was at its peak 19-22/6/44

AARO 1,426/25 British, ex-Danish (MoWT/*Aln) – taken up 12/5/44 for Stores
• Swansea 3/6; vehicles and troops	BC 5/6 EBC2Z	Omaha 8/6
• Southampton 25/6	Solent 27/6 EBC22W	Utah 27/6
• Southampton 16/7	Solent 17/7 EBC42W	Omaha 17/7
• Sharpness 11/8	BC 12/8 EBC70	US area 14/8

Returned to Barry 26/8 to load for US area
(Vessel seriously damaged at beachhead 6/10/44 and became a total loss: see Section 4)

ABILITY 881/43 British (Everard) – taken up 7/6/44 for Cased Petrol
Taken up for one voyage only, to replace coaster *Varegg*, which switched to Southampton
| • London | Thames 12/6 ETC8 | Sword 14/6 |

Returned 18/6; arrived Humber 24/6 for release 11/7

ACTINIA 352/37 Dutch – taken up 1/5/44 for Cased Petrol
• Port Talbot 1/6; left BC 2/6; embarked 65 troops in Solent
	Solent 8/6 EBC3W	Omaha 9/6
• Southampton 25/6	Solent 26/6 ETC18W	Sword 26/6
• Southampton 6/7	Solent 7/7 ETC29W	Sword 7/7
• Southampton 15/7	Solent 16/7 ETC38W	Sword 16/7
• Southampton 22/7	Solent 23/7 ETC45W	Gold 23/7
• Southampton 28/7	Solent 29/7 ETC51W	Gold 29/7
• Southampton 3/8	Solent 4/8 ETC57W	Arromanches 4/8
• Southampton 8/8	Solent 9/8 ETC62W	Port-en-Bessin 9/8
• Southampton 13/8	Solent 14/8 ETC67W	Arromanches 14/8
• Southampton 25/8	Solent 26/8 ETC79W	Arromanches 26/8
• Southampton 31/8	Solent 1/9 ETC85W	Arromanches 1/9

Returned to Southampton 6/9 to load for Dieppe

ACTIVITY 358/31 British (Everard) – taken up 26/4/44 for Cased Petrol
• London (King George V); small fire broke out in ship's accommodation at loading berth 20/5; 358 tons; left London 21/5 and Thames 5/6
| | Solent 8/6 ETC3W | British area 9/6 |

• Southampton 16/6	Solent 17/6 ETC11W	Port-en-Bessin 17/6
• Southampton 28/6	Solent 28/6 ETC20W	Gold 28/6
• Southampton 4/7	Solent 5/7 ETC27W	Juno 5/7
• Southampton 11/7	Solent 12/7 ETC34W	Port-en-Bessin 12/7
• Poole 19/7	Solent 20/7 ETC42W	Gold 20/7
• Poole 25/7	Solent 26/7 ETC48W	Gold 26/7
• London 11/8	Thames 12/8 ETC66	

Detached to Newhaven with engine defects; left 15/8
| | joined ETC69 | Arromanches 16/8 |
| • Southampton 25/8 | Solent 26/8 ETC79W | Port-en-Bessin 26/8 |

Returned to Southampton 1/9 to load for Caen

ALACRITY 554/40 British (Everard) – taken up 31/3/44 for Cased Petrol
• London (King George V); 561 tons; left Thames 7/6
| | Solent 10/6 ETC5W | Sword 11/6 |

• London 18/6; left Thames 22/6; turned back
| | Thames 24/6 ETC17 | Sword 25/6 |

On return, collided with ocean-going cargo ship *Empire Canyon* in Thames 30/6
• London 1/7	Thames 2/7 ETC25	Gold 3/7
• London (Tilbury) 12/7	Thames 14/7 ETC37	Sword 15/7
• Southampton 23/7	Solent 24/7 EBC49W	Utah 24/7
• Poole 4/8	Solent 5/8 EBC60W	Utah 5/8
• Poole 12/8	Solent 13/8 EBC69W	US area 13/8
• Poole 26/8	Solent 27/8 EBC83W	US area 27/8

Returned to Poole 7/9 to load for US area

Sixteen coasters under Everard management served Normandy in 1944-45: one of these was the cased petrol coaster *Alacrity*, photographed in 1960.
[FotoFlite/J. and M. Clarkson collection]

ALBERT C FIELD 1,764/23 **Canadian** – taken up 4/44 for Ammunition
• Penarth 16/6; 2,500 tons   BC 17/6 EBC14
Lost. S of Isle of Wight on passage to Utah at 2340 18/6, hit starboard side amidships by aerial torpedo thought to have been from a Ju88 aircraft; vessel broke in two and sank within three minutes; Master and three crew members killed, 17 others injured; most survivors rescued by HM trawler *Herschell*

ALCYONE 359/38 **Dutch** – taken up 22/7/44 for Stores
• Southampton 31/7   Solent 1/8 ETC54W   Arromanches 1/8
Assigned to French coastal ferry service: returned 10/9 to load at Falmouth for St Brieuc

ALGOL 1,566/24 **British (Kyle/*Monroe)** – taken up 9/5/44 for Stores
• Grimsby 20/5; 1,040 tons   Thames 10/6 ETC6   Juno 12/6
• Southampton 24/6   Solent 25/6 ETC17W   Gold 25/6
• Southampton 9/7   Solent 10/7 ETC32W   Gold 10/7
• Southampton 25/7   Solent 26/7 ETC48W   Juno 26/7
• Southampton 8/8   Solent 9/8 ETC62W   Arromanches 9/8
Returned to Southampton 15/8 to discharge import cargo and for repairs
• Southampton 30/8   Solent 31/8 ETC84W
Turned back   Solent 1/9 ETC85W   Arromanches 1/9
Returned to Southampton 5/9 to load for Caen

The stores coaster *Algol* loaded her first consignment for Normandy at Grimsby, then moved south to the Thames to await her convoy departure for the beachhead. *[National Maritime Museum, P21388]*

ALNWICK 508/36 **British (Tyne-Tees)** – taken up 18/5/44 for Stores
• Southampton 7/6   Solent 8/6 ETC3W   British area 9/6
• Southampton 16/6   Solent 17/6 ETC11W   Port-en-Bessin 17/6
• Southampton 4/7   Solent 5/7 ETC27W   Port-en-Bessin 5/7
• Southampton 14/7   Solent 15/7 ETC37W   Port-en-Bessin 15/7
• Southampton 23/7   Solent 24/7 ETC46W   Port-en-Bessin 24/7
• Southampton 1/8   Solent 2/8 ETC55W   Port-en-Bessin 2/8
• Southampton 10/8   Solent 12/8 ETC65W   Port-en-Bessin 12/8
• Southampton 18/8   Solent 20/8 ETC73W   Port-en-Bessin 20/8
Returned to Southampton 27/8 with heavy weather damage

AMAZONE 250/39 **Dutch** – taken up 7/44 for Stores
• Southampton 23/7   Solent 24/7 ETC46W   Port-en-Bessin 24/7
Assigned to French coastal ferry service; returned to Plymouth 10/9 to load at Torquay for St Brieuc

ANDONI 678/37 **British (Evans)** – taken up 5/44 for Cased Petrol
• Garston 27/5; called Swansea 31/5-2/6; left BC 6/6
    Solent 10/6 EBC5W   Utah 11/6
• Sharpness 22/6   BC 23/6 EBC20   Isigny 25/6
Whilst proceeding out of Isigny, vessel struck alternate banks of the channel, went aground and stuck fast, with propeller badly damaged and rudder twisted and useless 1500 28/6; proceeded in tow of tug *ST248* 0450 30/6; tug grounded 0610 30/6; *Andoni* grounded 0715 30/6; both vessels refloated 1555-1700 30/6 and proceeded to anchorage; *Andoni* left beachhead in tow of tug *Empire Larch*; anchored in Solent 9-22/7; arrived in Thames 23/7 in tow of tug *Moose Peak*; arrived Tyne 25/7 for repairs and subsequent release

ANTHONY ENRIGHT 1,791/43 **British, ex-US (MoWT/*Witherington)** – taken up 5/44 for Stores
• Swansea 12/6   BC 13/6 EBC10   Omaha 16/6
• Swansea 2/7   BC 2/7 EBC29   Omaha 4/7
• Loading switched from Swansea after vessel put into Plymouth for engine repairs; left 21/7 but turned back with further engine trouble; left 22/7
    joined EBC48   Omaha 23/7
• Swansea 30/8   BC 31/8 EBC89
Convoy sheltered in Weymouth Bay; left 3/9   Cherbourg 3/9

ANTICOSTI 1,925/21 **Canadian** – taken up 5/44 for Stores
• London (Royal Albert); 35 vehicles and 140 troops
    Thames 5/6 ETC2Z   British area 7/6
• London (Tilbury) 21/6; ammunition
    Thames 25/6 ETC18   Juno 26/6
• London; left Thames 9/7   Solent 11/7 ETC33W   Arromanches 11/7
Returned to London 16/7 for temporary release

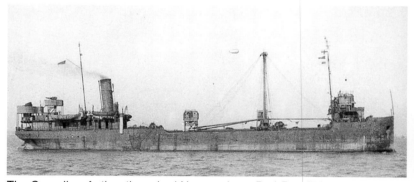

The Canadian *Anticosti* reached Normandy on D+1 Day (7th June 1944) carrying 35 vehicles and 140 troops from London. *[National Maritime Museum, P21443]*

ANTILOPE 206/39 **Dutch** – taken up 8/44 for Stores
• Southampton 28/8   Solent 29/8 EBC85W   Barfleur 29/8
Assigned to French coastal ferry service in US area

ANTIQUITY 311/33 **British (Everard)** – taken up 19/4/44 for Cased Petrol
• London (Purfleet) 14/5; 240 tons   Thames 7/6 ETC22   Sword 8/6
• Southampton 15/6   Solent 16/6 ETC10W   Sword 16/6

On return, coming alongside at Southampton in tow of tug *TID69* caused damage to coaster *Lowestoft Trader* 2015 21/6; adjudged in need of lengthy repairs and unfit for further operations; left Solent 19/7, arrived in Thames 20/7 in tow of coaster *Accruity*

ANTRIM COAST 646/37 British (Coast) – taken up 25/4/44 for Cased Petrol
• Port Talbot 2/6; left BC 5/6   Solent 9/6 EBC4W   Omaha 10/6
In return convoy, was struck a glancing blow by a landing craft 0147 17/6; arrived Portishead 19/6
• Portishead 23/6   BC 24/6 EBC21   Utah 26/6
At beachhead, tip of stem bent over when hit hard on port bow by a US tank landing ship, thought to have been *LST283*, 1410 27/6
• Port Talbot 8/7   BC 9/7 EBC36   Omaha 11/7
Rudder slightly damaged when vessel struck unknown object whilst discharging at anchor 1315 13/7; on return, underwent repairs at Llanelly 19/7-5/8
• Port Talbot 7/8   BC 8/8 EBC66   US area 10/8
• Southampton 23/8   Solent 23/8 ETC76W
Convoy turned back to Solent; left 24/8   Arromanches 24/8
Returned to Southampton 1/9 to load for Arromanches

APRICITY 402/33 British (Everard) – taken up 4/4/44 for Cased Petrol
• London (King George V); 265 tons cased petrol and stores; left Thames 31/5; coming alongside in heavy swell in Solent, paddle steamer *Duchess of Cornwall* buckled *Apricity*'s starboard side main deck plating 1530 4/6; embarked 59 troops in Solent   Solent 5/6 Force L1   Gold 6/6 (D-Day)
• Poole   Solent 13/6 ETC8W   Port-en-Bessin 14/6
• Poole   Solent 22/6 ETC15W   Gold 22/6
• Southampton 27/6   Solent 29/6 ETC21W   Port-en-Bessin 29/6
Port bow dented on entering port as a result of vessel touching ground then striking dock wall 1900 30/6
• Poole 6/7   Solent 7/7 ETC29W   Port-en-Bessin 7/7
• Poole 13/7   Solent 14/7 ETC36W   Juno 14/7
• Poole   Solent 22/7 ETC44W   British area 22/7
• Southampton 6/8   Solent 7/8 ETC60W   Port-en-Bessin 7/8
• Poole 16/8   Solent 17/8 ETC70W   Port-en-Bessin 17/8
• Poole 24/8 with craft in tow   Solent 25/8 ETC78W   Port-en-Bessin 25/8
Returned to Poole 28/8 to load for Port-en-Bessin

Following heavy weather damage sustained on her first round voyage to Normandy, the Norwegian stores coaster *Ara* played no further part in the operation. *[National Maritime Museum, P21456]*

ARA 965/19 Norwegian – taken up 12/6/44 for Stores
• Southampton 14/6   Solent 15/6 ETC9W   Gold 15/6
Returned to Solent 23/6 with heavy weather damage to shell plating and frames and slight leakage in engine room and bilges; arrived Thames 7/7 on passage to Tyne for release 3/9

ARBROATH 553/35 British (Dundee, Perth & London) – taken up 8/4/44 for Cased Petrol
• London (Purfleet) 4/5; 540 tons; left Thames 9/6
          Solent 12/6 ETC7W   Juno 13/6
• Poole 23/6   Solent 24/6 EBC17W   Omaha 24/6
• Poole 28/6   Solent 29/6 EBC24W   Utah 29/6
• Poole 5/7   Solent 6/7 EBC31W   Isigny 6/7
Whilst approaching port in a strong eddy current, vessel slewed to starboard and sliced channel bank; after sliding off, stern pounded causing propeller blades to become chipped 2303 6/7
• Poole 11/7   Solent 12/7 EBC37W   Omaha 12/7
• Poole 20/7   Solent 21/7 EBC46W   Omaha 21/7
• Poole 27/7   Solent 28/7 EBC53W   US area 28/7
On being called forward to Isigny, again sliced bank whilst entering port 0012 4/8; contact with forecastle head of coaster *Vliestroom* damaged *Arbroath*'s boat deck structure 0035 4/8; on departure, bumped heavily on bilge 2244 5/8
• Poole 10/8   Solent 12/8 EBC68W   US area 12/8
• Poole 24/8   Solent 25/8 EBC81W   US area 25/8
Returned to Poole 31/8 to load for US area

Mishaps distinctly marred the two calls made by *Arbroath* at the small Normandy port of Isigny in July and August 1944. *[Ships in Focus]*

ARDGRYFE 975/18 British (MacCallum) – taken up 1/5/44 for Stores
• London (Royal Albert) 4/6; 358 tons; left Thames 7/6
          Solent 9/6 ETC4W
Convoy heavily attacked in English Channel by E-boats 10/6 Juno 10/6
• London 17/6   Thames 18/6 ETC13   Gold 19/6
• London (Tilbury) 9/7   Thames 10/7 ETC33   Sword 11/7
• Southampton 24/7   Solent 25/7 ETC47W   Juno 25/7

In August 1944, *Ardgryfe*'s cargo of maps was of such vital importance that she completed her crossing to Cherbourg, despite collision damage rendering the ship incapable of anchoring: the photograph shows the vessel in 1937. *[Captain J. F. van Puyvelde]*

• Southampton 5/8	Solent 5/8 EBC60W	Utah 5/8	
• Southampton 14/8; cargo of maps	Solent 15/8 EBC71W		

In the vicinity of the Needles, sustained considerable stem, hawse pipe and forecastle damage when struck on the port bow right forward by an unknown incoming tank landing ship, which then scraped down *Ardgryfe*'s port side causing damage to lifeboat and davits 0220 15/8; turned back, then left escorted by tug, as unable to anchor Solent 16/8 EBC72W Cherbourg 16/8
Returned to Thames 29/8 and Grangemouth 2/9

ARIDITY **336/31 British (Everard)** – taken up 4/4/44 for Cased Petrol
• London (Purfleet); 240 tons	Thames 7/6 ETC22	Gold 8/6
• Southampton 14/6	Solent 17/6 ETC11W	Gold 17/6
• Southampton 23/6	Solent 24/6 ETC16W	Gold 24/6
• Southampton 28/6	Solent 29/6 ETC21W	Juno 29/6
• Southampton 7/7	Solent 8/7 ETC30W	Juno 8/7

Assigned to French coastal ferry service from ocean-going store ships; returned 14/8
• Southampton 26/8	Solent 27/8 ETC80W	Arromanches 27/8
• Southampton 31/8	Solent 3/9 ETC87W	Port-en-Bessin 3/9

Returned to Southampton 7/9 and London 12/9

ASA ELDRIDGE **1,791/43 British, ex-US (MoWT/*Witherington)** – taken up 24/4/44 for Stores
• Grimsby 3/6; 1,000 tons	Thames 7/6 ETC22	Gold 8/6

Bottom, steering gear and boilers damaged by grounding in the storm 20/6; refloated 21/6; returned in tow of tug *Cheerly* 23/6; withdrawn for extensive repairs; arrived Hull 28/7

ASEITY **416/35 British (Everard)** – taken up 25/4/44 for Cased Petrol
• London (Purfleet); 450 tons; left Thames 8/6		
	Solent 11/6 ETC6W	Juno 12/6

Whilst at anchor, port side amidships and steering gear damaged by stern of ocean-going cargo ship *Stanridge* 2330 12/6; 10 minutes later, *Stanridge*'s stern again collided with *Aseity*, on this occasion causing damage to vessel's port bow and forecastle head; returned to London 18/6

• London 25/6	Thames 26/6 ETC19	Sword 27/6
• London 1/7	Thames 3/7 ETC26	Gold 4/7
• Poole 17/7	Solent 18/7 EBC43W	Omaha 18/7
• Poole 23/7	Solent 24/7 EBC49W	Utah 24/7
• Poole 1/8	Solent 2/8 EBC58W	US area 2/8
• Poole 10/8	Solent 12/8 EBC68W	US area 12/8
• Poole 24/8	Solent 25/8 EBC81W	US area 25/8

Returned to Poole to load for US area

An ocean-going cargo ship twice damaged *Aseity*, whilst she was anchored off the Normandy beaches on 12th June 1944. *[Ships in Focus]*

ASHANTI **534/36 British (Evans)** – taken up 31/3/44 for Cased Petrol
• London (King George V); 480 tons; left Thames 7/6	
	Solent 9/6 ETC4W

Lost. On passage to Juno at 0315 10/6, vessel hit port side amidships by E-boat torpedo from *S177* or *S178*; fire rapidly spread through the ship which then disintegrated in a massive explosion; nine lives, including Master, lost; only two bodies recovered, one two weeks later

ASHBEL HUBBARD **1,793/43 British, ex-US (MoWT/*Heyn)** – taken up 4/44 for Stores
• Barry 9/6	BC 10/6 EBC7	Omaha 13/6
• Portishead 12/7	BC 13/7 EBC40	Omaha 15/7
• Swansea 27/7	BC 28/7 EBC55	

Diverted to Solent; at anchor for over four weeks
	Solent 28/8 EBC84W	Utah 28/8

Returned to Newport 12/9 to load for Cherbourg

ASHMUN J CLOUGH **1,791/43 British, ex-US (MoWT/*Stephenson Clarke)** – taken up 4/44 for Stores
• Cardiff 5/6	BC 7/6 EBC4	Omaha 10/6
• Cardiff 5/7	BC 5/7 EBC32	Omaha 7/7
• Swansea 24/7	BC 24/7 EBC51	Cherbourg 26/7
• Barry 22/8; 1,200 tons; turned back with engine defects; left 24/8		
	BC 24/8 EBC82	

Lost. On passage to Utah at 0832 26/8, engine room hit starboard side amidships by torpedo from *U-989*; vessel settled by the stern and quickly sank 23 miles N of Cherbourg; 15 crew members rescued, one with injuries; Master and Chief Engineer amongst the 12 killed

ASK 1,541/17 Norwegian – taken up 6/4/44 for Ammunition

• Newport 10/6	BC 11/6 EBC8	Omaha 14/6
• Newport	BC 4/7 EBC31	Utah 6/7
• Swansea 24/7; stores	BC 24/7 EBC51	Utah 26/7
• Swansea 27/8; stores	BC 27/8 EBC85	Utah 29/8

Returned to Barry 17/9

The Norwegian steamer *Ask* was initially based in the Bristol Channel to load ammunition and stores for the US Army. *[National Maritime Museum, P21485]*

ASSIDUITY 350/30 British (Everard) – taken up 31/3/44 for Cased Petrol

• London (Purfleet); 315 tons; left Thames 5/6		
	Solent 8/6 ETC3W	British area 9/6
• Southampton 16/6	Solent 17/6 ETC11W	Gold 17/6
• Southampton 30/6	Solent 2/7 ETC24W	Sword 2/7
• Southampton 8/7	Solent 9/7 ETC31W	Sword 9/7
• Southampton 13/7	Solent 14/7 ETC36W	Juno 14/7
• Southampton 20/7	Solent 21/7 ETC43W	Gold 21/7
• Southampton 28/7	Solent 29/7 ETC51W	Gold 29/7
• Southampton 2/8	Solent 3/8 ETC56W	Arromanches 3/8
• Southampton 15/8	Solent 16/8 ETC69W	Arromanches 16/8
• Southampton 21/8	Solent 23/8 ETC76W	
Convoy turned back to Solent; left 24/8		Arromanches 24/8
• Southampton 30/8	Solent 2/9 ETC86W	
Turned back to Solent	Solent 7/9 ETC90W	Arromanches 7/9

Returned to Southampton 15/9

ASTERIA 649/26 British (Robertson) – taken up 21/4/44 for Ammunition

• London (Tilbury) 5/6; 630 tons; left Thames 7/6		
	Solent 9/6 ETC4W	
Convoy heavily attacked in English Channel by E-boats		Sword 10/6
• Newhaven 20/6	joined ETC15	
Convoy sheltered in Solent; left 22/6		Gold 22/6

Port side of hull damaged by lighters bumping alongside 23/6

• Newhaven 28/6	Solent 29/6 ETC21W	Gold 29/6

• Newhaven 3/7; in the process of relaying orders, an HM motor launch steered too close, damaging vessel's port lifeboat and davit 3/7

	joined ETC26	Gold 4/7
• Newhaven 11/7	joined ETC34	Gold 12/7
• Newhaven 20/7	joined ETC43	Juno 21/7

• Newhaven 28/7	joined ETC51	Gold 29/7
• Newhaven 4/8	joined ETC58	Arromanches 5/8
• Newhaven 12/8	joined ETC65	
Convoy diverted to Solent; left 13/8		Arromanches 13/8
• Newhaven 23/8	joined ETC77	Arromanches 24/8

Returned to Newhaven 3/9 to load for Dieppe

ATLANTIC COAST 890/34 British (Coast) – taken up 6/5/44 for Cased Petrol

• Sharpness 10/6	BC 12/6 EBC9	Utah 15/6
• Sharpness 2/7	BC 3/7 EBC30	Utah 5/7
• Port Talbot 18/7	BC 19/7 EBC46	Omaha 21/7
• Plymouth 31/7	joined EBC58	US area 2/8
Returned 8/8 for repairs at Plymouth		
• Plymouth 19/8	joined EBC77	
Convoy sheltered in Solent; left 23/8		Utah 23/8

Returned to Plymouth 28/8 to load for US area

AVANCE 1,582/20 British, ex-Danish (MoWT/*Cory) – taken up 4/44 for Stores

• Swansea 3/6; vehicles and troops	BC 5/6 EBC2Z	Omaha 8/6
• Avonmouth 25/6	BC 26/6 EBC23	Omaha 28/6
• Newport 15/7; ammunition	BC 16/7 EBC43	Omaha 18/7

Whilst at anchor, barge collided with vessel, denting starboard side shell plates 2024 20/7

• Cardiff 1/8	BC 1/8 EBC59	
Straggled from convoy; called Dartmouth 3/8		
	Solent 5/8 EBC60W	Omaha 5/8
• Grimsby 30/8	Thames 7/9 ETC91	Arromanches 8/9

Returned to Grimsby 26/9

Avance was a part of the ex-Danish fleet: for war service, her port of registry was switched to London. *[National Maritime Museum, P21521]*

AVANCE I 1,300/12 Norwegian – taken up 3/5/44 for Ammunition

• Newport 11/6	BC 12/6 EBC9	Omaha 15/6
• Newport 9/7	BC 10/7 EBC37	Utah 12/7
• Penarth	BC 27/7 EBC54	Omaha 29/7
• Barry	BC 10/8 EBC68	US area 12/8
• Swansea 27/8	BC 27/8 EBC85	US area 29/8

Returned to Penarth 27/9

AVANVILLE 683/20 British (Monks) – taken up 10/4/44 for Ammunition
• London (Tilbury); 740 tons; left Thames 31/5; embarked 63 troops in Solent

	Solent 6/6 EWC1B	Sword 7/6
• Newhaven 16/6 | Solent 17/6 ETC11W | Sword 17/6 |

Keel and shell plating set up whilst beached at Sword 23/6: refloated 5/7; arrived Thames 13/7 and Humber 15/7 for repairs at Hull

• Southampton 15/8	Solent 15/8 EBC72W	US area 16/8
• Southampton 31/8	Solent 3/9 EBC89W	US area 3/9

Returned to Southampton 11/9

Bottom damage whilst beached at Normandy during the June gales resulted in *Avanville* being declared unfit for operations pending repairs. *[World Ship Society Ltd.]*

BAILEY FOSTER 1,791/43 British, ex-US (MoWT/*Currie) – taken up 4/44 for Stores

• Barry 3/6; stores and 69 troops	BC 6/6 EBC3	Omaha 9/6

Whilst at anchor off the beachhead in heavy weather, bumped the ground aft several times 17/6; sustained damage on bulwarks, side and poop from landing craft 18/6 and lost starboard anchor and 10 fathoms of cable in the 19/6 storm

• Cardiff 1/7	BC 2/7 EBC29	Utah 4/7
• Penarth 24/7	BC 25/7 EBC52	Utah 27/7
• Cardiff 10/8	BC 10/8 EBC68	

Called Falmouth to tow lighter for Cherbourg; left 12/8

	joined EBC70	Omaha 14/8
• Avonmouth 29/8	BC 29/8 EBC87	Omaha 31/8

Arrived Swansea 10/9 to load for Omaha

BALDUIN 1,164/21 Norwegian – taken up 12/6/44 for Stores

• Southampton 14/6	Solent 15/6 ETC9W	Gold 16/6
• Southampton 28/6	Solent 29/6 ETC21W	Gold 29/6

Returned to Solent 3/7 for release 22/8

BARONSCOURT 869/35 British (Kelly/*Clint) – taken up 1/5/44 for Stores
• London (Royal Albert) 2/6; 344 tons; left Thames 5/6

	Solent 8/6 ETC3W	Juno 9/6
• Southampton 17/6	Solent 18/6 EBC13W	Utah 18/6
• Southampton 28/6	Solent 29/6 EBC24W	Omaha 29/6
• Southampton 9/7	Solent 10/7 EBC35W	
Turned back due bad weather	Solent 11/7 EBC36W	Omaha 11/7
• Southampton 19/7	Solent 20/7 EBC45W	Omaha 20/7
• Plymouth 5/8	joined EBC63	Utah 7/8
• Plymouth 28/8	joined EBC85	St Vaast 29/8

Returned to Plymouth 6/9 to load coal for Granville

Baronscourt, pictured here at anchor in the Mersey, was one of the first coasters to load coal for Granville in September 1944. *[J. and M. Clarkson collection]*

BEAL 504/36 British (Tyne-Tees) – taken up 13/5/44 for Stores

• Southampton 9/6	Solent 9/6 ETC4W	
Convoy heavily attacked in English Channel by E-boats		Port-en-Bessin 10/6
• Southampton 15/6	Solent 16/6 ETC10W	Gold 16/6

Grounding indented and set up keel and adjoining strakes, port and starboard 17-18/6

• Southampton 27/6	Solent 29/6 ETC21W	Port-en-Bessin 29/6
• Southampton 7/7; tanks and heavy lifts		
	Solent 8/7 ETC30W	Port-en-Bessin 8/7
• Southampton 15/7	Solent 16/7 ETC38W	Port-en-Bessin 16/7

Two steel plates damaged in collision with landing craft 16/7; temporarily unfit for operations; left Southampton 24/7; arrived Tyne 29/7 for survey at Jarrow of June and July damage

BEECHFIELD 449/22 British (Zillah/*Savage) – taken up 4/44 for Stores
• London (Tilbury) 2/6; 380 tons ammunition; left Thames 5/6; embarked 39 troops in Solent

	Solent 7/6 ETC22W	Sword 8/6
• Southampton 16/6	Solent 17/6 ETC11W	Gold 17/6

US Army tug, dragging anchor in the storm, fouled vessel's port bow and lifeboat 2335 21/6

• Southampton 24/6	Solent 25/6 ETC17W	Gold 25/6
• Southampton 2/7	Solent 3/7 ETC25W	Gold 3/7
• Southampton 9/7	Solent 10/7 ETC32W	Gold 10/7
• Southampton 15/7	Solent 16/7 ETC38W	Gold 16/7
• Southampton 20/7	Solent 21/7 EBC46W	Utah 21/7

• Southampton 30/7	Solent 31/7 EBC56W	Utah 31/7	
• Southampton 6/8	Solent 7/8 EBC63W	US area 7/8	
• Southampton 15/8	Solent 15/8 EBC72W	US area 16/8	

On return to Solent, starboard bow struck by coaster, said to be, *Rockleaze* 2355 19/8 but not reported by that vessel

• Southampton 28/8	Solent 30/8 EBC86W	Isigny 30/8	

Returned to Southampton 9/9 to load for US area

After frequent Channel crossings carrying ammunition and stores, *Beechfield* was released from service in December 1944. [World Ship Society Ltd.]

BEESTON 466/21 British (ICI) – taken up 18/4/44 for Stores
• Avonmouth 17/5; called Portishead 19/5-1/6; left BC 2/6; embarked 21 troops in Solent

	Solent 7/6 EBC2W	Utah 8/6	
• Southampton 15/6	Solent 17/6 ETC11W	Gold 17/6	
• Southampton 29/6	Solent 30/6 ETC22W	Gold 30/6	
• Littlehampton 7/7; ammunition	joined ETC29	Sword 7/7	
• Littlehampton 12/7; ammunition	joined ETC35	Juno 13/7	
• Southampton 24/7	Solent 25/7 ETC47W	Gold 25/7	
• Southampton 30/7	Solent 31/7 ETC53W	Arromanches 31/7	
• Southampton 4/8	Solent 5/8 ETC58W	Arromanches 5/8	
• Southampton 9/8	Solent 10/8 ETC63W	Arromanches 10/8	
• Southampton 14/8	Solent 15/8 ETC68W	Arromanches 15/8	
• Southampton 19/8	Solent 20/8 ETC73W	Arromanches 20/8	
• Southampton 24/8	Solent 25/8 ETC78W	Arromanches 25/8	

Returned to Southampton 28/8 to load for British area

BELFORD 366/20 British (Piggins) – taken up 25/4/44 for Stores

• London 4/6; left Thames 5/6	Solent 7/6 ETC22W	Sword 8/6	

Stem damaged in collision with coaster *Dicky* 0830 9/6

• Southampton 14/6	Solent 16/6 ETC10W	Gold 16/6	
• Southampton 21/6	Solent 22/6 ETC15W	Gold 22/6	
• Southampton 28/6	Solent 29/6 ETC21W	Gold 29/6	
• Southampton 7/7	Solent 8/7 ETC30W	Gold 8/7	

Seventeen shell plates set up through pounding in rough weather 10/7; returned to Thames 15/7 on passage to Dundee for release 14/8

BELLATRIX 281/38 Dutch – taken up 5/8/44 for Stores

• Southampton 25/8	Solent 25/8 EBC81W	Isigny 25/8	

Assigned to French coastal ferry service in US area; returned to Southampton 14/10

BENGUELA 534/36 British (Metcalf) – taken up 9/5/44 for Ammunition
• London (Tilbury); 580 tons; left Thames 9/6

	Solent 12/6 ETC7W	Gold 13/6	
• London (London Dock) 19/6	Thames 20/6 ETC15		

Convoy sheltered in Solent; left 22/6

		Gold 22/6	

• Harwich 4/7; awaited orders for over four weeks; left Thames 2/8

	Solent 5/8 ETC58W	Juno 5/8	
• Southampton 23/8	Solent 24/8 ETC77W	Arromanches 24/8	
• Southampton 31/8	Solent 1/9 ETC85W	Arromanches 1/9	

Returned to London 11/9, then Hull 20/9 for release 20/10

BENJAMIN SHERBURN 1,814/43 British, ex-US (MoWT/*Glen & Co) – taken up 4/44 for Stores
• London (Royal Albert) 8/6; 1,148 tons

	Thames 9/6 ETC5	Juno 11/6	
• London 27/6	Thames 28/6 ETC21	Juno 29/6	
• London 13/7	Thames 14/7 ETC37	Sword 15/7	

In collision with a landing craft at beachhead 1000 18/7

• Swansea 29/7	BC 29/7 EBC56		

Diverted to Solent; at anchor for over four weeks

	Solent 28/8 EBC84W	Omaha 28/8	

Returned to Grimsby 10/9 to load for Dieppe

BERRYDEN 506/04 British (Taylor/*Gillie & Blair) – taken up 22/4/44 for Ammunition
• London (Tilbury Jetty) 4/6; 500 tons; left Thames 5/6

	Solent 7/6 ETC22W	Gold 8/6	
• Southampton 18/6; stores	Solent 19/6 ETC13W		

On passage, steam steering gear became inoperative 1100 19/6; vessel almost unmanageable in rough seas when relying on hand steering gear

		Juno 19/6	

Steering problems caused vessel to run aground in the storm 1900-2030 20/6; temporary repairs enabled cargo discharge to start 0900 22/6; returned to Southampton 27/6; unfit for further service; left Southampton 5/7; arrived Blyth 9/7, where survey on 13/7 revealed extensive pounding damage to shell and deck plating, frames, rudder and propeller; released 15/9

BIDASSOA 558/01 British, ex-French (MoWT/*Bristol) – taken up 4/44 for Ammunition
• Swansea 29/5; ammunition and stores; left BC 30/5; embarked 23 troops in Solent

	Solent 5/6 Force O3	Omaha 6/6 (D-Day)	

Bow damaged when struck by HM landing craft *LCT883* at beachhead 1135 11/6; steering gear broke down whilst returning to Fowey 0720 16/6

• Fowey 24/6	joined EBC20	Utah 25/6	
• Fowey 7/7	joined EBC33		

Called Dartmouth with bunker trouble; left Portland 9/7

	joined EBC35		

Heavy seas shipped fore and aft caused 2ft 6in flooding in firemen's quarters 10/7

		Utah 10/7	

• Fowey 22/7	joined EBC48	Utah 23/7
• Fowey 30/7	joined EBC57	Utah 1/8
• Fowey 19/8	joined EBC76	US area 20/8

Returned to Fowey 27/8 and Newport 2/9 to load for US area

BIRKER FORCE 953/19 British (West Coast/*Kennaugh) – taken up 14/5/44 for Stores
• London (Royal Albert); 572 tons Thames 8/6 ETC4
Convoy heavily attacked in English Channel by E-boats 10/6

		Juno 10/6
• Southampton 21/6	Solent 22/6 ETC15W	Gold 22/6

After return to Southampton, struck on starboard quarter by coaster *Larchfield* 1930 27/6

• Southampton 3/7	Solent 4/7 ETC26W	Sword 4/7
• Southampton 14/7	Solent 16/7 ETC38W	British area 16/7
• Southampton 25/7	Solent 26/7 ETC48W	Juno 26/7
• Southampton 3/8	Solent 4/8 ETC57W	Arromanches 4/8

• Southampton 11/8	Solent 12/8 ETC65W	Arromanches 12/8
• Southampton 21/8	Solent 22/8 ETC75W	Arromanches 22/8

Returned to Southampton 31/8 to load for British area

BLACKTOFT 1,109/10 British (Toft/*Donking) – taken up 1/5/44 for Stores
• London (Royal Albert) 2/6; 780 tons; left Thames 5/6

	Solent 8/6 ETC3W	British area 9/6
• London 21/6	Thames 24/6 ETC17	

When transitting Strait of Dover, shell plating pierced in 12 places in hull and upper superstructure and a lifeboat damaged by splinters from long-range gunfire 1445 24/6

		Gold 25/6
• Harwich 5/7	Thames 6/7 ETC29	Sword 7/7
• Harwich 19/7; ammunition	Thames 21/7 ETC44	Juno 22/7
• Newhaven 4/8; ammunition	joined ETC58	Arromanches 5/8
• London (Tilbury) 17/8	Thames 18/8 ETC72	Juno 19/8

Returned to London (Tilbury) 23/8 to load for Arromanches
(Vessel sunk by enemy action 20/2/45: see Section 4)

The importance of Southampton can be judged from the fact that *Birker Force* was one of 15 coasters to leave the port for Normandy on 11th August 1944.
[Fotoflite/J and M. Clarkson collection]

Blackwater used the ammunition loading port of Newhaven as her base from mid-June 1944 onwards. *[World Ship Society Ltd.]*

BLACKWATER 707/07 British (Kelly/*Clint) – taken up 20/4/44 for Ammunition
• London (Tilbury); 690 tons; left Thames 5/6

	Solent 7/6 ETC22W	Sword 8/6
• Newhaven 18/6	joined ETC13	Juno 19/6
• Newhaven 1/7	joined ETC24	Gold 2/7
• Newhaven 10/7	joined ETC33	Gold 11/7
• Newhaven 18/7	joined ETC41	Juno 19/7
• Newhaven 27/7	joined ETC50	Gold 28/7
• Newhaven 7/8	joined ETC60	Arromanches 7/8
• Newhaven 14/8	joined ETC67	Arromanches 14/8
• Newhaven 21/8	joined ETC75	Arromanches 22/8

Returned to Southampton 28/8

BONAWE 355/19 British (Gardner) – taken up 12/4/44 for Ammunition
• London (Tilbury Jetty) 2/6; 340 tons; left Thames 5/6; embarked 43 troops in Solent

	Solent 7/6 ETC22W	Gold 8/6
• Littlehampton 14/6	Solent 15/6 ETC9W	Gold 15/6
• Littlehampton 27/6	joined ETC19	Sword 27/6
• Littlehampton 4/7	joined ETC27	Juno 5/7
• Littlehampton 9/7	joined ETC32	Juno 10/7
• Littlehampton 16/7	joined ETC38	Juno 16/7
• Littlehampton 2/8	Solent 3/8 ETC56W	Juno 3/8
• Littlehampton 11/8	Solent 12/8 ETC65W	Juno 12/8
• Littlehampton 17/8	Solent 18/8 ETC71W	Juno 18/8
• Littlehampton 23/8	joined ETC76	

Convoy diverted to Solent; left 24/8 — Arromanches 24/8
| • Littlehampton 30/8 | Solent 31/8 ETC84W | Juno 31/8 |

Returned to Littlehampton 10/9 to load for Caen

BOSTON TRADER 371/36 British (Gt Yarmouth) – taken up 29/3/44 for Cased Petrol
• London (Purfleet); 312 tons; left Thames 7/6

	Solent 9/6 ETC4W	

Convoy heavily attacked in English Channel by E-boats: near missed by torpedo 10/6
| | | Sword 10/6 |

Subjected to field artillery fire at beachhead 10/6

• London	Thames 16/6 ETC11	Juno 17/6
• Southampton 25/6	Solent 26/6 ETC18W	Gold 26/6
• Southampton 1/7	Solent 2/7 ETC24W	Sword 2/7
• Southampton 7/7	Solent 8/7 ETC30W	Juno 8/7
• Southampton 12/7	Solent 13/7 ETC35W	Gold 13/7
• Littlehampton 20/7; ammunition	joined ETC43	Juno 21/7
• Southampton 26/7	Solent 27/7 ETC49W	Gold 27/7
• Southampton 1/8	Solent 2/8 ETC55W	Arromanches 2/8
• Southampton 6/8	Solent 7/8 ETC60W	Arromanches 7/8
• Southampton 11/8	Solent 12/8 ETC65W	Arromanches 12/8

Whilst approaching Isle of Wight on return, lost port lifeboat and sustained structural damage to port quarter and accommodation in collision with a landing craft 2245 14/8
| • Southampton 28/8 | Solent 29/8 ETC82W | Arromanches 29/8 |

Returned to Southampton 3/9 to load for Dieppe

Having completed a full programme of sailings to Normandy, *Boston Trader* was included in the first coaster convoy to enter the port of Dieppe. *[J. and M. Clarkson collection]*

BRACKENFIELD 657/37 British (Zillah/*Savage) – taken up 25/4/44 for Ammunition
• London (Tilbury); 660 tons; left Thames 7/6

	Solent 9/6 ETC4W	

Lost. At 0314 10/6, struck port side aft by E-boat torpedo from *S177* or *S178* when 50 miles S of Nab Tower, whilst on passage to Juno; aft end blown off; bows rose into the air, then vessel rolled over to port and rapidly sank; only two survivors from crew of 19

BRAMHILL 1,834/23 British (Hudson) – taken up 3/5/44 for Stores
Assigned to load vehicles at Swansea for early convoys to US area but, at short notice, not used

• Swansea 12/6	BC 13/6 EBC10	Omaha 16/6
• Swansea 2/7	BC 2/7 EBC29	Omaha 4/7
• Swansea 16/7	BC 16/7 EBC43	Utah 18/7
• Swansea 13/8	BC 13/8 EBC71	

Called Falmouth to tow lighter for Cherbourg, left 15/8
| | joined EBC72 | US area 16/8 |

Returned to Solent 29/8 in tow; arrived Southampton 6/9; subsequent survey at Blyth revealed damage to 14 shell plates; required lengthy repairs prior to release

BREM 428/39 **Dutch** – taken up 26/4/44 for Cased Petrol
• London (Purfleet); 384 tons; left Thames 8/6

	Solent 11/6 ETC6W	Juno 12/6
• Poole	Solent 18/6 ETC12W	Juno 18/6
• Poole 28/6	Solent 29/6 ETC21W	Gold 29/6
• Poole 4/7	Solent 5/7 ETC27W	British area 5/7
• Poole 15/7	Solent 16/7 ETC38W	Gold 16/7
• Poole 21/7	Solent 22/7 ETC44W	Gold 22/7
• Poole 27/7	Solent 28/7 ETC50W	Juno 28/7
• Poole 2/8	Solent 4/8 ETC57W	Port-en-Bessin 4/8
• Poole 8/8	Solent 9/8 ETC62W	Port-en-Bessin 9/8
• Poole 15/8	Solent 16/8 ETC69W	Port-en-Bessin 16/8
• Poole 24/8	Solent 25/8 ETC78W	Port-en-Bessin 25/8
• Poole 31/8	Solent 1/9 ETC85W	Port-en-Bessin 1/9

Returned to Poole 7/9 to load for Arromanches

During the first three months of the operation, the Dutch *Brem* made 12 outward crossings to Normandy carrying cased petrol, mainly from Poole. *[Captain J. F. van Puyvelde]*

BRIARFIELD 446/20 **British (Zillah/*Savage)** – taken up 18/4/44 for Stores
• Cardiff 7/6; left BC 8/6   Solent 12/6 EBC7W   Omaha 13/6
Whilst at anchor, considerable starboard side damage inflicted by US landing craft *LCT550* coming alongside to receive cargo 16/6; vessel further damaged by US *LCT644* 17/6

• Southampton 23/6	Solent 24/6 ETC16W	Gold 24/6
• Southampton 1/7	Solent 2/7 ETC24W	Gold 2/7
• Southampton 9/7	Solent 10/7 ETC32W	Gold 10/7
• Southampton 16/7	Solent 17/7 ETC39W	Gold 17/7
• Southampton 23/7	Solent 24/7 ETC46W	Port-en-Bessin 24/7
• Southampton 31/7	Solent 1/8 EBC57W	Utah 1/8
• Southampton 13/8	Solent 14/8 EBC70W	US area 14/8

Port hawse pipe and plates damaged by US barge under tow 16/8; returned to Southampton 22/8 to load for US area

BRITISH COAST 889/34 **British (Coast)** – on return from W Africa, assigned 22/7/44 for Cased Petrol
• Penarth 31/7   BC 1/8 EBC59

Convoy diverted to Solent; left 4/8   Omaha 4/8
• Portishead 18/8   BC 19/8 EBC77
Convoy sheltered in Solent; left 23/8   Utah 23/8
Returned to Penarth 5/9 to load for US area

BROCKLEY COMBE 662/38 **British (Ald)** – taken up 31/3/44 for Cased Petrol
• Port Talbot 2/6; cased petrol and 104 troops

	BC 5/6 EBC2Y	Omaha 8/6
• Llanelly 18/6	BC 20/6 EBC17	
Convoy sheltered in Poole Bay		Utah 24/6
• Llanelly 2/7	BC 3/7 EBC30	Omaha 5/7
• Llanelly 16/7	BC 17/7 EBC44	Isigny 19/7
• Southampton 28/7	Solent 29/7 EBC54W	Isigny 29/7

• Southampton 5/8; vessel's earlier departure than scheduled caused Chief Engineer to miss ship   Solent 6/8 EBC61W   St Vaast 6/8
On departure from St Vaast, US Navy pilot ignored Master's protests regarding insufficiency of room between sunken barge and bank; Master's concern proved justified when ship fouled barge and stuck fast 1700 12/8; floated off 1545 13/8; inflow of water through damage on starboard side stemmed by cement box; left 0630 14/8; arrived Southampton 16/8
• Southampton 21/8   Solent 23/8 EBC77W   Isigny 23/8
Returned to Southampton 30/8 to load for Omaha

BROOMFIELD 657/38 **British (Zillah/*Savage)** – taken up 30/4/44 for Ammunition
• London (Tilbury) 3/6; 643 tons; left Thames 5/6

	Solent 7/6 ETC22W	Juno 8/6
• Newhaven 17/6	joined ETC12	Gold 18/6
• Newhaven 1/7	joined ETC24	Gold 2/7
• Newhaven 9/7	joined ETC33	Gold 11/7
• Newhaven 19/7	joined ETC41	Juno 19/7
• Newhaven 29/7	joined ETC52	Arromanches 30/7
• Newhaven 10/8	joined ETC65	
Convoy diverted to Solent; left 13/8		Arromanches 13/8
• Newhaven 21/8	joined ETC75	Arromanches 22/8

Returned to Newhaven 27/8 to load for Arromanches

BROOMLANDS 518/20 **British (Chester)** – taken up 8/4/44 for Ammunition
• London (Tilbury) 26/5; 321 tons ammunition and stores; left Thames 31/5; embarked 59 troops in Solent   Solent 5/6 Force L1   Juno 6/6 (D-Day)
• Newhaven 17/6   joined ETC12   Gold 18/6
Sustained heavy weather damage whilst beached during the 19-22/6 storm; temporarily repaired, then refloated 3/7; returned to Newhaven 6/7: survey at Blyth 25/7 revealed 15 shell plates in need of replacement and frames requiring repair; released 27/9

BRYNHILD 2,195/07 **British, ex-Danish (MoWT/*Gibson)** – taken up 4/44 for Stores
• Grimsby; 784 tons engineers' stores; left London 10/6
      Thames 11/6 ETC7   Gold 13/6
In return convoy, vessel struck by a landing craft 0115 19/6; arrived Thames 19/6
• London 25/6   Thames 26/6 ETC19   Gold 27/6

• London 11/7   Thames 11/7 ETC34   Sword 12/7
• London 29/7, after completion of repairs
                Thames 30/7 ETC53   Arromanches 31/7
Going alongside at Arromanches, fractured shell plate on corner of pier 2145 31/7
• Grimsby 16/8   Thames 18/8 ETC72   Arromanches 19/8
Returned to London (Tilbury) 2/9, then left for Hull to load coal for Cherbourg

BUCKLAW 424/43 British (Gibson) – taken up 11/4/44 for Cased Petrol
• London (King George V) 17/5; 548 tons; left Thames 7/6
                Solent 9/6 ETC4W
Convoy heavily attacked in English Channel by E-boats 10/6   Gold 10/6
• London (Purfleet) 22/6   Thames 24/6 ETC17   Arromanches 25/6
• London 1/7   Thames 2/7 ETC25   Gold 3/7
• London 12/7   Thames 13/7 ETC36   Juno 14/7
• London 21/7   Thames 22/7 ETC45   Arromanches 23/7
• London 29/7   Thames 30/7 ETC53   Arromanches 31/7
• London 6/8   Thames 9/8 ETM58   Arromanches 10/8
• London 17/8   Thames 19/8 ETM63   Arromanches 20/8
• Southampton 28/8   Solent 29/8 EWL82B   Arromanches 29/8
Returned to London 7/9 to load for Dieppe

BUSIRIS 943/29 British (Moss Hutchison) – taken up 12/6/44 for Stores
• Southampton 15/6   Solent 17/6 ETC11W   Gold 17/6
Returned to Southampton with 4 tons of mail and 25 tons of empty gas cylinders
• Southampton 28/6   Solent 29/6 ETC21W   Gold 29/6
Returned to Southampton 5/7 and Tyne 11/7 for release 26/8

CAIRNGORM 394/38 British (Robertson) – taken up 22/4/44 for Cased Petrol
• Sharpness 25/5; called Port Talbot 26/5-1/6; left BC 2/6
                Solent 8/6 EBC3W   Utah 9/6
• Poole 19/6   Solent 20/6 ETC14W   Gold 20/6
Two crew members, ashore without permission, wounded by shell blast 26/6
• Poole 29/6   Solent 30/6 ETC22W   Port-en-Bessin 30/6
• Poole 4/7   Solent 4/7 ETC26W   British area 4/7
• Poole 11/7   Solent 12/7 ETC34W   Arromanches 12/7
• Poole 17/7   Solent 18/7 ETC40W   Port-en-Bessin 18/7
• Poole 24/7   Solent 25/7 ETC47W   Gold 25/7
• Poole 20/8   Solent 21/8 ETC74W   Port-en-Bessin 21/8
• Poole 26/8   Solent 27/8 ETC80W   Port-en-Bessin 27/8
Returned to Poole 31/8 to load for Port-en-Bessin

CALVIN COGGIN 1,791/43 British, ex-US (MoWT/*Lawson) – taken up 4/44
for Stores
• Cardiff 11/6   BC 12/6 EBC9   Omaha 15/6
• Swansea 1/7   BC 2/7 EBC29   Omaha 4/7
• Swansea 16/7   BC 17/7 EBC44   St Vaast 19/7
One crew member injured in air raid on St Vaast 24/7
• Swansea 9/8   BC 10/8 EBC68
Called Falmouth to tow barge for Cherbourg; left 12/8
                joined EBC69   Omaha 13/8
• Belfast 26/8, after delay due to engine trouble
                sd BC 30/8 EBC88   Omaha 1/9
Returned to Swansea 8/9 to load for Omaha and Cherbourg

CAMEO 946/37 British (Robertson) – taken up 22/4/44 for Cased Petrol
• Sharpness 27/5; cased petrol and stores; called Avonmouth 27/5-30/5; left BC 30/5;
embarked 124 troops in Solent   Solent 5/6 Force O3
                then U3   Utah 6/6 (D-Day)
• Portishead 20/6   BC 23/6 EBC20   Omaha 25/6
• Southampton 9/7   Solent 10/7 EBC35W
Turned back owing to bad weather Solent 11/7 EBC36W   Omaha 11/7
• Southampton 24/7   Solent 25/7 EBC50W   St Vaast 25/7
Underwent repairs at Southampton after 3/8 return
• Southampton 26/8   Solent 27/8 ETC80W   Arromanches 27/8
Returned to Southampton 1/9 to load for Dieppe

CAPITO 968/18 British (Bristol) – taken up 15/4/44 for Ammunition
• Portishead 7/6; left BC 8/6   Solent 12/6 EBC7W   Utah 13/6
Struck unmarked sunken object whilst proceeding to anchorage 0900 15/6; in the
storm, starboard anchor cable parted 0230 20/6, followed by port anchor 0640
20/6, so spare anchor rigged
• Swansea 2/7   BC 2/7 EBC29   US area 4/7
• Cardiff 3/8; engineers repaired boiler tubes at sea 5/8
                BC 6/8 EBC64   Utah 8/8
• Southampton 16/8   Solent 16/8 EBC73W   Cherbourg 17/8
Returned to Southampton 7/9

CARNALEA 619/13 British (Barkley/*Clint) – taken up 29/4/44 for Ammunition
• London (Tilbury) 7/6; 550 tons; left Thames 8/6
                Solent 11/6 ETC6W   Gold 12/6
• Southampton 22/6   Solent 23/6 EBC16W   Utah 23/6
• Plymouth 7/7   joined EBC33   Utah 8/7
• Southampton 16/7   Solent 17/7 EBC42W   Omaha 17/7
• Southampton 24/7   Solent 25/7 EBC50W   Utah 25/7
• Southampton 5/8   Solent 6/8 EBC61W   US area 6/8
• Southampton 25/8   Solent 26/8 EBC82W   US area 26/8
Returned to Southampton 3/9 to load for US area

Carrick Coast began unloading at Sword beachhead at 1045 on 9th July 1944: all cased petrol having been discharged, she left again at 1510 that day. *[J. and M. Clarkson collection]*

CARRICK COAST 369/34 British (Coast) – taken up 1/4/44 for Cased Petrol
- Garston 29/5; called Swansea 31/5-2/6; left BC 5/6

	Solent 9/6 EBC4W	Omaha 10/6
• Southampton 19/6	Solent 20/6 ETC14W	Gold 20/6
• Southampton 30/6	Solent 1/7 ETC23W	Gold 1/7
• Southampton 7/7	Solent 8/7 ETC30W	Sword 8/7

Completed discharge in under 5 hours
• Southampton 27/7	Solent 28/7 ETC50W	Juno 28/7
• Plymouth 5/8	joined EBC63	Utah 7/8
• Plymouth 16/8	joined EBC73	
Detached to Solent	Solent 19/8 EBC75W	US area 19/8
• Plymouth 31/8	joined EBC88	
Put into Solent	Solent 3/9 EBC89W	US area 3/9

Returned to Plymouth 10/9 to load for Cherbourg

CASSARD 1,602/20 British, ex-French (MoWT/*Harries) – taken up 5/44 for Stores
Assigned to load vehicles at Swansea for early convoys to US area but, at short notice, not used
• Southampton 25/6; 2,000 tons	Solent 26/6 EBC21W	Omaha 26/6
• Swansea 11/7	BC 12/7 EBC39	Omaha 14/7
• Swansea 28/7	BC 29/7 EBC56	

Diverted to Solent; at anchor for over four weeks; whilst there, in collision with unidentified vessel 0600 23/8 Solent 28/8 EBC84W Omaha 28/8
Returned to Newport 10/9 to load coal for Cherbourg

CASTLE COMBE 454/36 British (Ald) – taken up 6/5/44 for Cased Petrol
• Sharpness 7/6; left BC 7/6	Solent 11/6 EBC6W	Utah 12/6
• Port Talbot 23/6; 1,350 tons	BC 24/6 EBC21	Utah 26/6
• Llanelly 7/7	BC 8/7 EBC35	St Vaast 10/7
• Llanelly 2/8	BC 2/8 EBC60	
Convoy diverted to Solent; left 5/8		Isigny 5/8
• Poole 17/8	Solent 18/8 EBC74W	Isigny 18/8
• Poole 27/8	Solent 28/8 EBC84W	Cherbourg 28/8

Returned to Poole 3/9 to load for Barfleur

CEDARWOOD 899/33 British (Constantine) – taken up 27/4/44 for Ammunition
• Portishead 1/6; left BC 2/6	Solent 8/6 EBC3W	Utah 9/6
• Swansea 23/6	BC 23/6 EBC20	Utah 25/6
• Newport 6/7	BC 7/7 EBC34	Utah 9/7
• Avonmouth 27/7	BC 28/7 EBC55	Utah 30/7
• Harwich 18/8	Thames 19/8 ETC73	Arromanches 20/8

Returned to Harwich 26/8 to load for Dieppe

CHANNEL FISHER 700/21 British (Woodtown/*Comben Longstaff) – taken up 11/6/44 for Stores
• London 26/6	Thames 27/6 ETC20	

Turned back 27/6, unable maintain convoy speed
	Thames 29/6 ETC22	Gold 30/6
• London (Tilbury) 12/7	Thames 12/7 ETC35	Sword 13/7
• Southampton 23/7	Solent 23/7 ETC45W	Port-en-Bessin 23/7
• Southampton 30/7	Solent 31/7 EBC56W	Utah 31/7

After serving Normandy and Dieppe, *Cedarwood* sank at the Ostend quayside on 1st October 1944 as a result of a mine explosion. *[J. and M. Clarkson collection]*

Stem bar and five shell plates damaged in collision with US Liberty ship *William C Endicott*, whilst at anchor off beachhead 7/8
• Southampton 17/8	Solent 18/8 EBC74W	US area 18/8

Returned to Solent 24/8; left 29/8 for collision damage survey at Greenock; subsequently underwent bow repairs, which unsuccessful until new forecastle deck fitted

CHANNEL QUEEN 567/40 British (British Channel Islands) – taken up 6/5/44 for Cased Petrol
• London (Purfleet); 480 tons; left Thames 7/6		
	Solent 10/6 ETC5W	Juno 11/6
• London 18/6	Thames 20/6 ETC15	
Convoy sheltered in Solent; left 22/6		Juno 22/6
• London	Thames 4/7 ETC27	Gold 5/7
• London 12/7	Thames 13/7 ETC36	Sword 14/7
• London 23/7	Thames 24/7 ETC47	Arromanches 25/7
• Plymouth 2/8	joined EBC59	
Sheltered in Solent	Solent 6/8 EBC61W	Utah 6/8
• Plymouth 30/8	joined EBC87	US area 31/8

Returned to Plymouth 8/9 to load for US area

CHARLES H SALTER 1,814/42 British, ex-US (MoWT/*Stephenson Clarke) – taken up 4/44 for Ammunition
• London (Tilbury Jetty) 8/6; 2,555 tons		
	Thames 8/6 ETC4	
Convoy heavily attacked in English Channel by E-boats 10/6		Gold 10/6
• London (Royal Albert) 21/6	Thames 24/6 ETC17	Gold 25/6
• Grimsby 10/7; stores	Thames 12/7 ETC35	Arromanches 13/7
• Grimsby 24/7; stores	Thames 26/7 ETC49	Arromanches 27/7
• Grimsby 5/8; stores	Thames 7/8 ETC61	Arromanches 8/8

Returned to London (Tilbury) 13/8; left 17/8 for Sunderland, then loaded at Grimsby for Arromanches

CHARLES TREADWELL 1,814/43 British, ex-US (MoWT/*Constantine) – taken up 4/44 for Stores
• Penarth 29/6	BC 30/6 EBC27	Utah 2/7

• Newport 20/7	BC 21/7 EBC48	Utah 23/7
• Avonmouth 4/8	BC 5/8 EBC63	

Called Falmouth to tow lighter for Cherbourg; left 7/8

	joined EBC64	Cherbourg 8/8
• Swansea 23/8	BC 23/8 EBC81	US area 25/8

Returned to Swansea 15/9

CHELWOOD 2,742/28 British (France, Fenwick) – taken up 6/5/44 for Stores
• London (Royal Albert) 4/6; 48 vehicles and 140 troops

	Thames 5/6 ETC2Y	Gold 7/6
• London (Tilbury) 16/6	Thames 17/6 ETC12	Sword 18/6

Grounded on Calvados Reef, off Normandy coast, during the storm 20/6; refloated 21/6 and berthed Arromanches 22/6; required major repairs to Nos 3 and 4 holds on return to Thames 1/7; sustained shell plate damage by striking Tilbury quay 11/7; subsequent survey at Sunderland revealed 80 shell plates set up or indented; released 22/8

Damage by grounding, when the June 1944 storm struck the Normandy coast, prevented *Chelwood* from playing any further part in the cross-Channel build-up. [*National Maritime Museum, P21819*]

CHORZOW 845/21 Polish – taken up 28/4/44 for Ammunition
• Penarth 2/6; left BC 2/6; embarked 44 troops in Solent

	Solent 7/6 EBC2W	Utah 8/6

Grounded two miles W of Arromanches in the storm 20/6 but refloated

• Southampton 26/6	Solent 27/6 ETC19W	Gold 27/6
• Southampton 9/7	Solent 10/7 ETC32W	Juno 10/7
• Southampton 22/7	Solent 23/7 ETC45W	Juno 23/7
• Southampton 1/8	Solent 2/8 EBC58W	US area 2/8

Returned to Southampton 14/8 for release

CIRCE II 2,031/26 British, ex-French (MoWT/*Brown, Atkinson) – taken up 22/5/44 for Stores

• Swansea 3/6; vehicles and troops BC 5/6 EBC2Z		Utah 8/6
• Cardiff 29/6	BC 30/6 EBC27	Omaha 2/7
• Newport 19/7	BC 20/7 EBC47	Utah 22/7
• Newport 3/8	BC 4/8 EBC61	

Convoy diverted to Solent; left 6/8

		US area 6/8

Returned to Cardiff 27/8 to load coal for Cherbourg

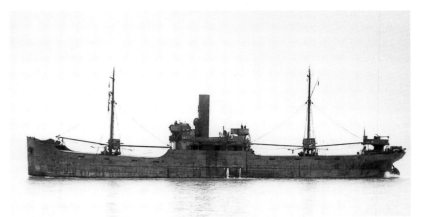

The French *Circe II* was transferred to Hull registry for war service and initially formed part of the US vehicle-carrying fleet sailing to Utah beachhead. [*National Maritime Museum, P21847*]

CITRINE 783/39 British (Robertson) – taken up 19/4/44 for Cased Petrol
• Sharpness 26/5; called Avonmouth 26/5-3/6

	BC 5/6 EBC2Y	US area 8/6

Damage by landing craft bumping alongside resulted in 47 shell plates being set in 8/6
• Sharpness 16/6

• Sharpness 16/6	BC 17/6 EBC14	Utah 19/6

Rudder and propeller struck submerged object, rock or wreck during the storm 0500 20/6; beaching revealed hull to be holed, rudder stock bent and stern frame fractured in two places 22/6; rudder stock straightened from 45° by bulldozer and vessel refloated; in return convoy, sustained damage to starboard bow in collision with unknown vessel 26/6; withdrawn for substantial repairs; arrived Tyne 9/7; surveyed at South Shields 17/7

CITY OF CHARLEROY 869/33 British (Brussels) – taken up 30/4/44 for Ammunition
• London (Tilbury) 7/6; 1,040 tons; left Thames 8/6

	Solent 11/6 ETC6W	Juno 12/6

On beaching, heavily struck then passed over a half-submerged Army tank, heeling to port in so doing; vessel holed in several places; arrived London 17/6 for repairs

• London (Tilbury) 12/7	Thames 13/7 ETC36	Juno 14/7
• London (Tilbury) 22/7	Thames 23/7 ETC46	Juno 24/7
• London 1/8	Thames 1/8 ETC55	Arromanches 2/8
• London (Tilbury) 13/8	Thames 14/8 ETC68	Juno 15/8

Returned to London 21/8 to load for Dieppe

CITY OF MALINES 373/05 British (Gt Yarmouth) – taken up 11/6/44 for Ammunition
• London 24/6

• London 24/6	Thames 28/6 ETC21	

Sustained damage in collision with HM tank landing ship *LST451*; called Dover for repairs to leaking stern 28-29/6 joined ETC22 Sword 30/6

• London (Purfleet) 5/7	Thames 7/7 ETC30	Gold 8/7
• Newhaven 15/7	joined ETC37	Sword 15/7
• Littlehampton 22/7	joined ETC45	Juno 23/7
• Littlehampton 28/7	joined ETC52	Juno 30/7
• Littlehampton 3/8		

Departure delayed awaiting replacement for Chief Engineer, who incoherent and seemingly intoxicated   joined ETC57   Juno 4/8
• Littlehampton 10/8   joined ETC65
Convoy diverted to Solent; left 13/8   Juno 13/8
• Littlehampton 16/8   joined ETC70   Juno 17/8
• Littlehampton 28/8   Solent 29/8 ETC82W   Juno 29/8
Returned to Littlehampton 3/9 to load for Caen

CLARA MONKS 577/20 British (Monks) – taken up 21/4/44 for Ammunition
• London (Tilbury) 20/5; 550 tons; left Thames 7/6

	Solent 10/6 ETC5W	Sword 11/6
• London (Tilbury) 20/6	Thames 23/6 ETC16	Juno 24/6
• Littlehampton 1/7	joined ETC23	Juno 1/7
• Newhaven 8/7	joined ETC30	Gold 8/7
• Newhaven 13/7	joined ETC36	Juno 14/7
• Newhaven 20/7	joined ETC43	Juno 21/7
• Newhaven 30/7	joined ETC53	Arromanches 31/7
• Southampton 7/8	Solent 8/8 EBC64W	US area 8/8
• Southampton 23/8	Solent 24/8 EBC78W	US area 24/8

Returned to Southampton 3/9 to load for US area

CLAUDIUS MAGNIN 2,310/21 British, ex-French (MoWT/*Stockwood, Rees) – taken up 4/44 for Stores
• Swansea 2/6; vehicles and troops BC 5/6 EBC2Z   Utah 8/6
• Barry 18/6   BC 19/6 EBC16
Convoy sheltered in Poole Bay   Utah 23/6
• Newport 12/7   BC 13/7 EBC40   Omaha 15/7
• Barry 26/7   BC 27/7 EBC54
Diverted to Solent; at anchor for nearly five weeks
     Solent 29/8 EBC85W   US area 29/8
Ordered firstly to Cherbourg 4/9, back to Utah 5/9, then finally to Omaha 12/9 for food supplies for crew and for cargo discharge; returned to London 22/9

CLEMENT T JAYNE 1,793/43 British, ex-US (MoWT/*Heyn) – taken up 4/44 for Stores
• Avonmouth 6/6
On departure, severely dented starboard side of shell plating by striking lock wall 0836 6/6   BC 7/6 EBC4   Utah 10/6
Touching bottom, whilst shifting anchorage, caused heavy list to starboard 1012 10/6; bumped heavily on bottom 0530 18/6, then hit repeatedly on starboard side by HM landing barge *LBE30*, which not under command during storm
• Swansea 1/7   BC 1/7 EBC28   Omaha 3/7
• Barry 22/7   BC 23/7 EBC50   St Vaast 25/7
On being called forward to enter St Vaast inner harbour, again bumped bottom heavily 0955 3/8; fouled propeller and sustained damage to starboard quarter, whilst being manoeuvred by tug *TID65* 2238 4/8
• Avonmouth 17/8   BC 18/8 EBC76   US area 20/8
Returned to Cardiff 29/8 to load for US area

CLERMISTON 1,498/21 British (London & Edinburgh) – taken up 12/5/44 for Ammunition
• Penarth 14/6   BC 15/6 EBC12   Omaha 17/6

Bilge keel buckled and plates holed and set up, whilst beached during the storm 19-20/6
• Portishead 8/7   BC 9/7 EBC36
Put into Falmouth; left 11/7   joined EBC37   Omaha 12/7
• Cardiff 30/7   BC 30/7 EBC57   Cherbourg 1/8
Returned for June damage survey at Leith 22-29/8, then arrived Hull 1/9 to load for Arromanches

The ammunition carrier *Clermiston* could not be spared until August for a survey of June 1944 grounding damage and not until January 1945 for repair work to be started. *[National Maritime Museum]*

COEN 290/35 Dutch – taken up 8/44 for Stores
• Southampton 24/8   Solent 25/8 EBC81W   Isigny 25/8
Assigned to French coastal ferry service in US area

CORAL 638/19 British (Robertson) – taken up 23/4/44 for Ammunition

• Penarth; left BC 2/6	Solent 8/6 EBC3W	Utah 9/6
• Southampton 21/6	Solent 22/6 ETC15W	Sword 22/6
• Southampton 27/6	Solent 28/6 ETC20W	Gold 28/6
• Southampton 7/7	Solent 8/7 ETC30W	Sword 8/7
• Southampton 17/7	Solent 18/7 ETC40W	Gold 18/7
• Southampton 28/7	Solent 29/7 ETC51W	Juno 29/7
• Southampton 5/8	Solent 6/8 ETC59W	Port-en-Bessin 6/8
• Southampton 10/8	Solent 11/8 ETC64W	Arromanches 11/8
• Southampton 16/8	Solent 17/8 ETC70W	Arromanches 17/8

Lost. Left Arromanches for Southampton 0830 20/8; at 1715 20/8 hit on the port side abreast No 1 hold by torpedo from *U-764*; vessel listed to port before rapidly settling by the head; six men killed, 11 survived, two with serious injuries

CORAL QUEEN 303/41 British (British Channel Traders) – taken up 29/3/44 for Cased Petrol
• Port Talbot 2/6; cased petrol and 44 troops
     BC 5/6 EBC2Y   US area 8/6
• Southampton 14/6   Solent 15/6 ETC9W   Mulberry B 15/6
• Southampton 23/6   Solent 24/6 ETC16W   Port-en-Bessin 24/6
At anchor, awaiting return convoy, HM landing craft *LCT855* towing *LCT807* struck ship's port bow causing dents, holes and a buckled frame 1855 26/6
• Southampton 4/7   Solent 5/7 ETC27W   Port-en-Bessin 5/7

• Southampton 10/7	Solent 11/7 ETC33W	Port-en-Bessin 11/7
• Southampton 17/7	Solent 18/7 ETC40W	Gold 18/7
• Southampton 29/7	Solent 30/7 ETC52W	Gold 30/7
• Southampton 4/8	Solent 5/8 ETC58W	Arromanches 5/8
• Southampton 15/8	Solent 16/8 ETC69W	Arromanches 16/8

Returned to Southampton 21/8

CORBRIDGE 1,703/28 British (Cory) – taken up 9/4/44 for Stores
• London 10/6	Thames 11/6 ETC7	Gold 13/6
• London 26/6	Thames 28/6 ETC21	Gold 29/6
• London 12/7	Thames 13/7 ETC36	Gold 14/7
• Harwich 3/8; ammunition	Thames 4/8 ETC58	Juno 5/8
• London 24/8	Thames 25/8 ETC79	Arromanches 26/8

Returned to London 2/9

CORDALE 2,143/25 British (Cory) – taken up 25/4/44 for Ammunition
• London (Tilbury) 9/6; 3,250 tons	Thames 10/6 ETC6	Gold 12/6
• London 6/7	Thames 7/7 ETC30	Gold 8/7
• London (Millwall) 22/7	Thames 23/7 ETC46	Arromanches 24/7
• London 6/8	Thames 7/8 ETC61	Arromanches 8/8

Sustained indented plates in collision with ocean-going cargo ship *Fort Steele* at Arromanches 8/8
• London 19/8	Thames 20/8 ETC74	Arromanches 21/8

Returned to London 29/8

CORGLEN 2,822/29 British (Cory) – taken up 4/5/44 for Stores
• London (King George V) 3/6; 35 vehicles, 140 troops		
	Thames 5/6 ETC2Z	British area 7/6
• London 19/6	Thames 20/6 ETC15	
Convoy sheltered in Solent; left 22/6		Sword 22/6

Subjected to field artillery fire 26/6; sustained damage to shell plates when grounded 26-28/6
• Grimsby 17/7	Thames 20/7 ETC43	Gold 21/7

Returned to London 27/7; arrived Tyne 4/8 for drydocking at Jarrow for June damage survey and release 12/9

CORSEA 2,764/21 British (Cory) – taken up 8/5/44 for Stores
• London (Royal Albert) 4/6; 56 vehicles and 140 troops		
	Thames 5/6 ETC2Y	British area 7/6
• London 17/6	Thames 18/6 ETC13	Gold 19/6
• Grimsby 12/7	Thames 15/7 ETC38	Arromanches 16/7
• London (Millwall) 8/8; cased petrol	Thames 9/8 ETC63	Arromanches 10/8

Returned to London 16/8, subsequently to load on Humber for Cherbourg

CORUNDUM 929/25 British (Robertson) – taken up 19/4/44 for Ammunition
• London (Tilbury) 15/5; 1,000 tons; left Thames 5/6; embarked 78 troops in Solent		
	Solent 7/6 ETC22W	Juno 8/6
• Southampton 22/6	Solent 23/6 EBC16W	Omaha 23/6
• Fowey 6/7	joined EBC32	Utah 7/7
• Fowey 18/7	joined EBC44	US area 19/7
• Southampton 31/7	Solent 1/8 EBC57W	Utah 1/8
• Southampton 23/8	Solent 24/8 EBC78W	Barfleur 24/8

With a gross tonnage of 2,822, the stores ship *Corglen* was one of the largest coasters in the Normandy invasion fleet: her return to London in late July 1944 concluded her service. *[National Maritime Museum, P21907]*

Corsea loaded a variety of cargoes for France: originally taken up for stores, she carried vehicles and troops from London on her first sailing in June 1944, cased petrol on her fourth and coal from the Humber thereafter. *[National Maritime Museum, P21882]*

Whilst discharging at Barfleur, starboard quarter struck by coaster *Munin* 1120 3/9; on return to Solent, stem and plating severely damaged by a landing craft 2355 6/9; returned to Southampton 10/9 to load for US area

COXWOLD 1,124/38 British (Yorkshire Dale/*Atkinson & Prickett) – taken up 16/5/44 for Cased Petrol
• Penarth 8/6	BC 8/6 EBC5	Omaha 11/6

Grounded at anchorage on two successive low tides 11/6; sustained hull indentations from craft alongside for cargo discharge in NW swell 14-15/6
• Sharpness 24/6; 1,118 tons	BC 25/6 EBC22	

Sustained damage when vessel's port anchor fouled by another ship in same convoy, as two columns merged into one during Channel crossing 1759 26/6 (other ship's name recorded as *Torkell* but no such vessel traced)   Utah 27/6
Rough seas whilst discharging resulted in vessel grounding, with hull indentations caused by landing craft bumping heavily alongside 27-29/6
• Sharpness 15/7	BC 16/7 EBC43	Omaha 18/7
• Llanelly 2/8	BC 2/8 EBC60	

Convoy diverted to Solent; left 5/8   Barfleur 5/8

Whilst at anchor off Barfleur, vessel subjected to blast vibrations from 21 mines being exploded by sweepers 9-10/8
• Southampton 27/8   Solent 28/8 EBC84W   Barfleur 28/8
Returned to Southampton 11/9 for stem and hawse pipe replacement

CRAGSIDE 496/35 British (Tyne-Tees) – taken up 9/4/44 for Stores
• London (King George V) 6/6; 275 tons
                              Thames 7/6 ETC22   Gold 8/6
At beachhead, sustained shell plating, hawse pipe and stem post damage when struck by barge, which also dragged heavily across starboard anchor cable 0230 14/6
• Plymouth 26/6; cased petrol   joined EBC22   Omaha 27/6
Stokehold found to be making water after vessel struck submerged object 2000 27/6; beached for temporary repairs until 1/7; returned to Plymouth 4/7 for drydocking
• Plymouth 14/7   joined EBC40   Utah 15/7
• Plymouth 26/7   joined EBC52   Barfleur 27/7
Ship's balloon cable brought down an enemy aircraft at Barfleur; returned to Solent 3/8 requiring repairs; left 1/9 for Hull in tow of tug *Assiduous*

CRESCENDO 348/38 Dutch – taken up 18/5/44 for Cased Petrol
• Port Talbot 2/6; left BC 6/6   Solent 10/6 EBC5W   Omaha 11/6
• Southampton 18/6   Solent 19/6 ETC13W   Gold 19/6
• Southampton 5/7   Solent 6/7 ETC28W   Sword 6/7
• Southampton 12/7   Solent 13/7 ETC35W   Port-en-Bessin 13/7
• Southampton 18/7   Solent 19/7 ETC41W   Gold 19/7
• Littlehampton 26/7; ammunition   joined ETC48   Gold 26/7
• Southampton 30/7   Solent 31/7 ETC53W   Arromanches 31/7
• Southampton 5/8   Solent 6/8 ETC59W   Arromanches 6/8
• Southampton 10/8   Solent 11/8 ETC64W   Arromanches 11/8
• Southampton 15/8   Solent 16/8 ETC69W   Arromanches 16/8
• Southampton 20/8   Solent 21/8 ETC74W   Port-en-Bessin 21/8
• Southampton 26/8   Solent 27/8 ETC80W   Port-en-Bessin 27/8
Returned to Southampton 30/8 to load for Port-en-Bessin

CRESCO 1,270/16 Norwegian – taken up 28/4/44 for Ammunition
• London (Tilbury) 6/6; 1,720 tons; left Thames 7/6
                              Solent 9/6 ETC4W
Convoy heavily attacked in English Channel by E-boats 10/6 Sword 10/6
• London 27/6   Thames 28/6 ETC21   Gold 29/6
• London 8/7   Thames 9/7 ETC32   Gold 10/7
• London (Tilbury) 22/7   Thames 23/7 ETC46   Juno 24/7
• London   Thames 4/8 ETC58   Arromanches 5/8
• London 19/8   Thames 20/8 ETC74   Arromanches 21/8
Returned to London 25/8, then assigned to load vegetables on Humber

CREWHILL 695/23 British (Kelly/*Clint) – taken up 10/4/44 for Stores
• Barry; left BC 30/5; embarked 44 troops in Solent
                              Solent 6/6 EWC1A   Omaha 7/6
• Southampton 28/6   Solent 29/6 EBC24W   Omaha 29/6
• Southampton 7/7   Solent 8/7 EBC33W   Omaha 8/7
• Southampton   Solent 14/7 ETC36W   Arromanches 14/7

• Southampton 20/7   Solent 22/7 ETC44W   Juno 22/7
• Newhaven 2/8; ammunition   Solent 3/8 ETC56W   Arromanches 3/8
• Newhaven 10/8; ammunition   joined ETC65
Convoy diverted to Solent; left 13/8   Arromanches 13/8
Returned to Southampton 16/8 for repairs
• Southampton 29/8   Solent 30/8 ETC83W   Arromanches 30/8
Returned to Solent 3/9 for onward routing to Newhaven

CUSHENDUN 646/04 British (Brook/*Comben Longstaff) – taken up 28/4/44 for Ammunition
• Penarth; called Portishead, left 30/5; left BC 30/5; embarked 65 troops in Solent
                              Solent 6/6 EWC1A   Utah 7/6
• Southampton 14/6   Solent 15/6 ETC9W   Mulberry B 15/6
Shell plates slightly damaged in collision with destroyer, probably HMS *Jervis*, 18/6
• Southampton 30/6   Solent 1/7 ETC23W   Gold 1/7
• Southampton 9/7   Solent 10/7 ETC32W   Sword 10/7
• Southampton 17/7   Solent 18/7 ETC40W   Gold 18/7
• Southampton 4/8; turned back; left 5/8
                              Solent 6/8 ETC59W   Arromanches 6/8
• Southampton 11/8   Solent 12/8 ETC65W   Port-en-Bessin 12/8
• Southampton 18/8   Solent 19/8 ETC72W   Arromanches 19/8
Returned to Solent 24/8 for survey of June collision damage at South Shields and release 17/9

CYRUS SEARS 1,814/43 British, ex-US (MoWT/*Stephenson Clarke) – taken up 4/44 for Stores
• Grimsby 23/5; 1,134 tons;   called London 26/5-7/6
                              Thames 8/6 ETC4
Convoy heavily attacked in English Channel by E-boats 10/6 Gold 10/6
• London (Tilbury) 25/6   Thames 25/6 ETC18   Arromanches 26/6
• London (Tilbury) 8/7   Thames 9/7 ETC32   Juno 10/7
• Grimsby 26/7   Thames 29/7 ETC52   Arromanches 30/7
• Grimsby 9/8   Thames 12/8 ETC66   Arromanches 13/8
Returned 22/8, subsequently to load at Grimsby for Arromanches

The Norwegian *Cresco* photographed in the Mersey: she survived when her first outward convoy in June 1944 suffered three coaster losses in an attack by E-boats. *[B. and A. Feilden/J. and M. Clarkson collection]*

DA COSTA 243/37 Dutch – taken up 7/44 for Stores
• Southampton 25/7   Solent 26/7 ETC48W   Port-en-Bessin 26/7
Assigned to French coastal ferry service; returned to Plymouth 11/9 to load for St Brieuc

DAGENHAM 2,178/19 British (Hudson) – taken up 9/4/44 for Stores
• London (Tilbury) 11/6   Thames 12/6 ETC8   Sword 14/6
Boat, funnel and ventilator damaged during air attack at beachhead 17/6
• London 26/6   Thames 27/6 ETC20   Sword 28/6
• London 11/7   Thames 11/7 ETC34   Juno 12/7
• London 26/7   Thames 27/7 ETC50   Gold 28/7
• London 29/8; left Thames 30/8   Solent 3/9 EBC89W   Cherbourg 3/9
Returned to Grimsby 17/9 to load for Dieppe

The stores coaster *Dagenham* sustained superficial damage at Sword on 17th June 1944 in one of the night-time raids on the beachheads by German aircraft. *[National Maritime Museum, P22135]*

DALEWOOD 2,774/31 British (France, Fenwick) – taken up 6/5/44 for Stores
• Swansea 2/6; vehicles and troops; in Swansea Bay anchorage, coaster *Empire Sedge* dragged anchor and struck *Dalewood*'s stern 1448 4/6
     BC 5/6 EBC2Z   Utah 8/6
Shaken by bombs exploding close to ship's port quarter 0055 9/6
• Barry 24/6; 1,973 tons   BC 25/6 EBC22   Omaha 27/6
• Newport 27/7   BC 28/7 EBC55   Omaha 30/7
• Barry 20/8; stores and US mail   BC 23/8 EBC81   US area 25/8
Returned to Solent, then arrived Hull 24/9

DAWLISH 248/37 British (Ridley) – taken up 3/44 for Cased Petrol
• Introduction into service delayed for repairs after sustaining starboard quarter damage, when hit by coaster *Topaz* at Southampton 1200 13/6; further delayed by auxiliary engine trouble 18/7
Southampton 19/7   Solent 20/7 ETC42W   Arromanches 20/7
• Littlehampton 26/7; ammunition   joined ETC49   Arromanches 27/7
• Littlehampton 30/7; ammunition   joined ETC53   Juno 31/7
• Littlehampton 4/8; ammunition   joined ETC58   Juno 5/8
• Littlehampton 10/8; ammunition   joined ETC64   Juno 11/8
• Littlehampton 16/8; ammunition   joined ETC69   Juno 16/8
• Littlehampton 21/8; ammunition   joined ETC75   Arromanches 22/8
Returned to Littlehampton 3/9 to load for Caen

DEEMOUNT 569/33 British (Border) – taken up 7/4/44 for Stores
• London (Royal Albert) 4/6; 297 tons Thames 7/6 ETC22   Sword 8/6
• Plymouth 17/6; cased petrol   joined EBC13   Omaha 18/6
• Plymouth 28/6; cased petrol   joined EBC24   Utah 29/6
• Plymouth 7/7   joined EBC33   Omaha 8/7
• Plymouth 14/7   joined EBC41   Utah 16/7
• Plymouth 23/7; with barge in tow joined EBC49   Cherbourg 24/7
• Southampton 10/8   Solent 12/8 EBC68W   US area 12/8
• Southampton 20/8   Solent 23/8 EBC77W   Utah 23/8
Returned to Southampton 27/8 to load for US area

DENBIGH COAST 484/37 British (Coast) – taken up 22/4/44 for Cased Petrol
• Port Talbot 7/6; left BC 8/6   Solent 12/6 EBC7W   Omaha 13/6
• Port Talbot 22/6   BC 23/6 EBC20   Omaha 25/6
• Southampton 4/7; ammunition   Solent 6/7 EBC31W   Omaha 6/7
• Plymouth 24/7; with tow   joined EBC50
Unable maintain convoy speed, put into Dartmouth
     joined EBC51   Isigny 26/7
Grounded 27/7; heavy air raid on Isigny 28/7; propeller chipped when struck obstruction in shallow water 1640 28/7
• Poole 4/8   Solent 5/8 ETC58W   Port-en-Bessin 5/8
• Poole 12/8   Solent 13/8 ETC66W   Port-en-Bessin 13/8
On refloating in heavy swell, struck harbour bottom and quay wall causing heavy indentations to shell plating port side forward 1800 14/8
• Poole 18/8   Solent 19/8 ETC72W   Port-en-Bessin 19/8
• Poole 29/8   Solent 30/8 ETC83W   Port-en-Bessin 30/8
Returned to Poole 6/9

DICKY 507/01 British (Culliford) – taken up 3/5/44 for Ammunition
• London (Tilbury) 5/6; 520 tons; left Thames 5/6
     Solent 7/6 ETC22W   Sword 8/6
Starboard quarter plates and lifeboat davit damaged in collision with coaster *Belford* 0830 8/6
• Plymouth 19/6; cased petrol   joined EBC15   Utah 20/6
At Plymouth, port side plates and bulwark damaged by US Liberty ship *Stephen W Kearny* 29/6
• Plymouth 30/6; cased petrol   joined EBC26   Omaha 1/7
• Plymouth 11/7; cased petrol   joined EBC37   Utah 12/7
• Plymouth 18/7   joined EBC44   Utah 19/7
Sustained collision damage to lifeboats and counter in contact with HM landing craft *LCT783* 22/7, then grounded several times in Isigny channel same day; returned 25/7; drydocked at Plymouth for repairs 28/7-9/8
• Plymouth 12/8   joined EBC69   US area 13/8
• Southampton 28/8   Solent 29/8 EBC85W   St Vaast 29/8
Returned 6/9 to load for US area

DOGGERSBANK 208/39 Dutch – taken up 7/44 for Stores
• Southampton 26/7   Solent 27/7 ETC49W   British area 27/7
Assigned to French coastal ferry service; returned 10/9

DONA FLORA 1,179/24 British (Kingdon/*Donking) – taken up 4/5/44 for Stores
• Southampton 13/6   Solent 14/6 EBC9W   Utah 14/6

Rudder damaged by beaching during the 19-22/6 storm; returned without assistance 8/7 for repairs
- Southampton 21/7   Solent 22/7 EBC47W   Utah 22/7
- Plymouth 3/8   joined EBC60
Convoy diverted to Solent; left 5/8   Barfleur 5/8
Magnetic mine exploded 50yds ahead of vessel at Barfleur 7/8; returned to Plymouth 16/8 for repairs (22/8-4/9) and to load for US area

DORRIEN ROSE 1,039/22 British (Hughes) – taken up 15/4/44 for Stores
- London (Royal Albert); 558 tons; left Thames 9/6
                           Solent 12/6 ETC7W   Sword 13/6
- Southampton 21/6   Solent 22/6 ETC15W   Gold 22/6
- Southampton 2/7   Solent 3/7 ETC25W   British area 3/7
Arrived Southampton 13/7 for repairs
- Southampton 6/8   Solent 7/8 ETC60W   Port-en-Bessin 7/8
- Southampton 15/8   Solent 16/8 ETC69W   Port-en-Bessin 16/8
Coming alongside at Port-en-Bessin, vessel's starboard quarter damaged bulwark of coaster *Holburn Head* 16/8
- Southampton 26/8   Solent 27/8 ETC80W   Juno 27/8
Returned to Southampton 1/9 to load for Dieppe

DOWNLEAZE 486/24 British (Osborn & Wallis) – taken up 21/4/44 for Cased Petrol
- Poole 17/6   Solent 18/6 EBC13W   Utah 18/6
During the storm, bow of a landing craft, in difficulties and attempting to moor, hit ship's counter, damaging side, belting and deck plates 1000 19/6; stem buckled when struck by coaster *Rowanfield* 0200 20/6; temporary repairs at Poole 26-30/6
- Poole   Solent 2/7 EBC27W   Utah 2/7
- Poole 8/7   Solent 9/7 EBC34W   Utah 9/7
- Weymouth 2/8; cargo from coaster *Parknasilla*
                           joined EBC58   Omaha 2/8
- Southampton 11/8   Solent 12/8 EBC68W   US area 12/8
- Southampton 24/8   Solent 25/8 EBC81W   US area 25/8
Returned to Solent 30/8 to load at Southampton for US area

DOWNSHIRE 398/25 British (East Downshire) – taken up 30/4/44 for Ammunition
- Newport; left BC 7/6   Solent 10/6 EBC5W   Omaha 11/6
- Southampton 17/6   Solent 18/6 ETC12W   Arromanches 18/6
- Southampton 29/6   Solent 30/6 ETC22W   Sword 30/6
- Southampton 8/7   Solent 9/7 ETC31W   Port-en-Bessin 9/7
- Southampton 15/7   Solent 15/7 ETC37W   British area 15/7
Returned to Solent 21/7 for release 16/8

DRAKE 531/38 British (General Steam) – taken up 26/4/44 for Cased Petrol
- Sharpness 30/5; called Avonmouth 31/5-3/6; left BC 5/6
                           Solent 9/6 EBC4W   Utah 10/6
Attacked by aircraft at beachhead 12, 13, 15/6
- Portishead 27/6   BC 28/6 EBC25   Utah 30/6
- Llanelly 13/7   BC 14/7 EBC41   Omaha 16/7
- Poole 25/7   Solent 26/7 EBC51W   Isigny 26/7
- Poole 9/8   Solent 10/8 EBC66W   Grandcamp 10/8

On return to Solent, bow plates damaged and stem twisted when struck by a landing craft 2235 19/8
- Southampton 26/8   Solent 29/8 ETC82W   Arromanches 29/8
Returned to Southampton 3/9 to load for US area

Drake, which saw service carrying cased petrol to Normandy, was commended for outstanding efficiency when acting as Convoy Vice Commodore's ship. *[Author's collection]*

DRITTURA 187/28 Dutch – taken up 8/44 for Stores
- Southampton 25/8   Solent 26/8 EBC82W   US area 26/8
Assigned to French coastal ferry service in US area

DUNGRANGE 621/14 British (Dungrange/*Buchan & Hogg) – taken up 1/5/44 for Ammunition
- London (Tilbury) 5/6; 680 tons; left Thames 7/6
                           Solent 9/6 ETC4W
Lost. On passage to Juno, hit on starboard quarter by E-boat torpedo from *S177* or *S178* at 0400 10/6, 25 miles from the French coast; stern blown into the air before vessel quickly sank, with only two survivors, the Master and 11 others being killed; ship's barrage balloon, still attached, marked the exact spot

DUNVEGAN HEAD 638/20 British (Henry & MacGregor) – taken up 8/4/44 for Ammunition
- London (Tilbury) 30/5; 560 tons; left Thames 31/5
                           Solent 6/6 EWC1B   Sword 7/6
- Southampton 18/6; 574 tons including bombs
                           Solent 19/6 ETC13W   Sword 19/6
Lost. Steamed at anchors during the 19-22/6 storm, then beached for cargo discharge; after crew had gone ashore for safety, ship hit by two field artillery shells 2130 22/6, the first on the after end, while the second punched hole below the water-line port side; exploding ammunition caused fire which not extinguished by the tide until 24/6, despite engine room flooding at high water; vessel, although burnt out, initially considered salvable but, by 28/8, deemed a constructive total loss

DURWARD 419/40 British (Gibson) – taken up 12/4/44 for Cased Petrol
- London (Purfleet) 31/5; 480 tons; left Thames 31/5; embarked 40 troops in Solent
                           Solent 6/6 EWC1B   Gold 7/6

- London (Royal Albert) 17/6 | Thames 18/6 ETC13 | Gold 19/6
- London (Royal Albert) 1/7 | Thames 2/7 ETC25 | Gold 3/7
- London 10/7 | Thames 12/7 ETC35 | Juno 13/7
- London 18/7 | Thames 19/7 ETC42 | Juno 20/7
- Southampton 13/8 | Solent 14/8 ETC67W | Arromanches 14/8
- Southampton 20/8 | Solent 21/8 ETC74W | Arromanches 21/8
- Southampton 30/8 | Solent 31/8 ETC84W | Arromanches 31/8
Returned to Southampton 4/9 to load for Dieppe

DUURSWOLD 199/36 Dutch – taken up 7/44 for Stores
- Southampton | Solent 30/7 ETC52W | Port-en-Bessin 30/7
After coastal ferrying duties, returned to Plymouth 11/9 to load for St Brieuc

EAST COASTER 469/19 British (British Isles) – taken up 11/4/44 for Ammunition
- Penarth 3/6; sd BC 5/6 | Solent 9/6 EBC4W | Utah 10/6
Laden barge struck ship's stern damaging rudder and steering gear 13/6; repaired at beachhead
- Plymouth 24/6; 353 tons cased petrol
  | | joined EBC20 | Utah 25/6
- Plymouth 1/7; cased petrol | joined EBC27 | Utah 2/7
- Plymouth 8/7; cased petrol | joined EBC34 | Utah 9/7
- Plymouth 16/7; with barge in tow | joined EBC42 | US area 17/7
- Plymouth 25/7; with barge in tow | joined EBC51 | Omaha 26/7
Returned to Solent 31/7, then left for Mersey

EASTWOOD 1,551/24 British (France, Fenwick) – taken up 30/4/44 for Ammunition
- Port Talbot 3/6; vehicles and troops BC 5/6 EBC2Z | Omaha 8/6
- London (Tilbury) 21/6 | Thames 24/6 ETC17 | Juno 25/6
- London (Tilbury) 6/7 | Thames 7/7 ETC30 | Gold 8/7
- London 23/7; oil installation pipes Thames 23/7 ETC46 | Port-en-Bessin 24/7
- London 25/8 | Thames 26/8 ETC80 | Arromanches 27/8
Returned to London 9/9 to load bridging materials for Dieppe

EBBRIX 258/38 British (Rix) – taken up 12/43 for Cased Petrol
- London (Purfleet) 9/5; 240 tons; left Thames 31/5; embarked 40 troops in Solent
  | | Solent 6/6 EWC1B | Juno 7/6
- Southampton 13/6; 151 tons aviation fuel
  | | Solent 13/6 ETC8W | Juno 14/6
- Southampton 19/6 | Solent 20/6 ETC14W | Juno 20/6
- Southampton 29/6 | Solent 30/6 ETC22W | Gold 30/6
- Southampton 16/7 | Solent 17/7 ETC39W | Gold 17/7
- Poole 23/7 | Solent 24/7 ETC46W | Gold 24/7
- Southampton 29/7 | Solent 30/7 ETC52W | Gold 30/7
- Southampton 4/8 | Solent 5/8 ETC58W | Arromanches 5/8
- Southampton 9/8 | Solent 10/8 ETC63W | Arromanches 10/8
- Southampton 14/8 | Solent 15/8 ETC68W | Arromanches 15/8
- Southampton 19/8 | Solent 20/8 ETC73W | Arromanches 20/8
- Southampton 26/8 | Solent 27/8 ETC80W | Arromanches 27/8
Returned to Southampton 31/8 to load for Port-en-Bessin

EDENSIDE 366/21 British (Rose) – taken up 15/5/44 for Ammunition
- Southampton 15/6 | Solent 16/6 ETC10W | Juno 16/6

- Southampton 21/6 | Solent 22/6 ETC15W | Gold 22/6
- Southampton 27/6 | Solent 28/6 ETC20W | Gold 28/6
- Southampton 3/7 | Solent 4/7 ETC26W | Gold 4/7
- Southampton 8/7 | Solent 9/7 ETC31W | Gold 9/7
- Southampton 13/7 | Solent 14/7 ETC36W | Gold 14/7
- Southampton 18/7 | Solent 19/7 ETC41W | Gold 19/7
- Littlehampton 25/7 | joined ETC47 | Gold 25/7
Returned to Littlehampton with 43 tons of miscellaneous cargo
- Littlehampton 30/7 | joined ETC53 | Juno 31/7
- Littlehampton 5/8 | joined ETC58 | Juno 5/8
- Littlehampton 12/8 | joined ETC65
Convoy diverted to Solent; left 13/8 | | Juno 13/8
- Littlehampton 19/8 | joined ETC73 | Arromanches 20/8
- Littlehampton 25/8 | Solent 26/8 ETC79W | Arromanches 26/8
- Littlehampton 31/8 | Solent 2/9 ETC86W
Destined for Arromanches but turned back; arrived Solent 3/9

From Littlehampton, *Edenside* joined Normandy convoys from the Thames, as they passed along the English south coast. *[J. and M. Clarkson collection]*

EDINA 489/39 British (Currie) – taken up 7/4/44 for Cased Petrol
- Garston 29/5; called Swansea, left 4/6; left BC 7/6
  | | Solent 11/6 EBC6W | Omaha 12/6
- Llanelly 21/6 | BC 23/6 EBC20 | Omaha 25/6
Went aground 0800-1100 26/6; on departure from beachhead, damaged starboard bulwark in collision with coaster *Jade* 28/6; returned to Swansea for repairs
- Llanelly 5/7 | BC 6/7 EBC33 | Utah 8/7
- Llanelly 22/7 | BC 22/7 EBC49 | Omaha 24/7
- Poole 29/7 | Solent 30/7 EBC55W | Utah 30/7
- Poole 5/8 | Solent 6/8 EBC61W | US area 6/8
- Poole 14/8 | Solent 15/8 EBC71W | US area 15/8
- Poole 25/8 | Solent 26/8 EBC82W | US area 26/8
Returned to Poole 5/9

EDLE 654/16 Norwegian – taken up 15/4/44 for Ammunition
- Swansea; ammunition and stores; left BC 30/5; embarked 65 troops in Solent

	Solent 5/6 Force O3	Omaha 6/6 (D-Day)
• Fowey 18/6	joined EBC14	Omaha 19/6
• Fowey 1/7	joined EBC27	Utah 2/7
• Fowey 9/7	joined EBC35	Omaha 10/7
• Fowey 24/7	joined EBC50	Utah 25/7
• Fowey 8/8	joined EBC66	US area 10/8
• Fowey 25/8	joined EBC82	US area 26/8

Returned to Plymouth 3/9 to load for US area

EGEE 2,667/40 British, ex-French (MoWT/*Duncan) – taken up 5/44 for
Stores

• Penarth 18/6	BC 19/6 EBC16	
Convoy sheltered in Poole Bay		Omaha 23/6
• Sharpness 18/7	BC 18/7 EBC45	Cherbourg 20/7
• Newport 6/8	BC 7/8 EBC65	US area 9/8

After beaching for cargo discharge, first attempt to refloat at 1700 13/8 proved
unsuccessful; after adjusting ballast, further attempts finally succeeded at 0820 15/8
- London (Millwall) 27/8   Thames 28/8 ETC82

Sustained blast damage to chart room and lifeboat from German flying bomb hit by
British anti-aircraft guns deployed on Kent coast 28/8   Arromanches 29/8
Returned to London 13/9 to load for Arromanches

In August 1944, it took a number of attempts before the ex-French *Egee*
succeeded in refloating after beaching for cargo work. *[J. and M. Clarkson
collection]*

EILDON 1,447/36 British (Gibson) – taken up 13/5/44 for Stores

• Avonmouth 5/6; left BC 7/6	Solent 11/6 EBC6W	Utah 12/6
• Portishead 1/7; ammunition	BC 2/7 EBC29	Utah 4/7
• Port Talbot 21/7; cased petrol	BC 22/7 EBC49	Omaha 24/7
• Port Talbot 5/8; cased petrol	BC 5/8 EBC63	US area 7/8
• Port Talbot 18/8; cased petrol	BC 19/8 EBC77	
Convoy sheltered in Solent; left 23/8		Utah 23/8

Returned to Cardiff 29/8 to load for US area

EILIAN HILL 781/13 British (Thomas) – taken up 30/4/44 for Ammunition
- London (Tilbury Jetty) 7/6; 740 tons; left Thames 7/6

	Solent 10/6 ETC5W	Port-en-Bessin 11/6

Extensively damaged shell plating and frames on both sides and slightly fractured
bottom through striking the quay and grounding during the 19-22/6 storm; fitting
of cement boxes enabled vessel to arrive London 24/6, then leave for Tyne for
survey and subsequent release

ELIDIR 398/03 British (Coppack) – taken up 5/44 for Stores

• Southampton 7/6	Solent 8/6 ETC3W	Gold 9/6
• Southampton 19/6	Solent 20/6 ETC14W	British area 20/6
• Southampton 27/6	Solent 29/6 ETC21W	Gold 29/6
• Southampton 5/7	Solent 6/7 ETC28W	Gold 6/7
• Southampton 10/7	Solent 11/7 ETC33W	Gold 11/7
• Southampton 16/7	Solent 17/7 ETC39W	Gold 17/7
• Southampton 22/7	Solent 23/7 ETC45W	Gold 23/7
• Southampton 27/7	Solent 28/7 ETC50W	Gold 28/7
• Southampton 3/8	Solent 4/8 ETC57W	Port-en-Bessin 4/8
• Southampton 8/8	Solent 9/8 ETC62W	Arromanches 9/8
• Southampton 13/8	Solent 14/8 ETC67W	Arromanches 14/8
• Southampton 18/8	Solent 19/8 ETC72W	Arromanches 19/8
• Southampton 26/8	Solent 27/8 ETC80W	Port-en-Bessin 27/8

Returned to Southampton 2/9

In July and August 1944, *Elidir* was, on some occasions, achieving a
departure from Southampton for Normandy every five days. *[J. and M.
Clarkson collection]*

ELKANAH CROWELL 1,791/43 British, ex-US (MoWT/*Cory) – taken up
4/44 for Stores

• Avonmouth 5/6	BC 6/6 EBC3	US area 9/6
• Cardiff 23/6	BC 24/6 EBC21	Omaha 26/6
• Swansea 8/7	BC 9/7 EBC36	Omaha 11/7
• Swansea 24/7	BC 25/7 EBC52	
Detached to Falmouth 26/7 with boiler trouble; left 29/7		
	joined EBC55	
Diverted to Solent; at anchor for over four weeks		
	Solent 28/8 EBC84W	Omaha 28/8

Returned to Port Talbot 8/9 to load for US area

EMERALD QUEEN 481/37 British (British Channel Islands) – taken up 25/6/44 for Ammunition

• Newhaven 13/7	joined ETC36	Juno 14/7	
• Southampton 21/7	Solent 22/7 ETC44W	Port-en-Bessin 22/7	
• Southampton 27/7	Solent 28/7 ETC50W	Port-en-Bessin 28/7	
• Southampton 4/8	Solent 5/8 ETC58W	Port-en-Bessin 5/8	
• Southampton 10/8	Solent 11/8 ETC64W	Arromanches 11/8	

Returned to Southampton 14/8 for repairs and to load cased petrol for Dieppe

EMPIRE BANK 402/41 British (MoWT/*Metcalf) – taken up 4/44 for Cased Petrol

• London (Purfleet); 333 tons; left Thames 7/6

	Solent 10/6 ETC5W	Gold 11/6
• London	Thames 18/6 ETC13	Port-en-Bessin 19/6

Tug *TID12*, delivering pilot in anchorage, damaged port side bulwarks when twice striking ship heavily 0030 23/6; on return to London, ship surveyed at Rotherhithe for damage through straining in heavy weather 28/6

• London	Thames 3/7 ETC26	Arromanches 4/7
• London 12/7	Thames 13/7 ETC36	Juno 14/7
• London 19/7	Thames 20/7 ETC43	Port-en-Bessin 21/7

When departing stern first, sustained heavy indentation in stern plating on port quarter, as a result of contact with the outer harbour knuckle 22/7

• Southampton 28/7	Solent 29/7 ETC51W	Arromanches 29/7
• Southampton 3/8	Solent 4/8 ETC57W	Arromanches 4/8
• Southampton 9/8	Solent 10/8 ETC63W	Arromanches 10/8
• Southampton 14/8	Solent 15/8 ETC68W	Port-en-Bessin 15/8

Port bow heavily indented in collision with stone wall on entering harbour in moderate swell 2045 15/8

• Southampton 19/8	Solent 20/8 ETC73W	Arromanches 20/8
• Southampton 27/8	Solent 28/8 ETC81W	Arromanches 28/8

Heavy weather on return passage resulted in vessel's hold making water; arrived Southampton 1/9 to load for Dieppe

By the end of August 1944, *Empire Bank*'s 11 voyages to Normandy had been punctuated by a number of minor incidents: she is pictured after her 1946 renaming as *Rose-Julie M. [World Ship Society Ltd.]*

EMPIRE BOND 2,088/06 British (MoWT/*Gillespie & Nicol) – taken up 5/44 for Stores

• Cardiff 13/6	BC 14/6 EBC11	Utah 16/6	
• Penarth 8/7	BC 9/7 EBC36		
Put into Falmouth; left 11/7	joined EBC37	Omaha 12/7	
• Swansea 30/8	BC 31/8 EBC89		

Convoy sheltered in Weymouth Bay; vessel detached from convoy because of crew trouble; arrived Weymouth 3/9; left Portland 7/9

	joined EBC95	Cherbourg 8/9

Returned to Falmouth 26/9 and Newport 30/9

EMPIRE CAPE 872/41 British (MoWT/*Tyne-Tees then Dundee, Perth & London) – taken up 4/44 for Cased Petrol

• Port Talbot 28/5; cased petrol and stores; left BC 30/5; embarked 121 troops in Solent

	Solent 5/6 Force O3	Omaha 6/6 (D-Day)
• Portishead 15/6	BC 17/6 EBC14	Omaha 19/6
• Poole 1/7	Solent 2/7 EBC27W	Utah 2/7
• Poole 9/7	Solent 10/7 EBC35W	Omaha 10/7
• Poole 17/7	Solent 18/7 EBC43W	Omaha 18/7
• Poole 25/7	Solent 26/7 EBC51W	Utah 26/7
• Poole 1/8	Solent 2/8 EBC58W	US area 2/8
• Southampton 16/8	Solent 16/8 EBC73W	US area 17/8

Returned to Southampton 27/8

EMPIRE CLIFF 873/40 British (MoWT/*Salvesen) – taken up 3/44 for Cased Petrol

• Garston 13/5; called Swansea 31/5-2/6; left BC 8/6

	Solent 12/6 EBC7W	Omaha 13/6

Water entered engine room to a depth of 2ft as a result of grounding 2115 13/6; beached 14/6 for repairs which completed 15/6; sustained hull damage when moorings of US landing craft *LCT639* parted and craft collided with ship's port quarter 1307 16/6; vessel's bulwark torn by a DUKW in heavy swell 17/6; hull on starboard side severely indented when hit by stern of US landing craft *LCT520* 21/6

• Newport 4/7	BC 5/7 EBC32	Utah 7/7
• Southampton 23/7	Solent 24/7 ETC46W	Gold 24/7
• Southampton 31/7	Solent 1/8 ETC54W	Arromanches 1/8
• Southampton 9/8	Solent 10/8 ETC63W	Arromanches 10/8
• Southampton 16/8	Solent 18/8 ETC71W	Arromanches 18/8

Struck by coaster *Enid Mary* whose anchor dragged 0730 20/8

• Southampton 26/8	Solent 27/8 ETC80W	Port-en-Bessin 27/8

Returned to Southampton 3/9 to load for Caen

EMPIRE CREEK 332/41 British (MoWT/*Springwell) – taken up 5/44 for Cased Petrol

• Plymouth 16/6; 384 tons	joined EBC12	Utah 17/6
• Plymouth 25/6	joined EBC21	Utah 26/6
• Plymouth 1/7	joined EBC27	

Straggled in fog, so crossed to beachhead independently Omaha 2/7

• Plymouth 8/7	joined EBC36	Utah 11/7
• Plymouth 16/7	joined EBC42	US area 17/7
• Plymouth 23/7 with barge in tow		
Put into Dartmouth 23/7	joined EBC50	Utah 25/7

• Plymouth 31/7	joined EBC57	Utah 1/8
• Plymouth 18/8	joined EBC75	US area 19/8
• Plymouth 26/8	joined EBC83	US area 27/8

Returned to Plymouth 3/9 to load for US area

EMPIRE ESTUARY 319/40 British (MoWT/*Craggs & Jenkin) – taken up
3/44 for Cased Petrol
• Port Talbot 1/6; left BC 2/6; embarked 65 troops in Solent

	Solent 8/6 EBC3W	Omaha 9/6

Port bow damaged in collision with barge 0330 10/6
• Southampton 19/6	Solent 20/6 ETC14W	Gold 20/6

On return to Southampton, starboard quarter holed and indented in contact with
vessel, possibly HM landing craft *LCT517*, 27/6; cement box fitted
• Southampton 29/6	Solent 30/6 ETC22W	Gold 30/6
• Southampton 6/7	Solent 7/7 ETC29W	Juno 7/7
• Southampton 12/7	Solent 13/7 ETC35W	Port-en-Bessin 13/7
• Southampton 17/7	Solent 18/7 ETC40W	Gold 18/7
• Southampton 26/7	Solent 27/7 ETC49W	Port-en-Bessin 27/7

Returned to Southampton 30/7 with 58 tons of empty ammunition boxes and two
Army deserters, who discovered in ship's hold
• Southampton 2/8	Solent 3/8 ETC56W	Port-en-Bessin 3/8
• Southampton 8/8	Solent 8/8 ETC61W	Arromanches 8/8
• Southampton 12/8	Solent 13/8 ETC66W	Arromanches 13/8
• Southampton 17/8	Solent 18/8 ETC71W	Arromanches 18/8
• Southampton 22/8	Solent 23/8 ETC76W	
Convoy turned back to Solent; left 24/8		Arromanches 24/8
• Southampton 28/8	Solent 29/8 ETC82W	Port-en-Bessin 29/8

Returned to Southampton 1/9 to load for Dieppe

EMPIRE FABIAN 411/44 British (MoWT/*Fisher) – taken up 8/44 for Stores
• Southampton	Solent 28/8 EBC84W	Cherbourg 28/8

Returned to Southampton 7/9 load for US area

EMPIRE FACTOR 410/44 British (MoWT/*Ellerman's Wilson) – taken up
6/7/44 for Stores
• Southampton 3/8	Solent 4/8 ETC57W	Port-en-Bessin 4/8
• Southampton 8/8	Solent 9/8 ETC62W	Port-en-Bessin 9/8
• Southampton 17/8	Solent 18/8 ETC71W	Arromanches 18/8

Broached to whilst beached; sustained twisted rudder post and rudder, broken
propeller blade and other damage; returned to Southampton 29/8 in tow of tug
Empire Betsy

EMPIRE FAVOURITE 410/44 British (MoWT/*Rix) – taken up 25/7/44 for
Stores
• Southampton 11/8	Solent 12/8 ETC65W	Port-en-Bessin 12/8
• Southampton 17/8	Solent 18/8 ETC71W	Arromanches 18/8
• Southampton 23/8	Solent 23/8 ETC76W	
Convoy turned back to Solent;	left 24/8	Port-en-Bessin 24/8
• Southampton 29/8	Solent 29/8 ETC82W	Arromanches 29/8

Returned to Southampton 2/9 to load for British area

EMPIRE FORELAND 873/41 British (MoWT/*Comben Longstaff) – taken up
5/44 for Cased Petrol
• Garston; called Swansea 30/5-4/6; left BC 8/6
	Solent 12/6 EBC7W	Omaha 13/6
• Port Talbot 23/6	BC 24/6 EBC21	Utah 26/6
• Portishead	BC 11/7 EBC38	Omaha 13/7
• Southampton 23/7	Solent 24/7 ETC46W	Sword 24/7
• Southampton 4/8	Solent 5/8 ETC58W	Arromanches 5/8

Whilst beached, sustained damaged plates on port quarter when struck by barge
7/8; after return to Solent, lost lifeboat and sustained damage to davits, plates and
bulwarks in collision with unknown vessel 0335 17/8; arrived Southampton 18/8
for repairs

EMPIRE HEARTH 2,020/42 British (MoWT/*Tyne & Wear) – taken up 4/44
for Stores
• London (Royal Albert); 33 vehicles and 132 troops
	Thames 5/6 ETC2Z	British area 7/6
• London	Thames 20/6 ETC15	
Convoy sheltered in Solent; left 22/6		Gold 22/6
• Grimsby 5/7	Thames 8/7 ETC31	Gold 9/7

Returned to London 15/7 after going aground previous day

The 1942-built *Empire Hearth* arrived in London on 29th May 1944 to load
vehicles and troops at King George V Dock: these she duly delivered to
Normandy on D+1 Day (7th June 1944). *[National Maritime Museum,
P22328]*

EMPIRE JONQUIL 369/39 British (MoWT/*Monroe) – taken up 3/44 for
Cased Petrol
• Port Talbot 1/6; left BC 2/6; embarked 39 troops in Solent
	Solent 8/6 EBC3W	Omaha 9/6
• Southampton 19/6	Solent 22/6 ETC15W	Gold 22/6
• Southampton 30/6	Solent 1/7 ETC23W	Gold 1/7
• Southampton 6/7	Solent 7/7 ETC29W	Juno 7/7
• Southampton 15/7	Solent 16/7 ETC38W	
Turned back owing to fog	Solent 17/7 ETC39W	Courseulles 17/7

Returned to Southampton 28/7 with 170 tons of salvaged engines and landing craft parts
• Southampton 7/8	Solent 8/8 ETC61W	Arromanches 8/8
• Southampton 12/8	Solent 13/8 ETC66W	Arromanches 13/8
• Southampton 17/8	Solent 18/8 ETC71W	Arromanches 18/8
• Southampton 26/8	Solent 27/8 ETC80W	Arromanches 27/8

Returned to Southampton 7/9 to load for Dieppe

EMPIRE LAGOON 2,013/41 British (MoWT/*Hudson) – taken up 5/44 for Stores
• London (King George V) 3/6; 34 vehicles, 136 troops

	Thames 5/6 ETC2Z	Gold 7/6
• London 15/6	Thames 16/6 ETC11	Gold 17/6
• London 1/7	Thames 2/7 ETC25	Gold 3/7
• London (Purfleet) 22/7; cased petrol		
	Thames 23/7 ETC46	Arromanches 24/7
• London 3/8	Thames 4/8 ETC58	Arromanches 5/8
• London 15/8	Thames 16/8 ETC70	Juno 17/8

Returned to London 25/8

EMPIRE LOUGH 2,824/40 British (MoWT/*Stanhope) – taken up 4/44 for Stores
• London (Millwall); 36 vehicles and 140 troops

	Thames 5/6 ETC2Z	British area 7/6
• London 23/6; 2,800 tons cased petrol		
	Thames 24/6 ETC17	

Lost. Whilst transitting Strait of Dover 1510 24/6, subjected to long-range gunfire; third salvo exploded on No 4 hold; the following two salvoes ripped holes in port side; vessel caught fire and burned intensely; crew abandoned ship by 1527 24/6; Master died from effect of immersion in the sea; one Maltese crewman killed, three others wounded; vessel subsequently beached by tug *Lady Brassey* three miles W of Dover; 29/6 survey revealed fire extinguished but masts and derricks collapsed, all hatches and decks littered with empty petrol containers and hull so badly damaged on port side that vessel subsequently declared a constructive total loss

EMPIRE NESS 2,922/41 British (MoWT/*Souter) – taken up 4/44 for Stores
• London (Millwall); 36 vehicles and 140 troops

	Thames 5/6 ETC2Z	British area 7/6
• London 16/6	Thames 17/6 ETC12	Gold 18/6
• London 5/7	Thames 6/7 ETC29	Gold 7/7
• London (Purfleet) 21/7; cased petrol		
	Thames 22/7 ETC45	Juno 23/7

Subjected to field artillery fire whilst discharging 28/7
• London (Tilbury) 8/8   Thames 11/8 ETC65
Convoy diverted to Solent; left 13/8   Juno 13/8
Returned to London 21/8; subsequently loaded bridging materials at Grimsby for Dieppe

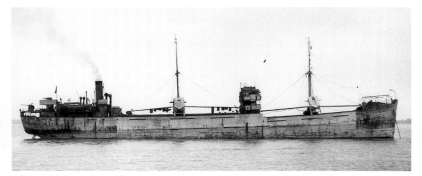

After initially serving Normandy, the intended destination of *Empire Ness* on 30th November 1944 was Antwerp when she collided with a Liberty ship and sank. [*National Maritime Museum, P22397*]

EMPIRE NUTFIELD 1,561/19 British (MoWT/*Lindley) – taken up 5/44 for Stores
• London (Royal Albert) 3/6; 25 vehicles, 100 troops

	Thames 5/6 ETC2Z	British area 7/6
• Southampton 19/6	Solent 20/6 ETC14W	

Experienced difficulty in maintaining speed, so sailed independently after convoy disappeared out of sight 0130 20/6   Sword 20/6
On return, further steam problems resulted in vessel sailing five miles astern of convoy; arrived Thames 28/6

• London 4/7	Thames 5/7 ETC28	Gold 6/7
• London (Millwall) 18/7	Thames 19/7 ETC42	Sword 20/7
• London 27/7	Thames 29/7 ETC52	Arromanches 30/7
• London (Purfleet) 12/8	Thames 13/8 ETC67	Juno 14/8

Returned to London 21/8; subsequently loaded bridging materials at Grimsby for Dieppe

EMPIRE RESISTANCE 1,631/08 British (MoWT/*Jones) – taken up 5/44 for Ammunition

• Newport 11/6	BC 12/6 EBC9	Omaha 15/6

During the storm, 50 US dock operating troops marooned on board 19-22/6

• Portishead 4/7	BC 5/7 EBC32	Omaha 7/7
• Portishead 25/7	BC 26/7 EBC53	Omaha 28/7
• Grimsby 15/8	Thames 17/8 ETC71	Arromanches 18/8

Returned to Grimsby 25/8 to load for Arromanches

EMPIRE RIDER 965/43 British (MoWT/*Hay) – taken up 6/44 for Ammunition

• London (Millwall) 14/6	Thames 16/6 ETC11	Juno 17/6

Beached 18/6; required repairs before refloating 4/7

• London (Tilbury Jetty) 18/7; stores	Thames 19/7 ETC42	Juno 20/7
• London (Tilbury) 28/7	Thames 30/7 ETC53	Arromanches 31/7
• London 12/8	Thames 12/8 ETC66	Juno 13/8
• London 30/8	Thames 30/8 ETC84	Arromanches 31/8

Returned to London (Tilbury Jetty) 10/9 to load for Dieppe

Completed on the Clyde in 1943, *Empire Rider* was exclusively based in the Thames during her first three months of cross-Channel service, carrying ammunition or general stores to the British beachheads. [*National Maritime Museum*]

EMPIRE SCOUT 2,229/36 British (MoWT/*Capper, Alexander) – taken up 5/44 for Cased Petrol
• Port Talbot 12/6 | BC 13/6 EBC10 | Omaha 16/6
Whilst manoeuvring to anchorage to resume cargo discharge, grounded near coaster *Freeman Hatch*; on refloating, latter vessel's port counter hit *Empire Scout*'s port side bulwarks and raft frame 2020 22/6
• Swansea 6/7 | BC 6/7 EBC33 | Utah 8/7
• Port Talbot 25/7 | BC 26/7 EBC53 | Omaha 28/7
In strong wind and rough seas, vessel drifted onto breakwater blockships, partly smashing ship's jolly boat and bending forward all propeller blades, some badly, 2000 1/8; returned to Solent 8/8, then to Immingham Dock and later Hull
• Grimsby 29/8 | Thames 1/9 ETC86 | Arromanches 2/9
Returned to Thames 15/9 to load at London (Purfleet) for Dieppe

EMPIRE SEDGE 2,852/41 British (MoWT/*Burnett) – taken up 5/44 for Stores
• Swansea 4/6; vehicles and troops; in Swansea Bay anchorage, dragging of anchor in gale caused ship's starboard quarter to hit coaster *Dalewood* 1448 4/6; *Empire Sedge* sustained indenting of hull from deck to water-line; cement box fitted over two damaged rivets; when weighing port anchor to join convoy, frame fracture rendered windlass unserviceable 1352 5/6; the hoving home of anchor and cable by means of wires to fore deck winches enabled vessel to catch up convoy
| | BC 5/6 EBC2Z | Omaha 8/6 |
Whilst discharging, US landing craft *LCT545* indented hull and a barge struck starboard quarter 11/6; scheduled to load at Grimsby but returned to Swansea 14/6 for windlass repairs
• Swansea 22/6 | BC 23/6 EBC20 | Utah 25/6
• Grimsby 20/7 | Thames 23/7 ETC46 | Arromanches 24/7
• Grimsby 16/8 | Thames 19/8 ETC73 | Arromanches 20/8
Returned to London 29/8 and Grimsby 1/9 to load for Caen

Grimsby became the loading port for some of the larger coasters sailing to the British area: *Empire Sedge* was one such vessel. *[National Maritime Museum, P22459]*

EMPIRE SHOAL 878/41 British (MoWT/*Everard) – taken up 4/44 for Cased Petrol
• Sharpness 27/5; called Avonmouth, left 3/6; left BC 5/6
| | Solent 9/6 EBC4W | Utah 10/6 |
• Portishead 23/6 | BC 24/6 EBC21 | Omaha 26/6

• Llanelly 18/7 | BC 19/7 EBC46 | Omaha 21/7
• Southampton 29/7 | Solent 30/7 ETC52W | Gold 30/7
• Southampton 6/8 | Solent 7/8 ETC60W | Arromanches 7/8
• Southampton 14/8 | Solent 15/8 ETC68W | Arromanches 15/8
• Southampton 27/8 | Solent 28/8 ETC81W | Juno 28/8
Returned to Southampton 3/9 to load for Dieppe

EMPIRE STRAIT 2,824/40 British (MoWT/*Witherington) – taken up 5/44 for Stores
• Swansea 3/6; vehicles and troops BC 5/6 EBC2Z | Omaha 8/6
• Grimsby 21/6 | Thames 24/6 ETC17 | Sword 25/6
Returned to London 10/7 for repairs and release 27/7

ENID MARY 582/21 British (British Isles) – taken up 9/4/44 for Ammunition
• London (Tilbury) 12/5; 560 tons; left Thames 31/5; embarked 39 troops in Solent
| | Solent 6/6 EWC1B | Juno 7/6 |
Sustained damage as a result of being ordered to beach when depth of water insufficient
• Southampton 23/6 | Solent 24/6 ETC16W | Gold 24/6
• Southampton 10/7 | Solent 11/7 ETC33W | Juno 11/7
• Southampton 18/7 | Solent 19/7 ETC41W | Gold 19/7
• Newhaven 26/7 | joined ETC49 | Gold 27/7
• Southampton 2/8 | Solent 3/8 ETC56W | Arromanches 3/8
• Southampton 8/8 | Solent 9/8 ETC62W | Port-en-Bessin 9/8
• Southampton 16/8 | Solent 17/8 ETC70W | Arromanches 17/8
Dragged anchor and collided with coaster *Empire Cliff* 0730 20/8
• Southampton 23/8 | Solent 24/8 ETC77W | Arromanches 24/8
• Southampton 28/8 | Solent 29/8 ETC82W | Arromanches 29/8
Returned to Southampton 1/9 to load for Arromanches

ERICA 1,592/19 Norwegian – taken up 11/5/44 for Ammunition
• Swansea 4/6; vehicles and troops BC 5/6 EBC2Z | Omaha 8/6
• Newport 24/6; 1,881 tons | BC 25/6 EBC22 | Omaha 27/6
• Swansea 8/7 | BC 9/7 EBC36 | Omaha 11/7
• Portishead 29/7 | BC 30/7 EBC57 | Omaha 1/8
• Grimsby 22/8; coal | Thames 27/8 ETC81 | Caen 28/8
Returned to Grimsby 11/9 to load for Dieppe

ERNA 361/40 Dutch – taken up 3/44 for Cased Petrol
• Port Talbot; left BC 30/5; embarked 65 troops in Solent
| | Solent 6/6 EWC1A | Omaha 7/6 |
• Southampton 15/6 | Solent 16/6 ETC10W | Gold 16/6
• Southampton 25/6 | Solent 26/6 ETC18W | Sword 26/6
• Southampton 8/7 | Solent 12/7 ETC34W | Port-en-Bessin 12/7
• Southampton 17/7 | Solent 18/7 ETC40W | Gold 18/7
• Southampton 25/7 | Solent 26/7 ETC48W | Port-en-Bessin 26/7
• Southampton 1/8 | Solent 2/8 ETC55W | Arromanches 2/8
• Southampton 6/8 | Solent 7/8 ETC60W | Arromanches 7/8
• Southampton 11/8 | Solent 12/8 ETC65W | Arromanches 12/8
• Southampton 19/8 | Solent 20/8 ETC73W | Arromanches 20/8
• Southampton 26/8 | Solent 27/8 ETC80W | Arromanches 27/8
Returned to Southampton 31/8

Erna was one of 14 coasters allocated to load their first Normandy-bound cargoes of cased petrol at Port Talbot's Talbot Wharf. *[Ben Scholten collection]*

ESKWOOD 791/11 British (Grand Union) – taken up 4/44 for Stores
• London (Royal Albert) 2/6; 466 tons; left Thames 5/6

	Solent 8/6 ETC3W	British area 9/6
• Southampton 18/6	Solent 19/6 EBC14W	Isigny 19/6
• Southampton 2/7	Solent 3/7 EBC28W	Omaha 3/7
• Southampton 11/7	Solent 12/7 EBC37W	Omaha 12/7
• Southampton 21/7	Solent 22/7 EBC47W	Omaha 22/7
• Southampton 31/7	Solent 1/8 EBC57W	Utah 1/8
• Southampton 10/8	Solent 12/8 EBC68W	Utah 12/8

Whilst beached in high wind, vessel's stern and steering gear extensively damaged when fouled by coaster *Westburn* (qv) 14/8; swell lifted vessels against each other 14-15/8: floated and shifted to deeper water 16/8; returned under tow, arrived Southampton 24/8

EUTERPE 897/03 Dutch – taken up 29/4/44 for Stores

• Southampton 26/6	Solent 28/6 ETC20W	Gold 28/6
• Southampton 13/7	Solent 15/7 ETC37W	Gold 15/7
• Southampton 26/7	Solent 27/7 ETC49W	Juno 27/7
• Southampton 5/8	Solent 6/8 ETC59W	Arromanches 6/8
• Southampton 16/8	Solent 17/8 ETC70W	Arromanches 17/8
• Southampton 25/8	Solent 26/8 ETC79W	Arromanches 26/8

Returned to Southampton 2/9 to load for Arromanches

EVERTSEN 392/29 Dutch – taken up 18/5/44 for Cased Petrol

• Poole	Solent 15/6 ETC9W	Gold 15/6
• Poole 27/6	Solent 28/6 ETC20W	Juno 28/6
• Poole 6/7	Solent 7/7 ETC29W	Gold 7/7
• Poole 13/7	Solent 13/7 ETC35W	Gold 13/7
• Poole 17/7	Solent 17/7 ETC39W	British area 17/7
• Poole 28/7	Solent 29/7 ETC51W	Port-en-Bessin 29/7
• Poole 2/8	Solent 3/8 ETC56W	Gold 3/8
• Poole 9/8; loaded overside from coaster *Zuidland*		
	Solent 10/8 ETC63W	Port-en-Bessin 10/8
• Poole 16/8	Solent 17/8 ETC70W	Port-en-Bessin 17/8
• Poole 24/8	Solent 25/8 ETC78W	Port-en-Bessin 25/8
• Poole 31/8	Solent 1/9 ETC85W	Port-en-Bessin 1/9

Returned to Poole 6/9 to load for Dieppe

EXPRESS 195/29 Dutch – taken up 8/44 for Stores

• Southampton 20/8	Solent 23/8 EBC77W	Utah 23/8

Returned to Poole 28/8

One of the small Dutch coasters which joined the Normandy cross-Channel fleet in August 1944 was *Express*. *[Dick Gorter collection]*

FAGERBRO 994/23 Norwegian – taken up 22/5/44 for Stores

• Southampton 13/6	Solent 14/6 EBC9W	Utah 14/6
• Southampton 16/7	Solent 17/7 EBC42W	Omaha 17/7
• Southampton 23/7	Solent 24/7 EBC49W	Omaha 24/7
• Southampton 31/7	Solent 1/8 ETC54W	Arromanches 1/8
• Southampton 6/8	Solent 7/8 ETC60W	Port-en-Bessin 7/8
• Southampton 13/8	Solent 14/8 ETC67W	Arromanches 14/8

Returned to Harwich 20/8 to load 1,128 tons ammunition for Dieppe

FANO 1,889/22 British, ex-Danish (MoWT/*Souter) – taken up 4/44 for Stores

• Swansea 3/6; vehicles and troops BC 5/6 EBC2Z		Omaha 8/6
• Barry 19/6	BC 20/6 EBC17	
Convoy sheltered in Poole Bay		Omaha 24/6
• Barry 11/7	BC 12/7 EBC39	Utah 14/7
• Swansea 2/8	BC 4/8 EBC61	
Convoy diverted to Solent; left 6/8		Barfleur 6/8

On leaving Barfleur, involved in collision with coaster *Lilleaa* 11/8

• Southampton 23/8	Solent 24/8 EBC78W	Omaha 24/8

Returned to Solent 12/9, Southampton 20/9 and London 26/9

FENJA 847/24 British (South Georgia/*Chr Salvesen) – taken up 11/5/44 for Stores

• London (Millwall) 11/6	Thames 12/6 ETC8	Sword 14/6

On departure from beachhead, sustained damage in collision with a landing craft 0200 16/6

• London 26/6	Thames 28/6 ETC21	Sword 29/6

Rolling in heavy seas on return passage caused starboard after raft to be swept overboard 1405 3/7

- London (Millwall) 7/7   Thames 8/7 ETC31   Gold 9/7
- Harwich 20/7; 1,056 tons ammunition

         Thames 21/7 ETC44   Juno 22/7
- Southampton 2/8   Solent 3/8 ETC56W   Arromanches 3/8

In return convoy, sustained damage to shell plating and hawse pipe when hit by coaster *Naviedale*, with jammed steering gear, 1140 6/8; examination by Chief Officer of extent of damage revealed an Army deserter stowaway, who was disembarked into boat sent by escorting corvette, HMCS *Calgary*, 1205 6/8
- Southampton 11/8   Solent 12/8 ETC65W   Arromanches 12/8
- Southampton 19/8   Solent 20/8 ETC73W   Arromanches 20/8
- Southampton 28/8   Solent 29/8 ETC82W   Arromanches 29/8

Returned to Hull 4/9 for release 27/9

FIRE QUEEN 650/21 **British (Coast)** – taken up 1/5/44 for Ammunition
- Newport 3/6; left BC 5/6   Solent 9/6 EBC4W   Omaha 10/6
- Southampton 24/6; stores   Solent 24/6 ETC16W   Gold 24/6
- Southampton 9/7; stores   Solent 10/7 ETC32W   Juno 10/7
- Southampton 18/7   Solent 19/7 ETC41W   Gold 19/7
- Southampton 27/7   Solent 28/7 ETC50W   Juno 28/7
- Southampton 3/8   Solent 4/8 EBC59W   US area 4/8

On returning to Solent, sustained damage to hull, above the waterline, and starboard lifeboat in collision with coaster *William Howland* 0400 6/8; under repair at Southampton (Northam) from 9/8; next sailing 16/9 to Barfleur

FLATHOUSE 1,546/31 **British (Stephenson Clarke)** – taken up 7/4/44 for Stores
- London (King George V); 1,000 tons; left Thames 7/6

         Solent 9/6 ETC4W

Convoy heavily attacked in English Channel by E-boats 10/6   Mulberry B 10/6
Was the first coaster to discharge her cargo inside Mulberry B (later renamed Arromanches)
- London (Tilbury) 21/6; ammunition Thames 23/6 ETC16   Gold 24/6
- London 8/7; ammunition   Thames 9/7 ETC32   Sword 10/7
- London (Tilbury) 2/8;   Thames 3/8 ETC57   Arromanches 4/8

Returned to London 12/8

FLUOR 914/25 **British (Robertson)** – taken up 23/4/44 for Stores
- Avonmouth 30/5; left BC 30/5; embarked 89 troops in Solent

         Solent 6/6 EWC1A   US area 7/6
- Southampton 22/6; ammunition Solent 23/6 EBC16W   Utah 23/6

Steel plate on port bow set in by US tank landing ship *LST355* at Southampton 0600 1/7
- Southampton 2/7   Solent 3/7 EBC28W   Omaha 3/7
- Southampton 10/7   Solent 11/7 EBC36W   Omaha 11/7
- Southampton 20/7   Solent 21/7 EBC46W   Omaha 21/7
- Plymouth 3/8   joined EBC60

Convoy diverted to Solent; left 5/8   Isigny 5/8
Fouled by anchor of fleet oiler *Rapidol* at Plymouth 0730 19/8
- Plymouth 25/8   joined EBC82   St Vaast 26/8

Returned to Plymouth 6/9 to load for Barfleur

FOLDA 1,165/20 **British (South Georgia/*Chr Salvesen)** – taken up 28/4/44 for Stores
- London (King George V) 10/6; 636 tons

         Thames 11/6 ETC7

Whilst acting as Commodore ship leading port column, another convoy sighted proceeding in opposite direction; after several ships had passed on either side, a vessel was observed immediately ahead; evasive action failed to prevent *Folda*'s stem striking coaster *Reias* at 0050 13/6: vessels swung clear and, leaving the escorts to attend to *Reias*, *Folda* ordered to resume station in convoy, her Master being unaware of the fate or identity of *Reias*, which sank; *Folda* sustained buckled stem bar, fractured hawse pipe and forecastle plates set in on both port and starboard sides   Gold 13/6
Temporary repairs effected at Southampton on return
- Southampton 2/7   Solent 4/7 ETC26W   Sword 4/7
- Southampton 16/7   Solent 17/7 ETC39W   Gold 17/7
- Harwich 27/7; ammunition   Thames 28/7 ETC51   Juno 29/7
- Harwich 9/8; ammunition   Thames 11/8 ETC65

Convoy diverted to Solent; left 13/8   Arromanches 13/8
- Harwich 25/8; ammunition   Thames 26/8 ETC80   Juno 27/8

Returned to Harwich 1/9 to load ammunition for Dieppe

Reaching Normandy on 10th June 1944, with 1,000 tons of stores from London, *Flathouse* was accorded the privilege of being the first coaster to discharge inside the prefabricated Mulberry harbour at Arromanches. [*National Maritime Museum, P22618*]

In the darkness of her first outbound crossing to Normandy, *Folda* had the misfortune to ram and sink the returning coaster *Reias* on 13th June 1944. [*Author's collection*]

FORELAND 1,870/39 British (Shipping & Coal) – taken up 23/4/44 for Stores
• London (Royal Albert) 2/6; 1,258 tons; small fire broke out in No 2 hold while ship anchored in Thames 2/6; left Thames 5/6

	Solent 8/6 ETC3W	Sword 9/6
• London 22/6	Thames 24/6 ETC17	Juno 25/6
• London 8/7	Thames 9/7 ETC32	Juno 10/7
• London 23/7	Thames 24/7 ETC47	Arromanches 25/7
• London (Millwall) 12/8	Thames 13/8 ETC67	Juno 14/8

Returned to London 23/8 to load for Caen

After leaving Berth 24 in London's Royal Albert Dock, the stores coaster *Foreland* was directed to Erith Reach as her anchorage position, until being ordered to leave the Thames for her first voyage to Normandy. *[National Maritime Museum, P22630]*

FREEMAN HATCH 1,793/43 British, ex-US (MoWT/*Cory) – taken up 5/44 for Stores
• Barry 9/6	BC 11/6 EBC8	Omaha 14/6
• Barry 1/7; cased petrol	BC 2/7 EBC29	Omaha 4/7

Dragging of anchor resulted in collision with coaster *Greyfriars* 7/7
• Barry 23/7	BC 23/7 EBC50	Omaha 25/7
• Barry 12/8	BC 13/8 EBC71	

Called Falmouth 14-15/8 to tow lighter for Cherbourg
	joined EBC72	Utah 16/8
• Barry 31/8	BC 31/8 EBC89	

Convoy sheltered in Weymouth Bay; left 3/9 — Utah 3/9
Returned to Swansea 17/9

FYLLA 792/06 British, ex-Danish (MoWT/*Duncan) – taken up 4/44 for Ammunition
• Swansea 2/6; ammunition and 65 troops
	BC 5/6 EBC2Y	US area 8/6
• Newport 20/6	BC 23/6 EBC20	Omaha 25/6
• Avonmouth 11/7	BC 12/7 EBC39	Utah 14/7
• Cardiff 31/7	BC 1/8 EBC59	

Straggled and put into Dartmouth; left 3/8
	Solent 5/8 EBC60W	Omaha 5/8

Did not commence discharge until 22/8; returned to Harwich 30/8 to load for Dieppe

GALACUM 585/15 British (Derwent/*Anthony & Bainbridge) – taken up 22/4/44 for Ammunition
• London (Tilbury Jetty) 31/5; 618 tons; left Thames 31/5; embarked 39 troops in Solent
	Solent 6/6 EWC1B	Gold 7/6
• Southampton 3/7	Solent 4/7 ETC26W	Sword 4/7
• Southampton 13/7	Solent 14/7 ETC36W	Gold 14/7

Returned to Southampton 19/7 and Tyne 3/8; surveyed at South Shields 16/8 for damage caused by grounding and by landing craft bumping alongside between 7/6 and 18/7

GARESFIELD 2,168/24 British (Consett Iron/*Dickinson) – taken up 1/5/44 for Stores
• London (King George V); 35 vehicles, 140 troops
	Thames 5/6 ETC2Z	British area 7/6
• London 25/6	Thames 26/6 ETC19	Sword 27/6

Arrived London 3/7 with bottom damage from beaching
• London 10/7	Thames 11/7 ETC34	Gold 12/7
• Grimsby 4/8	Thames 7/8 ETC61	Arromanches 8/8

Returned to London 14/8 to load for Arromanches

Garesfield began her Normandy sailings in June 1944 loaded with vehicles and troops, continued it by carrying cross-Channel stores, was transporting engine assemblies from Caen to London in February 1945, then was used as a collier. *[National Maritime Museum, P10423]*

GASTON MICARD 982/17 Norwegian – taken up 9/5/44 for Stores
Assigned to load vehicles at Swansea for early convoys to US area but, at short notice, not used
• Fowey 28/6; ammunition	joined EBC24	Omaha 29/6
• Fowey 8/7; ammunition	joined EBC34	US area 9/7
• Fowey 19/7; ammunition	joined EBC45	Omaha 20/7
• Plymouth 10/8	joined EBC67	US area 11/8
• Cardiff 27/8	BC 28/8 EBC86	Cherbourg 30/8

Returned to Barry 7/9 to load for Cherbourg

GATESHEAD 744/19 British (Tyne-Tees) – taken up 9/4/44 for Stores
• London (Royal Albert) 4/6; 283 tons
	Thames 7/6 ETC22	Sword 8/6
• Plymouth 17/6; cased petrol	joined EBC13	Omaha 18/6

| • Southampton 24/6 | Solent 25/6 EBC20W | Omaha 25/6 |
| • Plymouth 2/7 | joined EBC29 | Utah 4/7 |

Arrived Plymouth 7/7 with two shell plates holed, others indented, counter plates buckled and torn and bulwark plating damaged; temporary repairs effected at Devonport

• Plymouth 21/7; with barge in tow	joined EBC48	Utah 23/7
• Fowey 1/8; ammunition	joined EBC58	Omaha 2/8
• Fowey 12/8; ammunition	joined EBC69	US area 13/8
• Fowey 21/8; ammunition	Solent 24/8 EBC78W	US area 24/8

Returned to Fowey 6/9 and Belfast (Albert Quay) 10/9 to load for US area

GEM 640/24 British (Robertson) – 19/4/44 for Ammunition

• Penarth 13/5; called Portishead 13-30/5; left BC 30/5; embarked 65 troops in Solent

	Solent 6/6 EWC1A	Utah 7/6
• Southampton 17/6	Solent 17/6 ETC11W	Port-en-Bessin 17/6
• Southampton 1/7	Solent 1/7 ETC23W	Port-en-Bessin 1/7
• Southampton 15/7	Solent 16/7 ETC38W	Gold 16/7
• Southampton 26/7	Solent 26/7 ETC48W	Gold 26/7
• Southampton 3/8	Solent 3/8 ETC56W	Arromanches 3/8

Returned to Solent, where stowaway found on board 7/8

• Southampton 10/8	Solent 10/8 ETC63W	Port-en-Bessin 10/8
• Southampton 17/8	Solent 17/8 ETC70W	Port-en-Bessin 17/8
• Southampton 24/8	Solent 25/8 ETC78W	British area 25/8

Returned to Southampton 28/8 to load for Arromanches

GIRONDE 1,770/20 Belgian – taken up 7/5/44 for Stores

| • Avonmouth 9/6 | BC 10/6 EBC7 | Utah 13/6 |

On return passage, struck on starboard bow by unknown ship 0137 26/6; arrived Barry 27/6

• Barry 2/7	BC 3/7 EBC30	Utah 5/7
• Cardiff 23/7	BC 24/7 EBC51	Utah 26/7
• Avonmouth 29/8	BC 30/8 EBC88	US area 1/9

Returned to Newport 15/9

GLADONIA 360/39 British (Wharton) – taken up 30/3/44 for Cased Petrol

• London (Purfleet) 30/5; 345 tons; left Thames 31/5; embarked 42 troops in Solent

| | Solent 6/6 EWC1B | Sword 7/6 |
| • Southampton 20/6 | Solent 22/6 ETC15W | |

On leaving Solent, vessel holed in the stern when rammed by tanker *British Princess* 0230 22/6; turned back for temporary repairs

	Solent 26/6 ETC18W	Port-en-Bessin 26/6
• Southampton 6/7	Solent 7/7 ETC29W	Sword 7/7
• Southampton 16/7	Solent 17/7 ETC39W	Port-en-Bessin 17/7
• Southampton 21/7	Solent 22/7 ETC44W	Gold 22/7
• Plymouth 29/7	joined EBC56	Omaha 31/7
• Plymouth 8/8	joined EBC66	US area 10/8
• Plymouth 19/8	joined EBC77	

Convoy sheltered in Solent; left 23/8

| | | Utah 23/8 |

Returned to Plymouth 27/8 for repairs and to load for US area

GLAMIS 555/36 British (Dundee, Perth & London) – taken up 8/4/44 for Cased Petrol

• London (King George V) 14/5; 524 tons; in Thames, motor barge, out of control with steering and engine trouble, dented ship's starboard side 1245 16/5 and another barge gave vessel glancing blow also on starboard side 0800 25/5

| | Thames 7/6 ETC22 | Juno 8/6 |

Vessel touched bottom at anchorage and was involved in collision with a landing craft 8-10/6

• London (Purfleet) 17/6	Thames 18/6 ETC13	Juno 19/6
• London (Purfleet) 30/6	Thames 30/6 ETC23	Juno 1/7
• London 6/7	Thames 7/7 ETC30	Gold 8/7
• London 14/7	Thames 15/7 ETC38	Sword 16/7
• London 24/7	Thames 25/7 ETC48	Arromanches 26/7
• London 31/7	Thames 1/8 ETC55	Arromanches 2/8
• London 10/8	Thames 11/8 ETC65	

Convoy diverted to Solent; left 13/8

| | | Arromanches 13/8 |
| • Southampton 22/8 | Solent 22/8 ETC75W | British area 22/8 |

Coaster *Soborg* collided with vessel's port quarter 0030 25/8; returned to Southampton 29/8 to load bridging equipment for Caen

Transporting Army stores from Avonmouth, *Gironde* was one of four Belgian pre-loaders for Normandy: those four were joined by two others in the equally important build-up phase of the operation. *[National Maritime Museum, P22821]*

Glanton and 33 other coasters were assembled at anchor off the Mumbles, near Swansea, on 4th June 1944, awaiting the order to sail for Normandy. *[National Maritime Museum, P22826]*

GLANTON 2,822/29 British (Sharp) – taken up 4/5/44 for Stores
- Swansea 3/6; vehicles and troops BC 5/6 EBC2Z   Omaha 8/6
- Grimsby 24/6   Thames 26/6 ETC19   Sword 27/6
- Grimsby 14/7   Thames 16/7 ETC39   Gold 17/7
- Hull 17/8   Thames 19/8 ETC73   Arromanches 20/8

Returned to Hull 3/9 to load for Arromanches

GLEN 471/35 British (Tyne-Tees) – taken up 30/3/44 for Stores
- London (Royal Albert) 7/6; 222 tons
                                      Thames 8/6 ETC4

Convoy heavily attacked in English Channel by E-boats 10/6   Port-en-Bessin 10/6
- Southampton 14/6   Solent 15/6 ETC9W   Juno 15/6
- Southampton 22/6   Solent 23/6 EWC2B   Port-en-Bessin 23/6
- Southampton 7/7   Solent 8/7 ETC30W   Port-en-Bessin 8/7
- Southampton 23/7   Solent 24/7 ETC46W   Port-en-Bessin 24/7
- Southampton 30/7   Solent 31/7 ETC53W   Port-en-Bessin 31/7
- Southampton 7/8   Solent 8/8 ETC61W   Port-en-Bessin 8/8
- Southampton 17/8   Solent 18/8 ETC71W   Port-en-Bessin 18/8
- Southampton 23/8   Solent 24/8 ETC77W   Arromanches 24/8

Returned to Southampton 2/9 to load for Dieppe

GLEN GAIRN 904/22 British (Brook/*Comben Longstaff) – taken up 4/44 for Stores
- London 11/6   Thames 12/6 ETC8   Gold 14/6
- Southampton 27/6   Solent 28/6 EBC23W   Omaha 28/6
- Southampton 14/7   Solent 15/7 EBC40W

Whilst leaving Solent, unidentified US Liberty ship (in Southampton-bound nine-vessel convoy FPM4) observed right ahead; course altered but ship failed to swing clear and collision resulted; other vessel's starboard side twisted *Glen Gairn's* stem bar to starboard 0110 15/7   Utah 15/7
- Southampton 22/7   Solent 23/7 EBC48W   Omaha 23/7
- Southampton 8/8   Solent 9/8 EBC65W   US area 9/8
- Southampton 17/8   Solent 18/8 EBC74W   US area 18/8

Returned to Barry 3/9 to load for US area

GLENDINNING 1,927/21 British (Gibson) – taken up 1/5/44 for Stores
- London (Royal Albert); 35 vehicles and 140 troops
                                      Thames 5/6 ETC2Z   British area 7/6
- Portsmouth; 35 vehicles and troops Solent 11/6 ETC6W   Gold 12/6
- Portsmouth; 35 vehicles and troops Solent 16/6 ETC10W   Sword 16/6
- London 29/6   Thames 30/6 ETC23   Gold 1/7

Lost. Whilst returning at 2156 5/7, hit between No 2 hatch and bridge by torpedo from *U-953*; stern rose high in the air and vessel sank in 30 minutes

GLENGARRIFF 868/36 British (Kelly/*Clint) – taken up 27/4/44 for Ammunition
- London (Tilbury) 31/5; 389 tons ammunition and stores; left Thames 31/5; embarked 78 troops in Solent   Solent 5/6 Force L1   Sword 6/6 (D-Day)
- London (Tilbury Jetty) 13/6   Thames 13/6 ETC9   Juno 15/6
- London (Tilbury Jetty) 24/6   Thames 26/6 ETC19
Turned back with defects 26/6   Thames 27/6 ETC20   Gold 28/6
- London (Tilbury)   Thames 8/7 ETC31   Juno 9/7
- London (Tilbury Jetty)   Thames 21/7 ETC44   Juno 22/7

- London (Tilbury) 30/7   Thames 31/7 ETC54   Arromanches 1/8
- London (Tilbury) 15/8   Thames 16/8 ETC70   Juno 17/8

Returned to London (Tilbury) 21/8 to load for Arromanches

GOLDFINCH 454/37 British (General Steam) – taken up 27/4/44 for Cased Petrol
- Plymouth 11/6   joined ECM4   Utah 12/6
- Plymouth 21/6
Sheltered at Dartmouth   joined EBC17   Omaha 24/6
- Plymouth 29/6   joined EBC25   Utah 30/6
- Plymouth 8/7   joined EBC34   Utah 9/7
- Plymouth 14/7   joined EBC41
Put into Solent   Solent 18/7 EBC43W   Utah 18/7
- Plymouth 25/7 with barge in tow   joined EBC51   Isigny 26/7
- London 5/8   Thames 6/8 ETC60   Port-en-Bessin 7/8
- Southampton 22/8   Solent 23/8 ETC76W

Convoy turned back to Solent; left 24/8   Juno 24/8

Returned to Southampton 30/8 to load bridging equipment for Arromanches

GRANBY 2,051/22 Canadian – taken up 5/44 for Stores
- London (Royal Albert) 4/6; 35 vehicles and 140 troops
                                      Thames 5/6 ETC2Z   British area 7/6
- London 12/6   Thames 14/6 ETC9   Gold 15/6
- London 1/7

Sustained damage to bulwarks, deck and port side of bridge when struck by unknown vessel in Thames 0200 2/7   Thames 2/7 ETC25   Gold 3/7

Returned to London 9/7; temporarily released for major repairs; planned Harwich loading cancelled

GRANFOSS 1,461/13 Norwegian – taken up 9/5/44 for Stores
- Barry 8/6   BC 9/6 EBC6   Omaha 12/6
- Port Talbot 10/7   BC 11/7 EBC38   Utah 13/7
- Southampton 24/7   Solent 25/7 ETC47W   Gold 25/7
- London 7/8   Thames 8/8 ETC62   Arromanches 9/8
- London 19/8   Thames 20/8 ETC74   Arromanches 21/8

Returned to London 29/8 to load for Arromanches

Scheduled to commence loading at London on 16th June 1944 for her second crossing to Normandy, the Norwegian stores ship *Granfoss*, seen here in the Mersey, was so seriously delayed at the beachhead after her first arrival that the London voyage was cancelled. *[National Maritime Museum, P22862]*

GRANGETOFT 975/20 British (Toft/*Donking) – taken up 14/4/44 for Ammunition

• Portishead 6/6; left BC 7/6	Solent 11/6 EBC6W	Utah 12/6

Bottom damaged whilst beached during the storm; vessel became stranded 20/6-6/7; drydocked at Swansea for repairs 9-13/7

• Swansea 18/7	BC 19/7 EBC46	Omaha 21/7
• Plymouth 9/8	joined EBC66	US area 10/8
• Plymouth 25/8	joined EBC82	Omaha 26/8

Returned to Plymouth 6/9 to load coal for Granville

GRASLIN 2,323/24 British, ex-French (MoWT/*Dawson) – taken up 5/44 for Stores

• Swansea 3/6; vehicles and troops BC 5/6 EBC2Z		Utah 8/6

On return, lost port anchor and 15 fathoms of cable 2230 14/6, then experienced difficulties with port boiler 2359 14/6; arrived Tyne 5/7; temporarily released for substantial boiler repairs

Graslin had been re-registered at Cardiff for war service under the Red Ensign: she was one of 13 ships of French origin which ultimately took part in the liberation of their country. *[National Maritime Museum, P22863]*

GRENAA 1,262/17 British, ex-Danish (MoWT/*Stone & Rolfe) – taken up 4/44 for Ammunition

• Newport 1/6	BC 9/6 EBC6	Omaha 12/6

Vessel hit the ground several times at beachhead 14/6 and 16/6

• Newport 1/7	BC 2/7 EBC29	Utah 4/7
• Sharpness 18/7	BC 19/7 EBC46	St Vaast 21/7
• Portishead 11/8	BC 12/8 EBC70	Omaha 14/8
• Cardiff 28/8	BC 28/8 EBC86	St Vaast 30/8

Returned to Portishead 11/9 to load for St Vaast

GRETA FORCE 914/28 British (West Coast/*Kennaugh) – taken up 19/4/44 for Stores

• Cardiff 2/6; left BC 5/6	Solent 9/6 EBC4W	Omaha 10/6
• Southampton 22/6; 673 tons	Solent 23/6 EBC16W	Omaha 23/6
• Southampton 30/6	Solent 1/7 EBC26W	Omaha 1/7
• Southampton 9/7	Solent 10/7 EBC35W	
Turned back due bad weather	Solent 11/7 EBC36W	Omaha 11/7
• Southampton 18/7	Solent 19/7 EBC44W	Isigny 19/7

• Plymouth 4/8	joined EBC61	
Convoy diverted to Solent; left 6/8		St Vaast 6/8
• Fowey 24/8	joined EBC81	St Vaast 25/8

Returned to Plymouth 6/9 to load coal for Cherbourg

GREYFRIARS 1,142/23 British (Newbigin) – taken up 13/5/44 for Ammunition

Assigned to load vehicles at Swansea for early convoys to US area but, at short notice, not used; caused slight damage to coaster *Kenrix* whilst berthing at Southampton 16/6

• Southampton 22/6; 1,200 tons	Solent 23/6 EBC16W	Omaha 23/6
• Southampton 4/7	Solent 5/7 EBC30W	Omaha 5/7

Handrails damaged in collision with coaster *Freeman Hatch* when latter dragged anchor 7/7

• Fowey 19/7	joined EBC45	Omaha 20/7

Whilst beached, sustained heavy pounding in high wind 20/7; No 2 tank, starboard side, damaged, floors buckled and mud found in tanks

• Fowey 30/7	joined EBC56	Omaha 31/7
• Harwich 16/8	Thames 17/8 ETC71	Arromanches 18/8

Returned to Harwich 27/8 to load for Dieppe

GUDRUN MAERSK 2,294/37 British, ex-Danish (MoWT/*Brocklebank) – taken up 5/44 for Cased Petrol

• Port Talbot 14/6	BC 16/6 EBC13	Omaha 18/6

Whilst at anchor during the storm, starboard bow sharply indented when run into by HM landing craft *LCT753* 1530 19/6; vessel grounded in heavy swell 22/6, required tug assistance

• Swansea 8/7	BC 9/7 EBC36	Omaha 11/7
• Swansea 25/7	BC 26/7 EBC53	Omaha 28/7

Constant bumping by US landing craft *LCT542*, during discharge of heavy cargo, damaged ship's stern 4/8

• Newport 18/8	BC 19/8 EBC77	
Convoy sheltered in Solent: left 23/8		Utah 23/8

Poor handling of tug towing cargo lighter at beachhead caused three severe indentations in vessel's side 29/8; left the beachhead 1/9 for release for voyage to Australia

A veteran of the 1942 invasion of North Africa and the 1943 landings in Sicily, *Gudrun Maersk* was detached from the Normandy invasion fleet in September 1944 to prepare for a voyage to Australia. *[Captain J. F. van Puyvelde]*

GUERNSEY QUEEN 567/39 British (British Channel Islands) – taken up 20/4/44 for Cased Petrol

• London (Purfleet); 480 tons; left Thames 8/6		
	Solent 11/6 ETC6W	Sword 12/6
• London 18/6	Thames 20/6 ETC15	
Convoy sheltered in Solent; left 22/6		Gold 22/6
• London	Thames 1/7 ETC24	Gold 2/7
• London 10/7	Thames 10/7 ETC33	Juno 11/7
• Harwich 21/7; ammunition	Thames 22/7 ETC45	Juno 23/7
• London 29/7	Thames 30/7 ETC53	Arromanches 31/7
• London 6/8	Thames 7/8 ETC61	Arromanches 8/8
• London 16/8	Thames 17/8 ETC71	Arromanches 18/8
• Southampton 26/8	Solent 27/8 ETC80W	Arromanches 27/8

Returned to Southampton 1/9 to load for Caen

GUN 670/18 Norwegian – taken up 8/5/44 for Ammunition

• Penarth 1/6; left BC 2/6	Solent 8/6 EBC3W	Utah 9/6
• Fowey 24/6; 665 tons	joined EBC20	Utah 25/6
• Fowey 5/7	joined EBC31	Utah 6/7
• Fowey 15/7	joined EBC41	Omaha 16/7
• Fowey 23/7	joined EBC49	Utah 24/7
• Fowey 10/8	joined EBC67	US area 11/8

Returned to Fowey 20/8 for repairs, before loading in BC for US area

GURDEN GATES 1,791/43 British, ex-US (MoWT/*France, Fenwick) – taken up 5/44 for Stores

• Grimsby 25/5; 1,116 tons; called London 27/5-8/6		
	Thames 9/6 ETC5	Sword 11/6

Ship shaken when beachhead subjected to artillery fire and/or heavy air attacks 11-13/6 and 15/6
• London (Tilbury) 23/6; ammunition Thames 24/6 ETC17
Whilst transitting Strait of Dover on passage to Gold, long-range shell exploded 30ft to port 1520 24/6; fire broke out fore and aft, which extinguished by crew; accommodation severely damaged, port side holed, derricks, rafts, lifeboats, Oerlikon gun and balloon gear damaged; one crew member killed and four wounded, latter transferred ashore at Dungeness; vessel diverted for cargo discharge and repairs; arrived Southampton 1/7

• Southampton 22/7	Solent 23/7 EBC48W	Omaha 23/7

Life raft smashed during cargo discharge 29/7
• Grimsby 8/8; on departure, starboard bow dented against quayside due to an HM trawler fouling fairway 0915 8/8   Thames 10/8 ETC64   Arromanches 11/8
Returned to Sunderland 18/8; on arrival at Hull to load coal collided with bunkering barge, whilst backing down dock with two tugs in attendance in gale-force conditions 2030 31/8; next outward voyage to Dieppe on 3/9 prolonged by need to put into Dover 6-12/9 to clear fouled propeller

GWENTHILLS 868/37 British (British Channel Traders) – taken up 7/4/44 for Ammunition

• London (Tilbury) 3/6; 1,070 tons	Thames 5/6 ETC2Y	British area 7/6
• London (Tilbury) 23/6	Thames 24/6 ETC17	Gold 25/6
• London (Tilbury) 3/7	Thames 4/7 ETC27	Gold 5/7
• London 12/7	Thames 13/7 ETC36	Juno 14/7

• London (Tilbury) 24/7	Thames 25/7 ETC48	Arromanches 26/7
• London (Tilbury) 11/8	Thames 12/8 ETC66	Juno 13/8

Returned to London (Tilbury) 18/8 to load for Arromanches

HAARLEM 970/17 British (Strubin) – taken up 13/5/44 for Stores

• London 27/6	Thames 28/6 ETC21	Juno 29/6
• London 12/7	Thames 12/7 ETC35	

Owing to condenser trouble, ship had difficulty in maintaining convoy speed

		Juno 13/7
• Harwich 25/7; ammunition	Thames 26/7 ETC49	

Detached to Solent with bilges full and stokehold awash 27/7

	Solent 30/7 ETC52W	Juno 30/7

Returned to London 4/8, then Tyne 17/8 for release 27/9

HALO 2,365/19 British (*Stephenson Clarke) – taken up 1/5/44 for Stores

• Grimsby 25/5; 1,447 tons; called London 27/5-8/6		
	Thames 9/6 ETC5	Gold 11/6
• Grimsby 24/6	Thames 27/6 ETC20	Gold 28/6
• Harwich 13/7	Thames 14/7 ETC37	Gold 15/7
• Grimsby 1/8	Thames 3/8 ETC57	Arromanches 4/8
• London (Tilbury) 29/8	Thames 30/8 ETC84	Arromanches 31/8

Returned to Grimsby 9/9 to load coal for Cherbourg
(Vessel sunk by enemy action 23/1/45: see Section 4)

HARPTREE COMBE 439/12 British (Ohlson) – taken up 8/4/44 for Ammunition

• Penarth 4/6; left BC 6/6	Solent 10/6 EBC5W	Utah 11/6
• Plymouth 24/6; cased petrol	joined EBC20	Utah 25/6
• Plymouth 1/7; cased petrol	joined EBC27	Omaha 2/7
• Plymouth 10/7	joined EBC36	Isigny 11/7

Went aground entering Isigny 1700 12/7; refloated 0400 13/7 but grounded again under tow with rudder pressed heavily into bank of the waterway 0515 13/7; whilst discharging cargo, forestay to mainmast carried away, weight imposed caused mast to split at foot 0550 14/7; returned to Plymouth 17/7 for repairs 29/7-12/8

• Plymouth 14/8	joined EBC71	US area 15/8
• Southampton 28/8	Solent 29/8 EBC85W	US area 29/8

Returned to Solent 3/9 to load at Southampton for US area

HAWARDEN BRIDGE 297/40 British (Summers) – taken up 3/44 for Cased Petrol

• Sharpness 30/5; left BC 30/5; embarked 44 troops in Solent		
	Solent 6/6 EWC1A	Utah 7/6
• Southampton 13/6	Solent 13/6 ETC8W	Juno 14/6
• Southampton 21/6	Solent 22/6 ETC15W	Gold 22/6
• Southampton 27/6	Solent 28/6 ETC20W	Sword 28/6
• Southampton 3/7	Solent 4/7 ETC26W	Juno 4/7
• Southampton 10/7	Solent 11/7 ETC33W	Juno 11/7

Assigned to French coastal ferry service from ocean-going store ships: returned to Solent 15/8

• Southampton 17/8	Solent 18/8 ETC71W	Arromanches 18/8
• Southampton 23/8	Solent 23/8 ETC76W	

Convoy turned back to Solent; left 24/8

		Arromanches 24/8
• Southampton 28/8	Solent 29/8 ETC82W	Arromanches 29/8

Returned to Newhaven 3/9 to load ammunition for Dieppe

HEIEN 995/26 Norwegian – taken up 9/4/44 for Ammunition
• Penarth 30/5; ammunition and stores; left BC 30/5; embarked 99 troops in Solent

	Solent 5/6 Force O3	
	then U3	Utah 6/6 (D-Day)
• Swansea	BC 18/6 EBC15	Utah 20/6
• Penarth	BC 5/7 EBC32	Utah 7/7
• Penarth	BC 19/7 EBC46	Omaha 21/7
• Portishead 4/8	BC 5/8 EBC63	US area 7/8
• Southampton 19/8	Solent 20/8 EBC76W	US area 20/8

Returned to Southampton 30/8 to load for US area

HEIRE 807/17 Norwegian – taken up 3/5/44 for Ammunition

• London (Tilbury) 9/6; 982 tons	Thames 10/6 ETC6	Juno 12/6

After return to Swansea, in slight collision with coaster *Majorca* 1850 22/6

• Swansea; 1,410 tons	BC 24/6 EBC21	Omaha 26/6
• Portishead 10/7	BC 11/7 EBC38	Utah 13/7
• Sharpness 24/7; 678 tons dismantled huts		
	BC 28/7 EBC55	Utah 30/7
• Plymouth 31/8; stores	joined EBC88	
Detached to Solent	Solent 8/9 EBC95W	US area 8/9

Returned to Plymouth 15/9 and Portishead 20/9

After arrival at Juno beachhead on 12th June 1944, cargo discharge time for the Norwegian *Heire*'s 982 tons of ammunition was 49 hours, enabling the achievement of a satisfactory 11-day round voyage. [Captain J. F. van Puyvelde]

HELDER 979/20 British (Williamstown/*Comben Longstaff) – taken up 23/4/44 for Ammunition

• Portishead 8/6	BC 9/6 EBC6	Utah 12/6

Beachhead subjected to heavy air raids 12-14/6

• Falmouth 5/7	joined EBC32	
Detached to Weymouth; left 7/7	joined EBC33	Utah 8/7
• Portishead 26/7	BC 27/7 EBC54	
Detached to Weymouth Bay 29/7; left 2/8		
	joined EBC58	Omaha 2/8
• Portishead 17/8	BC 18/8 EBC76	
Detached to Falmouth for repairs; left 24/8		
	joined EBC81	Grandcamp 25/8

HELMOND 983/21 British (Strubin) – taken up 2/5/44 for Ammunition

• Newport 8/6	BC 9/6 EBC6	

Turned back to Barry Roads with boiler problems

	BC 11/6 EBC8	

Steering gear jammed 0200-0300 13/6   Omaha 14/6
Left beachhead 15/6; arrived BC 26/6 in tow; required lengthy repairs at Newport

Boiler and steering gear defects were responsible for *Helmond*'s first voyage to Normandy also being her last: on return, the need for at least three months' repairs prompted her release. [National Maritime Museum, P10669]

HENRI GERLINGER 1,219/06 Belgian – taken up 18/5/44 for Cased Petrol
• Sharpness 27/5; called Barry, left 2/6

	BC 9/6 EBC6	Utah 12/6
• Southampton 18/7	Solent 19/7 ETC41W	Juno 19/7
• Harwich 3/8; ammunition	Thames 4/8 ETC58	Juno 5/8
• Harwich 31/8; ammunition	Thames 1/9 ETC86	
Put into Shoreham	joined ETC88	Juno 5/9

Returned to London 16/9 to load for Caen

HERBERT W WALKER 365/21 British (Wilson/*Dixon) – taken up 19/4/44 for Ammunition

• London (Tilbury Jetty) 4/6; 290 tons; left Thames 7/6		
	Solent 9/6 ETC4W	

Convoy heavily attacked in English Channel by E-boats 10/6   Gold 10/6

• Littlehampton 16/6	Solent 17/6 ETC11W	Sword 17/6

Dragged anchor in the storm and grounded 0330-0500 19/6; returned to Littlehampton 25/6 making water, so withdrawn for repairs at Newhaven

• Littlehampton 15/7	joined ETC38	Juno 16/7
• Littlehampton 23/7	joined ETC46	Juno 24/7
• Southampton 29/7	Solent 30/7 ETC52W	British area 30/7
• Southampton 4/8	Solent 5/8 ETC58W	Port-en-Bessin 5/8
• Southampton 9/8	Solent 10/8 ETC63W	British area 10/8
• Southampton 17/8	Solent 18/8 ETC71W	Arromanches 18/8
• Southampton 25/8	Solent 26/8 ETC79W	Port-en-Bessin 26/8

Returned to Southampton 3/9 to load express cargo and mail for Dieppe

HERON 279/38 Dutch – taken up 7/44 for Stores

• Southampton 31/7	Solent 1/8 ETC54W	Arromanches 1/8

Assigned to French coastal ferry service: returned 8/9 to load coal at Penzance for St Brieuc

HETTON 2,714/24 British (Hudson) – taken up 16/4/44 for Stores
• London (Tilbury) 11/6   Thames 12/6 ETC8   Gold 14/6
• London 5/7   Thames 6/7 ETC29   Juno 7/7
Sustained grounding damage to side and bottom plating 7/7; returned to London 17/7, then left 28/7 for survey at North Shields and release 28/9

The 2,714 gross ton collier *Hetton* managed only two crossings to Normandy before grounding damage caused her premature release. [National Maritime Museum, P22941]

HIGHWEAR 1,173/36 British (High Hook) – taken up 5/4/44 for Ammunition
• Newport 8/6   BC 9/6 EBC6   Omaha 12/6
Touched bottom aft when anchors dragged during the storm 19/6; grounded when starboard cable parted, with vessel becoming entangled aft with wreckage and several landing craft 0640 20/6; in an attempt to get into deeper water, dragging of anchor resulted in vessel striking a wreck on shore, then drifting well up the beach athwartships to tide after both cables parted 2030 20/6; No 1 hold filled with water and heavy seas broke over vessel; hull holed starboard side forward; rudder and stern frame missing; propeller damaged and fouled with wire and numerous plates fractured and buckled; towed off beach to anchorage by tugs *Algorma*, *Bannock* and *Swivel* 8/7; arrived Solent 19/7; arrived Thames 27/7 in tow of tug *Kiowa*; subsequently moved to Tyne for preliminary survey at South Shields, which revealed repairs required to 90 shell plates, as well as to framing and rudder

HILDUR I 1,497/19 Norwegian – taken up 18/5/44 for Cased Petrol
• Sharpness 10/6   BC 12/6 EBC9   Omaha 15/6
• Sharpness 2/7   BC 3/7 EBC30   Utah 5/7
• Port Talbot 15/7   BC 15/7 EBC42   Omaha 17/7
• Barry 31/7   BC 31/7 EBC58   Utah 2/8
• Sharpness 17/8   BC 18/8 EBC76   US area 20/8
Returned initially to BC, then arrived on Mersey 1/9 for release for Mediterranean service 22/9

HOLBURN HEAD 489/25 British (Henry & MacGregor) – taken up 13/4/44 for Stores
• London (Royal Albert) 31/5; 275 tons; left Thames 31/5; embarked 52 troops in Solent   Solent 6/6 EWC1B   Sword 7/6
• Southampton 18/6   Solent 19/6 EBC14W   Utah 19/6
• Southampton 27/6   Solent 28/6 EBC23W   Omaha 28/6

Temporary repairs required after HM minesweeper *Sidmouth*, in berthing alongside at Southampton, struck vessel's starboard side abaft the bridge 0845 4/7
• Southampton 5/7   Solent 6/7 EBC31W   Isigny 6/7
Bumped bottom, when arriving Isigny 2320 6/7; starboard side holed by barges bumping beneath stern at beachhead; temporary repairs carried out after return to Plymouth 11/7
• Plymouth 15/7   joined EBC41   Utah 16/7
• Poole 24/7; cased petrol   Solent 25/7 ETC47W   Gold 25/7
• Southampton 1/8; in Solent, starboard bow holed by towed barge 2305 1/8
          Solent 2/8 ETC55W   Port-en-Bessin 2/8
At low water, bilge keel found to be damaged starboard side 5/8
• Southampton 9/8   Solent 10/8 ETC63W   Port-en-Bessin 10/8
• Southampton 15/8   Solent 16/8 ETC69W   Port-en-Bessin 16/8
Coaster *Dorrien Rose*, in mooring alongside at Port-en-Bessin, flattened part of vessel's starboard side bulwark 16/8
• Southampton 24/8; turned back; left 25/8
          Solent 26/8 ETC79W   Arromanches 26/8
Returned to Southampton 31/8 to load for Arromanches

HONDSRUG 227/37 Dutch – taken up 8/44 for Stores
• Southampton 24/8   Solent 25/8 EBC81W   US area 25/8

HOVE 435/13 British (Coppack) – taken up 13/5/44 for Stores
• Southampton 12/6   Solent 12/6 ETC7W   Gold 13/6
• Southampton 23/6   Solent 24/6 ETC16W   Port-en-Bessin 24/6
• Southampton 1/7   Solent 2/7 ETC24W   Gold 2/7
• Southampton 6/7   Solent 7/7 ETC29W   British area 7/7
• Southampton 11/7   Solent 12/7 ETC34W   Gold 12/7
• Southampton 17/7   Solent 18/7 ETC40W   Gold 18/7
Returned to Southampton 22/7 with 27 tons of miscellaneous cargo
• Southampton 28/7   Solent 29/7 EBC54W   Utah 29/7
• Southampton 7/8   Solent 8/8 EBC64W   US area 8/8
• Southampton 17/8   Solent 18/8 EBC74W   US area 18/8
• Southampton 28/8   Solent 29/8 EBC85W   US area 29/8
Returned to Southampton 6/9 to load for US area

IPSWICH TRADER 484/22 British (Horlock) – taken up 7/4/44 for Stores
• London (King George V) 26/5; 290 tons; left Thames 31/5; embarked 40 troops in Solent   Solent 6/6 EWC1B   Gold 7/6
• Southampton 13/6   Solent 13/6 ETC8W   Port-en-Bessin 14/6
• Southampton 18/6   Solent 19/6 ETC13W   Port-en-Bessin 19/6
• Southampton 24/6   Solent 25/6 ETC17W   Gold 25/6
• Southampton 30/6   Solent 1/7 ETC23W   Gold 1/7
• Southampton 6/7   Solent 7/7 ETC29W   Port-en-Bessin 7/7
Returned to Southampton 10/7, then to Grimsby for repairs
• Southampton 29/8   Solent 30/8 ETC83W   Arromanches 30/8
Returned to Southampton 8/9 to load for Arromanches

ISAC 2,385/26 British, ex-French (MoWT/*Ambrose, Davies & Matthews**) – taken up 5/44 for Stores
• Port Talbot 2/6; vehicles and troops BC 5/6 EBC2Z   Omaha 8/6
• London (King George V) 19/6   Thames 23/6 ETC16   Arromanches 24/6

Having loaded 290 tons of stores at Berth 9 in London's King George V Dock, *Ipswich Trader* later embarked 40 troops in the Solent. [Harry Stewart/J. and M. Clarkson collection]

On 10th October 1944, new cross-Channel designators were introduced and the formerly French stores carrier *Isac* left the Thames as a participant in convoy TMC1. [National Maritime Museum, P23004]

• Grimsby 12/7	Thames 15/7 ETC38	Arromanches 16/7
• London (Millwall) 30/7	Thames 31/7 ETC54	Juno 1/8
• London (Millwall) 15/8	Thames 16/8 ETC70	Arromanches 17/8
• London (Millwall) 31/8	Thames 1/9 ETC86	Arromanches 2/9

Returned to London (Millwall) 18/9 to load for British area

ISBJORN 597/07 Norwegian – taken up 5/5/44 for Ammunition

• Newport 1/6; left BC 8/6	Solent 12/6 EBC7W	Omaha 13/6
• Newhaven 23/6	joined ETC16	Port-en-Bessin 24/6
• Newhaven 1/7	joined ETC24	Gold 2/7
• Newhaven 10/7	joined ETC33	Gold 11/7
• Newhaven 18/7	joined ETC41	Juno 19/7
• Southampton 6/8	Solent 7/8 EBC63W	US area 7/8
• Southampton 20/8	Solent 24/8 EBC78W	US area 24/8

Returned to Southampton 31/8 to load for Isigny

J F V 515/09 British (Tom) – taken up 1/5/44 for Stores

• Southampton 15/6	Solent 16/6 ETC10W	Juno 16/6
• Southampton 22/6	Solent 23/6 EWC2B	Sword 23/6
• Southampton 5/7	Solent 6/7 ETC28W	Gold 6/7
• Southampton 13/7	Solent 14/7 ETC36W	Juno 14/7
• Southampton 24/7	Solent 25/7 EBC50W	Utah 25/7
• Southampton 2/8	Solent 4/8 EBC59W	Omaha 4/8
• Southampton 11/8	Solent 12/8 EBC68W	US area 12/8
• Southampton 23/8	Solent 23/8 ETC76W	

Convoy turned back to Solent; left 24/8   British area 24/8
Returned to Southampton 2/9 to load for US area

JADE 930/38 British (Robertson) – taken up 26/4/44 for Cased Petrol

• Port Talbot 4/6; left BC 7/6	Solent 10/6 EBC5W	Omaha 11/6
• Sharpness 21/6	BC 23/6 EBC20	Omaha 25/6

On departure from beachhead, collided with coaster *Edina* 28/6

• Sharpness 11/7	BC 12/7 EBC39	Omaha 14/7
• Cardiff 4/8	BC 5/8 EBC63	St Vaast 7/8
• Plymouth 24/8	joined EBC81	St Vaast 25/8

Returned to Plymouth 10/9 to load for St Vaast

JAN BRONS 400/39 Dutch – taken up 8/6/44 for Cased Petrol

• Poole 25/6	Solent 26/6 EBC21W	Utah 26/6
• Poole 2/7	Solent 3/7 EBC28W	Utah 3/7
• Poole 22/7	Solent 23/7 EBC48W	Omaha 23/7
• Plymouth 28/8	joined EBC85	US area 29/8

Returned to Plymouth 8/9 to load for US area

JARGOON 691/26 British (Robertson) – taken up 21/4/44 for Ammunition

• Swansea 1/6; left BC 2/6; embarked 65 troops in Solent		
	Solent 7/6 EBC2W	Omaha 8/6
• London (Tilbury) 23/6	Thames 25/6 ETC18	Gold 26/6
• London (King George V) 3/7	Thames 4/7 ETC27	Gold 5/7
• London 14/7	Thames 15/7 ETC38	Juno 16/7
• Newhaven 22/7	joined ETC45	Juno 23/7
• Newhaven 31/7	joined ETC54	Arromanches 1/8
• Newhaven 9/8	joined ETC63	Arromanches 10/8
• Newhaven 15/8	joined ETC69	Arromanches 16/8
• Newhaven 23/8	joined ETC77	Arromanches 24/8

Returned to Newhaven 30/8 to load for Arromanches

JELLICOE ROSE 1,118/20 British (Hughes) – taken up 12/4/44 for Stores
• Grimsby 20/5; 679 tons; called London

                        Thames 7/6 ETC22   Gold 8/6

On return to Southampton, collided with US Liberty ship *George G Crawford* 20/6
• Southampton 23/6   Solent 24/6 EBC17W   Omaha 24/6

Shell plates set up when finally beaching 12/7; returned to Leith 12/8, then arrived Harwich 31/8 to load ammunition for Dieppe

JERNFJELD 1,369/17 Norwegian – taken up 30/4/44 for Ammunition
• Newport 10/6   BC 11/6 EBC8   Utah 14/6

Beached and damaged during the 19-22/6 storm; required repairs on return
• Sharpness 26/7   BC 27/7 EBC54   Omaha 29/7

Returned to Thames 9/8, subsequently to load for Arromanches

JERNLAND 1,289/05 Norwegian – taken up -/44 for Stores
• London (Millwall) 4/6; 28 vehicles and 112 troops

	Thames 5/6 ETC2Z	British area 7/6

• Portsmouth; 35 vehicles and troops

	Solent 11/6 ETC6W	Gold 12/6

• London 25/6; ammunition Thames 26/6 ETC19 Gold 27/6
• London 8/7 Thames 9/7 ETC32 Juno 10/7
• Grimsby 29/7; left Thames 2/8 to anchor in Solent

	Solent 12/8 EBC68W	Cherbourg 12/8

• Grimsby 31/8 Thames 7/9 ETC91 Arromanches 8/9
Returned to London 18/9

JESSE G COTTING 1,791/43 British, ex-US (MoWT/*Lawson) – taken up 4/44 for Stores
• Barry 3/6; stores and 104 troops   BC 5/6 EBC2Y   Omaha 8/6
In collision with a landing craft whilst discharging at beachhead 14/6
• Cardiff 23/6; 1,076 tons   BC 24/6 EBC21   Utah 26/6
• Port Talbot 7/7   BC 8/7 EBC35   Omaha 10/7
On return in thick fog off Swansea, damaged above water-line by starboard anchor of coaster *Theseus* 0947 16/7; arrived Barry Roads 1355 16/7
• Port Talbot 3/8   BC 5/8 EBC63
Called Falmouth to tow lighter for Cherbourg; left 7/8

	joined EBC64	Utah 8/8

• Swansea 18/8   BC 19/8 EBC77
Called Dartmouth for medical assistance; left 21/8

	joined EBC78

Convoy diverted to Solent; left 24/8   Utah 24/8
Returned to Swansea, then arrived Cardiff 5/9 to load for US area

Immediately following the cessation of hostilities in Europe, the US-built *Jesse G Cotting* left Immingham bound for the north German port of Lubeck. *[National Maritime Museum, P23042]*

JIM 833/08 British (Strubin) – taken up 1/5/44 for Ammunition
• London (Tilbury Jetty) 7/6; 840 tons; left Thames 8/6

	Solent 12/6 ETC7W	Juno 13/6
• Southampton 20/6	Solent 23/6 EWL15	Gold 23/6
• Southampton 5/7	Solent 7/7 ETC29W	Sword 7/7
• Southampton 26/7	Solent 27/7 ETC49W	Gold 27/7
• Southampton 3/8	Solent 4/8 ETC57W	Arromanches 4/8

• Southampton 9/8	Solent 11/8 ETC64W	Arromanches 11/8
• Southampton 16/8	Solent 17/8 ETC70W	Arromanches 17/8
• Southampton 23/8	Solent 25/8 ETC78W	Arromanches 25/8

Returned to Southampton 29/8 to load for Arromanches
(Vessel sunk by enemy action 30/3/45: see Section 4)

JOFFRE ROSE 715/15 British (Hughes) – taken up 21/4/44 for Stores
• Avonmouth 28/5; departure delayed by crew shortage after four men went ashore without permission; called Portishead, left 1/6; left BC 2/6; embarked 23 troops in

Solent	Solent 7/6 EBC2W	Utah 8/6
• Southampton 22/6	Solent 24/6 ETC16W	Sword 24/6
• Southampton 9/7	Solent 10/7 ETC32W	Juno 10/7

Arrived Southampton 17/7 with leaking forecastle
• Fowey 31/7; ammunition   joined EBC57   Omaha 1/8
Conditions too rough for cargo discharge at anchorage, so beached 3/8
• Belfast 13/8; left Milford Haven 15/8

	joined EBC73	Isigny 17/8

Collided with channel bank on leaving Isigny stern first in strong NE wind 1300 22/8; returned via Fowey to Belfast 28/8 to load for Omaha

JOLA 269/35 Dutch – taken up 7/44 for Stores
• Southampton 20/7   Solent 21/7 ETC43W   Gold 21/7
Assigned to French coastal ferry service
• Southampton 24/8   Solent 25/8 ETC78W   Arromanches 25/8
Returned to Solent 9/9 to load coal at Torquay for St Brieuc

JOSEWYN 1,926/19 British (Dillwyn) – taken up 4/5/44 for Stores

• Swansea 3/6; vehicles and troops BC 5/6 EBC2Z	Omaha 8/6
• Swansea 17/6	BC 18/6 EBC15	Omaha 20/6
• Swansea 5/7	BC 6/7 EBC33	Omaha 8/7
• Swansea 18/7	BC 19/7 EBC46	Utah 21/7
• Barry 15/8	BC 16/8 EBC74	US area 18/8

Returned to Southampton 27/8 to load for Arromanches

Josewyn made five round voyages from the Bristol Channel with US military cargo, before being switched to Southampton to carry stores to the British Army. *[National Maritime Museum, P23074]*

JOSIAH P CRESSEY 1,791/43 British, ex-US (MoWT/*Tanfield) – taken up 4/44 for Stores

• Barry 3/6; stores and 104 troops	BC 5/6 EBC2Y	Omaha 8/6
• Grimsby 4/7	Thames 7/7 ETC30	Juno 8/7
• Grimsby 22/7	Thames 25/7 ETC48	Juno 26/7
• Grimsby 12/8	Thames 14/8 ETC68	Arromanches 15/8

Returned to Grimsby 25/8 to load for Arromanches

JULIA 549/07 Belgian – taken up 18/4/44 for Ammunition

• Swansea; ammunition and 65 troops	BC 5/6 EBC2Y	US area 8/6
• Southampton 23/6; 500 tons	Solent 24/6 EBC17W	Omaha 24/6
• Southampton 2/7	Solent 3/7 EBC28W	Omaha 3/7
• Southampton 7/8	Solent 8/8 EBC64W	US area 8/8
• Southampton 15/8	Solent 15/8 EBC72W	US area 16/8
• Southampton 29/8	Solent 30/8 EBC86W	Isigny 30/8

Returned to Solent 7/9, where in collision with coaster *Saint Bedan* 8/9, prior to loading at Plymouth for Cherbourg

The 1907 building date of *Julia* proved no handicap when carrying ammunition to the American sectors of Normandy. *[Photo GVM/Copyright Flor Van Otterdyk]*

JUNE 400/38 Dutch – taken up 20/5/44 for Cased Petrol

• Southampton 12/6	Solent 14/6 EBC9W	Utah 14/6
• Southampton 3/7	Solent 4/7 EBC29W	Utah 4/7
• Poole 11/7	Solent 12/7 EBC37W	Omaha 12/7
• Poole 30/7	Solent 31/7 EBC56W	Omaha 31/7

Returned to Southampton 9/8; moved to Poole 12/8, then towed to Southampton 30/8 by tug *Danube VI* for repairs

JUSTIN DOANE 1,791/43 British, ex-US (MoWT/*Cory) – taken up 4/44 for Stores

• Avonmouth 7/6	BC 8/6 EBC5	Utah 11/6

Air attack at beachhead 14/6; 30 US dock operating troops marooned on board for four days during the storm; vessel incorrectly ordered to return to BC by US authorities but diverted to Grimsby

• Grimsby 5/7	Thames 8/7 ETC31	Gold 9/7
• Grimsby 21/7	Thames 23/7 ETC46	Juno 24/7
• Grimsby 5/8	Thames 9/8 ETM58	Arromanches 10/8
• Grimsby 31/8	Thames 6/9 ETM72	Arromanches 7/9

Returned to London 15/9

JUTA 1,559/08 British, ex-Estonian (MoWT/*Tyne & Wear) – taken up 4/44 for Ammunition

• Swansea 3/6; vehicles and troops	BC 5/6 EBC2Z	Omaha 8/6
• Newport 23/6	BC 24/6 EBC21	Omaha 26/6
• Newport 8/7	BC 9/7 EBC36	
Put into Falmouth	joined EBC37	Omaha 12/7
• Swansea 23/7	BC 24/7 EBC51	Cherbourg 26/7
• Barry 5/8	BC 5/8 EBC63	Utah 7/8
• Newport 20/8	BC 23/8 EBC81	US area 25/8

Returned to Cardiff 7/9 to load for Cherbourg

KAIDA 510/02 British, ex-Estonian (MoWT/*Neil & Hannah) – taken up 4/44 for Ammunition

• London (Tilbury); 370 tons; left Thames 5/6; embarked 39 troops in Solent		
	Solent 7/6 ETC22W	Juno 8/6

Straggled from return coastal convoy; sheltered in Weymouth Bay 14/6; arrived Plymouth 17/6

• Plymouth 21/6; cased petrol		
Sheltered at Dartmouth 21-23/6	joined EBC17	Omaha 24/6
• Plymouth 5/7	joined EBC31	Utah 6/7
• Southampton 15/7	Solent 16/7 EBC41W	Omaha 16/7
• Southampton 31/7	Solent 1/8 EBC57W	Isigny 1/8

Rudder damaged whilst ship coming to anchor 3/8; grounded at Isigny owing to steering gear defect 1230 4/8; vessel badly strained at low water 4/8; rudder came into contact with channel bank whilst vessel under tow 2230 4/8; returned to Barry in tow for rudder and engine repairs 21/8; operational again 18/9 but regarded as suitable only for coal shipments

KALEV 1,867/17 British, ex-Estonian (MoWT/*Tulley) – taken up 4/44 for Stores

• Barry 7/6	BC 8/6 EBC5	Omaha 11/6

Whilst discharging at anchor, sustained heavy damage port side amidships to shell plates, decks and frames when struck by coaster *Westburn* 1610 24/6; returned to Grimsby 30/6 for repairs

• Grimsby 18/7	Thames 20/7 ETC43	Gold 21/7
• Grimsby 3/8	Thames 7/8 ETC61	Arromanches 8/8
• Hull 25/8; coal	Thames 29/8 ETC83	Caen 30/8

Returned to London 14/9 to load for Dieppe

KATOWICE 1,995/25 Polish – taken up 12/5/44 for Ammunition

Shortly before sailing, ship's cook ordered ashore by naval authorities, as women not allowed on ships of the invasion fleet

• Swansea 3/6; vehicles, stores and 161 troops		
	BC 5/6 EBC2Z	Omaha 8/6
• Penarth	BC 23/6 EBC20	Omaha 25/6
• Penarth; cargo for Cherbourg	BC 14/7 EBC41	Omaha 16/7

Returned to Swansea 27/7 for repairs to amidships damage caused by collision with coaster *Munin* during outward voyage, when a tug and tow unexpectedly crossed ship's bow

• Swansea	BC 19/8 EBC77	

Convoy sheltered in Solent; left 23/8 | | Utah 23/8 |

Returned to Newport 11/9 to load for US area

The cook aboard *Katowice* was ordered ashore, just before the ship's first sailing, because women were not allowed on invasion ships. *[National Maritime Museum, P23105]*

KATWIJK 1,589/21 Dutch – taken up 5/5/44 for Stores
Assigned to load vehicles at Swansea for early convoys to US area but, at short notice, not used

• Barry 14/6	BC 17/6 EBC14	Omaha 19/6
• Barry	BC 10/7 EBC37	Utah 12/7
• Swansea 25/7	BC 25/7 EBC52	
Diverted to Solent	Solent 30/7 EBC55W	Utah 30/7
• Avonmouth 18/8	BC 19/8 EBC77	
Convoy sheltered in Solent; left 23/8		Utah 23/8

Returned to Port Talbot 7/9 to load for US area

The Dutch *Katwijk* was one of the vessels allocated to load vehicles at Swansea, until the US authorities changed their plans at short notice. *[National Maritime Museum, P23107]*

KENRIX 692/21 British (Rix) – taken up 29/4/44 for Stores
• London (Royal Albert) 30/5; 387 tons; left Thames 31/5; embarked 59 troops in Solent   Solent 6/6 EWC1B   Juno 7/6
• Southampton 16/6
At Southampton, struck by coaster *Greyfriars* which berthing 16/6
                            Solent 17/6 EBC12W   Omaha 17/6
Whilst at beachhead with both anchors down during the storm, propeller became fouled with wires 19/6 and vessel sprang leak due to pounding bottom heavily

19-22/6; propeller cleared after beaching 23/6; returned to Solent 24/6 with ship's pumps controlling inflow of water

• Southampton 5/7	Solent 6/7 EBC31W	Omaha 6/7
• Port Talbot 18/7	BC 19/7 EBC46	Isigny 21/7
• Newhaven 30/7; ammunition	joined ETC53	Arromanches 31/7
• Newhaven 6/8; ammunition	joined ETC60	Arromanches 7/8
• Newhaven 14/8; ammunition	joined ETC68	Arromanches 15/8
• Newhaven 25/8; ammunition	joined ETC79	Arromanches 26/8

Returned to Newhaven 1/9 to load ammunition for Dieppe

KENTISH COAST 459/38 British (Coast) – taken up 3/5/44 for Cased Petrol
• Sharpness 6/6; left BC 7/6   Solent 11/6 EBC6W   Utah 12/6
Ship's side dented by landing barge *LBV174* manoeuvring alongside 2130 13/6 and 1530 14/6
• Llanelly 23/6; 1,333 tons   BC 24/6 EBC21   Omaha 26/6
• Port Talbot 4/7   BC 5/7 EBC32   Omaha 7/7
• Llanelly 20/7; lubricating oil   BC 21/7 EBC48   Omaha 23/7
Arrived Bristol 30/7 to load potatoes but rejected due to possibility of taint from previous cargo
• Llanelly 5/8   BC 5/8 EBC63   Isigny 7/8
Briefly grounded on channel bank at Isigny 1420 9/8; developed heavy list to port after settling on base of quay wall which set up starboard bilge keel 1600 9/8
• Poole 19/8   Solent 20/8 EBC76W   US area 20/8
Port windlass brake carried away as a result of vessel pitching heavily at anchor 21/8
• Poole 28/8   Solent 29/8 EBC85W   Isigny 29/8
Returned to Poole 8/9 to load for US area

KEYNOR 1,806/14 Canadian – taken up 5/44 for Ammunition
• London (Royal Albert) 5/6; 35 vehicles and 140 troops
                            Thames 5/6 ETC2Z   British area 7/6
• London (Tilbury) 15/6   Thames 17/6 ETC12
Put into Solent   Solent 23/6 EWL15   Gold 23/6
• London 7/7   Thames 9/7 ETC32   Gold 10/7
Returned to London 19/7 and Rochester 29/7 for temporary release, until leaving Grimsby for Caen 29/9

Although the Canadian *Keynor* was released after only three crossings to Normandy, she re-entered service in late September 1944. *[National Maritime Museum, P23121]*

KIMBALL HARLOW 1,793/42 British, ex-US (MoWT/*Currie) – taken up 4/44 for Stores
- Barry 7/6   BC 8/6 EBC5   Omaha 11/6
- Grimsby 1/7   Thames 4/7 ETC27   Juno 5/7
- Hull 18/7; coal   Thames 25/7 ETC48   Cherbourg 26/7

Whilst at anchor at Cherbourg, starboard boat davit hit by US transport *Marine Eagle* 0638 2/8; returned to London; arrived Leith 17/8 for repairs, then loaded at Grimsby for Arromanches

KMICIC 1,894/23 Polish – taken up 10/5/44 for Ammunition
- Port Talbot 3/6; vehicles and troops BC 5/6 EBC2Z   Omaha 8/6
- Newport 17/6   BC 19/6 EBC16

Convoy sheltered in Poole Bay   Omaha 23/6
- Newport   BC 7/7 EBC34   Omaha 9/7
- Penarth   BC 22/7 EBC49   Omaha 24/7
- Penarth   BC 17/8 EBC75   Barfleur 19/8

Port quarter hit by coaster *Marx* at Barfleur 31/8; returned to Southampton 6/9 to load for Caen

KNOWLTON 2,068/22 Canadian – taken up 4/44 for Ammunition
- London (Millwall) 3/6; 35 vehicles and 140 troops
                                   Thames 5/6 ETC2Z   British area 7/6
- London (Tilbury) 15/6   Thames 16/6 ETC11   Sword 17/6

Crew member killed by field artillery shell explosion at beachhead 1400 24/6
- London 8/7   Thames 9/7 ETC32

Put into Solent   Solent 12/7 ETC34W   Port-en-Bessin 12/7

Returned to Thames 23/7 for release until 5/10

KOLSDAL 1,269/20 Norwegian – taken up 16/5/44 for Ammunition
- Newport 9/6   BC 10/6 EBC7   Omaha 13/6
- Cardiff   BC 4/7 EBC31   Utah 6/7
- Sharpness 23/7   BC 24/7 EBC51   Omaha 26/7
- Barry 6/8; 1,000 tons coal   BC 6/8 EBC64   Arromanches 8/8
- Newport 18/8   BC 19/8 EBC77

Convoy sheltered in Solent; left 23/8   Cherbourg 23/8

Returned to Newport 31/8 to load for Cherbourg

KONGSHAVN 751/06 Norwegian – taken up 15/4/44 for Stores
- London (Royal Albert) 6/6; 413 tons; left Thames 7/6
                                   Solent 10/6 ETC5W   Sword 11/6
- Newhaven 21/6; ammunition   joined ETC15

Convoy sheltered in Solent; left 22/6   Juno 22/6
- Newhaven 29/6; ammunition   joined ETC22   Gold 30/6
- Newhaven 9/7; ammunition   joined ETC31   Gold 9/7
- Newhaven 18/7; ammunition   joined ETC40   Sword 18/7

Returned to Solent 25/7, then left for Mersey; subsequently loaded stores at Southampton for Dieppe

KORDECKI 1,975/30 Polish – taken up 11/5/44 for Ammunition
- Swansea 3/6; vehicles and troops BC 5/6 EBC2Z   Utah 8/6
- Newport 25/6   BC 26/6 EBC23   Omaha 28/6
- Newport 14/7   BC 15/7 EBC42   Omaha 17/7

Eight Polish ships played their part in the invasion: the photograph shows *Kordecki*, which carried US vehicles and troops on her first voyage and ammunition on her subsequent crossings from Bristol Channel ports. *[National Maritime Museum, P23143]*

- Newport 28/7   BC 29/7 EBC56   Omaha 31/7
- Sharpness 23/8   BC 24/8 EBC82   Utah 26/8

Diverted to Omaha 2/9; commenced cargo discharge 4/9; returned to Solent 16/9

KRAKOW 2,017/26 Polish – taken up 9/5/44 for Stores
- Swansea 3/6; vehicles and troops BC 5/6 EBC2Z   Omaha 8/6
- Cardiff   BC 17/6 EBC14   Omaha 19/6

Developed engine room leak after both anchors continually dragged during the 19-22/6 storm
- Barry 3/7   BC 4/7 EBC31   Omaha 6/7

Owing to slow cargo discharge, only 100 tons landed by 26/7; return departure delayed until 2/8
- Swansea   BC 14/8 EBC72   US area 16/8

Returned to Swansea 31/8 to load for US area

KUL 1,310/07 Norwegian – taken up 7/4/44 for Ammunition
- London (Tilbury Jetty); 1,580 tons; left Thames 5/6
                                   Solent 8/6 ETC3W   British area 9/6
- London (Tilbury Jetty) 24/6   Thames 26/6 ETC19   Sword 27/6
- London 9/7   Thames 11/7 ETC34   Gold 12/7

Returned to London 18/7; surveyed at Great Yarmouth for shell plate damage, then released 27/8

KYLE CASTLE 845/19 British (Walton/*FL Dawson) – taken up 19/4/44 for Ammunition
- London (Tilbury) 31/5; 800 tons; left Thames 31/5; embarked 59 troops in Solent
                                   Solent 6/6 EWC1B   Gold 7/6
- Southampton 18/6   Solent 19/6 ETC13W   Sword 19/6
- Southampton 3/7   Solent 4/7 ETC26W   Gold 4/7
- Southampton 14/7   Solent 15/7 ETC37W   Gold 15/7
- Southampton 24/7   Solent 25/7 EBC50W   Omaha 25/7
- Fowey 6/8   joined EBC63   US area 7/8
- Fowey 16/8   joined EBC73   US area 17/8

Returned to Fowey 28/8, then arrived Cardiff 2/9 to load for US area

KYLE QUEEN 616/13 British (Walton/*FL Dawson) – taken up 4/44 for Ammunition
• London (Tilbury) 1/6; 674 tons; embarked 78 troops in Solent

	Solent 6/6 EWC1B	Juno 7/6
• Southampton 15/6	Solent 16/6 ETC10W	Sword 16/6
• Southampton 24/6	Solent 29/6 ETC21W	Juno 29/6
• Southampton 7/7	Solent 8/7 ETC30W	Gold 8/7
• Southampton 17/7	Solent 18/7 ETC40W	Gold 18/7
• Newhaven 25/7	joined ETC48	Juno 26/7
• Southampton 1/8	Solent 2/8 EBC58W	US area 2/8
• Penarth	BC 14/8 EBC72	US area 16/8

Returned to Solent 24/8

KYLEBANK 969/25 British (Kyle/*Monroe) – taken up 26/4/44 for Stores
• Barry 3/6; left BC 5/6 — Solent 9/6 EBC4W — Omaha 10/6
• Plymouth 19/6; cased petrol — joined EBC15 — Isigny 20/6
Bottom damaged by grounding whilst entering Isigny 1340 23/6; listed badly when tide receded
• Plymouth 5/7 — joined EBC31 — Omaha 6/7
• Plymouth 14/7 — joined EBC40 — Omaha 15/7
Returned to Plymouth 15/7 for temporary repairs 21/7-1/8
• Fowey 4/8; ammunition — joined EBC61
Put into Solent — Solent 8/8 EBC64W — US area 8/8
• Southampton 20/8 — Solent 23/8 EBC77W — St Vaast 23/8
Grounding on rocky bottom, when entering St Vaast 1830 29/8, caused serious leaks into engine room and after peak tank; returned for drydocking at Southampton 7-15/9, then loaded for US area

KYLEGORM 622/14 British (Walton/*FL Dawson) – taken up 24/4/44 for Ammunition
• London (Tilbury) 30/5; 688 tons; left Thames 31/5; embarked 53 troops in Solent

	Solent 6/6 EWC1B	Sword 7/6
• Southampton 17/6	Solent 18/6 ETC12W	Sword 18/6

In danger of sinking during the 19-22/6 storm until pumped out by *Sea Salvor* 22/6

• Southampton 14/7	Solent 15/7 ETC37W	Juno 15/7
• Southampton 21/7	Solent 22/7 ETC44W	Gold 22/7
• Southampton 29/7	Solent 30/7 ETC52W	Gold 30/7
• Southampton 4/8	Solent 5/8 ETC58W	Port-en-Bessin 5/8
• Southampton 12/8	Solent 13/8 ETC66W	Arromanches 13/8
• Southampton 21/8	Solent 22/8 ETC75W	Arromanches 22/8

Returned to Southampton 31/8 to load for Caen; subsequently deemed suitable only for coal and loaded at Plymouth for Granville

KYLOE 2,820/30 British (Sharp) – taken up 8/5/44 for Stores
• Swansea 3/6; vehicles and troops BC 5/6 EBC2Z — Omaha 8/6
• Barry 18/6 — BC 19/6 EBC16
Convoy sheltered in Poole Bay — Omaha 23/6
• Barry 13/7 — BC 14/7 EBC41
At 0125 16/7, collision occurred in fog five miles off Isle of Wight involving *Kyloe*, HM destroyer *Vanquisher* and coaster *The President*, latter northbound and drifting not under command; *Kyloe* struck *The President* on her starboard bow, with *Kyloe's* starboard anchor becoming so embedded in the other vessel that it had to be slipped

and lost, with 15 fathoms of cable, to enable *Kyloe* to manoeuvre clear; in the process of proceeding at 0155 16/7, *Kyloe's* port lifeboat fouled a gun on *The President*; voyage completed despite extensive bow damage — Omaha 16/7
Returned to Barry 20/8, then moved to Avonmouth to load for US area

Heading for Omaha in night fog on 16th July 1944, *Kyloe* became involved in a messy collision with returning coaster *The President*, temporarily not under command. [National Maritime Museum, P23158]

LABAN HOWES 1,793/43 British, ex-US (MoWT/*France, Fenwick) – taken up 4/44 for Stores
• Avonmouth 8/6 — BC 9/6 EBC6 — Utah 12/6
• Barry 24/6; 1,400 tons — BC 25/6 EBC22 — Omaha 27/6
Fire discovered in forecastle head store 1615 30/6; brought under control by 1830 same day
• Penarth 19/7 — BC 20/7 EBC47 — Omaha 22/7
• Penarth 8/8 — BC 9/8 EBC67
Called Falmouth 10-11/8 to tow barge for Cherbourg
— joined EBC68 — US area 12/8
Returned to Cardiff 25/8 to load for US area

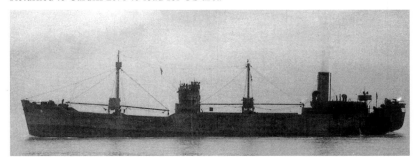

Most of the coasters carrying vehicles and drivers on their first crossing to Normandy were, like *Lambtonian*, afterwards employed as stores carriers. [National Maritime Museum, P23179]

LAMBTONIAN 2,781/42 British (Tanfield) – taken up 3/5/44 for Stores
• London (Royal Albert) 3/6; 45 vehicles and 140 troops

	Thames 5/6 ETC2Y	British area 7/6
• London 13/6	Thames 13/6 ETC9	Gold 15/6
• London (Tilbury) 29/6	Thames 30/6 ETC23	Gold 1/7
• London (Tilbury) 18/7	Thames 19/7 ETC42	Gold 20/7

Returned to London (Tilbury) 26/7 for release 17/8

LARCHFIELD 493/41 British (Zillah/*Savage) – taken up 29/4/44 for Ammunition

• Newport 7/6; left BC 8/6	Solent 12/6 EBC7W	Omaha 13/6
• Southampton 19/6	Solent 20/6 ETC14W	Gold 20/6

• Southampton 27/6; leaving berth, damaged port side lower bridge bulwarks when forced by strong wind under starboard quarter of coaster *Birker Force* 1930 27/6

	Solent 28/6 ETC20W	Gold 28/6
• Littlehampton 4/7	joined ETC26	Juno 4/7
• Southampton 10/7	Solent 11/7 ETC33W	Port-en-Bessin 11/7
• Southampton 17/7	Solent 19/7 ETC41W	Gold 19/7
• Southampton 27/7	Solent 28/7 ETC50W	Gold 28/7
• Southampton 1/8	Solent 2/8 ETC55W	Arromanches 2/8
• Southampton 6/8	Solent 7/8 ETC60W	Arromanches 7/8
• Southampton 11/8	Solent 12/8 ETC65W	Arromanches 12/8
• Southampton 16/8	Solent 17/8 ETC70W	Arromanches 17/8
• Southampton 21/8	Solent 22/8 ETC75W	Arromanches 22/8
• Southampton 26/8	Solent 27/8 ETC80W	Arromanches 27/8

Returned to Southampton 29/8 to load stores for Dieppe

LEKA 1,599/22 Norwegian – taken up 19/5/44 for Stores

• Barry 9/6	BC 11/6 EBC8	Omaha 14/6
• Barry 20/7	BC 20/7 EBC47	Omaha 22/7
• Swansea 4/8	BC 5/8 EBC63	

Called Falmouth to tow lighter for Cherbourg; left 7/8

	joined EBC64	Cherbourg 8/8
• Swansea 24/8	BC 24/8 EBC82	Omaha 26/8

Returned to Swansea 13/9

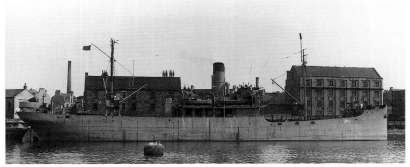

Still in military service, the Norwegian *Leka,* seen at Aberdeen, was switched in April 1945 from carrying US stores from Southampton to loading cement at Swanscombe on the Thames. *[National Maritime Museum, P23209]*

LEOVILLE 1,050/22 British, ex-French (MoWT/*Bennett) – taken up 4/44 for Stores

• London (King George V) 30/5; 510 tons; left Thames 31/5; embarked 59 troops in Solent

	Solent 6/6 EWC1B	Gold 7/6
• Southampton 25/6	Solent 26/6 EBC21W	

In convoy three miles S of Isle of Wight, starboard bow of unknown vessel, seen too late for collision to be averted, struck *Leoville's* port bow 0141 26/6

		Omaha 26/6

• Southampton 2/7; cased petrol	Solent 3/7 EBC28W	Omaha 3/7
• Southampton 11/7	Solent 12/7 EBC37W	Omaha 12/7
• Southampton 18/7; 600 tons ammunition		
	Solent 19/7 EBC44W	Omaha 19/7
• Southampton 28/7	Solent 29/7 ETC51W	Gold 29/7
• Newport 16/8	BC 17/8 EBC75	US area 19/8
• Southampton 31/8	Solent 1/9 ETC85W	Juno 1/9

Returned to Southampton 9/9 to load for Arromanches

LESTO 1,893/18 British (Pelton) – on return from Mediterranean, assigned 1/8/44 for Stores

• Grimsby 15/8	Thames 19/8 ETC73	Juno 20/8

Returned to Grimsby 29/8 to load engineering and general stores for Dieppe

LILIAN I 1,271/24 British, ex-Danish (MoWT/*JT Salvesen) – taken up 4/44 for Ammunition

• Portishead 6/6; ammunition and stores

	BC 7/6 EBC4	Omaha 10/6

In heavy swell, starboard side damaged by US landing craft *LCT541* 16/6 and port side by *LCT553* 17/6; vessel temporarily grounded 17/6

• Swansea 25/6	BC 26/6 EBC23	Omaha 28/6
• Swansea 18/7	BC 19/7 EBC46	Utah 21/7

On heaving in cable for departure, anchor lost 27/7

• Penarth 4/8	BC 5/8 EBC63	Omaha 7/8
• Portishead 20/8	BC 23/8 EBC81	Isigny 25/8

Returned to Penarth 17/9, subsequently to load at Barry for Utah

LILLEAA 921/22 British, ex-Danish (MoWT/*Dundee, Perth & London) – taken up 5/44 for Ammunition

• Plymouth 5/6; cargo from coaster *Valborg* (qv)

	joined EBC2Y	Utah 8/6

Whilst at anchor, bow hit by a US landing craft 2359 9/6

• Fowey 18/6; twice touched ground on leaving harbour 1330 18/6

	joined EBC15	Omaha 20/6

Nearby vessel, on refloating, damaged *Lilleaa's* starboard side engine ventilators 2359 23/6; on return, put into Falmouth where port lifeboat damaged in contact with US vessel 0400 10/7; left 11/7; arrived Sharpness 13/7

• Sharpness 28/7	BC 29/7 EBC46	Utah 31/7
• Southampton 2/8	Solent 5/8 EBC60W	Barfleur 5/8

At Barfleur, coaster *Fano* caught and distorted after davit of *Lilleaa's* port lifeboat 11/8

• Harwich 29/8	Thames 31/8 ETC85	Caen 1/9

Returned to Harwich to load for Arromanches

LOANDA 534/36 British (Evans) – taken up 28/3/44 for Cased Petrol

• Garston 29/5; called Swansea 30-31/5; embarked 65 troops at Swansea

	BC 5/6 EBC2Y	Omaha 8/6

• Port Talbot 20/6; lost starboard anchor whilst waiting in Swansea Bay 23/6

	BC 23/6 EBC20	Utah 25/6

On return, called Weymouth 30/6-7/7; arrived Port Talbot 9/7 for subsequent release; survey at Barry revealed eight indented shell plates and seven frames buckled as a result of beaching

LOCHEE 964/37 British (Dundee, Perth & London) – on return from
Mediterranean, assigned 17/8/44 for Cased Petrol
• Port Talbot 27/8 BC 28/8 EBC86
Off Portland, tanker *War Diwan*, approaching from astern, collided with ship's port
quarter, damaging lifeboat, bridge wing and Oerlikon gun mounting 0545 30/8
US area 30/8
Returned to London 16/9 to load for Dieppe

LOTTIE R 972/37 British (Stone & Rolfe) – taken up 1/4/44 for Cased Petrol
• Port Talbot 29/5; cased petrol and stores; left BC 30/5; embarked 121 troops in
Solent Solent 5/6 Force O3 Omaha 6/6 (D-Day)
• Port Talbot 16/6 BC 17/6 EBC14 Omaha 19/6
• Sharpness 2/7 BC 3/7 EBC30 Utah 5/7
• Plymouth 11/7 joined EBC37 Utah 12/7
• Llanelly 24/7 BC 24/7 EBC51 Omaha 26/7
• Southampton 13/8 Solent 13/8 EBC69W US area 13/8
• Southampton 24/8 Solent 25/8 EBC81W US area 25/8
Returned to Southampton 30/8 to load for US area

LOWESTOFT TRADER 311/34 British (Gt Yarmouth) – taken up 30/3/44 for
Cased Petrol
• Southampton 11/6 Solent 11/6 ETC6W Mulberry B 12/6
After return to Southampton, port quarter damaged by coaster *Antiquity* 2015 21/6
• Southampton 22/6 Solent 23/6 EWC2B Gold 23/6
• Southampton 29/6 Solent 30/6 ETC22W Juno 30/6
• Southampton 6/7 Solent 7/7 ETC29W Juno 7/7
At Southampton, starboard hull indented by balloon supply vessel coming
alongside 1630 13/7
• Southampton 13/7 Solent 14/7 ETC36W Gold 14/7
• Southampton 19/7 Solent 20/7 ETC42W Gold 20/7
• Poole 27/7 Solent 28/7 ETC50W Juno 28/7
• Southampton 4/8 Solent 5/8 ETC58W Arromanches 5/8
• Southampton 9/8 Solent 10/8 ETC63W Arromanches 10/8
• Southampton 14/8 Solent 15/8 ETC68W Arromanches 15/8
• Southampton 19/8 Solent 20/8 ETC73W Arromanches 20/8
• Southampton 25/8 Solent 26/8 ETC79W Port-en-Bessin 26/8
• Southampton 30/8 Solent 31/8 ETC84W
Turned back; left Southampton 31/8 Solent 1/9 ETC85W Port-en-Bessin 1/9
Returned to Southampton 6/9 to load for Dieppe

LYSAKER V 1,571/36 Norwegian – taken up -/44 for Cased Petrol
• London (King George V) 31/5; 1,736 tons
Thames 11/6 ETC7 Gold 13/6
• London 28/6 Thames 29/6 ETC22 Gold 30/6
Returned to Solent 5/7, prior to repairs at Newport
• Port Talbot 24/7 BC 25/7 EBC52 Utah 27/7
• Port Talbot 6/8 BC 7/8 EBC65 US area 9/8
• Port Talbot 19/8, left BC 20/8 Solent 24/8 EBC78W US area 24/8
Returned to Port Talbot 16/9

LYSLAND 1,335/07 Norwegian – taken up -/44 for Stores
• Swansea 3/6; vehicles and troops BC 5/6 EBC2Z Omaha 8/6
Allocated to load vehicles at Portsmouth but incorrectly routed to BC by US authorities

• Swansea 22/6 BC 23/6 EBC20 Omaha 25/6
• London 6/7 Thames 7/7 ETC30 Gold 8/7
• London (Tilbury) 18/7 Thames 19/7 ETC42 Gold 20/7
• Harwich 30/7; ammunition Thames 1/8 ETC55 Juno 2/8
• Harwich 21/8; ammunition Thames 22/8 ETC76
Convoy diverted to Solent; left 24/8 Juno 24/8
Returned to London 29/8 and arrived Grimsby 2/9 to load coal for Dieppe

Early in 1945, the Norwegian *Lysaker V* formed part of a 44-strong coaster
fleet assigned to carry stores from Southampton to the US Army on the
Continent. *[National Maritime Museum, P23286]*

MACVILLE 666/15 British (Western/*Scott) – taken up 11/5/44 for Ammunition
• Southampton 23/6 Solent 24/6 EBC17W Utah 24/6
• Southampton 4/7 Solent 5/7 EBC30W Omaha 5/7
• Southampton 12/7 Solent 13/7 EBC38W Omaha 13/7
• Southampton 21/7 Solent 22/7 ETC44W Gold 22/7
• Newhaven 29/7 joined ETC52 Arromanches 30/7
• Newhaven 6/8 joined ETC60 Arromanches 7/8
• Newhaven 13/8 joined ETC67 Arromanches 14/8
• Newhaven 23/8 joined ETC77 Arromanches 24/8
Returned to Newhaven 31/8 to load for Dieppe

MAJORCA 1,126/21 British (Currie) – taken up 28/4/44 for Ammunition
• Penarth 5/6 BC 7/6 EBC4 Utah 10/6
• Swansea 22/6; 1,173 tons; on departure, drifting across dock resulted in vessel's
port side rubbing along port side of coaster *Heire* 1850 22/6
BC 23/6 EBC20 Omaha 25/6
• Swansea 4/7 BC 5/7 EBC32 Omaha 7/7
• Swansea 16/7 BC 16/7 EBC43 Cherbourg 18/7
• Portishead 2/8 BC 2/8 EBC60
Convoy diverted to Solent; left 5/8; turned back
Solent 6/8 EBC61W US area 6/8
• Penarth 19/8 BC 20/8 EBC78
Straggled from convoy; called Plymouth 21/8-24/8
joined EBC81 Barfleur 25/8
Crew member, ashore without permission, shot and wounded by US Army sentry
2/9; vessel returned to Southampton 5/9 to load for St Vaast

MAKEFJELL 1,567/32 Norwegian – taken up 8/5/44 for Cased Petrol
• Port Talbot 8/6	BC 9/6 EBC6	Omaha 12/6
• Port Talbot 2/7	BC 2/7 EBC29	Utah 4/7
• Port Talbot 15/7	BC 15/7 EBC42	Omaha 17/7
• Port Talbot 31/7	BC 1/8 EBC59	
Convoy diverted to Solent; left 4/8		Omaha 4/8
• Port Talbot 13/8	BC 13/8 EBC71	US area 15/8

Returned to Mersey 2/9 for release for Mediterranean service 1/10

MAMMY 1,656/11 Norwegian – taken up 26/5/44 for Ammunition
• Portishead 5/6; ammunition and stores		
	BC 6/6 EBC3	Omaha 9/6
• Penarth	BC 2/7 EBC29	Omaha 4/7
• Penarth 16/7	BC 16/7 EBC43	Omaha 18/7
• Cardiff	BC 5/8 EBC63	US area 7/8
• Portishead 21/8	BC 23/8 EBC81	US area 25/8

Returned to Penarth 17/9

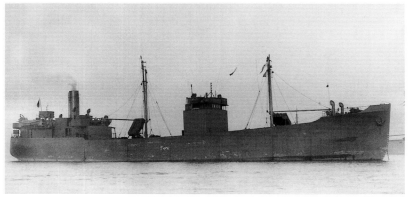

In August 1944, the Norwegian *Makefjell* left her base of Port Talbot for Normandy for the last time, prior to withdrawal for Mediterranean service. *[National Maritime Museum, P23313]*

MAPLEFIELD 492/41 British (Zillah/*Savage) – taken up 7/4/44 for Stores
• London (King George V) 8/6; 200 tons; left Thames 9/6		
	Solent 12/6 ETC7W	Gold 13/6
• Poole 24/6; cased petrol	Solent 25/6 EBC20W	Omaha 25/6
• Poole 1/7; cased petrol	Solent 2/7 EBC27W	Omaha 2/7
• Poole 6/7; cased petrol	Solent 7/7 EBC32W	Omaha 7/7
• Poole 13/7; cased petrol	Solent 14/7 EBC39W	Omaha 14/7
• Poole 18/7; cased petrol	Solent 20/7 EBC45W	Omaha 20/7
• Southampton 27/7	Solent 28/7 EBC53W	Utah 28/7
• Southampton 4/8	Solent 5/8 EBC60W	Barfleur 5/8
Stern post found to be bent over to starboard at Barfleur 14/8; returned 16/8		
• Southampton 25/8	Solent 26/8 EBC82W	Omaha 26/8

Returned to Solent 6/9

MARCEL 543/38 Belgian – taken up 24/4/44 for Cased Petrol
• London (King George V); 285 tons cased petrol and stores; left Thames 31/5;		
embarked 78 troops in Solent	Solent 5/6 Force L1	Sword 6/6 (D-Day)

• Southampton 11/6	Solent 11/6 ETC6W	Sword 12/6
• Southampton 21/7	Solent 22/7 ETC44W	British area 22/7
• Southampton 1/8	Solent 2/8 ETC55W	Arromanches 2/8

Returned to London 12/8 for subsequent release 12/10

MARGA 1,583/23 Norwegian – taken up 6/5/44 for Cased Petrol
• London (King George V) 26/5; 1,750 tons		
	Thames 10/6 ETC6	Gold 12/6
• Port Talbot 29/6	BC 29/6 EBC26	Omaha 1/7
• Portishead 15/7	BC 15/7 EBC42	Omaha 17/7
• Garston; left Mersey 4/8	BC 6/8 EBC64	US area 8/8
• Cardiff 18/8	BC 19/8 EBC77	
Convoy sheltered in Solent; left 23/8		Utah 23/8

Returned to Port Talbot 10/9 to load high octane fuel for Omaha

The Norwegian fleet is represented here by *Marga*, a cased petrol carrier: by far the largest non-British coaster contingent serving Normandy, the number of Norwegian coasters eventually grew to 44. *[National Maritime Museum, P23348]*

MARI 563/20-25 Norwegian – taken up 4/5/44 for Ammunition
• Swansea; ammunition and stores; left BC 30/5; embarked 42 troops in Solent		
	Solent 5/6 Force O3	Omaha 6/6 (D-Day)
• Fowey 18/6	joined EBC14	Omaha 19/6
• Fowey 29/6	joined EBC25	Utah 30/6
• Fowey 10/7	joined EBC36	Utah 11/7
• Fowey 23/7	joined EBC49	Utah 24/7
• Fowey 15/8, after repairs while loaded		
	joined EBC72	US area 16/8
• Plymouth 28/8	joined EBC85	US area 29/8

MARIANNE II 1,239/24 British, ex-Danish (MoWT/*Glen & Co) – taken up 5/44 for Ammunition
• Fowey 24/6; 1,300 tons	joined EBC20	Omaha 25/6
• Fowey 4/7	joined EBC30	Omaha 5/7
• Fowey 14/7	joined EBC40	Utah 15/7
• Fowey 27/7	joined EBC53	Omaha 28/7
• Penarth	BC 9/8 EBC67	US area 11/8
• Swansea 24/8	BC 24/8 EBC82	Cherbourg 26/8

Returned to Barry 16/9 to load coal for Granville

After loading ammunition and stores in Swansea's Prince of Wales Dock, the Norwegian coaster *Mari* was one of eight coasters to reach Omaha beachhead on D-Day (6th June 1944). *[Captain J. F. van Puyvelde]*

MARIE 1,409/24 Belgian – taken up 6/5/44 for Cased Petrol
• Sharpness 10/6	BC 12/6 EBC9	Omaha 15/6
• Sharpness 5/7	BC 7/7 EBC34	Utah 9/7
• Port Talbot 28/7	BC 28/7 EBC55	Omaha 30/7
• Port Talbot 10/8	BC 10/8 EBC68	US area 12/8
• Port Talbot 30/8	BC 31/8 EBC89	
Convoy sheltered in Weymouth Bay; left 3/9		US area 3/9
Returned to Port Talbot 14/9 to load for US area		

MARIE-FLORE 545/37 Belgian – taken up 12/6/44 for Stores
• Southampton 14/6	Solent 15/6 ETC9W	Gold 15/6
• Southampton 9/7	Solent 10/7 ETC32W	Port-en-Bessin 10/7
Returned to Southampton 18/7 with defective dynamos and winches		
• Southampton 26/7	Solent 27/7 EBC52W	Utah 27/7
• Southampton 5/8	Solent 6/8 EBC61W	US area 6/8
• Southampton 14/8	Solent 15/8 EBC71W	US area 15/8
Returned to Southampton 22/8		

Marie-Flore was one of only six Belgian coasters to supply the Allied forces in Normandy. *[Photo GVM/Copyright Flor Van Otterdyk]*

MARSDEN 2,874/24 British (Springfjord) – taken up 14/5/44 for Stores
• Port Talbot 15/6; 2,360 tons	BC 17/6 EBC14	Omaha 19/6
• Cardiff 8/7	BC 9/7 EBC36	Omaha 11/7
• Swansea 28/7	BC 29/7 EBC56	
Diverted to Solent; at anchor for over four weeks		
	Solent 28/8 EBC84W	Omaha 28/8
Returned to Grimsby 16/9 and Hull 19/9 to load for Cherbourg		

MARSWORTH 366/25 British (Grand Union) – taken up 2/5/44 for Stores
• Cardiff 7/6; left BC 8/6	Solent 12/6 EBC7W	Omaha 13/6
• Littlehampton 21/6	Solent 22/6 ETC15W	Gold 22/6
• Southampton 27/6	Solent 28/6 ETC20W	Gold 28/6
• Southampton 10/7	Solent 11/7 ETC33W	Port-en-Bessin 11/7
• Southampton 17/7	Solent 18/7 ETC40W	Gold 18/7
• Southampton 25/7	Solent 27/7 EBC52W	Barfleur 27/7
• Southampton 7/8	Solent 8/8 ETC61W	Port-en-Bessin 8/8
• Southampton 13/8	Solent 14/8 ETC67W	Port-en-Bessin 14/8
• Southampton 18/8	Solent 19/8 ETC72W	Arromanches 19/8
Returned to Southampton 22/8 and London 28/8		

MARX 1,259/24 British, ex-Danish (MoWT/*Dalgliesh) – taken up 5/44 for Ammunition
• Penarth 16/6; 1,600 tons	BC 17/6 EBC14	Utah 19/6
• Penarth 6/7	BC 7/7 EBC34	Omaha 9/7
• Portishead 3/8	BC 5/8 EBC63	US area 7/8
• Penarth 21/8	BC 23/8 EBC81	Barfleur 25/8
Commenced discharge in mid-harbour after grounding there; on refloating, collided with coaster *Kmicic* 31/8; returned to Newport 8/9 to load coal for Cherbourg		

MAURICE ROSE 1,600/30 British (Hughes) – taken up 28/5/44 for Stores
• London 23/6	Thames 24/6 ETC17	Juno 25/6
• London 7/7	Thames 7/7 ETC30	Sword 8/7
• Grimsby 22/7	Thames 24/7 ETC47	Arromanches 25/7
• Grimsby 9/8	Thames 12/8 ETC66	Juno 13/8
• Grimsby 30/8; anchored in Thames 1/9		
	Thames 7/9 ETC91	Arromanches 8/9

MELISSA 520/08 British (Alexander King) – taken up 16/6/44 for Stores
• Southampton 17/6	Solent 18/6 ETC12W	Gold 18/6
• Southampton 27/6	Solent 28/6 ETC20W	Gold 28/6
• Southampton 4/7	Solent 5/7 ETC27W	Port-en-Bessin 5/7
• Littlehampton 11/7; ammunition	joined ETC34	Juno 12/7
• Southampton 27/7; turned back; left 28/7		
	Solent 29/7 ETC51W	Port-en-Bessin 29/7
• Southampton 3/8	Solent 4/8 ETC57W	Arromanches 4/8
• Southampton 7/8	Solent 8/8 ETC61W	Arromanches 8/8
• Southampton 12/8	Solent 14/8 ETC67W	Port-en-Bessin 14/8
• Southampton 21/8	Solent 23/8 ETC76W	
Convoy turned back to Solent; left 24/8		Arromanches 24/8
• Southampton 30/8	Solent 31/8 ETC84W	Arromanches 31/8
Returned to Newhaven 3/9 to load ammunition for Dieppe		

At the end of November 1944, the port of Antwerp re-opened and *Maurice Rose* was one of the British coasters instructed to fly the Belgian ensign to mark the occasion. *[National Maritime Museum, P23404]*

MELITO 1,070/15 British (Bristol) – taken up 5/5/44 for Stores
• London (Royal Albert) 3/6; 36 vehicles and 140 troops
                         Thames 5/6 ETC2Y   British area 7/6
• Portsmouth 12/6; 35 vehicles and troops
                         Solent 13/6 ETC8W   Sword 14/6
Subjected to long-range gunfire during transit of Strait of Dover on return 19/6
• London 24/6   Thames 25/6 ETC18   Sword 26/6
Beachhead subjected to relentless field artillery fire 26/6
• London 3/7   Thames 4/7 ETC27   Gold 5/7
• Southampton 21/7   Solent 22/7 ETC44W   Juno 22/7
• Southampton 1/8   Solent 2/8 ETC55W   Port-en-Bessin 2/8
Whilst at anchor, sustained severe indentation of shell plating on port bow when struck by HM minesweeper *Gozo* 1945 4/8; starboard hawse pipe and shell plating damaged by port quarter of HM salvage vessel *Uplifter* 5/8; returned to Southampton 8/8 and BC 14/8

MR THERM 2,974/36 British (*Stephenson Clarke) – taken up 29/4/44 for Stores
• London (SW India) 3/6; 32 vehicles and 128 troops
                         Thames 5/6 ETC2Y   British area 7/6
On return to Thames 10/6, lost anchor and 15 fathoms of cable, which later recovered
• London 18/6   Thames 19/6 ETC14   Gold 20/6
Beaching during both visits to beachhead resulted in 57 shell plates being indented, with a further 45 affected by landing craft bumping alongside
• London 10/7   Thames 11/7 ETC34   Gold 12/7
Returned to London 18/7, prior to survey at South Shields and release 9/9

MOELFRE ROSE 631/31 British (Hughes) – taken up 8/4/44 for Ammunition
• Swansea 29/5; left BC 30/5; embarked 65 troops in Solent
                         Solent 6/6 EWC1A   Omaha 7/6
• Southampton 15/6   Solent 16/6 ETC10W   Gold 16/6
Damage sustained to vessel and to HM motor launch, when ship caught by high wind during the storm 1420 21/6, then two plates fractured when discharging into craft alongside in heavy swell 1630 same day
• Southampton 28/6   Solent 29/6 ETC21W   Juno 29/6
• Newhaven 7/7   joined ETC30   Gold 8/7
Whilst beached, shell plating on starboard quarter pierced above water-line when struck by barge 1540 9/7; two Army stowaways discovered in ship's stokehold 2015 10/7
• Southampton 17/7   Solent 18/7 ETC40W   Gold 18/7
Whilst beached, shell plating below water-line holed by US landing craft *LCT814* 1425 19/7
• Newhaven 24/7   joined ETC47   Gold 25/7
• Southampton 30/7   Solent 31/7 EBC56W   Utah 31/7
• Belfast 18/8   Solent 24/8 EBC78W   Cherbourg 24/8
Returned to Southampton 29/8 to load for St Vaast

MONKSTONE 867/23 British (Grace) – taken up 23/4/44 for Ammunition
• London (Tilbury); 442 tons ammunition and stores; left Thames 31/5; embarked 59 troops in Solent   Solent 5/6 Force L1   Sword 6/6 (D-Day)
• London 20/6   Thames 23/6 ETC16   Juno 24/6
• London 5/7   Thames 6/7 ETC29   Sword 7/7
• London 16/7   Thames 17/7 ETC40   Juno 18/7
• London 28/7   Thames 29/7 ETC52   Arromanches 30/7
• London 13/8   Thames 14/8 ETC68   Juno 15/8
Returned to London 20/8 to load for Dieppe

With a cargo of 442 tons of ammunition and stores from London (Tilbury), *Monkstone* arrived at Sword beachhead on D-Day (6th June 1944). [Captain J. F. van Puyvelde]

Monksville fared badly during the June 1944 storm, losing not only both anchors but also part of her mainmast. [J. and M. Clarkson collection]

MONKSVILLE 499/21 **British (Monks)** – taken up 6/4/44 for Ammunition
• Swansea; left BC 2/6; embarked 42 troops in Solent

	Solent 7/6 EBC2W	Omaha 8/6
• Fowey	joined EBC14	Utah 19/6

During the storm, starboard cable parted, losing anchor and 45 fathoms cable, 2345 19/6, then port anchor and 75 fathoms cable similarly lost 1410 20/6; topmast of mainmast broke 1500 20/6
At Fowey on return, two new anchors supplied, mainmast repaired and reshipped 28/6

• Fowey 29/6	joined EBC25	Utah 30/6
• Fowey 8/7	joined EBC34	

Straggled from convoy; put into Dartmouth, left 9/7

	joined EBC35	US area 10/7
• Fowey 20/7	joined EBC46	Omaha 21/7
• Southampton 2/8	Solent 3/8 ETC56W	Port-en-Bessin 3/8

In rough weather, vessel took ground heavily causing slight leak in port bilge 3/8

• Southampton 7/8	Solent 8/8 ETC61W	Arromanches 8/8
• Southampton 13/8	Solent 14/8 ETC67W	Port-en-Bessin 14/8
• Southampton 21/8	Solent 22/8 ETC75W	Port-en-Bessin 22/8
• Southampton 29/8	Solent 30/8 ETC83W	Arromanches 30/8

Returned to Southampton 11/9

MOORLANDS 420/21 **British (Taylor)** – taken up 10/4/44 for Stores
• London (Royal Albert) 2/6; 200 tons; left Thames 5/6; embarked 40 troops in Solent

	Solent 7/6 ETC22W	Juno 8/6
• Southampton 14/6	Solent 15/6 ETC9W	Gold 15/6
• Southampton 22/6	Solent 23/6 EWC2B	Gold 23/6
• Southampton 29/6	Solent 30/6 ETC22W	Gold 30/6
• Southampton 6/7	Solent 7/7 ETC29W	Juno 7/7
• Southampton 22/7	Solent 22/7 ETC44W	Gold 22/7
• Southampton 27/7	Solent 28/7 ETC50W	Gold 28/7
• Southampton 2/8	Solent 3/8 ETC56W	Port-en-Bessin 3/8
• Southampton 12/8	Solent 13/8 ETC66W	Arromanches 13/8

• Southampton 18/8	Solent 18/8 ETC71W	Arromanches 18/8
• Southampton 25/8	Solent 26/8 ETC79W	Arromanches 26/8

Returned to Southampton 30/8 to load for a voyage to Port-en-Bessin, during the course of which Master relieved of his command for being in a continuous state of intoxication since 1/8

MOSES GAY 1,791/43 **British, ex-US (MoWT/*France, Fenwick)** – taken up 4/44 for Stores

• Avonmouth 7/6	BC 8/6 EBC5	Utah 11/6
• Grimsby; left Humber 30/6	Thames 2/7 ETC25	Gold 3/7
• Grimsby 20/7	Thames 23/7 ETC46	Arromanches 24/7
• Grimsby 5/8	Thames 7/8 ETC61	Arromanches 8/8

Returned to London 17/8; subsequently loaded at Grimsby for Caen

MULAN 249/31 **Dutch** – taken up 7/44 for Stores

• Southampton 1/8	Solent 2/8 ETC55W	Port-en-Bessin 2/8

Assigned to French coastal ferry service; returned 8/9 to load coal for St Brieuc; arrived Penzance 11/9 with forepeak leaking

MUNIN 1,285/99 **Norwegian** – taken up 23/4/44 for Ammunition

• Newport 6/6	BC 7/6 EBC4	Omaha 10/6
• Barry 23/6; 1,529 tons	BC 24/6 EBC21	Omaha 26/6
• Penarth	BC 14/7 EBC41	

Collided with coaster *Katowice* on arrival off French coast Omaha 16/7

• Avonmouth 31/7	BC 1/8 EBC59	

Convoy diverted to Solent; left 4/8 Omaha 4/8

• Penarth	BC 23/8 EBC81	Barfleur 25/8

In collision with coaster *Corundum* at Barfleur 1120 3/9; returned to Cardiff 11/9

NAROCZ 1,795/15 **Polish** – taken up 14/5/44 for Stores
Assigned to load vehicles at Swansea for early convoys to US area but, at short notice, not used

• Cardiff 23/6; 784 tons	BC 24/6 EBC21	Omaha 26/6

• Portishead 19/7   BC 21/7 EBC48   Omaha 23/7
• Avonmouth 9/8   BC 9/8 EBC67
Called Falmouth to tow barge for Cherbourg; left 11/8
     joined EBC68   US area 12/8
Returned to Portishead 27/8, then moved to Swansea 5/9 to load coal for US area

NATO **399/39 Dutch** – taken up 18/5/44 for Cased Petrol
• Sharpness 6/6; left BC 8/6   Solent 12/6 EBC7W   Utah 13/6
• Poole 25/6   Solent 26/6 ETC18W   Juno 26/6
• Poole 2/7   Solent 3/7 ETC25W   Gold 3/7
• Poole 9/7   Solent 10/7 ETC32W   Gold 10/7
• Poole 16/7   Solent 17/7 ETC39W   Juno 17/7
• Poole 24/7   Solent 25/7 ETC47W   Gold 25/7
• Poole 30/7   Solent 31/7 ETC53W   Gold 31/7
• Poole 5/8   Solent 6/8 ETC59W   Port-en-Bessin 6/8
• Poole 13/8   Solent 14/8 ETC67W   Port-en-Bessin 14/8
• Poole 20/8   Solent 21/8 ETC74W   Port-en-Bessin 21/8
• Poole 29/8   Solent 30/8 ETC83W   Port-en-Bessin 30/8
Returned to Poole 3/9 to load for Port-en-Bessin

NAVIEDALE **383/06 British (Couper)** – taken up 22/4/44 for Ammunition
• London (Tilbury) 4/6; 280 tons; left Thames 5/6; embarked 39 troops in Solent
     Solent 7/6 ETC22W   Juno 8/6
• Littlehampton 14/6   Solent 15/6 ETC9W   Sword 15/6
• Littlehampton 19/6   joined ETC14   British area 20/6
• Newhaven 27/6   Solent 28/6 ETC20W   Arromanches 28/6
• Littlehampton 4/7   joined ETC27   Sword 5/7
• Littlehampton 10/7   joined ETC33   Juno 11/7
• Littlehampton 16/7   joined ETC39   Juno 17/7
• Littlehampton 21/7   joined ETC44   Juno 22/7
• Littlehampton 27/7   joined ETC50   Gold 28/7
After leaving beachhead, soldier surrendered as a stowaway 1700 30/7
• Littlehampton 1/8   joined ETC55   Juno 2/8
In return convoy, jamming of steering gear caused damage to starboard bow and lifeboat in collision with coaster *Fenja* 1140 6/8; at Southampton for repairs 6/8-16/8
• Littlehampton 20/8   joined ETC73   Arromanches 20/8
• Littlehampton 24/8   joined ETC78   Arromanches 25/8
Returned to Littlehampton 29/8, subsequently to load for Caen

NEPHRITE **927/27 British (Stephenson Clarke)** – taken up 24/4/44 for Stores
• London (Royal Albert); 550 tons; left Thames 5/6; embarked 58 troops in Solent
     Solent 7/6 ETC22W   Juno 8/6
• Southampton 21/6   Solent 23/6 EBC16W   Utah 23/6
• Southampton 5/7   Solent 6/7 EBC31W   Omaha 6/7
• Southampton 15/7; 1,000 tons ammunition
     Solent 16/7 EBC41W   Omaha 16/7
• Southampton 25/7   Solent 26/7 EBC51W   Utah 26/7
• Plymouth 6/8   joined EBC63   US area 7/8
• Plymouth 21/8   Solent 24/8 EBC78W   US area 24/8
Returned to Plymouth 30/8 to load for US area

Nephrite carried stores to the Normandy beaches, until becoming one of the first coasters to be routed to Le Havre after its opening in October. *[World Ship Society Ltd.]*

NESTTUN **1,271/17 Norwegian** – taken up 11/4/44 for Ammunition
• Penarth 11/6   BC 13/6 EBC10   Omaha 16/6
Settled on a mine at low water 17/6; with flooded after hold, vessel beached for cargo discharge; without a rudder, returned to Solent 17/7 towed by tug *LT152*; arrived in Thames 25/7 in tow of tug *Trinidad Head*, then left 27/7 for Tyne

After her first crossing, the Norwegian *Nesttun*, mine-damaged and rudderless, was at Normandy for a month before being towed back for repairs: the photo shows her in 1937. *[Captain J. F. van Puyvelde]*

NEWLANDS **1,556/21 British (Tulley)** – taken up 12/5/44 for Stores
• Swansea 3/6; vehicles and troops BC 5/6 EBC2Z   Omaha 8/6
• Penarth   BC 29/6 EBC26   Utah 1/7
• Sharpness 23/7   BC 24/7 EBC51   Omaha 26/7
• Grimsby 28/8   Thames 30/8 ETC84   Arromanches 31/8
Returned to London 10/9 to load bridging materials for Dieppe

NIVERNAIS 390/33 British, ex-French (MoWT/*Hull & Chicken) – taken up 3/44 for Cased Petrol
• London (Purfleet) 3/6; 240 tons; left Thames 5/6

	Solent 8/6 ETC3W	British area 9/6
• Southampton 14/6	Solent 15/6 ETC9W	Mulberry B 15/6
• Southampton 21/6; turned back with engine trouble; left 23/6		
	Solent 24/6 ETC16W	Gold 24/6
• Southampton 7/7	Solent 8/7 ETC30W	Sword 8/7
• Southampton 15/7	Solent 16/7 ETC38W	Juno 16/7
• Southampton 24/7	Solent 25/7 ETC47W	Port-en-Bessin 25/7
• Southampton 30/7	Solent 31/7 ETC53W	Arromanches 31/7
• Southampton 5/8	Solent 6/8 ETC59W	Arromanches 6/8
• Southampton 10/8	Solent 11/8 ETC64W	Arromanches 11/8
• Southampton 15/8	Solent 16/8 ETC69W	

Turned back for engine repairs; called Southampton 18-23/8

Solent 23/8 ETC76W	
Convoy turned back to Solent; left 24/8	Arromanches 24/8

Returned to Southampton 1/9

NJORD 374/39 Dutch – taken up 19/5/44 for Ammunition

• Newport 7/6; left BC 8/6	Solent 12/6 EBC7W	Omaha 13/6
• Southampton 22/6	Solent 23/6 EWC2B	Gold 23/6
• Southampton 1/7	Solent 2/7 ETC24W	Sword 2/7
• Southampton 8/7	Solent 9/7 ETC31W	Port-en-Bessin 9/7

Assigned to French coastal ferry service from ocean-going store ships; returned to Southampton 1/9

NORMANDY COAST 1,428/16 British (Coast) – taken up 6/4/44 for Cased Petrol
• Sharpness 27/5; called Avonmouth, left 5/6; left BC 7/6
Rocket projector on wheelhouse damaged, when guy carried away whilst bunkering from *Chemong* in Solent 2130 8/6

Solent 10/6 EBC5W	Utah 11/6

Hole torn in starboard hull when US landing craft *LCT532* came alongside 0830 14/6; vessel beached for 10 days; after being subjected to field artillery fire, moved to safer anchorage

• Port Talbot 28/6	BC 29/6 EBC26	Omaha 1/7
• Port Talbot 11/7	BC 12/7 EBC39	Omaha 14/7
• Port Talbot 26/7	BC 26/7 EBC53	Omaha 28/7
• Port Talbot 8/8	BC 9/8 EBC67	Utah 11/8

After beaching for cargo discharge, anchors and main engines failed to float vessel 1730 14/8-1110 15/8; finally refloated 0945 16/8 with aid of tug

• Port Talbot 25/8	BC 25/8 EBC83	Omaha 27/8

Returned to Southampton 6/9 to load for Omaha

NORTHGATE 429/41 British (Hull Gates) – taken up 25/4/44 for Cased Petrol
• London (King George V) 31/5; 256 tons cased petrol and stores; left Thames 31/5; embarked 78 troops in Solent

Solent 5/6 Force L1	Sword 6/6 (D-Day)

Whilst at anchor, attacked with three bombs, the nearest exploding 40ft from ship 2330 6/6

• Poole 10/6	Solent 11/6 ETM6W	Gold 12/6
• Poole 20/6	Solent 22/6 ETC15W	Gold 22/6
• Poole 27/6	Solent 29/6 ETC21W	Gold 29/6
• Poole 6/7	Solent 7/7 ETC29W	Gold 7/7
• Poole 12/7	Solent 13/7 ETC35W	Sword 13/7
• Poole 18/7	Solent 20/7 ETC42W	Gold 20/7
• Poole 26/7	Solent 28/7 ETC50W	Juno 28/7
• Poole 8/8	Solent 10/8 ETC63W	Port-en-Bessin 10/8
• Poole 17/8	Solent 18/8 ETC71W	Port-en-Bessin 18/8
• Poole 24/8	Solent 26/8 ETC79W	Port-en-Bessin 26/8

Returned to Poole 30/8 to load for Port-en-Bessin but next sailing delayed by engine trouble

Northgate was attacked with three bombs off the Normandy beaches on D-Day (6th June 1944) but was the first coaster to return. *[Fotoflite incorporating Skyfotos/J. and M. Clarkson collection]*

No fewer than 15 Robertson coasters were taken up for the Normandy invasion, including the 1913-built *Nugget*, a stores coaster until January 1945. *[World Ship Society Ltd.]*

NUGGET 515/13 British (Robertson) – taken up 27/4/44 for Stores

• Avonmouth 6/6; left BC 7/6	Solent 11/6 EBC6W	Utah 12/6
• Southampton 24/6	Solent 25/6 ETC17W	Gold 25/6
• Southampton 3/7	Solent 4/7 ETC26W	Port-en-Bessin 4/7
• Southampton 15/7	Solent 16/7 ETC38W	Juno 16/7
• Southampton 21/7	Solent 22/7 ETC44W	Gold 22/7
• Southampton 27/7	Solent 28/7 EBC53W	Omaha 28/7
• Southampton 5/8	Solent 6/8 EBC61W	US area 6/8
• Southampton 28/8	Solent 29/8 EBC85W	St Vaast 29/8

Returned to Southampton 6/9 to load for Barfleur

OBSIDIAN 811/22 British (Robertson) – taken up 21/4/44 for Stores

• Cardiff 2/6; stores and 65 troops	BC 5/6 EBC2Y	Omaha 8/6
• Plymouth 21/6; cased petrol		
Sheltered at Dartmouth 21-23/6	joined EBC20	Utah 25/6
• Plymouth 4/7; cased petrol	joined EBC30	Omaha 5/7
• Plymouth 12/7	joined EBC39	Utah 14/7
• Plymouth 21/7, after drydocking with cargo aboard		
	joined EBC47	Cherbourg 22/7
• Fowey 1/8; ammunition	joined EBC58	
Detached to shelter at Dartmouth; left 3/8		
	joined EBC60	
Convoy diverted to Solent; left 5/8		Omaha 5/8
• Fowey 16/8; ammunition	joined EBC73	US area 17/8

Returned to Fowey 27/8 and Port Talbot 2/9 to load for US area

OCEAN COAST 1,173/35 British (Coast) – taken up 13/5/44 for Cased Petrol

• Port Talbot 12/6	BC 13/6 EBC10	Utah 16/6
• Sharpness 4/7	BC 5/7 EBC32	Utah 7/7
• Llanelly 27/7	BC 28/7 EBC55	Omaha 30/7
• Sharpness 11/8	BC 12/8 EBC70	Utah 14/8
• Port Talbot 26/8	BC 27/8 EBC85	Morlaix 29/8

Returned to Port Talbot 10/9 to load high octane fuel for Omaha

OLEV 1,373/09 British, ex-Estonian (MoWT/*Tyne & Wear) – taken up 5/44 for Stores

• London (Royal Albert) 3/6; 34 vehicles and 136 troops		
	Thames 5/6 ETC2Y	British area 7/6
• Portsmouth 10/6; 35 vehicles and troops		
	Solent 11/6	Sword 11/6
• London 27/6	Thames 28/6 ETC21	
Diverted to Solent; at anchor for over five weeks		
	Solent 5/8 EBC60W	Cherbourg 5/8

Returned to London 18/8 to load at London (Tilbury) for Arromanches

OOSTERHAVEN 320/41 Dutch – taken up 9/6/44 for Ammunition

• Littlehampton	Solent 17/6 ETC11W	Juno 17/6
• Littlehampton 26/6	joined ETC18	Sword 26/6
• Littlehampton 3/7	joined ETC25	Sword 3/7
• Littlehampton 7/7	joined ETC30	Juno 8/7
• Littlehampton 13/7	joined ETC35	Juno 13/7
• Littlehampton 18/7	joined ETC40	Juno 18/7
• Littlehampton 24/7	joined ETC46	Gold 24/7
• Littlehampton 29/7	joined ETC52	Juno 30/7
• Littlehampton 10/8	joined ETC63	Juno 10/8
• Littlehampton 23/8	joined ETC77	Arromanches 24/8
• Littlehampton 30/8	Solent 1/9 ETC85W	Juno 1/9

Fouled anchor at beachhead 4/9; returned to Littlehampton 8/9 to load for Caen

ORANMORE 495/95 British (Kelly/*Clint) – taken up 5/5/44 for Cased Petrol

• Garston 19/5; called Swansea 31/5-2/6; left BC 2/6		
	Solent 9/6 EBC4W	Utah 10/6
• Poole 19/6	Solent 20/6 ETC14W	Sword 20/6
• Poole 1/7	Solent 2/7 ETC24W	Arromanches 2/7
• Poole 8/7	Solent 9/7 ETC31W	Arromanches 9/7
• Poole 16/7; 400 tons	Solent 17/7 ETC39W	Port-en-Bessin 17/7

Damaged by mine explosion 1345 17/7; towed to Port-en-Bessin for cargo discharge alongside breakwater 18/7; returned to Solent in tow with boilers empty and water above engine room floor level 20/7; arrived Southampton 26/7

• Southampton 12/8	Solent 14/8 ETC67W	Arromanches 14/8
• Southampton 21/8	Solent 22/8 ETC75W	Port-en-Bessin 22/8
• Southampton 27/8	Solent 28/8 ETC81W	Arromanches 28/8

Returned to Southampton 31/8 to load for Dieppe

ORIOLE 489/39 British (General Steam) – taken up 30/3/44 for Cased Petrol

• Sharpness 1/6; left BC 2/6	Solent 8/6 EBC3W	Utah 9/6
• Port Talbot 22/6	BC 23/6 EBC20	Utah 25/6
• Llanelly 4/7	BC 5/7 EBC32	Omaha 7/7
• Llanelly 18/7	BC 19/7 EBC46	Omaha 21/7
• Llanelly 31/7	BC 1/8 EBC59	

Convoy diverted to Solent; left 4/8 ... Utah 4/8

Whilst anchored in convoy assembly area, heavily struck on stempost and port side amiships when HM landing craft LCT1009 dragged anchor 1730 7/8

• Poole 11/8	Solent 12/8 EBC68W	US area 12/8

Sustained denting on starboard side of counter when stern swung onto unknown vessel 15/8

• Poole 25/8	Solent 26/8 EBC82W	US area 26/8

Returned to Poole 4/9 to load for US area

After the River Seine was opened to Allied shipping, the French destination for *Oriole* was switched to Rouen. *[J. and M. Clarkson collection]*

ORTOLAN 489/20 British (General Steam) – taken up 19/4/44 for Cased Petrol
• London (Purfleet); 470 tons; left Thames 7/6

	Solent 10/6 ETC5W	Gold 11/6
• London 26/6	Thames 28/6 ETC21	Juno 29/6
• London 4/7	Thames 5/7 ETC28	Gold 6/7
• Poole 13/7	Solent 14/7 EBC39W	Omaha 14/7
• Poole 18/7	Solent 19/7 EBC44W	Omaha 19/7
• Southampton 29/7	Solent 30/7 EBC55W	Utah 30/7
• Southampton 8/8	Solent 9/8 EBC65W	US area 9/8
• Southampton 24/8	Solent 25/8 EBC81W	US area 25/8

Returned to Southampton 6/9 to load for Barfleur

OXFORD 1,893/23 Canadian – taken up 5/44 for Stores
• London (Royal Albert) 3/6; 35 vehicles and 140 troops

	Thames 5/6 ETC2Y	British area 7/6
• London 18/6	Thames 19/6 ETC14	Gold 20/6
• Harwich 7/7	Thames 8/7 ETC31	Juno 9/7

Returned to London 19/7 for temporary release

PACIFIC 362/38 Dutch – taken up 7/44 for Stores
• Southampton 24/7   Solent 25/7 ETC47W   Gold 25/7
Assigned to French coastal ferry service; returned 5/9 to load coal at Torquay for St Brieuc

PALACIO 1,346/27 British (MacAndrews) – taken up 15/11/43 for Cased Petrol
• Sharpness 15/6, after delay due to windlass trouble

	BC 16/6 EBC13	Utah 18/6

• Sharpness 4/7   BC 5/7 EBC32   Utah 7/7
• Penarth 1/8   BC 1/8 EBC59
Convoy diverted to Solent; left 4/8   Omaha 4/8
• Avonmouth 17/8   BC 18/8 EBC76   US area 20/8
Returned to BC 31/8 and Penarth 4/9 to load for US area

PARKNASILLA 846/32 British (Kelly/*Clint) – taken up 10/4/44 for Cased Petrol
• Port Talbot 1/6; left BC 2/6; embarked 65 troops in Solent

	Solent 8/6 EBC3W	Omaha 9/6
• Llanelly 18/6	BC 25/6 EBC22	Omaha 27/6
• Port Talbot 5/7	BC 6/7 EBC33	Omaha 8/7
• Port Talbot 16/7	BC 16/7 EBC43	Omaha 18/7

Returned 22/7 with defective steering gear, no anchor, Army dock operating personnel still on board, short of food and with cargo only partially discharged; overcarried cargo transhipped to coaster *Downleaze* at Weymouth; laid up for repairs at Portsmouth 19/8-10/9, then arrived Southampton 11/9 to load for Dieppe

PARKWOOD 1,049/33 British (Constantine) – taken up 18/4/44 for Ammunition
• Penarth 4/6; left BC 6/6   Solent 10/6 EBC5W   Utah 11/6
• Swansea 23/6; 1,394 tons   BC 24/6 EBC21   Utah 26/6
• Portishead 15/7   BC 16/7 EBC43   Omaha 18/7
• Newport 31/7   BC 1/8 EBC59
Convoy diverted to Solent; left 4/8   Omaha 4/8
• Southampton 14/8   Solent 15/8 ETC68W   Arromanches 15/8
Returned to Southampton 19/8 to load for Ouistreham

Palacio went on to become one of the last military cargo coasters to remain on government service: she was finally released in August 1946.
[B. and A. Feilden/J. and M. Clarkson collection]

PAUL EMILE JAVARY 2,471/26 British, ex-French (MoWT/*JT Salvesen) – taken up 5/44 for Cased Petrol
• Port Talbot 13/6; after sailing, main engines temporarily broke down, so both anchors let go to prevent vessel grounding 1214 13/6

| | BC 14/6 EBC11 | Omaha 16/6 |

In the storm, port lifeboat smashed by one landing craft, then counter and steering gear damaged by another, the latter not under command, 1640 19/6; lost starboard anchor and 45 fathoms of cable 1700 19/6; vessel pitched and rolled heavily, shipping water fore and aft and making water in No 3 hold 1950 19/6; as a result of dragging anchor towards shore, engines put on stand-by and weighing anchor commenced 0320 21/6 but engines broke down; spare anchor rigged and vessel brought up 0640 21/6; starboard anchor temporarily fouled 2000 22/6; engines and steering gear deemed unreliable, so vessel towed to anchorage by tug *Cormorant*: returned to Swansea 2/7

| • Port Talbot 21/7 | BC 22/7 EBC49 | Omaha 24/7 |
| • Port Talbot 16/8 | BC 16/8 EBC74 | US area 18/8 |

Returned to Cardiff 5/9

The French *Paul Emile Javary* was re-registered at Cardiff for war service: engine trouble and bad weather ensured that her first round voyage to Normandy was anything but routine. [Captain J. F. van Puyvelde]

PEBBLE 597/25 British (Robertson) – taken up 23/4/44 for Ammunition
• Swansea 1/6; left BC 2/6; embarked 44 troops in Solent

	Solent 7/6 EBC2W	Omaha 8/6
• Southampton 20/6	Solent 22/6 ETC15W	Sword 22/6
• Newhaven 5/7	joined ETC28	Gold 6/7

• Southampton 16/7; sailing delayed awaiting three crew members, ashore without permission

	Solent 17/7 ETC39W	Gold 17/7
• Fowey 25/7	joined EBC51	Utah 26/7
• Fowey 9/8	joined EBC66	US area 10/8
• Fowey 24/8	joined EBC81	US area 25/8

Returned to Cardiff 2/9 to load for US area

POLGLEN 795/15 British (Strubin) – taken up 4/44 for Ammunition
• London (Tilbury); 429 tons ammunition and stores; left Thames 31/5; embarked 78 troops in Solent

	Solent 5/6 Force L1	Gold 6/6 (D-Day)
• Portishead 26/6	BC 27/6 EBC24	Omaha 29/6
• Swansea 11/7	BC 12/7 EBC39	Utah 14/7

• Cardiff 8/8	BC 8/8 EBC66	US area 10/8
• Southampton 20/8	Solent 21/8 ETC74W	Arromanches 21/8
• Southampton 28/8	Solent 29/8 ETC82W	Juno 29/8

Returned to Southampton 3/9 to load for Caen, which reached on 12/9 in tow by tug *Empire Doris*

POLLY M 380/37 British (Metcalf) – taken up 1/4/44 for Cased Petrol
• London (Purfleet); 360 tons; left Thames 5/6

	Solent 8/6 ETC3W	Courseulles 9/6
• Southampton 16/6	Solent 17/6 ETC11W	Courseulles 17/6
• Southampton 27/6	Solent 28/6 ETC20W	Juno 28/6

On return, arrived Cardiff 13/7 for repairs to broken rudder support which completed 12/8
• Port Talbot 14/8

| | BC 14/8 EBC72 | Utah 16/8 |

Returned to Southampton 28/8 to load for Port-en-Bessin

PORTAVOGIE 869/34 British (Kelly/*Clint) – taken up 18/8/44 for Ammunition
• Fowey 18/8

| | joined EBC75 | US area 19/8 |

PORTHREPTA 643/22 British (Care) – taken up 22/4/44 for Stores
• Avonmouth; called Portishead, left 1/6; left BC 2/6

	Solent 8/6 EBC3W	Utah 9/6
• Poole; cased petrol	Solent 19/6 EBC14W	Omaha 19/6
• Poole 27/6; cased petrol	Solent 28/6 EBC23W	Omaha 28/6
• Poole 4/7; cased petrol	Solent 5/7 EBC30W	Utah 5/7
• Poole 14/7; cased petrol	Solent 15/7 EBC40W	Omaha 15/7
• Plymouth 26/7	joined EBC52	Utah 27/7
• Southampton 8/8	Solent 9/8 EBC65W	US area 9/8
• Southampton 19/8	Solent 20/8 EBC76W	US area 20/8
• Southampton 30/8	Solent 31/8 EBC87W	Isigny 31/8

Returned to Southampton 12/9 to load for US area

On 18th September 1944 the ammunition carrier *Portia* completed her first crossing to Dieppe. [B. and A. Feilden/J. and M. Clarkson collection]

PORTIA 801/25 British (Coast) – taken up 6/4/44 for Stores
- Barry 3/6; left BC 5/6   Solent 9/6 EBC4W   Omaha 10/6
- London 27/6   Thames 27/6 ETC20   Gold 28/6
- London 2/8; left Thames 2/8 to anchor in Solent
                                    Solent 14/8 EBC70W   Cherbourg 14/8
Returned to Southampton 27/8 to load for Caen

POZNAN 2,017/26 Polish – taken up 22/5/44 for Ammunition
- Penarth   BC 16/6 EBC13   Omaha 18/6
Grounding on a sunken Army tank badly damaged 29 shell plates and
necessitated repairs to frames and floors; returned to Cardiff 13/7 for subsequent
release 26/9

PRASE 374/38 British (Robertson) – taken up 26/4/44 for Cased Petrol
- Port Talbot 4/6; left BC 7/6   Solent 10/6 EBC5W   Omaha 11/6
- Southampton 17/6   Solent 18/6 ETC12W   Juno 18/6
- Southampton 27/6   Solent 28/6 ETC20W   Gold 28/6
- Southampton 4/7   Solent 5/7 ETC27W   British area 5/7
- Southampton 13/7   Solent 14/7 ETC36W   Port-en-Bessin 14/7
- Southampton 21/7   Solent 22/7 ETC44W   Port-en-Bessin 22/7
- Southampton 28/7   Solent 29/7 ETC51W   Gold 29/7
- Southampton 22/8   Solent 23/8 ETC76W
Convoy turned back to Solent; left 24/8   Port-en-Bessin 24/8
Returned to Southampton 29/8 to load for Dieppe

QUENTIN 500/40 British (Gibson) – taken up 26/4/44 for Cased Petrol
- Port Talbot 2/6; cased petrol and 65 troops
                                    BC 5/6 EBC2Y   US area 8/6
- Llanelly 23/6; 1,334 tons   BC 25/6 EBC22   Utah 27/6
- Port Talbot 4/7   BC 5/7 EBC32   Omaha 7/7
- Llanelly 20/7   BC 21/7 EBC48   Omaha 23/7
- Port Talbot 1/8   BC 2/8 EBC60
Convoy diverted to Solent; left 5/8   Omaha 5/8
- Poole 20/8   Solent 23/8 EBC77W   Utah 23/8
- Poole 31/8   Solent 3/9 EBC89W   US area 3/9
Returned to Poole 11/9 to load for US area

RAFTSUND 610/19 Norwegian – taken up 5/6/44 for Ammunition
- Portishead 5/6; left BC 7/6   Solent 10/6 EBC5W   Utah 11/6
- Swansea 24/6; 1,392 tons   BC 24/6 EBC21   Utah 26/6
- Swansea 5/7   BC 5/7 EBC32   Utah 7/7
Straggled from return convoy 10/7; called Weymouth, left 12/7
- Swansea 20/7   BC 21/7 EBC48   Cherbourg 23/7
- Bristol 2/8; 500 tons potatoes   BC 4/8 EBC61
Convoy diverted to Solent; left 6/8   US area 6/8
- Newhaven 15/8   joined ETC69   Arromanches 16/8
- Newhaven 25/8   joined ETC79   Arromanches 26/8
Returned to Newhaven 30/8 to load for Dieppe

REDCAR 1,475/20 British (P&O) – taken up 30/4/44 for Stores
- London (King George V) 3/6; 30 vehicles, 135 troops
                                    Thames 5/6 ETC2Z   Sword 7/6
- London (Tilbury) 14/6   Thames 15/6 ETC10   Gold 16/6
Beachhead subjected to field artillery fire; after being beached during the 19-22/6

storm, moved to anchorage but, in the process, stern touched bottom, then bow
sustained deep denting by grazing coaster *Tres* 2130 23/6
- Grimsby 5/7   Thames 7/7 ETC30   Gold 8/7
- Grimsby 22/7   Thames 24/7 ETC47   Arromanches 25/7
- Grimsby 9/8   Thames 11/8 ETC65
Convoy diverted to Solent; left 13/8   Caen 13/8
Before return, vessel boarded by Military Police investigating theft of cargo during
discharge 0700 19/8; crew cleared of involvement; returned to Grimsby 25/8 to
load for Caen

REGFOS 1,548/10 British (Tyne & Wear) – taken up 5/5/44 for Stores
- London (Royal Albert) 4/6; 33 vehicles, 132 troops
                                    Thames 5/6 ETC2Y   Juno 7/6
Propeller struck underwater obstacle 8/6; vessel beached but broached to, then
driven further across the beach in the 19-22/6 storm; refloated 6/7; returned to
Solent 10/7 in tow of tug *Empire Sinew*; required services of salvage vessel to stem
tunnel leakage; arrived Sunderland 22/7 in tow of tug *Krooman* for survey and
release 29/8

REIAS 1,128/18 Norwegian – taken up 19/5/44 for Ammunition
- London (Royal Albert) 4/6; 32 vehicles, 128 troops
                                    Thames 5/6 ETC2Z   British area 7/6
- Portsmouth; 35 vehicles and troops
                                    Solent 11/6 ETC6W   Sword 12/6
Lost. Left beachhead 12/6; at 0050 13/6 rammed on starboard bow, at
approximately the break in the forecastle head, by outbound coaster *Folda* (qv);
abandoned one hour later when stern at angle of 45°

Whilst returning from Normandy on 13th June 1944 the Norwegian *Reias*
collided with the outward-bound coaster *Folda* and sank in mid-Channel.
[Captain J. F. van Puyvelde]

REUBEN SNOW 1,813/43 British, ex-US (MoWT/*Whimster) – taken up 4/44
for Stores
- Avonmouth 1/6; left BC 2/6   Solent 8/6 EBC3W   Utah 9/6
Deep indentation to shell plating created by US landing craft *LCT765* colliding
with starboard side 1400 9/6; air raids on beachhead 2359 9/6, 0300 11/6, 1400
12/6 and 0100 14/6
- Barry 24/6; 1,471 tons   BC 25/6 EBC22   Utah 27/6
Whilst beaching, kedge anchor lost when line severed on submerged wreckage 1650 27/6

• Avonmouth 11/7	BC 12/7 EBC39	Omaha 14/7
• Plymouth 6/8	joined EBC63	Omaha 7/8
• Avonmouth 30/8	BC 31/8 EBC89	
Convoy sheltered in Weymouth Bay; left 3/9		Omaha 3/9
Returned to Penarth 16/9 and Avonmouth 18/9		

RICHARD BEARSE 1,791/42 British, ex-US (MoWT/*Gibson) – taken up 4/44
for Stores
• Grimsby 25/5; 1,116 tons; called London 27/5-11/6

	Thames 11/6 ETC7	Gold 13/6
• Grimsby 25/6	Thames 27/6 ETC20	Sword 28/6
• Grimsby 18/7	Thames 20/7 ETC43	Gold 21/7
• Grimsby 3/8	Thames 6/8 ETM57	Juno 7/8
• Hull 30/8	Thames 6/9 ETM72	Caen 7/9

Returned to London 10/9 to load for a protracted voyage to Dieppe

RINGEN 1,499/17 Norwegian – taken up 15/5/44 for Stores
• London (King George V); 800 tons; left Thames 5/6

	Solent 8/6 ETC3W	British area 9/6
• London 18/6	Thames 20/6 ETC15	
Convoy sheltered in Solent; left 22/6		Juno 22/6
• London 2/7; 1,200 tons	Thames 3/7 ETC26	

Lost. On passage to Sword, at 0630 4/7, activated magnetic mine beneath her bridge
on the port side; after settling by the bow, vessel went down within a few minutes

ROCKLEAZE 486/24 British (Osborn & Wallis) – taken up 9/4/44 for
Ammunition
• Swansea; left BC 30/5; embarked 44 troops in Solent

	Solent 6/6 EWC1A	Omaha 7/6
• Southampton 23/6	Solent 24/6 ETC16W	Gold 24/6
• Newhaven 3/7	joined ETC26	Gold 4/7
• Southampton 16/7	Solent 16/7 ETC38W	British area 16/7
• Southampton 25/7	Solent 26/7 ETC48W	Port-en-Bessin 26/7

Curiously, the logbook completed by *Rockleaze* included no mention of a
19th August 1944 collision which, according to the other vessel, occurred in
the Solent. *[J. and M. Clarkson collection]*

| • Southampton 15/8 | Solent 15/8 EBC72W | US area 16/8 |

Coaster *Beechfield* reported collision between the two vessels in Solent 2355 19/8;
returned to Southampton to load for US area

ROCKVILLE 481/22 British (Monks) – taken up 23/4/44 for Ammunition
• London (Tilbury) 3/6; 535 tons; left Thames 5/6; embarked 40 troops in Solent

	Solent 6/6 EWC1B	Sword 7/6
• Southampton 18/6; stores	Solent 19/6 ETC13W	Sword 19/6
• Southampton 29/6	Solent 30/6 ETC22W	Juno 30/6
• Southampton 8/7	Solent 9/7 ETC31W	Juno 9/7
• Newhaven 18/7	joined ETC40	Juno 18/7
• Southampton 24/7	Solent 25/7 EBC50W	Isigny 25/7
• Southampton 7/8	Solent 8/8 EBC64W	Isigny 8/8
• Southampton 16/8	Solent 16/8 EBC73W	Barfleur 17/8
• Southampton 27/8	Solent 28/8 ETC81W	Arromanches 28/8

Returned to Southampton 3/9 to load for St Vaast

RODNEY BAXTER 1,791/42 British, ex-US (MoWT/*Stone & Rolfe) – taken
up 5/44 for Ammunition

| • Penarth 22/6; 1,939 tons | BC 23/6 EBC20 | Utah 25/6 |
| • Swansea 15/7 | BC 15/7 EBC42 | Utah 17/7 |

Bad weather marooned 46 US Army dock operating personnel on board 21/7

| • Swansea 1/8 | BC 2/8 EBC60 | |

Convoy diverted to Solent; left 5/8; whilst in Solent, crew's failure to produce sufficient
steam placed vessel in jeopardy when manoeuvring | | Utah 5/8 |

| • Swansea 22/8 | BC 23/8 EBC81 | St Vaast 25/8 |

Returned to Penarth 3/9 and Avonmouth 4/9 to load for Barfleur

RONAN 1,498/38 British (Gibson) – taken up 8/5/44 for Cased Petrol
• London (King George V) 20/5; 1,731 tons

	Thames 9/6 ETC5	Gold 11/6
• Port Talbot 28/6	BC 29/6 EBC26	Utah 1/7
• Port Talbot 10/7	BC 11/7 EBC38	Utah 13/7
• Sharpness 1/8; communications equipment		
	BC 2/8 EBC60	
Convoy diverted to Solent; left 5/8		Omaha 5/8
• Port Talbot 17/8	BC 18/8 EBC76	St Vaast 20/8

Returned to Port Talbot 12/9 to load for St Vaast

RONDO 2,750/27 British (Pelton) – taken up 29/4/44 for Stores

| • Cardiff 2/6 | BC 5/6 EBC2Y | Omaha 8/6 |

In collision with another vessel, possibly HM tank landing ship *LST386*, during the
storm 20/6; arrived Newport 28/6 for drydocking for repairs to hull and for deck, boiler
and engine work; at Barry, Master involved in road accident which proved fatal 8/7

| • Barry 13/7 | BC 14/7 EBC41 | Omaha 16/7 |
| • Barry 5/8 | BC 5/8 EBC63 | Cherbourg 7/8 |

Returned to Barry 10/9; vessel badly strained and requiring engine overhaul

ROSEMARIE 400/39 Dutch – taken up 18/5/44 for Stores

• London (Royal Albert); 222 tons	Thames 10/6 ETC6	Port-en-Bessin 12/6
• Southampton 19/6	Solent 20/6 ETC14W	Juno 20/6
• Southampton 27/6	Solent 28/6 ETC20W	Gold 28/6
• Southampton 5/7	Solent 6/7 ETC28W	Port-en-Bessin 6/7

- Southampton 13/7 | Solent 14/7 ETC36W | Port-en-Bessin 14/7
- Southampton 20/7 | Solent 21/7 ETC43W | Gold 21/7
- Southampton 26/7 | Solent 27/7 ETC49W | Gold 27/7
- Southampton 31/7 | Solent 1/8 ETC54W | Arromanches 1/8
- Southampton 5/8 | Solent 6/8 ETC59W | Arromanches 6/8
- Southampton 10/8 | Solent 11/8 ETC64W | Arromanches 11/8
- Southampton 15/8 | Solent 16/8 ETC69W | Arromanches 16/8
- Southampton 20/8 | Solent 21/8 ETC74W | Arromanches 21/8
- Southampton 25/8 | Solent 26/8 ETC79W | Arromanches 26/8

Returned to Southampton 29/8 to load for Arromanches

ROWANFIELD **495/38 British (Zillah/*Savage)** – taken up 7/4/44 for Stores
- London (Royal Albert) 8/6; 200 tons; left Thames 8/6; struck sunken wreckage off Goodwin Sands 2200 9/6 | Solent 12/6 ETC7W | Sword 13/6
- Poole 18/6; cased petrol | Solent 19/6 EBC14W | Omaha 19/6

In collision with coaster *Downleaze* in the storm 0200 20/6
- Poole 26/6; cased petrol | Solent 28/6 EBC23W | Utah 28/6
- Poole 3/7; cased petrol | Solent 4/7 EBC29W | Utah 4/7
- Poole 15/7; cased petrol | Solent 16/7 EBC41W | Omaha 16/7
- Poole 22/7; cased petrol | Solent 23/7 EBC48W | Omaha 23/7
- Southampton 30/7 | Solent 31/7 EBC56W | Utah 31/7
- Southampton 8/8 | Solent 9/8 EBC65W | US area 9/8
- Southampton 21/8 | Solent 23/8 EBC77W | Utah 23/8
- Southampton 31/8; whilst sheltering in Solent, damaged in collision with a landing craft 2/9 | Solent 3/9 EBC89W | Isigny 3/9

Returned to Southampton 8/9 to load for US area

ROYAL **759/18 Norwegian** – taken up 28/4/44 for Stores
- Cardiff 2/6; stores and 44 troops | BC 5/6 EBC2Y | US area 8/6
- Southampton 24/6 | Solent 25/6 EBC20W | Omaha 25/6
- Southampton 2/7 | Solent 3/7 EBC28W | Omaha 3/7
- Southampton 10/7 | Solent 11/7 EBC36W | Omaha 11/7
- Southampton 29/7 | Solent 30/7 EBC55W | Utah 30/7
- Southampton 11/8 | Solent 12/8 EBC68W | US area 12/8
- Southampton 24/8 | Solent 25/8 EBC81W | US area 25/8

Returned to Plymouth 20/9 to load coal for Cherbourg

RUNNELSTONE **869/23 British (Stone & Rolfe)** – taken up 20/4/44 for Ammunition
- London (Tilbury); 950 tons; left Thames 5/6 | Solent 8/6 ETC3W | British area 9/6
- London 18/6 | Thames 19/6 ETC14 | Gold 20/6
- London | Thames 30/6 ETC23 | Juno 1/7
- London 9/7 | Thames 10/7 ETC33 | Sword 11/7
- London 24/7 | Thames 25/7 ETC48 | Arromanches 26/7
- London | Thames 8/8 ETC62 | Juno 9/8
- London 26/8 | Thames 27/8 ETC81 | Arromanches 28/8

Returned to London 3/9 to load for Dieppe

S N A 8 **2,569/30 British, ex-French (MoWT/*Hogarth)** – taken up 5/44 for Stores
- London (Tilbury) 10/6 | Thames 11/6 ETC7 | Gold 13/6

Touching bottom by the stern damaged 40 shell plates 1545 17/6; other indentations caused by barges rolling alongside during cargo discharge; returned to London 26/6 for release 27/7 and major repairs

A pre-release survey in February 1945 revealed damage to *Runnelstone*'s shell and bulkhead plates and floors, caused when beaching at Normandy. *[Captain J. F. van Puyvelde]*

The French *S N A 10*, owned by Societe Nationale d'Affretements (SNA), was re-registered at Liverpool for war service and carried over 3,700 tons of ammunition to Omaha on her first Normandy voyage. *[National Maritime Museum, P12841]*

S N A 10 **2,921/20 British, ex-French (MoWT/*Constantine)** – taken up 4/44 for Ammunition
- Newport 22/6; 3,766 tons | BC 23/6 EBC20 | Omaha 25/6
- Avonmouth 15/7 | BC 15/7 EBC42 | Omaha 17/7
- Barry 29/7 | BC 30/7 EBC57 | Omaha 1/8
- Newport 12/8 | BC 13/8 EBC71 | Grandcamp 15/8

Steel plate burst on port side by barge whose mooring ropes parted 0300 21/8; returned to Newport 7/9 to load coal for Cherbourg

SAINT ANGUS **391/36 British (Gardner)** – taken up 22/4/44 for Cased Petrol
- London (Purfleet) 23/5; 330 tons; left Thames 7/6 | Solent 10/6 ETC5W | Gold 11/6
- Southampton 17/6 | Solent 18/6 ETC12W | Juno 18/6
- Southampton 27/6 | Solent 28/6 ETC20W | Juno 28/6
- Southampton 6/7 | Solent 7/7 ETC29W | Gold 7/7
- Southampton 13/7 | Solent 14/7 ETC36W | Juno 14/7

• Southampton 19/7	Solent 20/7 ETC42W	Gold 20/7
• Southampton 25/7	Solent 26/7 ETC48W	Gold 26/7
• Southampton 1/8	Solent 2/8 ETC55W	Arromanches 2/8
• Southampton 8/8	Solent 9/8 ETC62W	Arromanches 9/8
• Southampton 14/8	Solent 15/8 ETC68W	Arromanches 15/8
• Southampton 19/8	Solent 20/8 ETC73W	Arromanches 20/8
• Southampton 26/8	Solent 27/8 ETC80W	Port-en-Bessin 27/8

Returned to Southampton 1/9 to load for Arromanches

SAINT BEDAN 452/37 British (Gardner) – taken up 21/4/44 for Cased Petrol

• Port Talbot 2/6; left BC 5/6	Solent 9/6 EBC4W	Omaha 10/6
• Southampton 23/6	Solent 24/6 ETC16W	Juno 24/6
• London	Thames 4/7 ETC27	Gold 5/7
• London 11/7	Thames 12/7 ETC35	Juno 13/7
• London 18/7	Thames 19/7 ETC42	Gold 20/7
• Southampton 25/7	Solent 26/7 ETC48W	Port-en-Bessin 26/7
• Southampton 1/8	Solent 2/8 ETC55W	Arromanches 2/8
• Southampton 9/8	Solent 10/8 ETC63W	Arromanches 10/8
• Southampton 16/8	Solent 17/8 ETC70W	Arromanches 17/8
• Southampton 22/8	Solent 23/8 ETC76W	

Convoy turned back to Solent; left 24/8 — Arromanches 24/8
| • Southampton 29/8 | Solent 30/8 ETC83W | Arromanches 30/8 |

Returned to Southampton to load for Arromanches

After becoming the first sustained loader of stores at Grimsby in June 1944, the former French coaster *Saint-Enogat* was torpedoed by U-boat that August and went down whilst on passage to Juno beachhead. *[National Maritime Museum, P23922]*

SAINT-ENOGAT 2,360/18 British, ex-French (MoWT/*Wilton) – taken up 5/44 for Stores

Assigned to load vehicles at Swansea for early convoys to US area but, at short notice, not used
• Grimsby 20/6	Thames 23/6 ETC16	Juno 24/6
• Grimsby 15/7	Thames 17/7 ETC40	Arromanches 18/7
• London 4/8	Thames 5/8 ETC59	Arromanches 6/8
• London 17/8; 1,427 tons	Thames 18/8 ETC72	

Lost. On passage to Juno at 0820 19/8, torpedoed by *U-413* on starboard side of No 3 hold, with a second explosion, possibly the boilers, occurring five minutes later; ship broke in two amidships with after part submerging almost immediately and fore part rising out of the water then disappearing; three crew members killed, 31 survivors rescued by water ambulances from hospital carrier *Duke of Argyll*

SAINT RULE 524/41 British (Gardner) – taken up 27/4/44 for Cased Petrol
• Port Talbot 1/6; left BC 2/6; embarked 65 troops in Solent
	Solent 8/6 EBC3W	Omaha 9/6
• Llanelly 21/6	BC 23/6 EBC20	Omaha 25/6
• Llanelly 4/7	BC 5/7 EBC32	Omaha 7/7
• Llanelly 18/7	BC 19/7 EBC46	Omaha 21/7
• Llanelly 4/8	BC 5/8 EBC63	St Vaast 7/8
• Poole 20/8; delayed in Solent by engine trouble		
	Solent 25/8 EBC81W	Isigny 25/8

Returned to Poole 31/8 to load for Isigny

In August 1944, *Saint Rule* was directed to the small Normandy ports of St Vaast and Isigny for cargo discharge. *[J. and M. Clarkson collection]*

SAMBRE 349/30 Dutch – taken up 26/4/44 for Cased Petrol
• Port Talbot 2/6; left BC 5/6	Solent 9/6 EBC4W	Omaha 10/6
• Southampton 21/6	Solent 22/6 ETC15W	Gold 22/6
• Southampton 9/7	Solent 10/7 ETC32W	Gold 10/7
• Southampton 14/7	Solent 15/7 ETC37W	Gold 15/7
• Southampton 21/7	Solent 22/7 ETC44W	Port-en-Bessin 22/7
• Plymouth 31/7; put into Solent	Solent 5/8 EBC60W	Utah 5/8
• Plymouth 12/8	joined EBC69	US area 13/8
• Plymouth 24/8	joined EBC81	US area 25/8

Returned to Plymouth 29/8 to load for US area

SAMUEL VERY 1,814/43 British, ex-US (MoWT/*Constantine) – taken up 4/44 for Stores
• Avonmouth 9/6	BC 10/6 EBC7	Utah 13/6
• Swansea 2/7	BC 2/7 EBC29	Utah 4/7
• Plymouth 13/7	joined EBC40	St Vaast 15/7
• Barry 1/8	BC 1/8 EBC59	
Convoy diverted to Solent; left 4/8		Omaha 4/8
Newport 31/8	BC 1/9 EBC90	
Convoy diverted to Solent; left 6/9		Barfleur 6/9

Returned to Newport 14/9 to load for US area

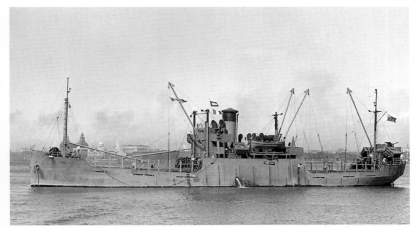

Samuel Very was one of the US coasters serving Normandy under the Red Ensign, 24 of them as pre-loaders: these and six subsequent joiners were mostly employed carrying stores for the British as well as the US Army. *[National Maritime Museum, P23965]*

SANDHILL 586/38 British (Tyne-Tees) – taken up 24/4/44 for Cased Petrol
• London (King George V) 16/5; 800 tons; left Thames 5/6

	Solent 8/6 ETC3W	British area 9/6

After return, whilst under tow to Cowes harbour by tugs *Empire Folk* and *TID69* for repairs to disabled engines, starboard side collided with anchored HM paddle steamer *Princess Elizabeth*, whose cable fouled *Sandhill's* rudder and propeller 2045 15/6; main engine under repair 26/6

• London (King George V) 2/7	Thames 3/7 ETC26	Gold 4/7
• London 16/7; ammunition	Thames 17/7 ETC40	Sword 18/7
• London 27/7	Thames 28/7 ETC51	Arromanches 29/7
• London 5/8	Thames 6/8 ETC60	Arromanches 7/8
• London 14/8	Thames 15/8 ETC69	Arromanches 16/8

Whilst leading return convoy, evasive action after spotting small blue light proved insufficient to avoid starboard bow and side striking what proved to be a tug 0514 20/8; arrived London 20/8 to load ammunition for Dieppe

SARD 410/09 British (Kinnes) – taken up 12/4/44 for Stores
• London (Royal Albert) 2/6; 200 tons; left Thames 5/6

	Solent 7/6 ETC22W	Juno 8/6
• Southampton 17/6	Solent 18/6 ETC12W	Gold 18/6
• Southampton 1/7	Solent 2/7 ETC24W	Gold 2/7
• Southampton 8/7	Solent 9/7 ETC31W	British area 9/7
• Southampton 17/7	Solent 18/7 ETC40W	Juno 18/7
• Southampton 4/8	Solent 5/8 ETC58W	Arromanches 5/8
• Southampton 11/8	Solent 13/8 ETC66W	Arromanches 13/8

Returned to Solent 17/8, then arrived Tyne 24/8

SARNIA 711/23 British (Dorey) – taken up 29/4/44 for Ammunition
• Swansea; ammunition and stores; left BC 30/5; embarked 65 troops in Solent

	Solent 5/6 Force O3	Omaha 6/6 (D-Day)

• Fowey 16/6; loaded ammunition vital to the capture of Cherbourg

	joined EBC12	Utah 17/6

The mid-June 1944 Fowey-loaded ammunition carried by *Sarnia*, pictured here leaving Ostend in 1938, was of high priority for the planned capture of Cherbourg. *[W. H. Brown/J. and M. Clarkson collection]*

Whilst beaching, lost port anchor and 30 fathoms of cable

• Southampton 1/7	Solent 2/7 EBC27W	Omaha 2/7
• Southampton 7/7	Solent 8/7 EBC33W	Utah 8/7
• Southampton 14/7	Solent 15/7 EBC40W	Omaha 15/7
• Southampton 24/7	Solent 25/7 EBC50W	Omaha 25/7
• Newhaven 8/8	joined ETC62	Arromanches 9/8
• Newhaven 20/8	joined ETC74	Arromanches 21/8
• Newhaven 29/8	joined ETC83	British area 30/8

• Returned to Newhaven 9/9 to load for Caen

SCHELDT 497/38 British (Vianda) – taken up 21/4/44 for Cased Petrol

• Port Talbot 7/6; left BC 8/6	Solent 12/6 EBC7W	Omaha 13/6
• Sharpness 23/6	BC 24/6 EBC21	Omaha 26/6
• Llanelly 12/7	BC 14/7 EBC41	Omaha 16/7
• Poole 26/7	Solent 27/7 EBC52W	Omaha 27/7
• Poole 3/8	Solent 5/8 EBC60W	US area 5/8
• Poole 14/8	Solent 15/8 EBC71W	US area 15/8
• Poole 24/8	Solent 25/8 EBC81W	US area 25/8

Returned to Poole 6/9

SEAVILLE 716/18 British (Monks) – taken up 5/5/44 for Ammunition
• London (Tilbury) 23/5; 690 tons; left Thames 5/6

	Solent 8/6 ETC3W	British area 9/6
• Newhaven 19/6	joined ETC14	Sword 20/6
• Newhaven 29/6	joined ETC22	Juno 30/6
• Newhaven 5/7	joined ETC28	Gold 6/7
• Newhaven 12/7	joined ETC35	Gold 13/7
• Newhaven 20/7	joined ETC43	Sword 21/7
• Newhaven 30/7	joined ETC53	Arromanches 31/7
• Newhaven 8/8	joined ETC62	Arromanches 9/8
• Newhaven 14/8	joined ETC68	Arromanches 15/8

Returned to Portsmouth 19/8 for wiping, then anchored in Solent where sustained hawse pipe and other damage when struck on starboard bow by unknown vessel 0110 22/8

SEDULITY 490/36 British (Everard) – taken up 30/3/44 for Cased Petrol
• London (King George V) 31/5; 262 tons cased petrol and engineers' stores; left Thames 31/5; embarked 59 troops in Solent

Solent 5/6 Force L1	Juno 6/6 (D-Day)
• London (Purfleet) 12/6 | Thames 12/6 ETC8 | Juno 14/6 |

Subjected to heavy pounding in rough seas; 1ft of water found in hold bilges on arrival London 18/6

• London 20/6	Thames 23/6 ETC16	Gold 24/6
• London 2/7	Thames 3/7 ETC26	Juno 4/7
• London 14/7	Thames 16/7 ETC39	

Detached to Solent due breakdown Solent 21/7 ETC43W   Sword 21/7

• London 30/7	Thames 31/7 ETC54	Arromanches 1/8
• London 9/8	Thames 10/8 ETC64	

On passage, collided with HM trawler *Sunlight* in dense fog 2305 10/8

Arromanches 11/8

Whilst at anchor, lost starboard anchor and 40 fathoms cable which severed by a minesweeper's sweep wire 1015 12/8

• Southampton 19/8	Solent 19/8 ETC72W	British area 19/8
• Southampton 28/8	Solent 28/8 ETC81W	British area 28/8

Returned to Southampton 2/9 to load for Caen

Discharge of *Sedulity*'s cargo of cased petrol, Bailey Bridging, coal, water and general stores commenced at Juno on D-Day (6th June 1944): the photograph shows the ship in 1960. *[Captain J. F. van Puyvelde]*

SERENITY 557/41 British (Everard) – taken up 3/5/44 for Cased Petrol
• London (King George V); 512 tons; left Thames 8/6

Solent 11/6 ETC6W	Juno 12/6
• London (Purfleet) 18/6	Thames 18/6 ETC13	Sword 19/6
• London (Purfleet) 29/6	Thames 30/6 ETC23	Juno 1/7
• London (Purfleet) 7/7	Thames 8/7 ETC31	Juno 9/7
• London 16/7	Thames 17/7 ETC40	Sword 18/7
• London 23/7	Thames 24/7 ETC47	Arromanches 25/7
• London 30/7	Thames 31/7 ETC54	Arromanches 1/8

Straining of ship, when beached, convinced Master that safety of vessel should not again be so endangered 2/8

• London 9/8	Thames 10/8 ETC64	Arromanches 11/8
• Southampton 17/8	Solent 18/8 ETC71W	Arromanches 18/8
• Southampton 25/8	Solent 26/8 ETC79W	Port-en-Bessin 26/8

Returned to Southampton 31/8 to load bridging equipment for Caen

SHERWOOD 1,530/24 British (France, Fenwick) – taken up 20/5/44 for Stores
• London (Millwall); 37 vehicles and 140 troops

Thames 5/6 ETC2Z	British area 7/6
• Portsmouth; 35 vehicles and troops		
Solent 11/6 ETC6W	British area 12/6
• London 29/6	Thames 30/6 ETC23	Gold 1/7
• London	Thames 17/7 ETC40	Gold 18/7
• London 31/7	Thames 1/8 ETC55	Juno 2/8
• London 16/8	Thames 17/8 ETC71	Arromanches 18/8

Returned to London 25/8 to load for Arromanches

SIAK 1,150/30 Norwegian – taken up 29/4/44 for Ammunition

• Penarth; ammunition and stores	BC 7/6 EBC4	Utah 10/6
• Penarth; 1,379 tons	BC 24/6 EBC21	Omaha 26/6
• Cardiff 10/7	BC 11/7 EBC38	Omaha 13/7
• Southampton 26/7	Solent 27/7 EBC52W	Omaha 27/7
• Penarth	BC 13/8 EBC71	US area 15/8

Returned to BC 29/8 to load at Newport for Cherbourg

SIGNALITY 487/37 British (Everard) – taken up 22/4/44 for Cased Petrol
• London (Tilbury); 176 tons cased petrol and engineers' stores; left Thames 31/5; embarked 78 troops in Solent   Solent 5/6 Force L1   Juno 6/6 (D-Day)

• London (Purfleet) 12/6	Thames 12/6 ETC8	Sword 14/6
• London (Purfleet) 21/6	Thames 23/6 ETC16	Gold 24/6
• London 1/7	Thames 2/7 ETC25	Sword 3/7
• London 11/7	Thames 12/7 ETC35	Sword 13/7

Beachhead subjected to field artillery fire 14/7

• London 19/7	Thames 20/7 ETC43	Gold 21/7
• London 26/7	Thames 27/7 ETC50	Arromanches 28/7
• London 3/8	Thames 4/8 ETC58	Arromanches 5/8
• London 11/8	Thames 12/8 ETC66	Arromanches 13/8
• Southampton 24/8	Solent 25/8 ETC78W	Arromanches 25/8

Returned to Southampton 31/8, on passage to London to load bridging equipment for Dieppe

SIR EVELYN WOOD 850/96 British (War Department) – Stores

• Southampton 13/6	Solent 16/6 ETC10W	Juno 16/6
• Littlehampton 14/7	joined ETC36	Juno 14/7
• Southampton 30/7	Solent 31/7 ETC53W	Port-en-Bessin 31/7
• Southampton 9/8	Solent 10/8 ETC63W	Arromanches 10/8

Returned to Solent 12/8

SKARV 852/23 Norwegian – taken up 8/4/44 for Ammunition
• Swansea; ammunition and stores; left BC 30/5; embarked 65 troops in Solent   Solent 5/6 Force O3   Omaha 6/6 (D-Day)

• Fowey 16/6	joined EBC12	Omaha 17/6
• Fowey 30/6	joined EBC26	Utah 1/7
• Fowey 10/7	joined EBC36	Utah 11/7
• Fowey 23/7	joined EBC49	Utah 24/7
• Southampton 10/8	Solent 12/8 EBC68W	US area 12/8

Returned to Solent 18/8 to load at Southampton for US area

SKELWITH FORCE 592/08 British (Spratt) – taken up 12/4/44 for Ammunition
• London (Tilbury) 30/5; 285 tons ammunition and engineers' stores; left Thames 31/5; embarked 59 troops in Solent Solent 5/6 Force L1 Juno 6/6 (D-Day)
• Newhaven 14/6 Solent 15/6 ETC9W Gold 15/6
Arrived Newhaven 25/6 with hull damage, which too serious for repairs to be undertaken at that port; arrived Swansea 20/7
• Swansea 7/8; potatoes BC 7/8 EBC65 Omaha 9/8
• Southampton 21/8 Solent 22/8 ETC75W Port-en-Bessin 22/8
• Southampton 29/8 Solent 30/8 ETC83W Arromanches 30/8
Returned to Southampton 2/9 to load for Caen

SKUM 1,304/16 Norwegian – taken up 30/4/44 for Ammunition
• Newport 6/6 BC 7/6 EBC4 Omaha 10/6
• Penarth BC 30/6 EBC27 Utah 2/7
• Portishead 17/7 BC 18/7 EBC45 Omaha 20/7
• Sharpness 5/8 BC 6/8 EBC64 Utah 8/8
• Newport 24/8 BC 25/8 EBC83 US area 27/8
Returned to Portishead 7/9 to load for US area

In the early months of the operation, *Skum* carried ammunition to the American beachheads: later in 1944, Rouen became her destination. *[Captain J.F. van Puyvelde]*

SLEMISH 1,536/09 British (Shamrock) – taken up 1/5/44 for Stores
• London (King George V); 29 vehicles, 116 troops
Thames 5/6 ETC2Y British area 7/6
• London 12/6 Thames 13/6 ETC9 Sword 15/6
Return convoy diverted to Solent for shelter; arrived Thames 22/6
• London 27/6 Thames 28/6 ETC21 Gold 29/6
• London 9/7 Thames 10/7 ETC33 Gold 11/7
Under repair on return to London 18/7
• London (Tilbury) 13/8 Thames 14/8 ETC68 Arromanches 15/8
• London (Tilbury) 28/8: left Thames 29/8
Solent 31/8 EBC87W Cherbourg 31/8
Returned to London 11/9, then Middlesbrough and Grimsby
(Vessel sunk by enemy action 23/12/44: see Section 4)

SOBORG 1,993/24 British, ex-Danish (MoWT/*Claymore) – taken up 5/44 for Stores
• London (Royal Albert) 4/6; vehicles and troops
Thames 5/6 ETC2Y British area 7/6

• London (King George V) 29/6 Thames 30/6 ETC23 Gold 1/7
Arrived London 6/7 for repairs at West India Dock 11-17/7
• London (Purfleet) 28/7 Thames 29/7 ETC52
Turned back, unable maintain convoy speed
Thames 31/7 ETC54 Juno 1/8
• Grimsby 18/8 Thames 21/8 ETC75 Arromanches 22/8
In collision with coaster *Glamis* 0030 25/8; returned to London 29/8 to load for Arromanches

SODALITY 829/38 British (Everard) – taken up 2/4/44 for Cased Petrol
• London (King George V); 720 tons; left Thames 5/6
Solent 8/6 ETC3W British area 9/6
• London (King George V) 16/6 Thames 17/6 ETC12 Sword 18/6
• London 28/6 Thames 29/6 ETC22 Arromanches 30/6
Struck submerged object on leaving beachhead 1720 3/7
• London 6/7 Thames 8/7 ETC31 Juno 9/7
Sustained damaged plating from barges alongside for cargo work during heavy weather 9-11/7
• London 16/7 Thames 17/7 ETC40 Juno 18/7
Whilst beaching, struck unspecified obstruction 1055 19/7
• London 25/7 Thames 26/7 ETC49 Arromanches 27/7
• London Thames 5/8 ETC59 Arromanches 6/8
• London Thames 13/8 ETC67 Arromanches 14/8
• London 19/8 Thames 21/8 ETC75 British area 22/8
• Southampton 26/8 Solent 27/8 ETC80W Arromanches 27/8
Returned to Southampton 3/9 to load for Caen

SOJOURNER 435/20 British (Taylor) – taken up 22/4/44 for Cased Petrol
• Poole 12/6 Solent 13/6 ETC8W
Found to be in wrong convoy, so turned back
Solent 17/6 EBC12W Omaha 17/6
• Poole 24/6 Solent 25/6 EBC20W Omaha 25/6
• Poole 2/7 Solent 3/7 EBC28W Omaha 3/7

The cased petrol carrier *Sojourner* was involved in the only reported instance of a coaster setting off for Normandy in the wrong convoy and consequently being turned back. *[Author's Collection]*

• Poole 10/7	Solent 11/7 EBC36W	Utah 11/7	
• Poole 18/7	Solent 19/7 EBC44W	Omaha 19/7	
• Southampton 7/8	Solent 8/8 EBC64W	US area 8/8	
• Southampton 16/8	Solent 16/8 EBC73W	US area 17/8	
• Southampton 28/8	Solent 29/8 EBC85W	St Vaast 29/8	

Returned to Southampton 9/9 to load for US area

SOLLUND 941/08 Norwegian – taken up -/44 for Ammunition
• London (Tilbury) 7/6; 1,025 tons; left Thames 8/6

	Solent 12/6 ETC7W	Sword 13/6	
• Southampton 21/6	Solent 23/6 EWL15	Gold 23/6	
• Southampton 5/7	Solent 6/7 ETC28W	Gold 6/7	
• Southampton 15/7	Solent 16/7 ETC38W	Juno 16/7	
• Harwich 28/7	Thames 29/7 ETC52	Juno 30/7	
• Harwich 12/8; 921 tons	Thames 13/8 ETC67	Arromanches 14/8	
• Harwich 26/8	Thames 27/8 ETC81	Juno 28/8	

Returned to London, then moved to Southampton to load stores for Dieppe

Originally an ammunition ship, *Southport* was switched to coal-carrying in November 1944, when she transported 526 tons from Swansea to Granville. *[J. and M. Clarkson collection]*

SOUTHPORT 572/14 British (Grace) – taken up 24/4/44 for Ammunition
• London (Tilbury) 30/5; 560 tons; left Thames 31/5; embarked 39 troops in Solent

	Solent 6/6 EWC1B	Juno 7/6	
• Southampton 15/6	Solent 16/6 ETC10W	Sword 16/6	
• Southampton 24/6	Solent 25/6 ETC17W	Gold 25/6	
• Southampton 3/7	Solent 4/7 ETC26W	Gold 4/7	
• Southampton 15/7	Solent 16/7 ETC38W	Juno 16/7	
• Southampton 23/7	Solent 24/7 ETC46W	Port-en-Bessin 24/7	
• Southampton 31/7	Solent 1/8 EBC57W	Utah 1/8	
• Southampton 12/8	Solent 13/8 EBC69W	US area 13/8	
• Southampton 28/8	Solent 29/8 ETC82W	Juno 29/8	

Returned to Southampton 4/9 to load for US area

SPARTA 291/40 Dutch – taken up 8/44 for Stores
• Southampton 25/8   Solent 26/8 EBC82W   Isigny 26/8
Assigned to French coastal ferry service in US area

SPES 1,142/18 Norwegian – taken up 17/5/44 for Ammunition
• London (Tilbury Jetty); 1,580 tons; left Thames 5/6

	Solent 7/6 ETC22W	Gold 8/6	
• London 30/6	Thames 1/7 ETC24	Sword 2/7	
• London 14/7	Thames 15/7 ETC38	Gold 16/7	

Returned 22/7 for repairs on Thames

• Harwich 21/8	Thames 22/8 ETC76		

Convoy diverted to Solent; left 24/8   Juno 24/8
Returned to London 29/8 to load cased petrol for Dieppe

SPHENE 815/20 British (Robertson) – taken up 22/4/44 for Stores

• Cardiff 10/6	BC 11/6 EBC8	Utah 14/6	
• Swansea 22/7	BC 22/7 EBC49		
Called Weymouth Bay 23/7		Omaha 24/7	
• Newhaven 4/8; ammunition	joined ETC58	Arromanches 5/8	
• Newhaven 12/8; ammunition	joined ETC66	Arromanches 13/8	
• Newhaven 21/8; ammunition	joined ETC75	Arromanches 22/8	

Returned to Newhaven 28/8 to load ammunition for Arromanches

SPIRALITY 554/39 British (Everard) – taken up 26/4/44 for Cased Petrol
• London (King George V); 883 tons; left Thames 5/6; embarked 38 troops in Solent

	Solent 7/6 ETC22W	Juno 8/6	
• Southampton 16/6	Solent 17/6 ETC11W	Sword 17/6	
• London 10/7	Thames 11/7 ETC34	Juno 12/7	
• London 22/7	Thames 24/7 ETC47	Arromanches 25/7	

• Southampton 2/8; in Solent anchorage, port bow, anchor and superstructure sustained considerable damage when struck by collier *Tyndall* 0120 3/8

	Solent 5/8 EBC60W	US area 5/8	
• Southampton 16/8	Solent 16/8 EBC73W	US area 17/8	

Returned to Solent, then left 29/8 for collision damage repairs at South Shields

STADION II 629/14 Norwegian – taken up 27/4/44 for Ammunition
• London (Tilbury) 3/6; 806 tons; left Thames 4/6; embarked 59 troops in Solent

	Solent 6/6 EWC1B	Juno 7/6	

The Norwegian *Stadion II*, seen here in 1954, was one of 63 coasters anchored in the Solent for shelter, when the June 1944 storms severely disrupted convoy movements. *[Captain J. F. van Puyvelde collection]*

• Southampton 23/6	Solent 24/6 EBC17W	Utah 24/6
• Southampton 3/7	Solent 4/7 EBC29W	Utah 4/7
• Southampton 15/7	Solent 18/7 EBC43W	St Vaast 18/7
• Southampton 24/7	Solent 25/7 EBC50W	Utah 25/7
• Belfast 14/8	BC 16/8 EBC74	Cherbourg 18/8

Returned to Belfast 30/8

STALEY BRIDGE 297/40 British (Summers) – taken up 4/44 for Cased Petrol

• Port Talbot 2/6; cased petrol and 44 troops

	BC 5/6 EBC2Y	Omaha 8/6
• Southampton 14/6	Solent 15/6 ETC9W	Juno 15/6
• Southampton 19/6	Solent 23/6 EWL15	Gold 23/6
• Southampton 27/6	Solent 28/6 ETC20W	Sword 28/6
• Southampton 4/7	Solent 5/7 ETC27W	Juno 5/7
• Southampton 10/7	Solent 11/7 ETC33W	Juno 11/7
• Southampton 17/7	Solent 18/7 ETC40W	Gold 18/7
• Southampton 23/7	Solent 24/7 ETC46W	Port-en-Bessin 24/7
• Southampton 29/7	Solent 30/7 ETC52W	Arromanches 30/7
• Southampton 3/8	Solent 4/8 ETC57W	Arromanches 4/8
• Southampton 9/8	Solent 10/8 ETC63W	Arromanches 10/8

On return passage, bombed but undamaged in air attack 2125 12/8

• Southampton 15/8	Solent 16/8 ETC69W	Arromanches 16/8
• Southampton 20/8	Solent 21/8 ETC74W	Arromanches 21/8
• Southampton 26/8	Solent 27/8 ETC80W	Port-en-Bessin 27/8

Returned to Southampton 31/8 to load for Arromanches

STANLEY FORCE 586/20 British (West Coast/*Kennaugh) – taken up 23/4/44 for Ammunition

• London (Tilbury) 30/5; 310 tons ammunition and stores; left Thames 31/5; embarked 59 troops in Solent

	Solent 5/6 Force L1	Gold 6/6 (D-Day)
• Southampton 14/6	Solent 15/6 ETC9W	Juno 15/6
• Southampton 24/6	Solent 25/6 ETC17W	Juno 25/6
• Southampton 7/7	Solent 8/7 ETC30W	Sword 8/7
• Southampton 16/7	Solent 17/7 ETC39W	Gold 17/7
• Southampton 27/7	Solent 28/7 ETC50W	Port-en-Bessin 28/7
• Southampton 14/8	Solent 15/8 EBC71W	US area 15/8

Returned to Solent 18/8 to load at Southampton for US area

STANVILLE 538/18 British (Monks) – taken up 6/5/44 for Cased Petrol

• Southampton 15/6	Solent 17/6 EBC12W	Utah 17/6
• Southampton 28/6	Solent 29/6 EBC24W	Omaha 29/6
• Southampton 8/7	Solent 9/7 EBC34W	Omaha 9/7
• Southampton 19/7	Solent 20/7 EBC45W	Omaha 20/7
• Southampton 30/7	Solent 31/7 ETC53W	Port-en-Bessin 31/7
• Southampton 12/8; stores	Solent 13/8 ETC66W	Arromanches 13/8
• Southampton 25/8, after repairs whilst loaded		
	Solent 26/8 ETC79W	Arromanches 26/8

Returned to Southampton 29/8 to load for Arromanches

STARKENBORGH 878/41 Dutch – taken up 27/4/44 for Cased Petrol

• Sharpness 30/5; cased petrol and stores; left BC 30/5; in fog, rammed stern of coaster Valborg off Plymouth 31/5; embarked 123 troops in Solent

	Solent 5/6 Force O3	
	then U3	Utah 6/6 (D-Day)

• Sharpness 18/6	BC 19/6 EBC16	
Convoy sheltered in Poole Bay		Omaha 23/6
• Sharpness 11/7	BC 12/7 EBC39	Omaha 14/7
• Llanelly 27/7	BC 28/7 EBC55	Cherbourg 30/7
• Southampton 14/8	Solent 15/8 ETC68W	Arromanches 15/8
• Southampton 22/8	Solent 23/8 ETC76W	
Convoy turned back to Solent; left 24/8		Arromanches 24/8
• Southampton 31/8	Solent 1/9 ETC85W	Arromanches 1/9

Returned to Solent 13/9 to load at Southampton for Dieppe

STUART QUEEN 1,224/41 British (British Channel Islands) – taken up 5/4/44 for Ammunition

• Barry 3/6; stores and five troops; left BC 5/6

	Solent 6/6 EWC1A	Omaha 7/6
• Fowey 24/6	joined EBC20	Utah 25/6
• Fowey 4/7	joined EBC30	Omaha 5/7
• Fowey 13/7	joined EBC39	Utah 14/7
• Fowey 24/7	joined EBC50	Omaha 25/7
• Southampton 4/8	Solent 5/8 EBC60W	Utah 5/8
• Southampton 16/8	Solent 16/8 EBC73W	St Vaast 17/8

After returning to Southampton and whilst undergoing boiler cleaning, port hawse pipe and bow plates hit when US tank landing ship LST21 backing out from loading ramp; all Stuart Queen's moorings carried away but vessel's momentum stopped by letting go starboard anchor 1145 31/8; left Southampton 8/9 to load coal at Plymouth for Cherbourg

SUMMITY 554/39 British (Everard) – taken up 22/4/44 for Cased Petrol

• London (King George V); 540 tons; left Thames 7/6

	Solent 10/6 ETC5W	Mulberry B 11/6
• London (King George V) 18/6	Thames 18/6 ETC13	Port-en-Bessin 19/6

Ship shaken by mine explosion 400ft away 0730 24/6

• London (Purfleet) 3/7	Thames 4/7 ETC27	Gold 5/7
• London (Tilbury) 14/7	Thames 15/7 ETC38	Sword 16/7
• Newhaven 22/7; ammunition	joined ETC45	Juno 23/7

On her second arrival in Normandy on 19th June 1944, Summity was affected by a mine exploding only 400 feet away. [Fotoflite/J. and M. Clarkson collection]

• Newhaven 31/7; ammunition	joined ETC54		Arromanches 1/8
• Poole 7/8	Solent 8/8 ETC61W		Port-en-Bessin 8/8
• Poole 13/8	Solent 14/8 ETC67W		Port-en-Bessin 14/8
• Newhaven 19/8; ammunition	joined ETC73		Arromanches 20/8

At beachhead, jolly boat carried away in gale 0430 21/8; after return to Newhaven, deck hand drowned after falling overboard 25/8

• Newhaven 29/8; ammunition	joined ETC83	British area 30/8

Returned to Newhaven 6/9 to load ammunition for Dieppe

TEESWOOD 864/15 British (Donking) – taken up 7/4/44 for Ammunition

• London (Tilbury); 1,000 tons; left Thames 31/5; embarked 59 troops in Solent

	Solent 6/6 EWC1B	Gold 7/6

As a result of beaching, bottom pierced below engine room 1600 7/6; cement box fitted

• London (Tilbury) 29/6	Thames 30/6 ETC23	Gold 1/7
• London	Thames 12/7 ETC35	Juno 13/7
• London (Tilbury) 26/7	Thames 27/7 ETC50	Arromanches 28/7
• London (Tilbury) 9/8	Thames 11/8 ETC65	

Convoy diverted to Solent; left 13/8

		Juno 13/8
• London (Tilbury) 29/8	Thames 30/8 ETC84	Ouistreham 31/8

Arrived Ouistreham with engine defects; whilst awaiting return convoy, lost anchor and 15 fathoms of cable at Arromanches 0830 7/9; subsequent grounding caused buckling of shell plating and deck starboard side abreast No 2 hatch; cement box fitted by crew enabled vessel to arrive London independently 11/9

On returning to Tilbury Dock, after surviving the war hazards of a late September 1944 voyage to France, *Teeswood* sustained damaged in collision with another coaster, then broke four propeller blades on an obstruction whilst in port. [World Ship Society Ltd.]

THE BARON 820/27 British (Hay) – taken up 4/6/44 for Stores

• Cardiff 10/6	BC 11/6 EBC8	Utah 14/6
• Southampton 1/7	Solent 2/7 ETC24W	Sword 2/7
• Southampton 22/7; 600 tons ammunition		
	Solent 23/7 EBC48W	

Leaving Solent as Commodore ship, collided with unknown vessel 0200 23/7

		Omaha 23/7

• Southampton 1/8	Solent 2/8 EBC58W	US area 2/8
• Southampton 12/8	Solent 13/8 EBC69W	US area 13/8
• Southampton 26/8	Solent 27/8 EBC83W	US area 27/8

Returned to Solent 3/9 to load at Southampton for US area

THE EARL 926/36 British (Hay) – taken up 7/4/44 for Ammunition

• Penarth 5/6; left BC 7/6	Solent 11/6 EBC6W	Utah 12/6

Whilst at anchor, sustained damage to starboard davit and bulwark plates when hit by HM landing craft *LCT1046*, which attempting to moor astern in the storm 0012 20/6

• Swansea 28/6	BC 29/6 EBC26	Omaha 1/7
• Portishead 17/7	BC 19/7 EBC46	St Vaast 21/7
• Harwich 12/8	Thames 13/8 ETC67	Arromanches 14/8
• Harwich 27/8	Thames 28/8 ETC82	Juno 29/8

Returned to Harwich 9/9 to load for Dieppe

THE PRESIDENT 926/36 British (Hay) – taken up 22/4/44 for Ammunition

• Swansea 29/5; ammunition and stores; left BC 30/5; embarked 65 troops in Solent

	Solent 5/6 Force O3	Omaha 6/6 (D-Day)

On return passage 11-12/6, crew member jumped overboard in a suicide attempt which failed; he was picked up by a warship and landed into hospital at Plymouth

• Fowey 16/6	joined EBC12	Utah 17/6

Damage sustained to crew accommodation and ship's bottom when beached during the 19-22/6 storm; left 15/7 in tow of tug *Bodie Island*; at 0125 16/7 in thick fog, tug collided with HM destroyer *Vanquisher* five miles off Isle of Wight; four minutes later *The President*, cast off from tug, without steam and not under command, received starboard side shell plating damage in collision with outward-bound coaster *Kyloe*; fire in a hole in *The President's* starboard forecastle was extinguished by *Kyloe*; *The President* subsequently reached Falmouth for lengthy repairs

June damage at the beachhead and a July collision during the northbound tow resulted in *The President* requiring extensive repairs. [W.H. Brown/J. and M. Clarkson collection]

THE VICEROY 824/29 British (Hay) – taken up 13/4/44 for Stores

• London (Royal Albert); 400 tons; left Thames 7/6

	Solent 9/6 ETC4W	

Convoy heavily attacked in English Channel by E-boats 10/6 Sword 10/6
Damaged by mine 13/6: on return, drydocked at Southampton for repairs

• Southampton 4/7	Solent 5/7 ETC27W	Juno 5/7
• Southampton 14/7	Solent 15/7 ETC37W	Gold 15/7
• Southampton 8/8	Solent 9/8 EBC65W	US area 9/8
• Southampton 15/8	Solent 15/8 EBC72W	US area 16/8
• Southampton 30/8	Solent 31/8 EBC87W	St Vaast 31/8

Returned to Southampton 9/9 to load for Barfleur

THESEUS 1,306/20 Dutch – taken up 18/5/44 for Ammunition
• Newport 1/6	BC 7/6 EBC4	Omaha 10/6
• Swansea 2/7	BC 2/7 EBC29	Omaha 4/7

• Penarth 16/7; hull damaged in collision with coaster *Jesse G Cotting* 0947 16/7;
called Swansea for repairs 17-20/7 BC 21/7 EBC48   Cherbourg 23/7
• Penarth	BC 27/8 EBC85	Cherbourg 29/8

Left for Morlaix 6/9 to ferry ammunition from Liberty ships; returned to
Portishead 18/9

During the June 1944 storm, *Thore Hafte* took refuge at Weymouth, before rejoining her convoy sheltering in Poole Bay. [Harry Stewart/J. and M. Clarkson collection]

THORE HAFTE 626/96 Norwegian – taken up 21/4/44 for Ammunition
• Swansea; ammunition and 39 troops
	BC 5/6 EBC2Y	US area 8/6
• Swansea	BC 19/6 EBC16	

Detached to Weymouth; left 22/6 to rejoin convoy sheltering in Poole Bay
		Utah 23/6
• Fowey 1/7	joined EBC27	
Put into Portland	joined EBC33	Omaha 8/7
• Fowey 22/7	Solent 24/7 EBC49W	Omaha 24/7
• Fowey 1/8	joined EBC58	Omaha 2/8

• Fowey 10/8; put into Plymouth for water
	joined EBC68	US area 12/8

Returned to Plymouth 26/8 to load for US area

THORNABY 1,174/35 British (Tyne-Tees) – taken up 4/5/44 for Stores
• London (Royal Albert) 3/6; 17 vehicles and 68 troops
	Thames 5/6 ETC2Z	British area 7/6

• Portsmouth 10/6; 35 vehicles and troops
	Solent 11/6 ETC6W	Sword 12/6
• London 23/6	Thames 25/6 ETC18	Gold 26/6

Beachhead under heavy field artillery fire 1600 26/6
• London 4/7	Thames 5/7 ETC28	

Sustained blast concussion from German flying bomb hit by British anti-aircraft guns
deployed on Kent coast 2000 5/7   Gold 6/7
• Harwich 16/7; ammunition	Thames 17/7 ETC40	Juno 18/7

Beachhead under air attack 18-19/7; vessel bumped bottom heavily in high wind and
rough sea 1730 20/7
• Harwich 30/7; ammunition	Thames 1/8 ETC55	Juno 2/8

Beachhead under air attack 0100 4/8
• Harwich 16/8; ammunition	Thames 17/8 ETC71	Arromanches 18/8

Returned to Harwich 25/8 to load ammunition for Dieppe

THYRA III 828/12 British, ex-Danish (MoWT/*Henry & MacGregor) – taken up
5/44 for Stores
• London (Tilbury); 27 vehicles and 108 troops
	Thames 5/6 ETC2Z	British area 7/6

Scheduled to load 35 vehicles at Portsmouth 10/6 but, in error, returned to London
• London (Tilbury)	Thames 15/6 ETC10	Juno 16/6

During the storm, port side struck by HM landing craft *LCT530*, causing severe
damage to forecastle head and ship's side, smashing lifeboat, bending davits and
jamming steering gear 0140 22/6; steering gear repaired; returned to London 28/6
• London 1/8	Thames 2/8 ETC56	

Detached to Solent; at anchor for two weeks
	Solent 18/8 EBC74W	Cherbourg 18/8

On entering Cherbourg, touched dock gate 18/8
• Southampton 30/8; turned back; left 1/9		
	Solent 2/9 ETC86W	Arromanches 2/9

Returned to Southampton 17/9 with 219 tons of engine assemblies, 64 tons RAF
equipment, 20 tons empty ammunition boxes, 105 tons empty cylinders and 29 tons
coal sacks

TILLY 381/39 Dutch – taken up 7/44 for Stores
• Southampton 31/7	Solent 1/8 ETC54W	Port-en-Bessin 1/8

Intended for French coastal ferry service but, on arrival, sustained collision damage just
above the water-line, so returned to Southampton 8/8 for repairs to frames and beams
• Southampton 25/8	Solent 26/8 ETC79W	Port-en-Bessin 26/8

TOMSK 1,229/11 British, ex-Danish (MoWT/*Richley, Halvorsen & Sample) –
taken up 2/5/44 for Ammunition
• Swansea 2/6; vehicles and troops	BC 5/6 EBC2Z	Utah 8/6
• Newport 27/6	BC 28/6 EBC25	Omaha 30/6

On departure from beachhead, struck wreck on starboard side 0700 3/7
• Newport 19/7	BC 20/7 EBC47	Omaha 22/7
• Swansea 4/8	BC 5/8 EBC63	Utah 7/8

On return to BC, between Barry and Newport, lost port anchor and 15 fathoms of cable
1615 16/8

• Newport 21/8; port side indented in collision with quay on departure in strong wind 2030 21/8   BC 23/8 EBC81   US area 25/8
Returned to BC 8/9 to load for US area

Seen in 1952, *Tomsk* was one of the former Danish vessels to serve at Normandy: she was re-registered in London for war service. *[Captain J. F. van Puyvelde]*

TON S 466/37 Dutch – taken up 11/6/44 for Stores
• Southampton 15/6   Solent 17/6 ETC11W   Juno 17/6
Returned 25/6 after going aground
Originally taken up for one voyage only, in view of condition which regarded as unreliable
• Southampton 30/6   Solent 1/7 ETC23W   Port-en-Bessin 1/7
• Southampton 10/7   Solent 11/7 ETC33W   Port-en-Bessin 11/7
• Newhaven 18/7; ammunition   joined ETC40   Sword 18/7
• Poole 27/7; cased petrol   Solent 28/7 EBC53W   Utah 28/7

So great was the demand for cargo space for Normandy stores that *Ton S* remained in service, despite serious doubts about her reliability. *[J. and M. Clarkson collection]*

• Southampton 4/8   Solent 5/8 EBC60W   US area 5/8
• Southampton 13/8   Solent 14/8 EBC70W   US area 14/8
• Southampton 24/8   Solent 25/8 EBC81W   US area 25/8
Returned to Southampton 3/9 to load for US area

TOPAZ 577/20 British (Robertson) – taken up 19/4/44 for Ammunition
• Penarth 1/6; left BC 2/6; embarked 42 troops in Solent
                              Solent 7/6 EBC2W   Utah 8/6
On return to Southampton, in collision with coaster *Dawlish* 13/6
• Southampton 14/6; stores   Solent 15/6 ETC9W   Sword 15/6
• Southampton 22/6; stores   Solent 23/6 EWC2B   Juno 23/6
• Southampton 4/7; stores   Solent 5/7 ETC27W   Gold 5/7
• Southampton 13/7; stores   Solent 14/7 ETC36W   Juno 14/7
• Southampton 22/7; stores   Solent 23/7 EBC48W   US area 23/7
• Southampton 10/8; stores   Solent 12/8 EBC68W   US area 12/8
• Southampton 29/8; stores   Solent 30/8 EBC86W   US area 30/8
Returned to Plymouth 12/9 to load for St Brieuc

TORFINN JARL 1,481/22 Norwegian – taken up 6/5/44 for Cased Petrol
• Port Talbot 8/6   BC 9/6 EBC6   Omaha 12/6
• Port Talbot 2/7   BC 2/7 EBC29   Omaha 4/7
• Port Talbot 17/7   BC 18/7 EBC45   Utah 20/7
• Port Talbot 31/7   BC 1/8 EBC59
Convoy diverted to Solent; left 4/8   Omaha 4/8
• Portishead 14/8   BC 15/8 EBC73   Grandcamp 17/8
Returned to Port Talbot 6/9 to load for US area

TORQUAY 870/14 British (Davidson) – taken up 10/4/44 for Stores
• London (Royal Albert) 26/5; 446 tons; left Thames 31/5; embarked 59 troops in Solent   Solent 6/6 EWC1B   Courseulles 7/6
Aground in Courseulles harbour (Juno sector) 1220-2300 8/6
• Southampton 17/6   Solent 18/6 EBC13W   Omaha 18/6
• Plymouth 5/7; cased petrol   joined EBC31   Utah 6/7
• Port Talbot 18/7; cased petrol   BC 19/7 EBC46   Omaha 21/7
• Southampton 30/7   Solent 31/7 EBC56W   Utah 31/7
• Southampton 11/8   Solent 12/8 EBC68W   US area 12/8
Returned to Southampton 29/8 to load for US area

TRES 946/17 Norwegian – taken up 29/4/44 for Ammunition
• London (Tilbury) 3/6; 1,050 tons; left Thames 5/6
                              Solent 8/6 ETC3W   British area 9/6
• London (Tilbury) 20/6   Thames 20/6 ETC15
Convoy sheltered in Solent; left 22/6   Sword 22/6
Subjected to field artillery fire at beachhead, then grazed by bow of coaster *Redcar*, resulting in bending to port of top of stem 2130 23/6
• London 1/7   Thames 2/7 ETC25   Gold 3/7
• London 13/7   Thames 14/7 ETC37   Juno 15/7
• Southampton 30/7   Solent 31/7 ETC53W   Gold 31/7
• Southampton 7/8   Solent 8/8 ETC61W   Port-en-Bessin 8/8
• Southampton 18/8   Solent 19/8 ETC72W   Arromanches 19/8
• Southampton 25/8   Solent 26/8 ETC79W   Arromanches 26/8
• Southampton 30/8; special ammunition
                              Solent 2/9 ETC86W   Arromanches 2/9
Returned to Solent 6/9 to load at Soutampton for Caen

TROMP 391/32 Dutch – taken up 19/4/44 for Cased Petrol
• London (King George V) 25/5; 360 tons; left Thames 7/6

	Solent 10/6 ETC5W	Juno 11/6
• Southampton 17/6	Solent 18/6 ETC12W	Gold 18/6
• Southampton 30/6	Solent 1/7 ETC23W	Sword 1/7
• Southampton 7/7	Solent 8/7 ETC30W	Sword 8/7

• Southampton 20/7; turned back; left 21/7

	Solent 22/7 ETC44W	British area 22/7
• Plymouth 2/8	joined EBC59	

Convoy diverted to Solent; left 4/8

		US area 4/8
• Plymouth 10/8	joined EBC67	US area 11/8
• Plymouth 20/8	joined EBC77	

Convoy sheltered in Solent; left 23/8

		Utah 23/8

Returned to Plymouth 27/8 to load for US area

For her first cargo, *Tromp* was assigned to load after *Sodality* and before *Ronan* at Berth 4 in London's King George V Dock. [Ben Scholten collection]

In August 1944 there was a requirement for a twice-daily coal shuttle service to Cherbourg and *Tudor Queen* was one of the coasters assigned. [J. and M. Clarkson collection]

TUDOR QUEEN 1,029/41 British (British Channel Islands) – taken up 29/4/44 for Ammunition
• London (Tilbury); 1,220 tons; left Thames 8/6

	Solent 11/6 ETC6W	Sword 12/6
• London	Thames 20/6 ETC15	

Convoy sheltered in Solent; left 22/6

		Gold 22/6
• Southampton 1/7	Solent 2/7 ETC24W	Juno 2/7
• Southampton 14/7	Solent 15/7 ETC37W	Arromanches 15/7
• Southampton 26/7	Solent 27/7 ETC49W	Arromanches 27/7
• Southampton 4/8	Solent 5/8 EBC60W	US area 5/8
• Southampton 10/8	Solent 12/8 EBC68W	US area 12/8
• Newport 29/8; coal	BC 29/8 EBC87	Cherbourg 31/8

Returned to Newport 6/9 to load coal for Cherbourg

TULLY CROSBY 1,791/43 British, ex-US (MoWT/*Stephenson Clarke) – taken up 4/44 for Stores
• Grimsby 25/5; 1,153 tons; called London (Purfleet) 28/5-8/6

	Thames 9/6 ETC5	Gold 11/6
• London 23/6	Thames 25/6 ETC18	Gold 26/6

Engine room affected by nearby mine explosion 30/6; under own steam, arrived London 5/7

• Grimsby 25/7	Thames 27/7 ETC50	Juno 28/7

• Grimsby 12/8; unable to maintain steam owing to coal being clagged in furnaces; returned under own power and docked with assistance of tug 13/8; left 16/8

	Thames 19/8 ETC73	Juno 20/8

Vessel bumped bottom in high wind 0700 21/8; dragged anchor in busy anchorage and relied on main engines to maintain position after windlass jammed 1400 same day; returned to Hull 28/8 to load for Caen

ULSTER HERO 483/24 British (Gardner) – taken up 8/4/44 for Stores

• Avonmouth 7/6; left BC 8/6	Solent 12/6 EBC7W	Utah 13/6
• Southampton 19/6	Solent 22/6 ETC15W	Gold 22/6
• Southampton 26/6	Solent 27/6 ETC19W	Gold 27/6
• Southampton 2/7		

Ulster Hero's scheduled departure from the Solent for Normandy on 3rd July 1944 was delayed by six days, firstly by a collision then by a lost anchor. [B. and A. Feilden/J. and M. Clarkson collection]

On passage to Normandy, main deck holed in collision with HM landing craft *LCT899* 0255 3/7; turned back; arrived Solent 0500 3/7; starboard anchor slipped with 15 fathoms of cable after fouling heavy object on sea bed in Solent 1330 3/7

	Solent 9/7 ETC31W	Gold 9/7
• Southampton 8/8	Solent 12/8 EBC68W	US area 12/8
• Southampton 29/8	Solent 30/8 EBC86W	Isigny 30/8

Returned to Southampton 9/9 to load for St Vaast

VALBORG 844/14 British, ex-Danish (**MoWT/*Hay**) – taken up 4/44 for Ammunition
• Penarth 30/5; ammunition and stores; left BC 30/5; in convoy to Solent (for onward passage to Utah), orders given to anchor in dense fog; vessel's starboard quarter rammed by coaster *Starkenborgh* causing considerable damage above water-line and rendering steering gear useless 31/5; vessel arrived Plymouth Roads towed by tug *Recovery* 0900 1/6; repairs commenced at Plymouth 6/6; cargo discharged and reloaded into coaster *Lilleaa*; left Plymouth 15/6

Fowey 21/6; 856 tons		
Arrived Dartmouth for shelter	joined EBC20	Utah 25/6
Indented bottom plates on beaching 25/6		
• Harwich 12/7; 665 tons stores	Thames 13/7 ETC36	Gold 14/7
• Harwich 22/7	Thames 23/7 ETC46	
Turned back, unable maintain convoy speed		
	Thames 25/7 ETC48	Juno 26/7

On return, called Hull for drydocking for repairs to bottom plates indented by beaching 14-16/8

• Grimsby 23/8	Thames 25/8 ETC79	Arromanches 26/8

Returned to Harwich Roads, where propeller fouled 1/9; subsequently loaded for Dieppe

VAN BRAKEL 398/29 Dutch – taken up 26/4/44 for Cased Petrol
• Sharpness 1/6; left BC 2/6	Solent 8/6 EBC3W	Utah 9/6

On return, required major repairs, so released

VAREGG 943/10 Norwegian – taken up 12/6/44 for Stores
• Southampton 16/6	Solent 17/6 EBC12W	Omaha 17/6
• Southampton 28/6	Solent 1/7 EBC26W	Omaha 1/7
• Southampton 12/7	Solent 13/7 EBC38W	Omaha 13/7
• Southampton 24/7	Solent 25/7 ETC47W	Gold 25/7
• Harwich 10/8; ammunition	Thames 11/8 ETC65	
Convoy diverted to Solent; left 13/8		Arromanches 13/8
• Harwich 24/8; 1,127 tons ammunition		
	Thames 25/8 ETC79	Juno 26/8

Returned to Harwich 2/9 to load ammunition for Dieppe

VESTMANROD 691/19 Norwegian – taken up 29/4/44 for Stores
• London (Royal Albert) 30/5; 405 tons; left Thames 31/5; embarked 59 troops in Solent

Solent	Solent 6/6 EWC1B	Juno 7/6
• Southampton 21/6	Solent 23/6 EBC16W	Utah 23/6
• Fowey 6/7; ammunition	joined EBC32	Omaha 7/7
Vessel considered to be in poor condition		
• Fowey 17/7; ammunition	joined EBC43	US area 18/7
• Southampton 31/7	Solent 1/8 EBC57W	Utah 1/8

Returned to London 15/8 for release 25/9

VILK 1,944/13 British, ex-Estonian (**MoWT/*Hudson**) – taken up 5/44 for Stores
• London (Royal Albert) 4/6; 31 vehicles and 124 troops

	Thames 5/6 ETC2Y	British area 7/6
• London (Millwall) 19/6	Thames 20/6 ETC15	
Convoy sheltered in Solent; left 22/6		Gold 22/6
• Grimsby 11/7	Thames 13/7 ETC36	Gold 14/7
• London 27/7	Thames 28/7 ETC51	Arromanches 29/7
• London 11/8	Thames 12/8 ETC66	Arromanches 13/8
• London (Millwall) 27/8	Thames 28/8 ETC82	Arromanches 29/8

Returned to London 6/9 to load for Arromanches

VLIESTROOM 655/12 Dutch – taken up 29/4/44 for Ammunition
• Swansea; left BC 2/6; embarked 42 troops in Solent

	Solent 7/6 EBC2W	Omaha 8/6
• Southampton 24/6	Solent 25/6 ETC17W	Gold 25/6
• Southampton 5/7	Solent 6/7 ETC28W	Juno 6/7
• Southampton 17/7	Solent 18/7 ETC40W	Gold 18/7
• Southampton 26/7	Solent 27/7 ETC49W	Gold 27/7
• Southampton 1/8	Solent 2/8 EBC58W	Omaha 2/8
In collision with coaster *Arbroath* at beachhead 0035 4/8		
• Southampton 11/8	Solent 13/8 EBC69W	US area 13/8
• Southampton 24/8	Solent 25/8 EBC81W	Barfleur 25/8

Returned to Southampton 5/9 to load for US area

Vliestroom reached Normandy on 8th June 1944, carrying ammunition from Swansea's Prince of Wales Dock and troops from the Solent.
[Willem H. Moojen collection]

VULCANUS 1,819/07 Dutch – taken up 1/5/44 for Stores
• Barry 9/6	BC 12/6 EBC9	Omaha 15/6
Returned to Barry 28/6 requiring repairs		
• Barry 3/7	BC 4/7 EBC31	Omaha 6/7
• Swansea 25/7	BC 25/7 EBC52	Utah 27/7
• Avonmouth 17/8	BC 18/8 EBC76	US area 20/8

Returned to Humber 11/9 to load for Caen

WALDO HILL 1,791/43 British, ex-US (MoWT/*Cory) – taken up 4/44 for Ammunition
• London (Tilbury) 5/6; 2,550 tons Thames 7/6 ETC3   Gold 9/6
Six ship's gunners injured ashore as a result of recklessly tampering with unexploded mortar bomb 1900 12/6; ship's plating set in amidships and aft at beachhead while taking on water from tanker *British Princess* in heavy swell 2010-2245 14/6
• London 24/6   Thames 25/6 ETC18   Arromanches 26/6
• Harwich 13/7; stores   Thames 14/7 ETC37   Arromanches 15/7
• Grimsby; left Thames 2/8 for Solent; at anchor for over three weeks; HM landing craft *LCT413* collided with vessel's port cable and stem 2250 19/8
                                 Solent 28/8 ETC81W
Leaving Solent, struck submerged object which scraped and bumped heavily along full length of ship's bottom 0200 28/8   Juno 28/8
Returned to London 13/9

WALENBURGH 496/38 Dutch – taken up 18/5/44 for Cased Petrol
• Sharpness 16/6   BC 17/6 EBC14   Omaha 19/6
• Llanelly 1/7   BC 2/7 EBC29   Omaha 4/7
• Llanelly 15/7   BC 16/7 EBC43   Omaha 18/7
• Llanelly 4/8   BC 5/8 EBC63   US area 7/8
Returned to Plymouth 18/8 for repairs

WALLACE ROSE 632/31 British (Hughes) – taken up 20/4/44 for Ammunition
• Penarth 30/5; ammunition and 65 troops; left BC 30/5
Diverted to Southampton; left 4/6 Solent 6/6 EWC1A   Utah 7/6
• Southampton 17/6   Solent 18/6 ETC12W   Gold 18/6
Lost both anchors during the 19-22/6 storm but used engines to hold position; vessel pounded and shipped heavy seas; Master offically commended Mate for exceptional courage and bravery, unparelled in his 18 years in command, in contributing to saving ship, cargo and crew
• Southampton 10/7   Solent 11/7 ETC33W   Juno 11/7
• Southampton 18/7   Solent 19/7 ETC41W   Gold 19/7
• Southampton 27/7   Solent 28/7 ETC50W   Port-en-Bessin 28/7
Returned to Solent 1/8; surveyed at Blyth for damage caused by explosions, heavy weather and pounding over the period 19/6-30/7

The Master of *Wallace Rose* glowingly commended the Mate for saving the ship in the June storm which struck the beachheads. *[Fotoflite/J. and M. Clarkson collection]*

WATERGATE 499/12 British (Coppack) – taken up 21/4/44 for Cased Petrol
• Plymouth 12/6   joined ECM5   Utah 13/6
• Plymouth 24/6   joined EBC20   Omaha 25/6
• Plymouth 3/7   joined EBC29   Omaha 4/7
• Plymouth 10/7   joined EBC36   Utah 11/7
• Plymouth 17/7   joined EBC43   Utah 18/7
• Plymouth 25/7, with barge in tow joined EBC51   Utah 26/7
• Southampton 11/8   Solent 12/8 EBC68W   US area 12/8
Returned to Thames 31/8, then arrived West Hartlepool 12/9 for survey of grounding damage sustained between 19/7 and 19/8

The service speed of some coasters was such that they could easily sail to Normandy in ocean-going cargo ship convoys: *Watergate*, pictured in 1938, did precisely this on her first June 1944 crossing. *[Captain J. F. van Puyvelde]*

WATSON FERRIS 1,791/43 British, ex-US (MoWT/*Cory) – taken up 5/44 for Stores
• Left Grimsby 7/6 for London where cargo had been delivered in error
London 11/6   Thames 12/6 ETC8   Mulberry B 14/6
• Grimsby 27/6   Thames 29/6 ETC22   Gold 30/6
• Harwich 17/7; 1,453 tons   Thames 18/7 ETC41   Juno 19/7
• Grimsby 1/8   Thames 3/8 ETC57   Arromanches 4/8
• Grimsby 29/8; left Thames 31/8 Solent 3/9 EPM52W   Utah 3/9
Returned to Grimsby 13/9

Scheduled to load at Grimsby, the stores carrier *Watson Ferris* was moved to London after it was found that her first cargo had been sent to the wrong port. *[National Maritime Museum, P24359]*

WESTBURN 2,842/29 British (*Westoll) – taken up 2/5/44 for Stores
• Swansea 3/6; vehicles and troops BC 5/6 EBC2Z		Omaha 8/6
• Barry 19/6	BC 20/6 EBC17	
Convoy sheltered in Poole Bay		Omaha 24/6

In collision with coaster *Kalev* at beachhead 1610 24/6
• Barry 19/7	BC 20/7 EBC47	Cherbourg 22/7

Ship's stores damaged by heavy rain and bad weather 25/7
• Cardiff 5/8	BC 6/8 EBC64	US area 8/8

In high wind, port anchor dragged and stern grounded; starboard anchor let go but, after paying out 40 fathoms cable, anchor lost 1800 14/8; fouled coaster *Eskwood*, both vessels being on the ground and rolling towards each other; tug's attempts to separate vessels failed when ropes parted; both ships damaged by the swell lifting the vessels towards each other; in further attempt to pull *Westburn* off beach, tug's wire broke 15/8; change of wind direction enabled ship to come off under own steam, with plates on starboard side heavily indented, frames set in and stern and rudder damaged 16/8; returned to Barry 21/8 to load for US area

WESTDALE 424/11 British (Ohlson) – taken up 19/4/44 for Stores
• Avonmouth 1/6; left BC 2/6; embarked 21 troops in Solent		
	Solent 7/6 EBC2W	Utah 8/6
• Southampton 17/6; 215 tons ammunition		
	Solent 18/6 ETC12W	Gold 18/6

Lost. Whilst steaming slowly ahead to anchors during the storm at 0200 20/6, nearby mine explosion, which sank a landing craft, caused leakage in engine room and stokehold; vessel began to settle by the stern, so anchors slipped and ship allowed to drift ashore but grounded 400 yards out; by 0930 20/6, only forecastle head rails and bridge top showed above water level; vessel refloated 24/6 but submerged again for further four days in bad weather, following which cargo discharged; ship, in derelict condition, left beachhead 5/7 in tow of tug *Assiduous*, with pumps controlling an inrush of 200 tons of water per hour; beached at Netley in Southampton Water 6/7; after inspection in drydock, vessel declared a constructive total loss

WESTLAND 426/31 Dutch – taken up 8/5/44 for Cased Petrol
• London (King George V); 265 tons cased petrol and stores; left Thames 31/5;		
embarked 59 troops in Solent	Solent 5/6 Force L1	Sword 6/6 (D-Day)
• Poole 13/6	Solent 13/6 ETC8W	British area 14/6
• Poole 28/6	Solent 29/6 ETC21W	Juno 29/6
• Poole 3/7	Solent 4/7 ETC26W	Juno 4/7
• Poole 9/7	Solent 10/7 ETC32W	Gold 10/7
• Poole 15/7	Solent 16/7 ETC38W	Gold 16/7
• Poole 22/7	Solent 23/7 ETC45W	Gold 23/7
• Poole 28/7	Solent 30/7 ETC52W	Port-en-Bessin 30/7
• Poole 4/8	Solent 5/8 ETC58W	Port-en-Bessin 5/8
• Poole 12/8	Solent 13/8 ETC66W	Arromanches 13/8
• Poole 21/8	Solent 22/8 ETC75W	Port-en-Bessin 22/8
• Poole 26/8	Solent 27/8 ETC80W	Port-en-Bessin 27/8

Returned to Poole 1/9 to load for Dieppe

WESTON 485/20 British (ICI) – taken up 5/44 for Stores
• London (Royal Albert) 2/6; 200 tons; left Thames 5/6; embarked 41 troops in		
Solent	Solent 7/6 ETC22W	Sword 8/6
• Southampton 12/6	Solent 12/6 ETC7W	Juno 13/6
• Southampton 17/6	Solent 18/6 ETC12W	Gold 18/6

Went aground 1/7; refloated 5/7 after temporary repairs effected; arrived Southampton 18/7
• Southampton 23/7	Solent 24/7 ETC46W	Gold 24/7
• Southampton 28/7	Solent 29/7 ETC51W	Gold 29/7
• Southampton 2/8	Solent 3/8 ETC56W	Arromanches 3/8
• Southampton 8/8	Solent 9/8 ETC62W	Port-en-Bessin 9/8
• Southampton 14/8	Solent 15/8 ETC68W	Port-en-Bessin 15/8

Returned to Southampton 21/8

Expected to be unfit for service after going aground on 1st July 1944, temporary repairs were sufficient to enable *Weston* to resume her sailings without further delay. *[J. and M. Clarkson collection]*

WESTOWN 710/21 British (Grace) – taken up 13/4/44 for Stores
• London (Royal Albert) 3/6; 393 tons; left Thames 6/6		
	Solent 9/6 ETC4W	
Convoy heavily attacked in English Channel by E-boats 10/6		Sword 10/6
• Poole 15/6; cased petrol	Solent 16/6 EBC11W	Utah 16/6

Vessel driven ashore after losing both anchors during the storm 19/6; heavy collision on port side with US landing craft *LCT511* caused severe denting to shell plating and bending and fracturing of frames 2330 21/6; arrived Poole 13/7 and Cardiff 19/7 for repairs
• Milford Haven 31/7; perishables	BC 1/8 EBC59	
Convoy diverted to Solent; left 4/8		Isigny 4/8
• Sharpness 16/8; left BC 18/8	Solent 24/8 EBC78W	Barfleur 24/8

Bottom damaged on rough ground in Barfleur, then, on departure, vessel's hull severely affected by grounding heavily outside the piers 0545 29/8; returned to Solent 15/9 and London 20/9

WHEATCROP 523/24 British (Spillers) – taken up 21/4/44 for Ammunition
• Penarth 1/6; left BC 2/6; embarked 44 troops in Solent		
	Solent 7/6 EBC2W	Utah 8/6
• Southampton 25/6; stores	Solent 26/6 ETC18W	Sword 26/6
• Southampton 3/7; stores	Solent 4/7 ETC26W	Port-en-Bessin 4/7
• Southampton 13/7	Solent 14/7 ETC36W	Gold 14/7
• Southampton 20/7	Solent 21/7 ETC43W	Arromanches 21/7
• Southampton 26/7	Solent 27/7 ETC49W	Arromanches 27/7

On return to Solent, sustained considerable bow and port side damage when struck by HM landing craft *LCT304* 2320 29/7; repairs carried out at Southampton (Northam)
• Southampton 27/8	Solent 28/8 ETC81W	Arromanches 28/8

Returned to Southampton 2/9 to load for Arromanches

Berth 3, North Side, Penarth was the loading point for *Wheatcrop*'s first cargo of US ammunition for Utah beachhead. *[Harry Stewart/J. and M. Clarkson collection]*

WILD ROSE **873/21 British (Hughes)** – taken up 20/4/44 for Ammunition
• Swansea 4/6; ammunition and 39 troops

	BC 5/6 EBC2Y	US area 8/6
• Southampton 25/6; stores	Solent 26/6 EBC21W	Omaha 26/6
• Southampton 10/7; stores	Solent 11/7 EBC36W	Omaha 11/7
• Southampton 18/7; 750 tons asphalt		
	Solent 19/7 EBC44W	Omaha 19/7
• Plymouth 11/8; stores	joined EBC68	US area 12/8
• Plymouth 27/8; stores	joined EBC84	St Vaast 28/8

Returned to Plymouth 6/9 to load for US area

WILLIAM BURSLEY **1,791/43 British, ex-US (MoWT/*Stephenson Clarke)** – taken up 4/44 for Stores

• Barry 9/6	BC 10/6 EBC7	Omaha 13/6
• Swansea 26/6	BC 27/6 EBC24	Omaha 29/6
• Swansea 9/7	BC 9/7 EBC36	Omaha 11/7
• Penarth 29/7	BC 2/8 EBC60	
Diverted to Solent; at anchor for nearly four weeks		
	Solent 13/8 EBC69W	Cherbourg 13/8
• Swansea 31/8	BC 31/8 EBC89	
Became detached from convoy; put into Dartmouth 2/9		
	joined EBC95	Utah 8/9

WILLIAM H DANIELS **1,772/23 Canadian** – taken up 5/44 for Stores
• London (Royal Albert) 4/6; 35 vehicles and 140 troops

	Thames 5/6 ETC2Y	British area 7/6

Beachhead subjected to concentrated air attack 0130 8/6 and further air raids 9/6
• London 13/6; 1,010 tons   Thames 13/6 ETC9   Juno 15/6

Failure of US tank landing ship *LST55* to clear vessel's bows, when both anchors down during the storm, caused heavy stem damage in resulting collision 1335 19/6
• London 28/6   Thames 29/6 ETC22
Convoy subjected to long-range gunfire in Strait of Dover for two hours 29/6

		Arromanches 30/6
• London (Tilbury) 16/7	Thames 17/7 ETC40	Gold 18/7

Whilst at anchor awaiting return convoy, HM trawler *King Emperor* crossed ship's bow towing oiling barges *LBO34*, *LBO59* and *LBO61*; *59* struck the vessel's port bow, causing large indentations, and *61* caused damage to plating on port side 1120 24/7; returned to London 25/7 for temporary release

WILLIAM HOMAN **1,793/43 British, ex-US (MoWT/*France, Fenwick)** – taken up 4/44 for Stores
• London 31/5; turned back, dynamo trouble; left 12/6

	Thames 13/6 ETC9	Gold 15/6
• Harwich 30/6	Thames 1/7 ETC24	Arromanches 2/7

Four dock operating soldiers injured in derrick accident during cargo discharge 4/7

• London 10/7	Thames 11/7 ETC34	Arromanches 12/7
• Grimsby 24/7	Thames 26/7 ETC49	
Turned back with engine defects	Thames 27/7 ETC50	Arromanches 28/7
• Grimsby 8/8	Thames 11/8 ETC65	Arromanches 12/8

Returned to Thames, then arrived Blyth 20/8, prior to loading at London for Dieppe

Dynamo trouble delayed by more than a week delivery of *William Homan*'s first shipment of stores for the British beachhead. *[National Maritime Museum, P24397]*

WILLIAM HOWLAND **1,792/43 British, ex-US (MoWT/*Heyn)** – taken up 4/44 for Stores
• Grimsby; 1,153 tons; called London, left 6/6

	Thames 7/6 ETC3	British area 9/6
• London 20/6	Thames 23/6 ETC16	Sword 24/6
• London 12/7	Thames 13/7 ETC36	Gold 14/7
• Grimsby 1/8	Thames 4/8 ETM55	

Involved in collision with returning coaster *Fire Queen* 0400 6/8; diverted to Solent, then to drydock at Southampton with cargo aboard 8/8; left 13/8

	Solent 13/8 EBC69W	Cherbourg 13/8

Returned to Grimsby 5/9 to load for Caen

WILNO 2,018/26 **Polish** – taken up 14/5/44 for Stores
• Failed to load 35 vehicles at London (Millwall) as scheduled, so transferred to Cardiff

Cardiff	BC 23/6 EBC20	Omaha 25/6
• Cardiff 8/7	BC 9/7 EBC36	Utah 11/7

Start of cargo discharge delayed for two weeks

• Barry 15/8	BC 15/8 EBC73	US area 17/8

Returned to Humber 11/9 to load for Cherbourg

Cargo arrangements in the US sector in July 1944 became so unpredictable that the Polish stores coaster *Wilno*, seen here in 1939, waited over two weeks before discharge even commenced. *[Captain J. F. van Puyvelde]*

WINONA 2,174/06 **Canadian** – taken up 5/44 for Stores
• London (Royal Albert) 4/6; 34 vehicles and 130 troops

	Thames 5/6 ETC2Z	British area 7/6
• London 15/6	Thames 16/6 ETC11	Juno 17/6
• London 4/7	Thames 5/7 ETC28	Gold 6/7

Whilst Vice Commodore of convoy, was unable to maintain designated speed, so convoy slowed accordingly

• London (Millwall) 19/7	Thames 19/7 ETC42	Juno 20/7

Under repair in Thames 4/8-15/8

• London 20/8	Thames 21/8 ETC75	Arromanches 22/8

Returned to London 29/8 to load cased aviation fuel for Dieppe

WOOLER 507/36 **British (Tyne-Tees)** – taken up 19/4/44 for Cased Petrol
• Garston 12/5; called Swansea 31/5-3/6; embarked 65 troops;

	BC 5/6 EBC2Y	Omaha 8/6
• Port Talbot 18/6	BC 19/6 EBC16	
Convoy sheltered in Poole Bay		Isigny 23/6
• Llanelly 2/7	BC 3/7 EBC30	Isigny 5/7
• Plymouth 10/7	joined EBC37	Utah 12/7
• Barry 23/7; 600 tons stores	BC 24/7 EBC51	Isigny 26/7
• Poole 4/8	Solent 6/8 EBC61W	Isigny 6/8
• Poole 16/8	Solent 18/8 EBC74W	Isigny 18/8
• Poole 30/8	Solent 3/9 EBC89W	Isigny 3/9

Returned to Poole 11/9 to load for St Vaast

YEWGLEN 607/15 **British (Stewart)** – taken up 2/5/44 for Ammunition
• London (Tilbury Jetty) 30/5; 610 tons; left Thames 31/5; embarked 59 troops in Solent

	Solent 6/6 EWC1B	Gold 7/6
• Southampton 15/6	Solent 16/6 ETC10W	Sword 16/6

At beachhead during the 19-22/6 storm; damaged and beached 23/6; refloated 4/7

• Southampton 18/7	Solent 19/7 ETC41W	Gold 19/7
• Newhaven 25/7	joined ETC48	Gold 26/7

• Southampton 31/7; went aground 1/8; refloated under own power and turned back

	Solent 5/8 EBC60W	US area 5/8
• Southampton 26/8	Solent 27/8 EBC83W	US area 27/8

Returned to Solent 3/9 to load at Southampton for US area

YEWMOUNT 859/39 **British (Stewart)** – taken up 26/4/44 for Cased Petrol
• London (King George V) 20/5; 852 tons; left Thames 8/6

	Solent 11/6 ETC6W	Gold 12/6
• Sharpness 25/6	BC 26/6 EBC23	Utah 28/6
• Llanelly 10/7	BC 11/7 EBC38	Omaha 13/7
• Southampton 23/7	Solent 24/7 EBC49W	Utah 24/7
• Southampton 1/8	Solent 2/8 EBC58W	US area 2/8
• Southampton 11/8	Solent 12/8 EBC68W	US area 12/8

Returned to Southampton 18/8

YEWPARK 827/30 **British (Stewart)** – taken up 7/4/44 for Stores
• London (King George V) 26/5; 1,035 tons; left Thames 31/5; embarked 58 troops in Solent

	Solent 6/6 EWC1B	Gold 7/6
• Southampton 15/6	Solent 17/6 EBC12W	Omaha 17/6

Grounded amidships with barges along each side 0045 19/6; the storm created heavy swell, with vessel pounding heavily; barge crews transferred to *Yewpark* and barges drifted ashore; vessel refloated with forepeak storeroom flooded 0800 19/6; cargo discharge resumed 22/6

• Southampton 4/7	Solent 5/7 EBC30W	St Vaast 5/7
• Plymouth 19/7	joined EBC46	Utah 21/7
• Southampton 28/7	Solent 29/7 EBC54W	Utah 29/7
• Southampton 9/8	Solent 10/8 EBC66W	Omaha 10/8
• Southampton 19/8	Solent 20/8 EBC76W	US area 20/8

Whilst ship at anchor, hatch fittings damaged when deck cargo of boat pontoons shifted due to heavy rolling in rough sea 21/8; returned to Southampton 29/8 to load for Barfleur

After months of cross-Channel service, *Yewtree* was withdrawn for extensive repairs at Plymouth on 1st March 1945. *[W.H. Brown/J. and M. Clarkson collection]*

YEWTREE 826/28 British (Stewart) – taken up 2/5/44 for Ammunition
- London (Tilbury) 23/5; 840 tons; left Thames 8/6

	Solent 12/6 ETC7W	Gold 13/6

Beachhead subjected to shelling and air attacks 13/6
- London (Tilbury Jetty) 20/6 — Thames 23/6 ETC16 — Juno 24/6
- London (Tilbury) 2/7 — Thames 3/7 ETC26 — Gold 4/7
- London (Tilbury Jetty) 14/7 — Thames 15/7 ETC38 — Gold 16/7
- London (Tilbury) 25/7 — Thames 26/7 ETC49 — Arromanches 27/7
- London (Tilbury) 8/8 — Thames 11/8 ETC65

Convoy diverted to Solent; left 13/8 — Juno 13/8
- Newhaven 19/8 — joined ETC73 — Arromanches 20/8
- Newhaven 29/8 — joined ETC83 — British area 30/8

Returned to Newhaven 7/9, then to Southampton to load for Arromanches

YOKEFLEET 844/10 British (Ouse/*Atkinson) – taken up 10/6/44 for Stores
- London 17/6 — Thames 18/6 ETC13 — Juno 19/6
- London 2/7 — Thames 3/7 ETC26 — Gold 4/7
- London (Tilbury) 15/7 — Thames 16/7 ETC39 — Gold 17/7
- Harwich 25/7; ammunition — Thames 26/7 ETC49 — Juno 27/7
- Southampton 6/8 — Solent 7/8 ETC60W — Port-en-Bessin 7/8
- Southampton 18/8 — Solent 19/8 ETC72W — Port-en-Bessin 19/8

Returned to Southampton 29/8, where in collision with train ferry *Hampton Ferry* 1958 2/9; subsequently loaded for Caen

Four days after D-Day, *Yokefleet* was already in the Thames when she was taken up for Normandy service as a London-loading stores carrier. *[Ships in Focus]*

ZEELAND (mv) 421/30 Dutch – taken up 26/4/44 for Cased Petrol
- London (Purfleet) 25/5; 420 tons; left Thames 9/6

	Solent 12/6 ETC7W	Gold 13/6
Poole 29/6	Solent 30/6 ETC22W	Gold 30/6
Poole 7/7	Solent 8/7 ETC30W	Juno 8/7
Poole 13/7	Solent 14/7 ETC36W	Gold 14/7
Poole 20/7	Solent 21/7 ETC43W	Gold 21/7
Poole	Solent 26/7 ETC48W	Gold 26/7
Poole	Solent 3/8 ETC56W	Gold 3/8
Poole 8/8	Solent 9/8 ETC62W	Port-en-Bessin 9/8
Poole 15/8	Solent 16/8 ETC69W	Port-en-Bessin 16/8
Poole 25/8	Solent 26/8 ETC79W	Port-en-Bessin 26/8

Returned to Poole 30/8 to load for Juno

ZEELAND (ss) 2,726/30 Dutch – taken up 9/5/44 for Stores
- Swansea 3/6; vehicles and troops — BC 5/6 EBC2Z — Omaha 8/6
- Barry 17/6 — BC 18/6 EBC15 — Omaha 20/6
- Barry 6/7 — BC 7/7 EBC34 — Omaha 9/7
- Barry 27/7 — BC 28/7 EBC55

Diverted to Solent for orders: left 4/8; turned back

	Solent 5/8 EBC60W	Cherbourg 5/8
Barry 26/8	BC 27/8 EBC85	Omaha 29/8

Returned to Southampton 18/9

The steamship *Zeeland*, photographed in 1954, was one of two coasters in the military cargo fleet of the same nationality and name but of very different size and propulsion. *[Captain J. F. van Puyvelde]*

After serving the British beachheads, *Zelo* was one of three coasters to reach Dieppe on 17th September 1944 carrying bridging materials. *[J. and M. Clarkson collection]*

ZELO 2,294/21 British (Pelton) – taken up 8/4/44 for Stores
- Grimsby 25/5; 1,500 tons; called London 27/5-9/6

	Thames 10/6 ETC6	Mulberry B 12/6

Whilst at anchor, touched bottom and suffered from heavy pounding 0800-1127 12/6; on return, called Portsmouth 20-23/6

• London 3/7	Thames 4/7 ETC27	Gold 5/7
• London 18/7	Thames 19/7 ETC42	Arromanches 20/7

Struck submerged object at beachhead 23/7

• London 30/7	Thames 31/7 ETC54	Arromanches 1/8
• London 11/8	Thames 12/8 ETC66	Juno 13/8

Whilst discharging cargo into landing craft in strong wind, sustained heavy indentation on starboard side 15/8

• London 27/8	Thames 28/8 ETC82	Juno 29/8

Returned to London 10/9 to load bridging materials for Dieppe

ZUIDERHAVEN 315/41 Dutch – taken up 18/5/44 for Ammunition
• London (Tilbury); 240 tons; left Thames 7/6

	Solent 9/6 ETC4W	

Convoy heavily attacked in English Channel by E-boats 10/6   Juno 10/6

• Littlehampton	Solent 16/6 ETC10W	Gold 16/6
• Littlehampton 27/6	joined ETC19	Gold 27/6
• Littlehampton 2/7	joined ETC25	Gold 3/7
• Littlehampton	joined ETC31	Sword 9/7
• Littlehampton 15/7	joined ETC37	Juno 15/7
• Littlehampton 20/7	joined ETC42	Juno 20/7
• Littlehampton 27/7	joined ETC50	Gold 28/7
• Littlehampton 2/8	joined ETC55	Arromanches 2/8

Thirteen shell plates indented by grounding; other plates damaged and frames buckled in collision with breakwater; returned to Littlehampton 6/8

• Littlehampton 10/8	joined ETC63	Juno 10/8
• Littlehampton 14/8	joined ETC68	Juno 15/8
• Littlehampton 20/8	joined ETC74	Arromanches 21/8

Returned to Littlehampton 26/8 to load for Dieppe

ZUIDLAND 426/31 Dutch – taken up 19/4/44 for Cased Petrol
• London (Purfleet); 396 tons; left Thames 8/6

	Solent 11/6 ETC6W	Juno 12/6
• Poole	Solent 18/6 ETC12W	Gold 18/6
• Poole 25/6	Solent 26/6 ETC18W	Gold 26/6
• Poole 30/6	Solent 1/7 ETC23W	Gold 1/7
• Poole 7/7	Solent 8/7 ETC30W	Gold 8/7
• Poole 14/7	Solent 15/7 ETC37W	Gold 15/7

Returned to Poole 18/7; loaded but unable to sail owing to rudder problems, so cargo transhipped overside to coaster *Evertsen*

ZUIJDERBURGH 2,630/06 Dutch – taken up 10/5/44 for Stores
• Barry 11/6	BC 13/6 EBC10	Utah 16/6
• Swansea 15/7	BC 15/7 EBC42	Omaha 17/7
• Newport 30/8	BC 30/8 EBC88	US area 1/9

In August 1944, the need for rudder repairs brought to a sudden end the scheduled sailings from Poole of the cased petrol carrier *Zuidland*. *[J. and M. Clarkson collection]*

After reaching Omaha beachhead on 17th July 1944, massive delays postponed *Zuijderburgh*'s return to Swansea until 21st August. *[Dick Gorter collection]*

Section 4
Supplying the Allied Armies in France and Belgium
September 1944 onwards

The speed and range of a military advance is heavily dependent upon the ability of the transport system to deliver supplies, particularly of ammunition, food and fuel. The crossing of the River Seine by Allied forces on 30th August and the German surrender of Dieppe two days later prompted a major reorganisation of the cross-Channel supply pattern, in which the main British discharge ports had latterly been Arromanches and Port-en-Bessin. Minesweepers completed their work to enable the first coasters to reach Ouistreham and pass along the canal to Caen on 4th September. *Erica, Glamis, Goldfinch, Kalev* and *Serenity* were the first of 91 coasters to be routed to Caen in September, a month during which 68 vehicles and over 40,000 tons of stores were discharged at the port, a cargo total almost equalling that handled at Arromanches during the same period. *Cairngorm, Henri Gerlinger* and the motor coaster *Zeeland* were the last ships to be directed to Juno beach on 5th September, before it was closed after having handled 349 coaster arrivals since D-Day and, during September, only 14, mainly cased petrol, coasters were directed to Port-en-Bessin. The lack of any threat from German surface vessels and U-boats prompted the early September removal of destroyers from the English Channel and the decision to permit merchant ships to burn dimmed running lights for the first time. Although Dieppe's port installations had been

demolished, the harbour had only been partially blocked, so the first WDC ([Isle of] Wight Dieppe Coaster) convoy was able to leave the exposed assembly anchorage off Newhaven at 2000 on 6th September. It was composed of three ammunition vessels, *Kenrix* and *Raftsund* from Newhaven harbour and *Zuiderhaven* from Littlehampton, and of six cased petrol carriers, *Westland* from Poole and *Boston Trader, Empire Estuary, Empire Shoal, Oranmore* and *Prase* from Southampton, all of which reached the French port the following day. Berths were soon available for 12 coasters but cargo discharge was initially hampered by a shortage of cranes and vehicles. The next eight of the daily WDC convoys were composed of the following military cargo coasters:
• WDC2: *Dorrien Rose* from Southampton; *Macville* from Newhaven and *Thornaby* from Harwich
• WDC3: *Evertsen* from Poole; *Cameo, Durward, Emerald Queen* and *Lowestoft Trader* from Southampton; *Asteria* and *Melissa* from Newhaven and *Fagerbro* from Harwich
• WDC4: *Actinia* from Southampton; *Hawarden Bridge* and *Summity* from Newhaven and *Glamis* and *Goldfinch* from London
• WDC5: *Larchfield* and *Polly M* from Southampton; *City of Charleroy, Sandhill* and *Serenity* from London and *Lysland* from Grimsby

When Dieppe was opened to coasters on 7th September, *Evertsen* was switched to that port to discharge her cased petrol cargo. *[Dick Gorter collection]*

For *Polly M*, sailings to Normandy were followed by calls at Dieppe and later Boulogne, prior to her February 1945 release. *[W. H. Brown/J. and M. Clarkson collection]*

- WDC6: *Cairngorm* from Poole; *Glen, Rosemarie, Sollund* and *Staley Bridge* from Southampton and *Cedarwood* from Harwich
- WDC7: *Antrim Coast, Empire Estuary, Erna, Kenrix* and *Njord* from Southampton and *Signality* from London
- WDC8: *Boston Trader, Lowestoft Trader* and *Saint Angus* from Southampton; *Guernsey Queen* and *Spes* from London; *Varegg* from Harwich and *Gurden Gates* with coal from Hull
- WDC9: *Northgate* from Poole; *Dorrien Rose, Ebbrix* and *Parknasilla* from Southampton and *Fylla* and *Greyfriars* from Harwich. The latter vessel sustained considerable bow damage at sea in the early hours of 15th September in a collision resulting from a sudden course alteration by the escorting trawler, HMS *Grenadier*. During September, Dieppe handled a total of 211 coasters carrying over 27,000 tons of ammunition, 32,500 tons of cased petrol and nearly 40,000 tons of stores, as well as a number of vehicles and railway locomotives.

Reviewing the situation in the US area on 4th September, we find coasters discharging cargoes at a range of locations: an east to west snapshot reveals 14 coasters at Omaha beach; 2 at Grandcamp; 11 at Isigny; 10 at St Vaast and 7 at Barfleur. *Rondo* was, after a long delay, finally discharging at Cherbourg, from where *Capito* and *Gaston Micard* were about to leave for Southampton and Barry respectively. Also in the US area were *Westown*, undergoing repairs to damage sustained at Barfleur, and *Channel Queen, Claudius Magnin, Dagenham, Marianne II* and *Topaz*, still loaded and awaiting orders as to their final destination. Further west, the Breton port of Morlaix was ready on 7th September to accommodate eight coasters, with St Brieuc becoming available four days later. With an

ever-increasing number of discharge ports, the American authorities estimated that their coaster requirements for the September–November period were likely to be 40 for service to Morlaix and St Brieuc; 57 for Barfleur, Isigny and St Vaast and 17 for Cherbourg: this total of 114 was in addition to the fleet required to handle the coal shipments to Granville, Cherbourg and St Brieuc. On 9th September, it was realised that US assault troops around Brest were running short of ammunition, so *Theseus* was sent to Morlaix to assist five Dutch coasters already engaged in transhipping supplies from Liberty ships discharging at the six anchorage positions established there. Other September developments included the

In September 1944, a shortage of ammunition prompted the sending of *Theseus* to ferry cargo from Liberty ships anchored at Morlaix. *[Dick Gorter collection]*

completion of mine clearance at Le Havre for coasters of up to 2,500 tons; the diversion of some Dieppe-bound vessels to nearby Le Treport, which was little damaged and offered direct cargo discharge to rail wagons, and the opening of Boulogne, to which port five cased petrol and stores coasters were directed. That month also saw the inauguration of sailings to Ostend after the removal of 14 sunken vessels, the first three coasters called forward being *Cedarwood, Fagerbro* and *Valborg*. *Cedarwood* had 640 tons of ammunition on board when a mine explosion beneath her No 2 hold at 1617 on 1st October resulted in the vessel heeling over to starboard towards the quay and sinking in 20 feet of water, before eventually settling on an even keel: it took until 23rd December for her cargo to be completely discharged by divers and until 12th May before she could be refloated for repairs at Antwerp.

New cross-Channel convoy designators were introduced in October, the first sailing from the Thames on the 10th being TMC1 (Thames Arromanches Coaster No 1) comprising *Carnalea*,

On her return from Cherbourg on 10th September 1944, *Rondo* was found to be badly strained and in need of engine overhaul. *[W. H. Brown/J. and M. Clarkson collection]*

Cordale was assigned to carry British supplies from London (Tilbury) to Ostend early in 1945: at the Belgian port in February she grounded, losing a propeller blade as a result. *[National Maritime Museum, P21896]*

Cordale, Crane, Erica, Goldfinch, Isac, Lesto, Newlands, Redcar, Sandhill and *Waldo Hill*, all of which were, despite the Arromanches designator, destined for Dieppe. On 24th October, *Empire Sedge* reached Dieppe with seven lifts of over five tons but the wooden quays proved of insufficient strength for discharge to be carried out. The number of coaster arrivals in October rose to 264 at Dieppe and to 38 at Boulogne, while at Ostend, where 12 berths became available, there was a massive increase to 110, over two-thirds carrying ammunition. Length of stay at Ostend for coasters was generally a few days but, in late October, *Kordecki*'s cargo of 1,477 tons of transportation stores took an exceptional 10 days to discharge. Consideration was given to the possibility of augmenting the facilities at Ostend by directing coasters onto the beach for discharge: although considered practical, the proposal was rejected in view of the inevitability of disruption due to autumn storms. Damage at Le Havre made Rouen the preferred alternative to St Vaast, Isigny and other small ports but a survey regarding its use revealed that the River Seine was blocked by sunken vessels in two places and that, in Rouen itself, 54 barges, 19 tugs and 67 other wrecks were on the bottom alongside the quays. Despite the damage, Le Havre was soon made fit for coaster use and *Nephrite* arrived on 22nd October; *East Coaster* and *Oxford* came in the following day and *Granby* on the 26th: a month later berths for 21 coasters became available. The eastward movement of the military front line prompted the need for the daily transportation from Caen to Boulogne or Ostend of about 2,500 tons of ammunition and stores and, to achieve this, coasters were required to make a triangular voyage, from London back to London, of up to 25 days duration.

In the US area of the Normandy beaches, the stranded naval collier *Yewdale* caused severe problems to two military coasters. On 5th October, *Dona Flora*, in the process of beaching for discharge, fractured her rudder post and sustained other damage when she struck *Yewdale* port side amidships. In strong winds the following day, *Aaro*, anchored near *Yewdale*, lost firstly her starboard anchor, then the port one and finally her spare. A 30 foot circular hole extending from her bilge keel to her bridge deck resulted from the weather forcing *Aaro*'s midship section onto the stern of *Yewdale* and her engine room was ripped open and flooded by the latter vessel's propeller. With heavy seas breaking over their ship, *Aaro*'s crew members and 40 dock operating troops transferred to *Yewdale*: the crew were sent back to England on 11th October and the vessel became a total loss. At Boulogne on 13th-14th October, *Porthrepta*, arriving from Dover with RAF stores, was holed beneath her boilers by grounding on a submerged wreck alongside the jetty and *Laban Howes* made an inauspicious arrival at Le Havre on 16th October carrying stores from Cardiff. She hit the lock gate, became holed in three places in her engine room on a submerged wreck, collided with the quay and grounded for five hours, with a heavy list to starboard and straining heavily amidships, before being swept into the dock by a strong flood tide. She was finally brought to a stop by her anchor, preparatory to completion of the unfortunate saga the following day, when a heavy case being discharged caused the receiving truck to collapse and come to rest with its front wheels resting on the quay and its after end overlapping the ship's bulwarks. On 21st October *Guernsey Queen* was completing a voyage from London with cased petrol: as she approached Boulogne basin at 1415, a mine explosion occurred

A catalogue of mishaps befell *Laban Howes* on her arrival at Le Havre on 16th October 1944, whilst carrying American stores from Cardiff. *[National Maritime Museum, N50027-154]*

near her port side, immediately forward of the bridge, killing the Mate, another crew member and two French pilots and injuring her Captain and four others. The ship's way carried her into the lock entrance, where she sank on her starboard side on top of a submerged wreck. Her cargo was unloaded and, on 2nd November, her forecastle was removed: eight days later the stern portion was severed and floated for a new forepart to be built and finally, on 14th November, the starboard side was removed. *Serenity* was one of the vessel's trapped inside the port until the entrance to the basin had been cleared. In early September, British troops reaching Antwerp had found its port facilities to be intact but German control of the islands at the mouth of the Scheldt seriously delayed use of the river. Finally, it was possible for the port to receive coasters, carrying stores but not ammunition or cased petrol, and the first three arrived on 26th November: for political considerations, it was decided that the inaugural coasters should fly the Belgian ensign and orders were given for these to be placed on board *Fano*, *Lysland*, *Maurice Rose*, *Moses Gay*, *Redcar* and *Thyra III*. In November *Empire Ness* was routed to Antwerp but failed to reach her destination: on her way up channel on the 30th, she was sunk in collision with the US Liberty ship *William Paca* near Terneuzen. With extensive damage to her hull forward of the bridge, the coaster slowly settled into the sand until her decks were 14 feet under water at low tide and salvage of both the ship and her cargo was impracticable.

Autumn gales seriously affected some of the coaster sailing schedules, with *Yewtree*, which had arrived in the Downs anchorage on 6th November from Newhaven, being forced to call at Dover for water and supplies before completing her voyage to Ostend, where 16 coasters could by that time be accommodated. This delay was not entirely due to weather conditions: it was also because the ammunition aboard *Gun*, *Jargoon* and *Sphene*, although loaded later, was given higher priority and these ships were therefore called forward in preference to *Yewtree*. The adverse conditions of 6th November also hit the outward-bound *Grenaa*, which lost her starboard anchor and 60 fathoms of cable in Barry Roads, then sustained damage on both sides of her forecastle in two collisions, the first with the Norwegian *Thoroy* and the second, when putting back into Barry Dock two days later, with another tanker, the recently-completed *Empire Crest*. The same bad weather was only one of the factors to affect *Jim*. She arrived at Barry on 9th November making water but, after stem repairs in drydock, was able to sail again one week late, only to sustain damage to

her derrick and to exhaust pipes on her funnel whilst crossing a storm-swept English Channel. When discharging her cargo of coal at Granville, the port wing of her bridge and other fittings were severely damaged by cranes and, by the time she reached Newport on 30th November, her starboard boiler had sprung a leak. *The Earl* encountered trouble at Boulogne on 7th November: striking a wreck when anchoring, she was holed and, with her engine room, stokehold and bunkers flooded, had to be beached and pumped out before entering port for cargo discharge. Arromanches, in the process of closing as a cargo terminal for use only as an assembly anchorage, was the 9th November departure point for *Crane* on a sailing which succeeded in attracting official displeasure, being performed independently and without permission. On a voyage

After striking a wreck at Boulogne on 7th November 1944, *The Earl* was beached for pumping out. *[J. and M. Clarkson]*

from Newport carrying US mails, fire severely damaged the midship accommodation of *J F V*, when she was 10 miles south of Swanage on 17th November. Further west, that same night, *Kylegorm* managed to reach port, despite being waterlogged, in a sinking condition and with her after hold leaking: her predicament had resulted from engine damage by sea water, followed by a collision in Plymouth Sound. That same month, *Krakow* was four miles from Rouen when she struck an underwater obstruction and subsequently sank forward alongside the quay: after temporary repairs, she was refloated and reached Southampton on 10th December for permanent work.

As would be expected, schedules had been carefully worked out for each type of ship and every category of cargo and for the applicable routes and convoy speeds. Calculations of ships' turn-

Although every effort had been made to clear the mass of river obstuctions left by the departing German forces, not all were removed as *Krakow* discovered prior to sinking forward on reaching Rouen in November 1944. *[National Maritime Museum, P23147]*

round times were based on the ability to load seven tons of stores, 10 tons of cased petrol or 12 tons of ammunition per gang hour, while discharge was based on 100 tons of stores, 120 tons of cased petrol or 140 tons of ammunition per 16-hour working day. For stores coasters, it was expected to take a full day to unload a small vessel, 1-2 days a medium one and 2-4 days a large one. To these cargo working times would be added, firstly, one day for undocking and convoy establishment; secondly, the relevant round trip passage durations and, thirdly, a further day for examination, berthing and bunkering on return. In practice, these turn-round times were becoming seriously undermined, and ships, excluding those on collier duty, were taking 61·5% more time than planned. Of the 213 round voyages completed during the second half of October, only 34 took the correct or less time and a colossal 179 were delayed, so that, instead of this fleet taking 1,846 ship/days to complete its voyages, the figure was nearer 3,000. Half of the problems were due to bad weather and the resultant bunching, with the other delays being attributed to slow cargo discharge; the lack of immediately available loading berths; the late arrival of cargo; diversions to alternative discharge ports and the need for repairs. Relevant to the latter was the fact that many of the coasters were of considerable age and all had been kept in service with the minimum of maintenance, despite being subjected to a degree of straining and damage to structure which would not have been tolerated in peacetime. However, boiler trouble in two 1943-built US ships showed that the need for running repairs was not exclusively confined to the older coasters. *Josiah P Cressey* reached London on 5th October in need of new boiler tubes and, nine weeks later, *Calvin Coggin* arrived in the Solent in the

tow of an Admiralty tug, not only with 90 tubes leaking in her boiler but also with her starboard bow damaged, as a result of striking the Herranville Bridge in the Caen Canal. Reports regarding the hazards of navigating the Caen Canal speak of sunken wrecks lining the banks and the fact that the bascule bridge could only lift half way: as a result it was necessary to angle ships one way to clear their foremasts and the other way to avoid damaging their mainmasts, a manoeuvre *Zelo* had failed to master in late September. On 19th November, the carrying away of the main bearing of *Drake*'s windlass resulted in the loss in the Solent of her starboard anchor and 45 fathoms of cable. Repairs were carried out at Southampton but, on her very first sailing three weeks later, the repaired part broke causing a repeat of the previous event, again in the Solent, except that this time only 30 fathoms of cable had to be slipped. To relieve the workload in British repair yards, the liberation of continental ports had made it possible to assign work elsewhere and a dozen coasters were drydocked at Dieppe during December, following the October opening of the graving dock there: Antwerp was able to share the repair burden soon afterwards and later Ghent also. The backlog of work continued to be a cause of concern, the extent of the problem being underlined by the fact that, on 20th March 1945, no fewer than 94 coasters were either awaiting, undergoing or completing repair.

From September, Military Cargo Branch coasters were in ever increasing numbers being allocated to meet the pressing demand to transport bulk coal for the use of Allied forces and essential civilian services, with *Heron*, one of the small Dutch coasters assigned to carry coal to St Brieuc, arriving there on 16th September. The

The Dutch coasters were ideally suited for utilising small ports: *Heron* loaded coal at Par and Penzance in Cornwall and her French destinations included St Brieuc in Brittany. *[Willem H. Moojen]*

tonnage of coal carried increased from 46,000 in October to 273,000 in March 1945, employing 113 vessels at its peak. In early November, *Dalewood*, *Empire Daughter* and *Juta* between them carried nearly 5,500 tons of coal from the Humber to Caen, a destination also served by *Amazone*, with 275 tons from Teignmouth in Devon, and by *Bidassoa* with 598 tons from Penarth. *Cassard* arrived at Cherbourg from Hull on 26th October with 1,939 tons but a 10-day discharge time and delays en route extended the duration of her round trip to a massive 34 days. A reminder that the U-boat threat was still alive came at 0932 on 23rd December when *Slemish*, proceeding into Cherbourg

carrying 1,650 tons of coal, was sunk by torpedo: the seven lives lost included three Greek crew members and one Arab. It was, however, Granville, with its nine discharge berths, which was the major destination for colliers: the cargo was discharged by German prisoners-of-war, then transported by railway wagon to its final destination. The sailing schedule, calling for a Channel crossing to Cherbourg and a daily coastal convoy, had been inaugurated on 16th September but was somewhat disrupted in mid-November when 14 Granville-bound coasters were forced to shelter off Plymouth, awaiting the abatement of the autumn gales referred to earlier. October-November sailings to Granville included *Edle*, *Gateshead*, *Kenrix* and *Mari*, carrying a combined total of 2,525 tons of coal from Barry; *Asteria*, *Cresco*, *Eskwood*, *Heire* and *Julia*, with 4,500 tons from Newport; *Baronscourt*, with 932 tons from the Humber, and *Heron* with 270 tons from Par in Cornwall. In early March the cargo flow through Granville was again interrupted when, berthed inside the harbour, were *Eskwood*, *Heien*, *Kyle Castle* and *Nephrite* from the Bristol Channel and *Parkwood* from the Humber, all of which had arrived on 7th March, had been unloaded and were waiting to sail. Outside the port was *Gem*, together with HM trawler *Pearl* which was on duty as convoy escort. At 2149 on 8th March, radar detected the approach of an enemy force of five craft: US *PC564* investigated and was disabled but *Gem* and *Pearl* got under way before two of the German vessels entered the harbour around 0100 on 9th March to land about 100 troops. Explosives badly damaged *Nephrite*'s boilers and wrecked *Parkwood*'s stokehold: *Kyle Castle* was set on fire amidships and, whilst *Heien* was unharmed, *Eskwood* was taken over with five crew members aboard, towed out of the harbour by a German tug and ended the war at the raiding party's base of Jersey.

By January 1945, US supplies shipped by coaster were exclusively directed to Ghent and Rouen, with Plymouth and Southampton being the loading ports

	TABLE 7	
	COASTERS ADDED TO THE CROSS-CHANNEL MILITARY CARGO FLEET: SEPTEMBER 1944-MAY 1945	
Ship's name	**Gross tonnage/year of build, nationality (Owners/*managers, if British)**	**Date taken up**
AINSLEY PARK	2,878/43 Canadian	25/4/45
ALF	2,178/09 British (MoWT/*Souter)	9/10/44
BRITA THORDEN	1,899/20 British (MoWT/*Kennaugh)	25/10/44
CAMP DEBERT	2,878/44 British ex-Canadian (MoWT/*Dickinson)	20/4/45
COTEAUDOC	1,975/29 British (MoWT/*Cory)	5/10/44
CRANE	785/37 British (General Steam)	24/9/43
DELFZIJL	227/39 Dutch	8/44
EAGLESCLIFFE HALL	1,900/28 Canadian	24/10/44
EMPIRE CITIZEN	2,066/43 British (MoWT/*Tanfield)	14/10/44
EMPIRE DAUGHTER	2,066/44 British (MoWT/*Stephenson Clarke)	29/10/44
EMPIRE FABLE	411/44 British (MoWT/*General Steam)	18/8/44
EMPIRE FAIRHAVEN	410/44 Britsh (MoWT/*Everard)	13/7/44
EMPIRE FASHION	410/44 British (MoWT/*Fisher)	21/8/44
EMPIRE HARCOURT	2,905/44 British (MoWT/*Hogarth)	8/5/45
EMPIRE ISLANDER	2,066/43 British (MoWT/*Donking)	1/11/44
EMPIRE PATRIOT	2,893/42 British (MoWT/*Currie)	22/4/45
EMPIRE PEGGOTTY	2,066/44 British (MoWT/*Stephenson Clarke)	25/4/45
EMPIRE VAUXHALL	2,025/45 British (MoWT)	1/5/45
EMPIRE VILLAGER	2,066/43 British (MoWT/*Marshall)	21/4/45
ESTER THORDEN	1,893/21 British (MoWT/*Penney)	10/44
FARRANDOC	1,925/29 British (MoWT/*Dalgliesh)	5/10/44
GANYMEDES	2,682/17 Dutch	9/10/44
HARDICANUTE	1,944/00 British (MoWT/*Chr Salvesen)	9/44
JACOBA	250/39 Dutch	8/44
KAIMANAWA	2,577/44 British (Union SS Co of New Zealand)	1/11/44
LACHINEDOC	1,990/27 British (MoWT/*Witherington)	10/11/44
NEZO	200/39 Dutch	8/44
SOLBRITT	1,885/18 British (MoWT/*Harper Hopps)	9/10/44
TROJAN III	1,797/17 British, ex-US (MoWT/*Cory)	11/11/44
WEGRO	281/38 Dutch	8/44
WELLANDOC	1,987/27 British (MoWT/*Dalgliesh)	23/10/44

Empire Daughter was completed in April 1944 and commenced her first cross-Channel sailing as a military cargo vessel on 3rd November 1944, carrying 1,845 tons of coal from Hull to Caen. *[National Maritime Museum, P22270]*

Quentin formed part of the fleet of 11 coasters carrying cased petrol to the Americans at Rouen. *[Mary Love/J. and M. Clarkson collection]*

for stores and Poole for cased petrol. Ostend featured very prominently in the schedules for the British Army, with coasters heading there from Poole and Southampton carrying cased petrol; from Dover with forces' mail and from Newhaven and London with ammunition. This latter category of cargo was also loaded for Antwerp at Dover. For British stores, Boulogne, Caen, Calais, Ghent and Ostend were all continental terminals for sailings from London's Millwall and Tilbury Docks. The 170 ships allocated to the various routes and cargoes, arranged by loading ports anti-clockwise from Plymouth and excluding vessels assigned to carry coal, are listed below.

Plymouth to Ghent with US stores

Alf	Empire Bond	Empire Citizen
Ganymedes	Graslin	Kyloe
Paul Emile Javary	Rondo	Westburn
Zuijderburgh		

Poole to Rouen with US cased petrol

Aseity	Channel Queen	Edina
June	Kentish Coast	Oriole
Quentin	Saint Rule	Sambre
Scheldt	Wooler	

Poole to Ostend with British cased petrol

Brockley Combe	Bucklaw	Denbigh Coast
Durward	Emerald Queen	Glamis
Goldfinch	Walenburgh	Westland

Southampton to Rouen and Ghent with US stores

Anthony Enright	Ask	Avance
Avance I	Bailey Foster	Brita Thorden
Charles Treadwell	Clement T Jayne	Coteaudoc
Eaglescliffe Hall	Eildon	Elkanah Crowell
Ester Thorden	Freeman Hatch	Gironde
Granby	Grenaa	Hardicanute
Jesse G Cotting	Katowice	Katwijk
Laban Howes	Lachinedoc	Leka
Lilian I	Lysaker V	Mammy
Marga	Marianne II	Marie
Munin	Ocean Coast	Palacio
Reuben Snow	Rodney Baxter	Ronan
Samuel Very	Skum	Solbritt
Theseus	Tomsk	Torfinn Jarl
Trojan III	William Bursley	

Southampton to Ostend with British cased petrol

Antrim Coast	Atlantic Coast	British Coast
Cameo	Empire Cape	Empire Cliff
Empire Foreland	Empire Shoal	Lochee

Newhaven to Ostend with British ammunition

Blackwater	Broomfield	Gun
Jargoon	Portia	Seaville
Sphene	Torquay	Yewtree

Coasters were called upon to deliver urgent food supplies to Rotterdam in May 1945: the ex-US *Elkanah Crowell* is pictured off Ostend at the time of that assignment. *[Captain J. F. van Puyvelde]*

Dover to Antwerp with British ammunition

Alnwick	*Beal*	*Drake*
Glen	*Sandhill*	*Sodality*
Starkenborgh	*Yewmount*	

Dover to Ostend with British forces mail

Brem	*Castle Combe*	*Empire Estuary*
Rosemarie	*Saint Angus*	*Saint Bedan*
Ton S	*Tromp*	

London (Tilbury Jetty) to Ostend with British ammunition

Asteria	*Fylla*	*Pebble*
Skelwith Force	*Stanley Force*	*Thyra III*
Valborg	*Yewglen*	

London (Tilbury Dock) to Ostend with British ammunition

Cordale	*Empire Islander*	*Empire Lagoon*
Granfoss	*Halo*	*Kaimanawa*
Lesto	*Vulcanus*	

London (Tilbury Dock) to Ostend with British medical, naval and NAAFI stores

Crane	*Euterpe*	*Leoville*

London (Tilbury Dock) to Ostend with British express stores

Arbroath	*Carnalea*	*Cragside*
Crewhill	*Holburn Head*	*Nato*
Oranmore	*Sedulity*	*Serenity*
Summity		

Euterpe began to show signs of her 42-year age in February 1945, experiencing defects firstly in her windlass, then in her boiler. *[Willem H. Moojen collection]*

London (Millwall) to Caen with British ammunition and stores, then reloading at Caen for Ostend

Benjamin Sherburn	*Charles H Salter*	*Cyrus Sears*
Empire Resistance	*Josiah P Cressey*	*Justin Doane*
Kimball Harlow	*Kmicic*	*Moses Gay*
Richard Bearse	*Waldo Hill*	*Watson Ferris*
William Homan	*William Howland*	

London (Millwall) to Boulogne or Calais with British stores

Egee	*Kordecki*	*Vilk*

London (Millwall) to Ostend with British stores

Algol	*Dagenham*	*Foreland*
Maurice Rose		

London (Millwall) to Ghent with British stores

Clermiston	*Corbridge*	*Empire Scout*
Erica	*Flathouse*	*Kalev*
Lilleaa	*Redcar*	

Ships in general reserve

Anticosti	*Jernfjeld*	*Oxford*
William H Daniels		

An indication of an October 1944-May 1945 coaster sailing pattern is set out below, covering *Empire Lagoon*'s movements during that period –

Loading Port	Sailing Date	Destination and Dates
London	27 Oct	Caen 30 Oct-3 Nov
Grimsby	15 Nov	Ostend 19-25 Nov
London	2 Dec	Dieppe 6-14 Dec
London	22 Dec	Antwerp 25-31 Dec
London	10 Jan	Ostend 12-16 Jan
London	21 Jan	Ostend 3-25 Jan
London	31 Jan	Ostend 3-6 Feb
London	14 Feb	Ostend 17-20 Feb
Hull	26 Feb	Dieppe 2-5 Mar
Hull	14 Mar	Dieppe 18-23 Mar
Hull	6 Apr	Cherbourg 9-16 Apr
Hull	23 Apr	Cherbourg 27 Apr-9 May

Returned to Newport 12 May

The sailing schedule of *Empire Lagoon*, between late October 1944 and the end of the war in Europe in May 1945, is shown in the accompanying narrative. *[National Maritime Museum, P22350]*

On 12th January, *Halo* arrived at Caen from Ostend: she then sailed from there for Antwerp on the 21st but failed to reach her destination. As she was heading for the Scheldt at 2300 next day, she took two E-boat torpedo hits on her port side forward and rapidly started to sink by the head. The escorting trawler *Turquoise* came alongside to take off all the crew, then, at 0140 on 23rd January, the tugs *TID110* and *TID115* commenced a tow but within five minutes *Halo* had gone down. The early part of 1945 also saw its fair share of marine casualties. Crossing the Channel from Rouen to Southampton in ballast on 16th January, *Charles Treadwell* collided with the US Liberty ship *Bert Williams*, resulting not only in a twisted bow but also in the coaster's deck plating becoming buckled as far back as No 2 hatch. Another Liberty ship accident occurred in the Thames Estuary eight days later when

Crane's stem and bows were extensively damaged in collision with the British *Samtrent*. Collisions also plagued *Wilno* causing her to spend most of February and March undergoing repairs, firstly at Grimsby, as a result of contact with another ship, then at Dieppe, for damage sustained on entering that port. To complete her misfortunes, *Wilno* went aground on 22nd April near Great Yarmouth and lost both anchors in the process. The workload of the hard-pressed military coasters was again being increased by the need to load return cargoes, mainly consisting of engine assemblies and ordnance stores from Antwerp and Caen to London (King George V, Millwall and Tilbury Docks). These also resulted in some unusual routings, such as *William Howland* loading scrap at Antwerp for Grangemouth in mid-January and *William Homan* transporting engine assemblies from Caen to Ipswich in early March. Some assignments proved particularly time-consuming with *Kmicic* being on the loading berth at Caen for nine days and *Kalev* for even longer. The final two military cargo coaster war losses both involved vessels sailing from Goole, as they headed down the English East Coast for the Thames Estuary assembly area on passage to France. The first was *Blacktoft* which left her loading port destined for Caen on 20th February and was sunk in a torpedo attack by three E-boats at 0120 on the 22nd: HM destroyer *Garth* reported that 20 survivors had been picked up but three men were lost. Five weeks later, on 28th March, *Jim* left Goole for Dieppe and, after passing Great Yarmouth Roads in the early hours of the 30th, went down at 0600 that day, as a result of an explosion aft: although her Master survived, the Chief Engineer and seven other

With the end of the conflict in Europe less than six weeks away, it was especially tragic for *Jim* to become a war loss on 30th March 1945. *[J. and M. Clarkson collection]*

crew members were killed. Meanwhile, in the English Channel in March, *Evertsen*, *Gladonia* and *Zuidland* were based at Newhaven to maintain a daily service to Dieppe carrying US mail and, the following month, military cargo coasters were switched to carry imported potatoes to Southampton, with *Ocean Coast*, *Tomsk* and *Vulcanus* loading at Rouen and *Crane*, *Empire Resistance*, *Euterpe*, *Leoville*, *Mammy*, *Theseus* and *Marianne II* at Antwerp. Whilst carrying 1,075 tons of potatoes on 4th April, the last named went aground in Yarmouth Roads and became embedded in soft sand. Two tugs were unable to refloat her and the use of a four-ton anchor, 120 fathoms of six-inch wire and heavy purchase blocks was equally unsuccessful. By 7th April, *Marianne II* was in danger of breaking her back, so naval working parties were employed to discharge part of her cargo: this proved effective and the following day she refloated, to continue her passage when all her cargo had been reloaded aboard.

Fano was still in service in May 1945, despite hitting a wreck at Ostend the previous 31st December. *[National Maritime Museum, P22589]*

In contrast to her previous military cargoes, *Vulcanus* was directed to carry potatoes from Rouen to Southampton in April 1945. *[Willem H. Moojen collection]*

The war in Europe came to an end on 8th May, a day which was routine in many other respects with *Fano* reaching Antwerp from London; *Charles Treadwell*, *Clement T Jayne*, *Elkanah Crowell*, *Kalev* and *Sedulity* arriving Ostend, also from London; *Theseus* calling at Ostend on passage from Grimsby to Ghent; *Saint Bedan* entering Calais harbour after crossing from Dover; *Coxwold* berthing in Dieppe after sailing from the Tyne; *Brita Thorden* and *Solbritt* proceeding into the Seine Estuary from Southampton; three coaster arrivals at Rouen in the form of *Channel Queen* from Poole, *Granfoss* from Southampton and *Siak* from the East Coast port of Seaham; *Baronscourt* arriving Caen from Newport, together with *Capito* and *Heien* from Cardiff and *Empire Foreland* from Goole; *Yewpark* reaching Cherbourg, also from Goole, and *Skarv*

heading into Granville from Swansea. Far from reducing the coaster commitments, the cessation of hostilities only added to them, with an early duty being the need to transport food to the people of Rotterdam. The large coasters *Charles Treadwell*, *Clement T Jayne*, *Elkanah Crowell* and *Richard Bearse* arrived there on 12th May; *Asa Eldridge*, *Benjamin Sherburn*, *Empire Scout* and *Isac* reached the port the next day, followed by *Anthony Enright*, *Empire Daughter*, *Kimball Harlow*, *Waldo Hill* and *William Howland* on the 14th and *Watson Ferris* and *William Bursley* three days after that. Another requirement was the shipment of urgently required supplies to the residents of the Channel Islands, who had endured five years of German occupation, the final months of it in total isolation. A fleet of coasters was assigned, with the first two flights carrying 2,660 tons of stores, 400 tons of coal and 1,249 tons of petrol, oil and lubricants to Jersey, while the respective tonnages for Guernsey were 5,547, 600 and 1,474. Leaving Plymouth for the Islands on 12th May were *Beal*, which went on from Guernsey with military cargo for Alderney, *Arbroath*, *Bucklaw*, *Cameo*, *Kenrix*, *Zeeland* (motor vessel), *Zuidland* and *Moelfre Rose*, the latter reaching Guernsey with 400 tons of coal, despite being extensively damaged forward in a collision near Eddystone with the defective trawler HMS *Rosevean*. These coasters were augmented from Southampton on 13th May by *Castle Combe*, *Glen* and *Sandhill*; by *Tromp* the next day, followed by *Macville*, *Portia* and *Tudor Queen*. Norway was another priority, with twelve coasters being allocated. *Ocean Coast* left Grimsby for the northern port of Tromso on 17th May, a day ahead of *Lochee* for Kristiansund and followed later in the month by *Ashbel Hubbard* from the Tyne and by *Kimball Harlow* from Newport. The latter ship was bound for Oslo, to

Kenrix formed part of the fleet assembled to re-supply the Channel Islands, after their May 1945 liberation from German occupation. *[J. and M. Clarkson collection]*

which destination *Alnwick* was routed from London (Tilbury), *William Bursley* from Newport, *Empire Sedge* and *Gurden Gates* from Immingham and also *Graslin*. During June, Stavanger was the intended Norwegian terminal of *Moses Gay* and Trondheim that of both *Calvin Coggin* and *Palacio*. On 1st June, *Jesse G Cotting* left Immingham for the German port of Lubeck and, a week later, *Kordecki* sailed from the Tyne with cargo for Kiel. Meanwhile, *Bailey Foster* and *Fano* were assigned the task of returning, from

Antwerp to the UK, initial stocks of ammunition no longer required on the Continent. These were independent sailings as all cross-Channel cargo convoys had been discontinued as from 22nd May.

During the twelve months from D-Day, over 460 coasters had, at one time or other, been maintaining the cross-Channel service of the Sea Transport Service's Military Cargo Branch and, at the end of May 1945, 246 still were – 68 for the British Army serving the ports of Rotterdam, Antwerp, Ostend, Calais and Caen; 78 sailing to Antwerp, Ghent, Le Havre, Rouen and Cherbourg for the US Army and 100 operating as colliers to Dieppe, Granville, St Malo and Morlaix. Provision of "Overlord" tonnage had been calculated on the basis of a loss rate of 10-15%. Fortunately this proved a highly pessimistic prediction, as, in reality, only 17 coasters were lost by enemy action, although three others were fatal victims of collisions and many required substantial repairs, mainly to bottom damage after beaching. Between D-Day and the end of August 1945 (when Japan surrendered), coasters completed 4,739 crossings to the Continent, as opposed to 1,837 by the large ocean-going cargo ships. Nearly 200 coasters were released from military service between June and September 1945; a further 33 by the end of that year and the final 20 between January and October 1946. They were the last of a total of 575 military cargo coasters which had set out for the Continent, through thick and thin, since the Second World War started in September 1939, their remarkable achievements undoubtedly justifying them a permanent place in maritime history.

The Canadian *Eaglescliffe Hall*, photographed at Cornwall Canal Lock in 1952, was assigned to carry vehicles from London to Normandy in one of the early June 1944 convoys. At the last minute she was found to be in need of substantial repairs and did not begin sailing to France until October that year. *[D. C. McCormick/W. A. Schell collection]*

Index of Ships

Illustrations in italics

Hetton 93,*93*
Hibernia 40
Highwear *49*,57,93
Hilda 11,15,28
Hildur I 93
Hodder 15,28,*28*,30
Holburn Head 78,93,138
Hondsrug 11,15,19,29,93
Horst 15,29
Hove 93
Hull Trader 15,29
Hythe 15,29,*29*
Ipswich Trader 93,94
Isac 93,*94*,133,140
Isbjorn 94
J F V 94,134
Jaba 13,15,30
Jacinth 7,30,*30*
Jacoba 136
Jade 7,15,30,79,94
Jaguar 38
Jan Brons 94
Jargoon 94,134,137
Java 30
Jellicoe Rose 94
Jernfjeld 94,138
Jernland 95
Jervis 76
Jesse G Cotting 95,*95*,121,137,141
Jim 95,134,139,*139*
Joffre Rose 95
Johanna 30
Jola 95
Jolly Girls 30
Josewyn 95,*95*
Josiah P Cressey 96,135,138
Julia 96,*96*,136
June 96,137
Justin Doane 57,60,96,138
Juta *50*,96,136
Jutland 15,28,30
Kaap Falga 10,15,17,31,*31*,43
Kaida 96
Kaimanawa 136,138
Kalev 96,126,131,138,139,140
Katowice 96,97,105,137
Katwijk 97,*97*,137
Keith 28
Kenrix 90,97,131,132,136,140,*141*
Kentish Coast 97,137
Keynor *97*,97
Kilrea 15,31,*31*
Kimball Harlow 98,138,140
King Emperor 127
Kingstown 15,31
Kiowa 93

Kmicic 98,103,138,139
Knowlton 56,98
Kolsdal 98
Kongshavn 98
Kordecki 98,*98*,133,138,141
Krakow 98,134,*135*
Krooman 111
Kul 98
Kyle Castle 56,98,136
Kyle Queen 99
Kylebank 56,99
Kylegorm 57,99,134
Kyloe 99,99,120,137
LBE30 74
LBO34 127
LBO59 127
LBO61 127
LBV174 97
LCT304 126
LCT413 125
LCT511 126
LCT517 82
LCT520 81
LCT530 121
LCT532 107
LCT541 100
LCT542 90
LCT545 84
LCT550 70
LCT553 100
LCT639 81
LCT644 70
LCT753 90
LCT765 111
LCT783 77
LCT807 74
LCT814 104
LCT855 74
LCT883 67
LCT899 124
LCT1009 108
LCT1046 120
LST21 119
LST55 127
LST283 63
LST355 86
LST386 112
LST451 73
LT152 106
Laban Howes 99,133,*133*,137
Lachinedoc 136,137
Lady Brassey 83
Lady Doris 40
Lady Haig 28
Lady Sheila 15,31
Lambtonian 99,*99*
Lancastria 14
Lansdowne 18
Larchfield 68,100,131

Leka 100,*100*,137
Lena 11,15,19,31
Leoville *51*,100,138,140
Lesrix 31
Lesto 100,133,138
Levenwood 15,31
Lilian I 100,137
Lilleaa 85,100,124,138
Loanda 100
Lochee 7,8,32,*32*,101,137,140
Lombardy 32
Lottie R 32,*32*,52,54,101
Lowestoft Trader 63,101,131,132
Lowick 9,12,15,*32*,33
Lysaker V 101,*101*,137
Lysland 57,101,131,134
Macville 101,131,140
Maidstone 15,33
Majorca 92,101
Makefjell 102,*102*
Mallard 33
Malrix 15,33
Mammy 102,137,140
Maplefield 102
Marcel 52,54,102
Marga 102,*102*,137
Mari 52,54,102,*103*,136
Marianne II 102,132,137,140
Marie 103,137
Marie-Flore 103,*103*
Marine Eagle 98
Marsden 58,103
Marsworth 15,33,103
Marx 98,103
Maurice Rose 103,*104*,134,138
Melissa 103,131
Melito 104
Mr Therm *46*,47,104
Moelfre Rose 56,104,140
Monkstone 52,104,*105*
Monksville 57,105,*105*
Mons 33
Montego Bay 40
Moorlands 105
Moose Peak 62
Moses Gay 105,134,138,141
Moss Rose 28
Mount 33,*33*
Mulan 105
Munin 75,96,105,137
Murrayfield 15,33
My Lassie 40
Narocz 105
Nato 106,138
Naviedale 86,106
Nephrite 9,15,33,106,*106*,133,136

Nesttun 56,106,*106*
Newlands 106,133
Nezo 136
Ngakoa 7,34
Ngaroma 15,34
Nivernais 107
Njord 107,132
Normandy Coast 107
Northgate 52,54,107,*107*,132
Nugget *107*,108
Nyroca 15,34
O280 13
Obsidian 15,34,*34*,108
Ocean Coast 34,*34*,108,137,140
Ocean Gift 40
Ocean Spray 40
Olev 108
Oosterhaven 108
Oranje 10,11,15,34
Oranmore 47,*48*,108,131,138
Oriole 108,*108*,137
Ortolan 35,109,*109*
Ouse 13,15,35
Ousel 6,7,35
Oxford 109,133,138
PC564 136
Pacific 15,35,58,109
Pacific Coast 7,35,*35*
Palacio 109,137,141
Paris 40
Parknasilla 15,35,*36*,78,109,132
Parkwood 109,136
Pascholl 11,12,15,35,*36*
Patria 11,*11*,15,36,43
Paul Emile Javary 37,57,110,*110*,137
Pearl 136
Pebble 110,138
Pembroke Coast 7,8,22,36
Perelle 13,15,36
Pinguin 15,36,*37*
Pizarro 8,20,36
Plover 37
Polglen 37,52,110
Polgrange 15,37
Polly M 56,110,131,*131*
Polperro 37,*37*
Portavogie 110
Porthrepta 110,133
Portia *110*,111,137,140
Portslade 37,*37*
Poznan *51*,111
Prase 111,131
Princess Elizabeth 115
Princess Iris *144*
Princess Maud 27,28
Queen of the Channel 10,24,34

Quentin 111,137,*137*
Raftsund 111,131
Rapidol 86
Ravonia 15,37,*38*
Recovery 124
Redcar 7,8,38,*38*,111,122,133,134,138
Regfos 57,111
Reias 56,86,111,*111*
Reiger 15,38
Reuben Snow 111,137
Rian 15,*15*,30,38
Richard Bearse 60,112,138,140
Rika 15,38
Ringen 56,58,112
Rockleaze 67,112,*112*
Rockville 56,112
Rodney Baxter 112,137
Roebuck 12,15,38,39
Ronan 8,39,*39*,112,123,137
Rondo 112,132,*132*,137
Rose Marie 28
Rose-Julie M 81
Rosemarie 112,132,138
Rosevean 140
Rowanfield 78,113
Royal 113
Royal Daffodil 42
Royal Sovereign 21
Ruja 15,18,39
Runnelstone 113,*113*
S177 64,69,78
S178 64,69,78
S N A 8 113
S N A 10 113,*113*
ST248 62
Saint Angus 56,113,132,138
Saint Bedan 96,114,138,140
Saint-Enogat 57,59,114,*114*
St Helier 41
Saint Rule 114,*114*,137
Sambre 114,137
Sambur 12,15,38,39,*39*
Samtrent 139
Samuel Very 114,*115*,137
San Antonio 15,39
Sandhill 7,9,12,15,39,115,131,133,138,140
Sard 115
Sarnia 52,54,115,*115*
Scheldt 15,40,*40*,115,137
Scimitar 28
Scotia 28
Scottish Co-operator 9,15,40
Sea Salvor 99
Seaville 115,137
Sedulity 52,54,116,*116*,138,140
Seine 15,40

Sequacity 10,*10*,15,40,45
Serenity 56,*56*,116,131,138,134
Sherwood *53*,116
Siak 116,140
Sidmouth 93
Signality 52,54,116,132
Silver Coast 15,40
Silver Spray 40
Sir Evelyn Wood 12,15,41,*41*,116
Skarv 52,*52*,54,116,140
Skelwith Force 52,117,138
Skipjack 28
Skum 117,*117*,137
Slemish 56,117,136
Soborg 88,117
Sodality 9,41,*41*,56,117,123,138
Sojourner 117,*117*
Solbritt 136,137,140
Sollund *50*,118,132
Southport *1,4*,118,*118*
Sparta (British) 13,15,25,42
Sparta (Dutch) 118
Spes 118,132
Sphene 118,134,137
Spinel 7,9,42,*42*,45
Spirality 118
Stadion II 118,*118*
Staley Bridge 60,*60*,119,132
Stanley Force 52,54,119,138
Stanridge 64
Stanville 119
Starkenborgh 52,*52*,54,119,124,138
Stephen W Kearny 77
Strijd voor Christus 42
Stuart Queen 119
Suffolk Coast 15,42
Summity 119,*119*,131,138
Sun X 35
Sunlight 116
Sursum Corda 11,15,28,42
Swift 42
Swivel 93
TID12 81
TID65 74
TID69 63,115
TID110 139
TID115 139
Teeswood 120,*120*
The Baron 15,42,*42*,120
The Countess 13,15,42,*43*
The Earl 120,134,*134*
The Marquis 9,43
The President 52,54,57,99,120,*120*
The Viceroy 120
Theems 13,15,43

The scene in Dieppe harbour on 14th October 1944, barely six weeks after the German surrender of the port, with the train ferry HMS *Princess Iris* unloading in the centre and the steamer *Claudius Magnin* on the move beyond. *[Imperial War Museum, B10888]*